Deposition Book

Clark County, Kentucky
Court Depositions
1795-1814

Harry G. Enoch

Diane Rogers

2005

Cover drawing: Map of the Indian Old Fields area from the Clark County Land Trials, 1812-1815, p. 488. *ABCD* is Cuthbert Combs' 400-acre survey and *CDJIHGFE* is Combs' 1,000-acre survey on Upper Howard's Creek (procession #59). *abcd*—Thomas Porter's 1,076$^{2}/_{3}$ acres. *8*—Beasley's cabin on Upper Howard's Creek and *13*—Beasley's cabin on Lulbegrud. *I I*—the gate posts in the "Old Indian Town," or Indian Old Fields.

ISBN 978-1-300-67726-0

Preface

The Clark County Court Deposition Book contains the testimony recorded in certain land actions between 1795 and 1814. These actions resulted from a law passed by the Kentucky General Assembly that allowed county courts to reestablish the boundaries of early land claims—especially those where the original corner trees had been lost—in a procedure referred to as a "procession." The Deposition Book contains the record of 222 depositions taken during the course of 96 processions.

The present work provides annotated transcriptions of these depositions, plus explanatory material that includes a description and location of 112 tracts of land, 235 biographical sketches of the individuals involved and 45 place name descriptions. A brief explanation of Kentucky's land grant system is also included.

The depositions are packed with significant information. There is not only a wealth of historical material but also a treasure-trove of genealogically important data. Particularly noteworthy are six depositions by Daniel Boone. We can examine Boone's own account of the naming of Lulbegrud Creek and the rescue of the Boone-Calloway girls after their capture by a band of Shawnees. We can learn of long-forgotten places (such as Fife Lick, John Baker's Station, the Sassafras Cabin and the Sycamore Forest) and the origin of obscure place names (Log Lick, Peeled Oak, Beaver Ponds, Mud Lick and others). We can review the contemporary observations of some of the most prominent figures in early Kentucky—Boone, George Rogers Clark, Michael Stoner, John "Wildcat" McKinney, and many more. And we can study the statements of some of Clark County's earliest settlers (William Bush, John Strode, William Sudduth, Josiah Hart, and numerous others).

Another option is simply to read with pleasure the testimony of Kentucky's first citizens, such as the following exchange: Daniel Boone gave a deposition at a place he called "the Plumb lick, which name I gave this Lick in the year 1770, at which time John Staurt was with me." Enoch Smith asked, "Why was this lick we now are at Distinguished by the Plumb lick, as there is no plumb Trees about it?" Boone replied,

> Because we Brought Plumbs neare a mile in our hats and eat them while we watched this lick. (procession #42)

This book includes an analysis of land data gleaned from the depositions. That analysis is found in the section entitled "Summary and Conclusions." Briefly stated, the data indicate that the land processioned in Clark County was claimed mostly for the purpose of speculation rather than settlement. The speculators were overwhelmingly Virginia men. Most had moved to Kentucky, and the majority lived in or near Clark County.

Finally, the Deposition Book contains a record of numerous individuals who were out on the Kentucky frontier when settlement began in 1775 and shortly thereafter. A list of pioneer names has been extracted from the depositions, along with the earliest corresponding date given showing when that person was in Kentucky. There are 88 names of men reported to have been in Clark County before 1780—long before

Kentucky became a state or Clark became a county. Many of these confirm other sources; however, 23 of the men are not mentioned in other compilations.

*   *   *

I would like to acknowledge the contribution of Diane Rogers that went into this publication. This book was really her idea, and she performed the groundbreaking work on it. In 2002, Diane gave me a copy of her draft transcription of all 222 depositions and asked if I would assist with editing. After spending several months on the transcriptions, it became apparent that a publication would be enhanced by providing some context for the depositions. That led to the task of locating 112 tracts of land, which was done by plotting all the original surveys and took almost a year to accomplish. The next task was to provide biographical data for all 235 owners and deponents. The research necessary to identify each of these individuals occupied another year or so. The last task was to format all of this information in a manner that would make it accessible to the casual reader and yet still be useful to the serious investigator. The whole process took the greater part of three years.

I am particularly grateful to Kathryn Owen of Winchester and Larry Meadows of Clay City for providing helpful information from their vast stores of knowledge and collections of documents. I am also indebted for the assistance provided by Claire McCann (now retired) and others at the Special Collections, M. I. King Library, University of Kentucky; Anita Jones and her assistants at the Clark County Clerk's office; and David Hunt, Clark Circuit Court Clerk. Finally, I would like to recognize the loving patience of my wife Brenda, without which this work could not have been completed.

Harry G. Enoch
Winchester, Kentucky
September 2005

Table of Contents

Processions and Depositions

Biographical Sketches

Place Names

Introduction

It may not be much of an exaggeration to state that the settlement of Kentucky was all about land. Acquiring land was the major goal of nearly all the tens of thousands of men and women who crossed the mountains before 1800 to settle the frontier. For many who came, the new land would provide a place to live and raise a family. For others, land represented different kinds of opportunities, foremost of which was the potential for profit. Virginia did not officially open Kentucky for settlement until 1773, after which adventurers and settlers poured into the region. Land was much on their minds. The Virginia commissioners appointed to settle claims held sessions in Kentucky from October 1779 through April 1780. During this short period—in the midst of the harshest winter ever remembered—1,340 claims were submitted to the commissioners for over 1,300,000 acres. Prior to that time, a large number of claims had been surveyed on military warrants awarded for service in the French and Indian War. These resulted in 570 surveys encompassing almost 500,000 acres. Nearly all of these early claims were in the central part of Kentucky.[1]

Because of Virginia's land laws, there were problems right from the start. Special preference was supposed to have been given for bona fide settlement, but it did not take long for speculators to figure out that one could qualify under the law by making an **improvement** on the land—building a small cabin and, perhaps, putting in a small plot of corn—without actually living on the land. In fact, one could have this done by men called "land jobbers" or "outlyers" without even leaving home. One early surveyor, John Floyd, criticized the practice:

> The Devel to pay here about land . . . Hundreds of wretches come down
> the Ohio & build pens or cabins [and] return to sell them [and] the people
> come down and settle on land they purchase. These same places are
> claimed by someone else, and then quarrels ensue.[2]

Land jobbers and outlyers show up repeatedly in the Deposition Book and are referred to in this work as **locators**. These men identified promising tracts of vacant land, which they marked in some fashion and sometimes made improvements. This process was referred to as **locating**, and the vacant tracts called **locations**. After 1775, there were frequently large companies of men in Kentucky locating land for others. Their locations were often sold to others who did not wish to risk going into the woods to find land.

Settlers complained over and over that nonresidents had claimed huge tracts of land and that the courts supported them—often to the extent of putting settlers off the

---

[1] For an excellent overview of land acquisition in Kentucky, see the following three works by Neal O. Hammon, "Land Acquisition on the Kentucky Frontier," *Register of the Kentucky Historical Society* (1980) 78:297; "Settlers, Land Jobbers, and Outlyers: A Quantitative Analysis of Land Acquisition on the Kentucky Frontier," *Register of the Kentucky Historical Society* (1986) 84:241; and *Early Kentucky Land Records, 1773-1780* (Louisville, 1992).

[2] John Floyd to William Preston, May 29, 1776, Draper MSS 33S96.

land (the legal process was referred to as **ejectment**). Thus, a man who had lived on the land for ten or twenty years, and had fought the British and Indians to protect his interests, could have his land taken away by a Virginia gentleman who had never set foot in Kentucky.[3]

That difficulty paled, however, compared to the problem of multiple patents issued for the same property. These overlapping land claims were a nightmare for Kentucky's pioneer settlers. Governor Isaac Shelby noted in his inaugural address that "the happiness and welfare of this country depends so much on the speedy settlement of our land dispute."[4] Sadly, it would take many years to disentangle thousands of conflicting claims.

One early attempt to address the problem was in 1795, when the Kentucky General Assembly passed "an Act for establishing the boundary of lands and for other purposes." By this time, many of the old trees marked as the corners of properties were beginning to rot and fall down. The act declared that

> the landmarks in this state, some of which are destroyed by fire and otherwise, particularly the corner trees, so that in a few years the bounds and corners cannot be ascertained.[5]

Also, the early locators, surveyors and their assistants, who were familiar with the boundaries, were aging and might not be available much longer to testify in court when boundaries were questioned. The law allowed landowners to petition the county court to appoint commissioners who would conduct a **procession** of their land, which was a process to reestablish their property boundaries—the corners and lines of their claim. The court in the county where the property was located would appoint several responsible citizens as commissioners "for the purpose of **processioning**," literally meaning to walk around his land. Commissioners were to visit the land in question and take sworn testimony (i.e., **depositions**) from persons who were familiar with the boundaries. Persons with conflicting claims could attend and ask questions of those who were testifying (**deponents**). Using the best information available to them, the commissioners were authorized to mark new boundary trees.[6]

While the law left most of the land problems unsolved, it did provide many valuable statements by the pioneers on the settlement of Kentucky, especially the period from 1775 to 1780. In Clark County, this information has been preserved in a court record called the Clark County Court Depositions, usually referred to as the **Deposition Book**. These depositions span the years from 1795 to 1814, and the testimony runs to 405 pages. At the beginning of that period, Clark County covered an area from which eighteen counties later were created. Thus, the processions found in the Deposition Book involve land that is in present-day Montgomery, Bath and Powell in addition to Clark

---

[3] Patricia Watlington, "Discontent in Frontier Kentucky," *Register of the Kentucky Historical Society* (1967) 65:77.

[4] George M. Chinn, *Kentucky Settlement and Statehood, 1750-1800* (Frankfort, 1975), p. 491.

[5] William Littell, *Statute Law of Kentucky, Vol. 1* (Frankfort, 1809), p. 554.

[6] Ibid.

County.[7]

Many notable figures appear in the Deposition Book: military heroes (George Rogers Clark and Nathaniel Gist), a future governor (James Garrard), a chief justice of the U.S. Supreme Court (John Marshall), wealthy landowners (Green Clay and Jacob Myers), state politicians (Aaron Lewis, John South, William Kennedy, Benjamin Harrison, etc.), Boonesborough pioneers (Nathaniel Hart, Samuel Henderson, etc.), and numerous representatives of the first families of Clark County (Bullocks, Burruses, Bushes, Combses, Couchmans, Dooleys, Dunaways, Eubanks, Halleys, McMillans, Pattons, Scholls, Sphars and many others).

There are six depositions by Daniel Boone, all of which have an important historic context (the naming of Lulbegrud Creek, for example). Numerous other early citizens of Clark and neighboring counties contributed their statements to this important record of the settlement period.

A Note on Format

The original Clark County Deposition Book contains 222 depositions taken in 96 processions. In the present work, each procession was placed in a separate, numbered section. The headings identify the deponents, followed by the processioner:

1. George Balla and Patrick Jordan for George Thompson

In the example above, George Balla and Patrick Jordan provided testimony to support the procession of George Thompson's land; the number (1.) indicates that this is the first procession in the book. Deponents, in most cases, were men who had been involved in locating or surveying the claim or who were familiar with landmarks on the claim. The processioner was usually but not always the property owner. Whenever possible, an explanation was provided to show the connection of the deponents and processioner to the property. In the original Deposition Book, only the surname of the processioner is given, but in each case, the individual could be identified by information provided in the deposition.

In order to give some context to the depositions, 235 brief biographies were prepared for processioners, deponents and other relevant individuals. Names headed in bold type had some interest or claim to the land, while deponents and others are shown in normal type. An alphabetized list of the biographies appears in the Table of Contents.

Numerous additional individuals were mentioned in the depositions. In most cases, these were the court-appointed commissioners or local citizens drafted to serve as witnesses to the proceedings. These names can be found in the "Index," but no biographies were prepared for them, as they had no other special relevance to the land claim. These persons were often neighbors of the processioners, so the depositions can provide information about where commissioners and witnesses were living at that time.

An effort was made to determine the location of each tract of land processioned. This includes identification of the present-day county, nearby watercourses or roads, and distance from Winchester or other towns (measured from the courthouse). In some cases, a plat of the tract showing landmarks or adjoining landowners was included.

---

[7] There is a second record book continuing this process: Clark County Processions, 1805-1857.

In transcribing the Deposition Book, original spelling and grammar were preserved (often a judgment call when it came to upper- and lower-case letters). The commonly used "[sic]" was not employed here, since it should be understood that contemporary writers used phonetic spelling and local dialect. Several formatting conventions were implemented to improve readability: Punctuation was added when required for clarity. The first letters of sentences were capitalized, consecutive repeated words were omitted, and most abbreviations were expanded. Clarifying material was added in brackets, though an attempt was made to limit the information to that necessary for comprehension. The transcription of each deposition was headed by the deponent's name and the page number, in brackets, corresponding to the page where the deposition is found in the original Deposition Book. A uniform format was adopted for "Questions" and "Answers" in the depositions. All material transcribed from the original Deposition Book appears as indented text and in a different font from the biographical material. While original spelling was maintained when transcribing the names of individuals and places, a consistent spelling was adopted for the headings and biographies. USGS topographic maps were used as the reference for the spelling of place names, streams, roads, etc.

The Process of Acquiring Land in Kentucky

The Deposition Book can be read on several levels. One can search for genealogical data, gather information about notable pioneers and place names of historic interest, or draw conclusions about settlement patterns. Even a casual reading, however, will require some basic knowledge of how one obtained land in early Kentucky. The quickest way to get property was to buy it from someone who had a good title to the land. Sadly, many immigrants purchased land that had defective titles. The other means to acquire property was to obtain a patent, or land grant, for "vacant and unused land," meaning land where no one else had yet obtained a right or entitlement.

The process for getting a patent was that used by Virginia and later adopted by the state of Kentucky. A helpful document for understanding this process is "The Kentucky Land Grant System" prepared by Kandie Adkinson, available from the Kentucky Secretary of State's office in Frankfort or on their web site.[8] An abbreviated version of this four-step process is described below, along with explanations for some of the most important terminology.

Step 1. The Warrant—A person wishing to obtain land first had to find and mark his claim. Only "vacant and unused" could be claimed; this meant land where no one was living, had made an improvement or had marked corners or lines. After the land was identified, one had to acquire an "entitlement" or "right" to the land, which was an official document usually referred to as a **warrant**. The most common types were military warrants, settlement and preemption warrants, and treasury warrants.

Military warrants, issued by Virginia for service in the French and Indian War, could be used to claim land in Clark County. The warrants—ranging from 50 acres for privates to 5,000 acres for field officers—were given in lieu of payment in currency,

---

[8] www.sos.state.ky.us.

which was in short supply in Virginia following the war.[9] As an example, Christopher Gist was issued a military warrant for 3,000 acres. In June 1775, James Douglass surveyed a tract located "on the north side of the Kentucky River, on Gist's Creek, a branch of the Licking." A note added to the warrant:

> Let the Patent issue in the name of Nathaniel Gist, who is oldest son and heir-at-law of Christopher Gist. William Preston, Surveyor of Fincastle County[10]

The tract was in Clark County near the Bourbon line. Early surveys made on military warrants trumped all other claims.

Under Virginia's land law of 1779, bona fide settlers could obtain a certificate for 400 acres of land and a preemption for an adjoining 1000 acres. Those who had not resided in Kentucky for a year or grown a crop of corn prior to 1778 could still obtain a 1000-acre preemption. These **settlement certificates** and **preemption warrants** were issued by the commissioners sent out from Virginia to hear the claims of settlers. They were referred to as the **Virginia Land Commission**, and they held their land court at various forts and stations during the "Hard Winter" of 1779-80. The complete record of their judgments and awards are found in the *Certificate Book of the Virginia Land Commission, 1779-1780*. An example of one of these awards is for a tract just south of the Indian Old Fields:

> Cuthbert Combs this day claimed a right to a settlement & preemption to a Tract of Land lying at an Indian Town on the North side of Kentucky between Lulbegrud Creek & Howards Creek, to include both side of the said Howards Creek for quantity, by making Corn in the Country in the year 1775 & Marking out the said place. Satisfactory proof being made to the Court, they are of Opinion that the said Combs has a right to a settlement of 400 Acres Land including the above mentioned place, and the preemption of 1000 Acres and that a Certificate issue for the same.[11]

Many of the commission's judgments are quoted extensively in the biographical sections of this work.

Another option was to purchase a certificate of entitlement from the state land office in the form of **treasury warrants**, which specified the name of the individual and the amount of acreage. Most of the patents in Kentucky were issued to holders of treasury warrants. However, the Deposition Book, dealing as it does with the very earliest claims, contains a higher than normal percentage of land granted on settlement certificates and preemption warrants.

---

[9] In spite of frequent claims to the contrary, land in Clark County was not granted for service in the Revolutionary War. Virginia set aside land below the Green River in Kentucky for her Revolutionary War veterans.

[10] Philip F. Taylor, *A Calendar of the Warrants for Land in Kentucky, Granted for Service in the French and Indian War* (Baltimore, 2001 reprint), p. 95.

[11] Kentucky Historical Society, *Certificate Book of the Virginia Land Commission, 1779-1780* (Frankfort, 1981), p. 14.

Virginia made provisions for poor settlers in Kentucky to obtain land by way of a **poor right**. The general assembly recognized that "by reason of great hardships they have encountered, and expenses incurred by them in their removal to that distant place . . . they have become unable to advance ready money to pay the state price of vacant lands." Therefore, the county courts were empowered to have their surveyors lay off up to 400 acres of vacant land for poor settlers. Such settlers had to be residing in the county with their families, could own no land and had to be "too poor to procure lands in the ordinary method."[12]

Step 2. The Entry—With a warrant in hand, an individual proceeded to the land office, where the county surveyor would **enter** the claim in a book, usually referred to as the Entry Book. Entering a claim was literally the process of writing down the particulars of a claim. Required information included the name of the individual, type of warrant used for the claim, acreage, and exact location of the tract. The following **entry** was made on April 26, 1780, in the land office at Wilson's Station near Harrodsburg:

> John Strode enters 1000 Acres in Kentucky by virtue of a preemption
> Warrant on Stouds fork joining James Stroud on the west and to include
> his Station.[13]

The purpose of the entry was to direct the county surveyor to conduct a survey of the property.

Step 3. The Survey—The **county surveyor** gave a copy of the entry to one of his assistants, a **deputy surveyor**, who then went to the property in question, usually attended by a **pilot** who was familiar with the corners of the claim. The deputy hired other individuals to assist him, usually two **chain carriers** who would measure the length of the property lines and a **marker** who would mark the corner trees. In conducting his survey, the deputy recorded the **metes and bounds** of the property—the distance and direction of each line—a description of each corner, and any other important features or landmarks (springs, streams, improvements, etc.). He also prepared a **plat** or map of the surveyed tract drawn to scale. The survey was then returned to the land office. (See example of a survey in Figure 1.)

Step 4. The Grant—After the county surveyor signed off on the survey, he forwarded it, along with a copy of the warrant, to the governor. The governor's office issued the **patent**, a document granting fee simple title to a specific piece of property. The patent was recorded in the state land office and the original was sent to the patentee. The term patent is synonymous with **grant**. (See example of a grant in Figure 2.)

By current usage, grant or land grant seems to imply that land was awarded to settlers at no charge. With the exception of military warrants, this was not the case. Holders of settlement certificates had to pay 40 shillings for their 400 acres, plus fees to the land office, clerks, deputy surveyors, etc. Preemption warrants cost 200 pounds per 1000 acres. Treasury warrants were strictly pay as you go.

---

[12] William Littell, *Statute Law of Kentucky, Vol. 1*, p. 430.

[13] Jefferson County Entry Book 1:85. The earliest entries for Fayette County are recorded in Jefferson County Entry Book 1.

Due to the haphazard manner of surveying (using vague terms such as "beginning at a white oak tree near a branch"), neither the county surveyor nor the governor could guarantee that patented land had no prior claims on it. Thus, multiple patents often were issued for the same property. Kentucky was the last state to use this survey system. In later territories and states, the government laid off the land in grids subdivided into sections, townships and ranges.

At each step in the land grant process, the claimant could dispose of his rights in a specific property. Thus, military warrants, settlement certificates, preemption warrants and treasury warrants could be sold, traded or assigned to another person. The same applied to entries and surveys. Patented land was sold and resold many times; the legal instrument for these sales is referred to as a **deed**.

Entries are indexed in Willard Rouse Jillson's *Old Kentucky Entries and Deeds*.[14] Surveys and patents are indexed in two books; *Master Index, Virginia Surveys and Grants, 1774-1791* and *Index for Old Kentucky Surveys & Grants*.[15] Deeds are recorded in county deed books, in the county where the property was located at the time the deed was made. Deed books can be found in the county clerks' offices. Most are indexed. The Clark County deed index was very helpful in identifying the owners of many of the processioned tracts, especially so when the owner had a common name or lived in another state. For example, James Davis patented 1,000 acres on Flat Creek, which he obtained by purchasing Thomas Clark's preemption warrant. The tract was processioned in 1796 (#18). By the year 1800, there were eighteen men named James Davis in Kentucky. A Clark County deed identifies "James Davis & Ann his wife of Mercer County" as the sellers of "part of the preemption Obtained in the name of Thomas Clark." As another example, Aaron Bledsoe patented 300 acres just south of Winchester. This tract was processioned in 1802 (procession #77). When Bledsoe sold this land, he was described in the deed as "Aaron Bledsoe and Mary, his wife, of Orange County, Virginia."

While legal jargon has been kept to a minimum in this work, technical terms associated with land acquisition are used repeatedly. A working knowledge of the terms appearing in bold type in this Introduction is essential to understanding the depositions.

---

[14] Originally published in 1926 and reprinted by the Genealogical Publishing Co., Baltimore, MD, 1987.

[15] Joan Brookes-Smith, editor, published by the Kentucky Historical Society, Frankfort, 1776 and 1975, respectively.

Figure 1

Example of a Survey

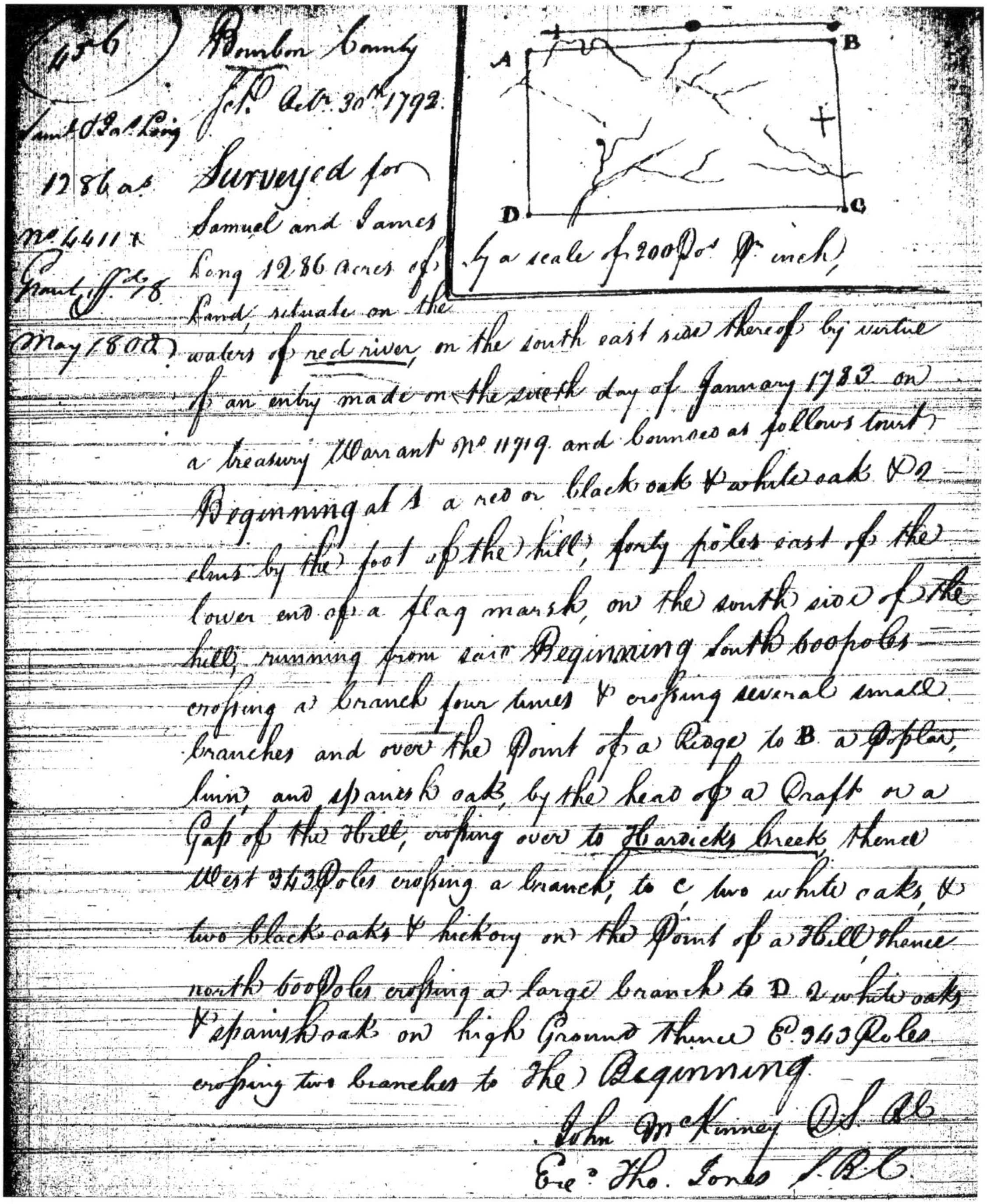

456

Saml & Jas Long

1286 as

No. 4411 ×

Grant iss'd 18 May 1800

Bourbon County

Sept. Octr. 30th 1792

Surveyed for Samuel and James Long 1286 acres of Land, situate on the waters of red river, on the south east side thereof by virtue of an entry made on the sixth day of January 1783 on a treasury Warrant No. 11719 and bounded as follows to wit Beginning at A a red or black oak & white oak & 2 elms by the foot of the hill, forty poles east of the lower end of a flag marsh, on the south side of the hill, running from said Beginning South 600 poles crossing a branch four times & crossing several small branches and over the Point of a Ridge to B a poplar, linn and spanish oak, by the head of a Draft or a Gap of the Hill, crossing over to Hardicks Creek thence West 343 Poles crossing a branch, to C two white oaks, & two black oaks & hickory on the Point of a Hill thence north 600 Poles crossing a large branch to D 2 white oaks & spanish oak on high Ground thence E. 343 Poles crossing two branches to the Beginning

John McKinney D.S. B.C.

Exd. Tho. Jones S.B.C.

A tract of 1,286 acres surveyed on a treasury warrant by John "Wildcat" McKinney for Samuel and James Long. The tract was situated on the "waters of red river," namely, Hardwick Creek and Mill Seat Creek. The beginning corner, "a red or black oak & white oak," was 40 poles east of "a flag marsh." (Old Kentucky Surveys 6:456)

Figure 2
Example of a Grant

PATRICK HENRY, Efquire; Governor of the Commonwealth of VIRGINIA; to all to whom thefe Prefents shall come; Greeting: KNOW YE that

by virtue and in consideration of part of a land office Treasury Warrant, Number 742, and issued the 15th day of October 1779 unto Jacob Myers

there is granted by the faid Commonwealth unto the faid *Jacob Myers* a certain Tract or parcel of Land, containing

5,000 acres by survey bearing date the 6th day of November 1783, lying and being in the county of Fayette, including part of big Slate creek and bounded as followeth, to wit, Beginning at a sycamore & bitty thorn trees standing on the bank of a branch of said creek, running thence east 800 poles crossing the branch twice and the creek three times to a double hickory and double black walnut, thence north 1,000 poles crossing the creek twice to two sugar trees and a hickory in a level, thence west 800 poles crossing the creek three times to a buckeye and sugar tree, thence south 1,000 poles crossing sundry branches of said creek to the beginning

with its Appurtenances to have and to hold the faid Tract or parcel of Land with its Appurtenances to the faid *Jacob Myers* and his Heirs forever. IN WITNESS whereof, the faid PATRICK HENRY, Efquire, Governor of the Commonwealth of Virginia; hath herewith fet his Hand and caufed the leffer Seal of the faid Commonwealth to be affixed at Richmond on the *Second* Day of *December* in the Year of our Lord One Thoufand Seven Hundred and Eighty *five* and of the Commonwealth the *Tenth*.

P Henry

Grant to Jacob Myers for 5,000 acres of land on Slate Creek, signed by Gov. Patrick Henry of Virginia. (*not an actual copy*) This land was later known as the "Morgan's Station Tract." (Old Virginia Grants 4:449)

Summary and Conclusions

The Deposition Book contains 96 processions for 112 different tracts of land. Five properties were processioned more than once. Basic data for each tract are summarized in Table 1.

A review of the land processioned was undertaken to characterize the size and location of the tracts involved. The average size of a processioned tract was 673 acres, however, the size ranged from 178 acres up to 19,934 acres. The most frequent sizes were 400 acres and 1000 acres. Most of the processions were for land located in present-day Clark County (72), followed by Montgomery, Bath and Powell.

Clark	72
Montgomery	29
Bath	10
Powell	5
Bourbon	2
Estill	1

Stoner Creek had by far the largest number of processions (36), followed by Lulbegrud, Flat, Hinkston, Somerset, Strodes and others. Counting all of its branches, there were 54 processions on the waters of Stoner.

Stoner	36
Lulbegrud	8
Flat	7
Hinkston	7
Somerset	7
Strodes	7

There were 5 processions on Georges Branch; 4 on Red River, Lower Howard's, Upper Howard's, Johnson and Grassy Lick; 3 on Fourmile and Little Stoner; 2 on Hancock, Greenbrier and Brush and 1 each on Kentucky River, Constants, Woodruff, Jouett, Spencer, Mud Lick and Sycamore.

The most prolific surveyor of processioned tracts was Enoch Smith with 12. Smith had been, at various times, deputy surveyor for Fayette, Bourbon and Mason and was the first county surveyor for both Clark and Montgomery. Other surveyors were William Hays (8), William Sudduth (7), Daniel Boone (6), John South (6), William Calk (6), John Fleming (6), James McMillan (6), Joshua Bennett (4), plus 27 others with 3 or fewer.

A review of owner data also was conducted in order to get an idea of the degree of land speculation that occurred with the processioned tracts. "Speculation" for this analysis is defined simply as ownership of land that the owner never lived on. Ownership included all those individuals with interests in the tract up to and including the patent. Eight of the owners were killed by Indians before the land was processioned; these were excluded from the analysis. Some tracts had multiple owners prior to processioning, and the residence or nonresidence of each owner was determined. A total of 23 owners lived on their tracts or had family members who did; 80 owners (78%) did not. One can say then that a large majority of the land processioned was purchased for speculation. Not all speculators stayed in Virginia. In fact, of the speculators whose residence could be determined, 49 resided in the state, while 20 did not. Thus, most of the speculators of the processioned land lived in Kentucky. Of the 49 Kentucky speculators, 29 (59%) lived in Clark or nearby counties (Fayette, Madison, Montgomery or Bourbon).

Most of the processioned land was entered on treasury warrants, followed by preemption warrants and settlement certificates.

treasury warrant	59
preemption warrant	34
settlement certificate	13
military warrant	5
poor right	2

One of the tracts included in these statistics (Tilley Emerson's) was entered on a combination of military warrant and treasury warrant.

Since settlement certificates were supposed to be issued for "actual settlement," one might presume that that few of the original owners of these tracts would be speculators. The data indicate otherwise. Of the 13 settlement certificates processioned, 8 were issued to speculators (including Daniel Boone) who never lived on the tract, 1 owner was killed by Indians, and 4 actually lived on their settlements (Jesse Copher, Enoch Smith, Cuthbert Combs and Thomas Kennedy). Even for the 2 tracts entered on a poor right (Edward Williams', procession #9, and James Townsend's, procession #39), only Edward Williams lived on his.

Procession data also were reviewed to determine the state from which the owners came. The large majority (85%) of those for whom residency could be determined were from Virginia.

Virginia	72
North Carolina	6
Maryland	3
Pennsylvania	2
Delaware	1
New Jersey	1

A sizeable number (25) came from five contiguous counties in northern Virginia— Fauquier, Fairfax, Stafford, Prince William and Loudoun.

In conclusion, the land processioned in early Clark County had been claimed by owners who were overwhelmingly Virginia men, mostly for the purpose of speculation rather than settlement. Most of these speculators lived in Kentucky, the majority in or near Clark County.

* * *

A total of 108 different men gave depositions in the processions. That number included 46 who gave multiple depositions. More of the deponents lived in the bounds of present-day Clark County (47) than any other county. Those who gave the most depositions are listed below, along with their residence at the time (present-day county):

Enoch Smith (Montgomery)	9
John Harper (Montgomery)	9
Elias Tolin (Montgomery)	8
Edward Williams (Montgomery)	7
Daniel Boone (Nicholas)	6
Joshua Stamper (Clark)	5
Nicholas Anderson (Montgomery)	5
Patrick Jordan (Mercer)	5
John McIntire (Fleming)	5
Lawrence Thompson (Madison)	5
William Hays (Madison)	5

When Boone gave his depositions, he was living near Carlisle on Big Brushy Creek, a branch of Hinkston. There were 7 men with 4 depositions, 10 men with 3, 17 with 2.

The Deposition Book also contains a record of numerous individuals who were in Kentucky when settlement began in 1775 and thereafter. A list of these pioneers has been extracted from the depositions, along with the earliest date that person was said to have been in Kentucky. Individuals were excluded from the list if they are known from other sources to have been here prior to the date given in the deposition. For example, Daniel Boone does not appear on the list; Boone's deposition states he was on Lulbegrud Creek in 1770, but from other sources we know he came into the country on his first Long Hunt in 1769.

The body of testimony in the Deposition Book includes a total of 89 men who were reported to have been in old Clark County before 1780. Many of these names confirm other sources; however, 27 of the men are not mentioned in previously published lists of pioneers, or the depositions place them in Kentucky at an earlier date than other sources.[16] The depositions name an additional 36 men who arrived in Kentucky after 1779 but before statehood (1792)—30 of these men have not been listed in previous compilations as having been in Kentucky as early as stated in these depositions. Table 2 lists the pioneers identified in the Deposition Book and gives the reported year of their arrival in Kentucky.

---

[16] The most comprehensive list of pre-1780 pioneers is the *Certificate Book of the Virginia Land Commission, 1779-1780*. Other compilations important for the Clark County area include H. Thomas Tudor, *Early Settlers of Fort Boonesborough* (Richmond, KY, 1975) and Neal O. Hammon, "Pioneers in Kentucky, 1773-1775," *Filson Club Historical Quarterly* (1981) 55:268; and for the period from 1776 to 1792, James R. Robertson, *Petitions of the Early Inhabitants of Kentucky* (Louisville, 1914). Also useful are the county tax lists beginning in 1787.

Table 1
Summary of Data for
Property Processioned by the Clark County Court
1795-1814

	Original Owner(s)	Acres	W	Location County/ Watercourse	Surveyor	Lived on land?	Lived in KY? County	From State/ County
1	George Thompson	5000	TW	Bath Slate	Ralph Morgan	N	Y Mercer	VA Albemarle
2	William Eustace	1000	PW	Clark Stoner	Richard Beale	N	N	VA Fauquier
3	Martin Hammond	400 1000	SC PW	Bath Flat	William Sudduth	N	N	NC
4	Walter Chiles (S)	150	MW	Clark Stoner	William Hays	N	Y Shelby	VA Spotsylvania
	Leonard Beall (G)					Y	Y Clark	VA Augusta
5	William Watson	950	TW	Bath Flat	Daniel Boone	N	Y Madison	VA Louisa
6	Richard Halley	400	TW	Clark Stoner	John South	Y	Y Clark	VA Fairfax
7	Benjamin Barton	400 1000	SC PW	Clark Stoner	Daniel Boone	N	N	
	Leonard Hall (S, G)					N	Y Barren	VA Bedford
8	Joshua Barton	400	SC	Clark Fourmile	William Calk		killed	NC Rowan
9	Edward Williams	400	PR	Montgomery Lulbegrud	James French	Y	Y Montgomery	VA Stafford
10	John Harper	400	PW	Montgomery Lulbegrud	James French	Y	Y Montgomery	VA Prince Wm
11	Nicholas Anderson	400	PW	Montgomery Hinkston	James French	Y	Y Montgomery	VA Stafford
12	John Lane	400 1000	SC PW	Montgomery Lulbegrud	John Payne	N	Y Montgomery	VA Loudoun
	Edward Payne (S, G)					Y*	Y Fayette	VA Fairfax
13	Benjamin White	400	PW	Montgomery Spencer	James McMillan		killed	
	David Crews (S, G)					N	Y Madison	
14	Ebenezer Corn	1000	PW	Clark Somerset	John Fleming	Y	Y Clark	PA
	John Craig and Robert Johnson (S, G)					N	Y Scott	VA

#	Name	Acres	Type	County/Place	Person			State/County
15	James Davis	1000	PW	Clark Stoner-Somerset	John Fleming	N	Y Mercer	
	John Craig and Robert Johnson (S, G)					N	Y Scott	VA
16	James Hendricks	1000	PW	Clark Somerset	John Fleming	N	Y Madison	
	John Craig and Robert Johnson (S, G)					N	Y Scott	VA
17	Mordecai Kelly	500	TW	Clark Stoner	James Morgan	Y	Y Clark	
18	Thomas Clark	1000	PW	Bath Flat	Joshua Bennett	N		
	James Davis (S, G)					N	Y Mercer	
19	John Poindexter	400 / 2000	TW / TW	Powell Lulbegrud	Enoch Smith	N	N	VA Campbell
20	Jesse Copher	400 / 1000	SC / PW	Clark Stoner	William Hays	Y	Y Clark	VA
21	Thomas Winn, George Winn, and Owen Winn	400 / 1000 / 500	TW / TW / TW	Clark Stoner	John South	N / N / N	Y, Clark / Y, Fayette / Y, Fayette	VA Loudoun
22	George Kilgore	800	TW	Clark Upper Howards	Enoch Smith	N	N	VA Loudoun
23	Samuel Meredith (same as #41)							
24	Tilley Emerson	750	TW MW	Clark Fourmile	Philip Detherage	Y	Y Clark	
25	John Strode	1000	PW	Clark Strodes	Benjamin Ashby	Y	Y Clark	VA Berkeley
26	Basil Stoker	981	PW	Montgomery Somerset	John Fleming	N	N	PA
27	Thomas Lewis	500	TW	Clark Stoner	John Payne	N	Y Fayette	VA Fairfax
28	Thomas Swearingen	1000	TW	Bath Hinkston	Thos. Swearingen	N	N	VA Berkeley
29	Mathias Sphar	500	TW	Clark Woodruff	Edward Wilson		killed	VA Berkeley
30	Anthony Buckner	400 / 1000	SC / PW	Montgomery Somerset	Tim Peyton John Peyton	N	N	VA Prince Wm
31	Jeremiah Moore	1000	TW	Clark Stoner	Enoch Smith	N	N	VA Fairfax
32	John Wilkerson	3050	TW	Bath Flat	Enoch Smith	N	Y Madison	VA Fairfax
33	William Bramblett	400	PW	Clark Stoner	William Sudduth		killed	VA Bedford

No.	Name	Acres	Type	Location	Entry			Origin
34	Thornton Farrow	1000	PW	Montgomery Grassy Lick	John Fleming	N	Y Fayette	VA Prince Wm
35	William Farrow	1000	PW	Montgomery Grassy Lick	John Fleming	Y*	Y Fleming	VA Prince Wm
36	Enos Hardin	1000	PW	Clark Stoner	Henry Martin	Y	Y Clark etc	VA
37	Joel Lipscomb	1000	TW	Montgomery Greenbrier	Enoch Smith	N	N	VA Spotsylvania
38	John White (S)	1000	TW	Bath Mud Lick	Enoch Smith	N	Y Madison	
	Walter Chiles and Lawrence Thompson (G)					N	Y Shelby-Madison	VA-NC
39	James Townsend	400	PR	Montgomery Brush	John South	N	Y Clark	
	John South Jr. (S, G)					N	Y Fayette	MD
40	Walter Carr	1000	TW	Montgomery Greenbrier	William Hays	N	Y Fayette	VA
41	Samuel Meredith	19934	TW	Montgomery Slate	William Sudduth	N		VA Amherst
42	George Smith	1500	TW	Montgomery Brush	Daniel Boone	N		
43	William Brent (no patent issued)	400 1000	SC PW	Clark Stoner	John McIntire	N	N	VA Stafford
44	Isaac Davis Jr.	1000	PW	Montgomery Hinkston	Enoch Smith	N		
45	Enoch Smith	400 1000	SC PW	Montgomery Hinkston	Henry Lane	Y	Y Montgomery	VA Stafford
46	Charles Morgan	1000	PW	Clark Stoner	John Bradford	N	N	VA Prince Wm
47	Peter King (S)	812½	PW	Montgomery Hinkston	William Calk	N	N	
	Peter Ringo (G)					Y	Y Montgomery	VA Prince Wm
48	Hugh Forbes	1000	PW	Clark Stoner	William Triplett	N	Y Montgomery	VA
49	Robert Fryer	500	TW	Clark Georges	Enoch Smith	Y*	Y Fayette	
50	Daniel Boone (S)	400 1000	SC PW	Clark Georges	William Hays	N	Y Madison etc	NC
	William Scholl (G)					N	Y Madison	VA
51	John Price	500	TW	Clark Georges	Enoch Smith	N	Y Jessamine	

#	Name	Acres		Location	Name			Origin
52	Bartholomew Dupuy	950	TW	Clark	Enoch Smith	Y*	Y	VA
		2000	TW	Stoner			Woodford	Amelia
53	William Smith	977	TW	Bath	William Sudduth	N		
				Flat				
54	Thomas Hart	800	TW	Clark	Benjamin Ashby	Y*	N	VA
				Constants				Berkeley
55	Philip Drake	1500	TW	Montgomery	Daniel Boone	N	Y	NJ
				Somerset			Bracken	
56	Jacob Myers	5000	TW	Montgomery	Thos. Swearingen	N	Y	MD
				Slate			Lincoln	Frederick
57	William Collinsworth (no survey made)	400	PW	Clark Lower Howards		N	N	
58	James Garrard and James McMillan	4000	TW	Clark-Montgomery Lulbegrud	James McMillan	N	Y Bourbon-Clark	VA Stafford-Frederick
59	Cuthbert Combs	400	SC	Clark	William Calk	Y	Y	VA
		1000	PW	Upper Howards			Clark	Stafford
60	Charles Morgan	975	TW	Montgomery	James Morgan	N	Y	VA
				Sycamore			Fayette	Prince Wm
61	William Davis	10000	TW	Montgomery-Bath Slate	John McIntire	N	N	VA Prince Geo
62	Forrest Webb	500	TW	Bath	James Parker	N	Y	VA
				Flat			Boone	
63	Stephen Collins	200	TW	Powell	John McKinney	Y	Y	VA
				Red			Fayette etc	Halifax
64	George Caldwell	1000	TW	Clark	Van Swearingen	N	Y	
				Stoner			Mercer	
65	David Shelton	1658	TW	Clark	William Hays	N	N	VA
		1000	TW	Johnson				Hanover
66	Archibald Woods (S)	1500	TW	Clark-Montgomery Lulbegrud	Philip Detherage	N	Y Madison	VA Albemarle
	Robert Craddock and John Wilson (G)					N	Y (Craddock) Mercer etc	
67	Joseph Combs	500	PW	Clark	William Calk	N	N	VA
				Lower Howards				Stafford
68	James Estill	400	PW	Clark	Green Clay		killed	VA
				Georges				Augusta
69	John Marshall	1600	TW	Clark	Benjamin Ashby	N	N	VA
	Thomas Marshall	1300	TW	Stoner-Strodes	Thos. Swearingen	N	Y Woodford	Fauquier
70	John Embry and Richard Embry	400	TW	Clark	William Sudduth	N		VA
		400	TW	Little Stoner		N		

71	James Ware	1500	TW	Clark-Montgomery Stoner-Hinkston	Joshua Bennett	N	Y Woodford	VA Gloucester
72	Aaron Lewis	1000	TW	Clark Stoner	Aaron Lewis	N	Y Madison etc	VA Washington
73	William Kennedy	189½ 200	TW TW	Clark Stoner	Charles Smith	N	Y Mercer etc	VA Charlotte
74	John Wilson	178	TW	Clark Jouett	James McMillan		killed	
75	Timothy Peyton	1000	TW	Clark Stoner	Timothy Peyton		killed	VA Prince Wm
76	James Speed	8200 4000	TW TW	Clark-Montgomery Stoner-Grassy Lick	Arthur Fox	N	Y Mercer	VA Botetourt
77	Aaron Bledsoe	300	TW	Clark Lower Howards	James McMillan	N	N	VA Orange
78	Charles Morgan (same as #46)							
79	Nathaniel Bullock	400	SC	Clark Strodes	John Constant	N	Y Fayette	VA
80	Thomas Kennedy	400 672	SC PW	Clark-Bourbon Strodes	Edward Wilson	Y	Y Bourbon	MD Frederick
81	William Dryden	250	TW	Clark Lower Howards	James McMillan	N	Y Madison	VA Augusta
82	Samuel Long and James Long	1286	TW	Powell Red	John McKinney	N		
83	Timothy Peyton (same as #75)							
84	Moses Kuykendall	1000	TW	Clark Stoner	William Triplett	N	Y Jefferson	VA Hampshire
85	William Farrow (same as #34 & 35)							
86	Alexander Barnett	500	TW	Estill Kentucky	William Orear	N	Y Bourbon	VA Culpeper
87	Stephen Collins	500	TW	Powell Red	William Calk	Y	Y Fayette etc	VA Halifax
88	Robert Boggs	1000	PW	Clark Stoner	Daniel Boone	N	Y Fayette	DE New Castle
89	Samuel Henderson	400 1000	SC PW	Clark Johnson-Hancock	Joshua Bennett	N	Y Madison	NC Granville
90	Mathias Sphar (same as #29)							

91	Benjamin Harrison	1000	PW	Clark Little Stoner	George Lewis	N	Y Harrison	VA	
92	Charles Tate	400	PW	Clark Strodes	Ralph Morgan	N	N	VA Bedford	
93	Nathaniel Gist	3000 3000	MW MW	Clark Stoner	James Douglass	Y	Y Clark	VA	
94	Thomas Maxwell	200	MW	Clark Upper Howards	John Floyd	N	Y Madison	VA Montgomery	
95	Nathaniel Hart	400	TW	Clark Fourmile	Asa Massie		killed	NC Orange	
96	Aaron Lewis	1000	TW	Clark Red	John South	N	Y Madison etc	VA Washington	

Explanation of table:

Original Owner(s)—the earliest owners of the property, from entry to grant. If the warrant was assigned, the person for whom the survey was made **(S)** and to whom the grant was issued **(G)** is also identified.

Acres—size of the tract(s) processioned.

W—type of warrant(s) used to enter the claim: **TW**, treasury warrant; **SC**, settlement certificate; **PW**, preemption warrant; **MW**, military warrant; **PR**, poor right.

Location—present-day county where the tract is located and the nearest watercourse.

Surveyor—deputy surveyor who made the official survey.

Lived on land?—indicates whether the owner ever lived on the processioned tract. **Y**, yes; **Y***, a family member of the owner lived on the tract; **N**, no evidence could be found that the owner lived on the tract.

Lived in KY?—indicates whether the owner ever lived in KY and, if known, the county where he resided. **Y**, yes; **N**, no evidence could be found that the owner lived in Kentucky; **killed**, the owner was killed by Indians prior to the procession. A blank means it was not possible to determine, usually due to multiple individuals of the same name.

From—the county and state from which the owner came to Kentucky.

Table 2
Pioneers in Clark County Prior to Statehood in 1792
Taken from the Deposition Book

(An asterisk beside a name means the Depositions give an earlier date for that person in Kentucky than shown by other conventional sources.)

1775

Benjamin Ashby*
Major Beasley
William Beasley*
Benjamin Berry
Thomas Brashear
William Bush
William Calk
Marquis Calmes Jr.
Marquis Calmes Sr.
Luke Cannon
George Rogers Clark
John Clark*
Thomas Clark

Benjamin Combs
Cuthbert Combs
Enos Combs*
John Combs*
Joseph Combs
Ebenezer Corn
John Crittenden
Isaac Davis Jr.
William Eustace*
James Galloway
___ Guy*
Evangelist Hardin
Thornton Farrow

Garrett Jordan
Patrick Jordan
Andrew Lynn
William Lynn
Robert McMillan
___ Paul
Enoch Smith
John Soverns
Elias Tolin
Samuel Tomlinson
Robert Whitledge
David Williams

1776

George Balla*
Lewis Barnett*
Elizamond Basye
William Bennett*
Thomas Clark Jr.*
Betts Collier*
James Davis
Hugh Forbes
Thomas French

Thomas Hardgrove
Benjamin Harrison
James Hendricks
Joshua Hughes
___ Keen*
Moses Killpatrick*
John Lane
Francis McDermid
Thomas Moore*

John Morgan
Peter Ringo
Hugh Sidwell
John Six
Oswald Townsend
George Ward*
John Warford
Daniel Whalen
Edward Wilson

1779

Nicholas Anderson
Charles Beall*
William Bramblett
Thomas Burrus*
Cooper Chancellor*
William Clinkenbeard
Benedict Couchman
Benjamin Dunaway
James Duncan

John Harper
John Henderson
Lucus Hood*
Beal Kelly
John Kelly
William Patterson
Lewis Reno*
Thomas Shald*
Richard Spurr*

Joshua Stamper
Jeremiah Starke
Charles Tate
John Taylor
Moses Thomas
Garrett Townsend*
Edward Williams

1780

Joshua Bennett*
John Embry*
John Halley
George James*
James Ledgerwood

Jeremiah Moore*
John Payne*
William Payne*
John Price*
Abraham Scholl

William Shortridge*
John Stevens*
John Vivion*

1781
John Clemons* Alexander McClain* James Townsend*
Samuel Martin* Richard Piles*

1782
Isaac Collins* John Donaldson*

1782 or 1783
Joseph Long*

1783
Michael Cassidy* Charles Morgan* Henry Payne*
George James* Achilles Morris*
Thomas Lewis* Edward Payne Sr.*

1784
David Hughes*

1785
Joseph Berry Leonard Hart* William Stribling*
William Foster*

1787 or 1788
Jacob Dooley*

1788
Benjamin Dod Wheeler

1789
Thomas Dawson

1791
Samuel Dawson*

Clark County Court Depositions

1795
Kentucky
Clarke County

Be it Remembered That the following are Depositions, Certificates and other Instruments of writing Committed to record pursuant to an Act of Assembly intitled "An Act for establishing the Boundary of Lands and for other purposes." attested
David Bullock, Clark County Clerk

1.

George Balla and Patrick Jordan for George Thompson

George Thompson

George Thompson was a wealthy landowner of Mercer County. He was born in Albermarle County, Virginia, where he resided when he was called into service in the Revolution in 1776. He was a lieutenant in the "Minute Men" under Capt. Roger Thompson. George built a fine colonial brick home 4 miles northeast of Harrodsburg, near Shawnee Springs, and kept 200 acres of his estate as a personal game preserve for elk, bear and deer. In 1795, Thompson bought into the Bourbon Furnace, built by Jacob Myers and then being operated by John Cockey Owings and Company. The iron furnace—Kentucky's first—was located less than 1 mile east of Thompson's claim on Slate Creek. Thompson's tract overlapped considerably with Myers' land. In 1800, Thompson petitioned the Mercer County court for permission to erect a water gristmill and sawmill on his lands on Shawnee Run.[1] His death notice appeared in the newspaper:

Col. George Thompson of Mercer county. Died April 22, 1834, aged 86 years.[2]

Ralph Morgan surveyed a 5000-acre tract on Slate Creek for Thompson on a treasury warrant in 1784, beginning the survey at a "pealed black oak." This huge tract lay entirely in present-day Bath County. The northeast corner is just south of I-64 near Owingsville; the southwest corner is near the village of Peeled Oak on KY 1331. Thompson also purchased a 1500-acre tract adjoining to the west, and in 1795 "George Thompson of Mercer County" sold 360 acres on Stepstone and Slate creeks to Abijah Brooks.[3]

George Balla

George Balla came to Kentucky in 1776 with Thomas Clark's company of Virginia locators. He stated in a land suit that they came down the Ohio River, ascended the Licking to Upper Blue Licks, and continued by water to the mouth of Little Flat Creek in present-day Bath County. The company built fourteen cabins to establish claims in the area. Balla eventually settled nearby on Balla Branch of Flat Creek, north and east of Sharpsburg.[4]

Patrick Jordan

Patrick Jordan was out with the Fincastle surveyors in 1775. He was a chain carrier for John Floyd's military surveys on North Elkhorn Creek and James Douglass' on Stoner Creek, including Nathaniel Gist's military surveys. Jordan recalled that "there was much cain here then." He later resided in Mercer County.[5]

Peeled Oak

Peeled Oak, a small rural community in Bath County, is located about ½ mile southwest of where this landmark tree stood. While there are various accounts of how the community got its name,[6] Jordan's deposition gives a clear description of the origin of the name "peeled oak." In

1776, Jordan accompanied James Harrod on an expedition in search of land on Slate Creek. While following a trail that led to the Mud Lick, they came upon "a pealed Black Oak which appeared was painted, as the said Harrod and the Deponant believed, by the Indians . . . but a short time before." Jordan said that Harrod was much taken with the area and intended to make a private survey on it, and that Harrod marked a beginning tree as follows: "[He] pealed one side of a much larger Black Oak standing on the right hand side of the road going to the Mud Lick." At the time of the deposition, the tree peeled and painted by the Indians had fallen down, but the tree peeled by Harrod was still standing. Jordan described how the Indians peeled the bark for use in their camps, and he found evidence of their marks in the fallen down oak.

Mud Lick

The Mud Lick was a notorious spot for buffalo in pioneer times. Hunters first called the place "sweet lick." The lick was later became the site of Olympian Springs, a famous resort spa that operated throughout the 1800s and well into the 1900s. The state's first stagecoach line, established in 1803, ran from Lexington to the Olympian Springs.[7]

Little Mountain

Little Mountain was the first name of Mt. Sterling. The name was derived from a massive Indian mound measuring 50 yards across at the base and 25 feet in height. Its discovery was described by Enoch Smith:

> William Calk and Robert Whitledge, who explored the cuntry, found the little Mount in the year 1775.[8]

The mound became a well-known landmark north of the Kentucky River. The Little Mountain, located at the corner of Locust Street and Queen Street, was unceremoniously leveled in 1846.[9]

Deposition of George Balla [1]

The Deposition of George Balla, of lawfull age, taken before us Commissioners appointed by an order of the court of Clarke County, the 28th day of April 1795, for taking Depositions in behalf of George Thompson to perpetuate Testimony respecting a *pealed Black Oak tree*, the beginning corner of a survey of 5000 acres lying on Slate Creek made for the said Thompson.

The said Balla being first sworn deposeth and saith That in November 1783 he was present when Thomas Swearingham [Swearingen] made A survey for himself which began at the place called the pealed Black Oak, which is the place where this Deponent now stands. That the place was then called the pealed Black Oak by those present & that this Deponent saw a pealed Black [oak] standing near the Buffaloe road which lead by the same, which he thinks is the same now lying & nearly rotton.

That in the year 1776 this Deponent with sundry others explored the country around the place now called the *mud Lick* and built a Cabbin at the said Lick. That in early times the said Lick was frequently called the sweet Lick & this Deponent does believe it was called & known by the name of the *sweet Lick* before it was called the mud Lick. That he was well acquainted with Slate Creek & its waters on the East side & that he knew no other place ever called the sweet Lick but the place now called the mud Lick, nor ever knew or heard any other place called "the pealed black Oak" but the place where this Deponent now stands & where the said Thomas Swearingham Began his survey as aforesaid.

This Deponent further saith that he was intimately acquainted with James Harrod while living and is satisfyed that he was well acquainted with slate Creek and the Country around the pealed Black [oak].

2

Question by James French: Had you ever seen the Pealed Black before the time
        aforesaid?
Answer: I had not.

Question by same: Who piloted you in 1783 to this place?
Answer: There were as many as 8 or 10 men along & he does not remember who
        piloted.

Question by same: Did you see the blazed tree on the side of the Hill said by
        Patrick Jordan to be pealed by Harrod, or were on the side of the Hill?
Answer: I do not remember that I was on the side of the Hill or saw the tree and
        to the best of my remembrance he began at the pealed Oak now lying
        down & he remembers seeing but that pealed tree & no other.

Question by same: What year did you know the mud Lick by the name & when
        slate Creek by that name?
Answer: In the year 1776.

Question by same: Did you know any other trace leading from slate Creek to the
        mud Lick?
Answer: I knew [one] which crossed at the mouth of the Prickly Ash [and] one
        other trace which crossed Slate above the mouth of Roes [Rose] Run
        which I think lead into the other trace before it reached the mud Lick &
        one other which went up a branch that headed towards *Little Mountain.*

Question by same: Did all these Traces lead from Hingston?
Answer: I cannot tell. They came, I believe, from that course and do not know
        whether this trace leads to Hingston.

Question by same: Did you ever see any other pealed Black Oak on any other
        trace leading to he mud Lick but this one?
Answer: I do not know that I did.

Question by same: When you came to survey here did Swearingham or any of his
        party call this the pealed Black Oak?
Answer: I think they did, perhaps Swearingham himself, for I carried the chain
        for Swearingham & he attended the making the Survey & paid me for
        carrying the chain.

Question by John Warford: Did you see two pealed trees at the Crossing of the
        war path of a fork between the mud Lick & Slate Creek?
Answer: I saw two trees scalped with a Tomahawk in November 1783 which
        appeared to have been marked but a few days before on a road which lead
        I do not know where but lead a southardly course.

Question by Thompson: Did you ever hear John Warford call the place where you now are the pealed Black Oak & did you ever see him at this place before?

Answer: John Warford was present in November 1783 when Swearingham made his survey as aforesaid & I have heard him call this place the pealed Black Oak.

Question by Thompson: Did the above John Warford ever request you not to divulge what you knew about Hugh Sidwells not having built a Cabbin at the Elkhorn Spring untill after he had conveyed away his right under Sidwells preemption?

Answer: He did, informing me he had sold to Jacob Myers & had only warranted against himself & his Heirs.

Question by Mr. Warford: When was this request made?
Answer: Last year.

Question by James French: Is the lying down tree before spoken of by you a black Oak?

Answer: I do not know, but believe it to be the same place Swearingham brought me to & the same place he began his survey from.

Question by same: Was any of the other traces spoken of before as large as this trace?

Answer: I believe there was but will not certify it.

Question by same: Was there as much of the Bark taken off the scalped trees aforesaid as there is off the tree shewed this day by Patrick Jordan & said by him to be pealed by Colonel Harrod in 1776?

Answer: There were two trees one on the right hand and the other on the left hand of a trace lying to the South East of this place leading from the mud Lick Southwardly. I cannot tell how much of the Bark was Hewed off with the Tommahock, but I believe it was not as long as this.

Question by Colonel Thompson: How far do you believe the two Trees that had the Bark Hewed off is from the peeled Black Oak where you now are?

Answer: I believe not nearer than two or three miles. And this Deponant further saith not.

[signed] George Balla
attested Enoch Smith, Jilson Payne, James Poage

Deposition of Patrick Jordan [7]

The Deposition of Patrick Jordan, of lawfull age, taken before us, Commissioners appointed by an order of the Court of Clarke County the 28th day of April 1795 for taking Depositions on behalf of George Thompson to perpetuate

Testimony respecting a pealed Black tree, the beginning Corner of a Survey of 5000 acres claimed by the said Thompson lying on Slate Creek.

The said Jordan being first sworn, Deposeth and Saith, That about the year 1776 Captain James Harrod (now deceased) & this Deponant explored Slate Creek and its waters for the purpose of examining & viewing the Land and during their route examined the Lands around the Lick now called the mud Lick.

That on their way to the mud Lick they Pursued a Buffoloe Road which lead from Hingston to the said Lick & passed by the place where this Deponant now stands at which there was a pealed Black Oak which appeared was painted, as the said Harrod and this Deponent believed, by the Indians and which appeared to have been painted & pealed but a short time before That. There is a tree now lying down nearly rotten which this Deponent does verily believe is the same tree above spoken of.

That the said Harrod seemed pleased with the land in that neighbourhood, and then pealed one side of a much larger Black Oak standing on the right hand side of the road going to the Mud Lick, and is the same tree which this Deponant has now shewed to the Commissioners & stands on a Bench of Rocks on the side of a Hill, and the said Harrod then declared that he intended to make that place the Beginning Corner of a large private survey.

This Deponent saith that the said Harrod & himself Camped several Days at the said Pealed Black Oak which is the place where he now stands and that it was a noted camping place for Indians as they passed & repassed. That he never saw the said place afterwards till about the year 1782 or 1783 when the said Black Oak tree, painted as aforesaid by the Indians, was standing but much decayed.

That the said Harrod at the time he marked the said tree called it the pealed Black Oak and whenever he heard the said Harrod afterwards, which he frequently did both before & since the opening of the Land Office, speak of the said place, he always called it "the Pealed Black Oak Tree." And this Deponant always afterwards knew it well by that name.

This Deponent saith that the place now called the Mud Lick was in former times known to a great many & called by the name of the Sweet Lick & was more generally called the Sweet Lick by those this Deponent heard speak of it. And this Deponent well knows was called the sweet Lick by James Harrod who was the first person who shewed it to this Deponent.

This Deponent saith that he does not recollect being at the said Pealed Black Oak from 1782 or 1783 till last winter, but this Deponent can speak with certainty & say it is the same place He saw Harrod mark in 1776, and is the same place he again was at in 1782 or 1783, it having undergone no change in appearance except the falling down of the tree pealed and painted by the Indians. That the Buffaloe road which lead from the said Sweet Lick, now Mud Lick, to the Pealed Black [Oak] & from thence to Hingston was in 1776 a plain much used & well trodden road and this Deponent never heard any other Lick called the Sweet Lick or any other place known by the name of the Pealed Black Oak.

Question by John Warford, who considers himself interested under Hugh Sidwells
    preemption right: Was there any other person in company but Colonel

Harrod with you in 1776?
Answer: No.

Question: When was you again at the pealed black Oak & who was with you?
Answer: I think it was in 1783 and Thomas Clarke & one Smit he thinks also.

Question by James French, who is interested on account of Entries made in the
        name Jeremiah Moore & John Farrer [Farrow]: Are you interested in the
        Establishment of this Pealed Black Oak tree?
Answer: I am not at all interested.

Question by same: Was Slate known by that name in 1776?
Answer: I do not know that it was then known by any name. I did not then hear
        it called Slate.

Question by same: Did you know whether it was the waters of Hingston or not?
Answer: I knew it was not the waters of Hingston, but knew that it was the waters
        of Licking.

Question by same: When did you first know it by the name of Slate?
Answer: I knew it by that name in 1779.

Question by same: Was you ever but once on Slate Creek with Colonel Harrod?
Answer: I was not.

Question by same: How early did you know the Mud Lick called so?
Answer: I think it was either in 1777 or 1778 or thereabouts.

Question by same: Did you know of any other Buffaloe road leading from
        Hingston to the Mud Lick or from Slate Creek to the Mud Lick?
Answer: I did not know of any other.

Question by same: Did Colonel Harrod peal any other Black Oak or other tree at
        any other place during your route together?
Answer: Not that I knew of or saw. This place where he pealed the black Oak
        was a remarkable place. We staid at it several Days and dressed skins.

Question by same: Do you know if Colonel Harrod was out on Slate after he
        pealed the black Oak & before the Land Office opened [in 1780]?
Answer: I think he informed me he was.

    This Deponent further saith that he hath now, since his Examination has
commenced, viewed the said Black Oak tree which was painted as aforesaid &
finds the plain & very visible marks of a Tomahawk or edged Instrument of that
size about 6 or 8 Inches above the root and that such is the Usual way that Indians
peal trees, the bark being intending by them to be made use of preparing their

6

camps with.

Question by Mr. French: Which tree did you always conceive to be the pealed
Black Oak & the one he meant to survey from?
Answer: The one Colonel Harrod marked I always conceived to be intended by
him for a marked tree & was called by him the pealed Black Oak.

Question: When Colonel Harrod ever afterwards mentioned the Pealed Black
Oak, did you Understand the Tree on the Hill only, or did you understand
the Camp & other pealed tree?
Answer: I understood the tree on the Hill & the Camp and the other pealed tree
which was painted by Indians. And this Deponant further Saith not.

Witness my hand,
[signed] Patrick Jordan
attested Enoch Smith, Jilson Payne, James Poage

The foregoing Depositions of George Balla and Patrick Jordan were taken
before us this 3rd day of June 1795 at the place called & known by the name of
"the Pealed Black Oak" lying on the East side of Slate Creek in Clarke County &
being the Beginning Corner of George Thompsons survey of 5000 acres by Entry
dated the 22d day of May 1780, present and attending thereto: John Hamilton,
Thomas Montgomery and John Story, three disinterested men residents of the
County of Clarke, as the Law directs, present also Hubbard Taylor, James Knox,
Jacob Myers, John McIntire, Valentine Stone, Abijah Brooks, David Hughes,
John McGuire & sundry other persons.
    And in order to perpetuate the place where the said Pealed Black [Oak]
stood, which is Now in a state of decay & which is deposed to in the two
foregoing Depositions, there being only a few marks made, by appearance with a
Tomahahawk, and within 6 or 8 inches of the root, We the said Commissioners
did mark on a large red Oak standing about 10 yards up the Branch from the said
lying pealed Black Oak (the same having stood on the North side of the Branch &
on the verge of the same nearly opposite to a White [oak] on the same side of the
Branch) the two first Letters of each of our names. The said large Black Oak
being formerly marked for a Corner & still bearing the marks thereof. Given
under our hands the Day Month and year above written. Enoch Smith
Jilson Payne
James Poage

2.

Benjamin Ashby and Hugh Forbes for William Eustace

William Eustace

Virginian William Eustace served in the Prince William County militia (1753) and later
(1770) reached the rank of colonel in the Fauquier County militia.[10]

Eustace's claim was placed before the Virginia land commission at Harrodsburg by his friend Hancock Lee on January 31, 1780.

> William Eustace . . . this day claimed a preemption of 1000 Acres of Land at the State price in the district of Kentucky On Account of Marking & improving the same in the year 1775, lying on the South side of Hi[n]gstons fork of licking Creek on a small branch running into the said Creek just above a small lick on the Bank of the said creek to include his improvement.[11]

The survey indicates that the tract is actually "on the waters of Stoners fork, a branch of Licking." The tract was surveyed by Richard Beale in 1783 and granted to Eustace in 1785. The land is situated about 6 miles northeast of Winchester and about 4 miles south of Bramblett's Lick. There is no record of Eustace ever moving his residence to Kentucky. In 1809, "William Eustace of the State of Virginia & County of Fauquier" gave his power of attorney to John Gibson to sell all his land in Kentucky.[12]

Benjamin Ashby

Benjamin Ashby was a surveyor from Frederick County, Virginia. He was in Kentucky in 1775 running surveys on behalf of the Ohio Company in what is now Clark County. In 1782 and 1783, he made numerous surveys for fellow Virginians in Clark and Montgomery. He surveyed for himself and patented a tract of 597 acres on Stoner adjoining Gist's military survey. Benjamin Ashby and wife Jane of Frederick County sold part of this tract to Joshua Singleton in 1795. In 1796, Ashby gave Enos Hardin of Clark County his power of attorney to dispose of his Kentucky lands. In 1804, Benjamin Ashby, age 57, gave a deposition at his home in Frederick County stating that he had been a surveyor in Kentucky.[13]

Gist Creek

Gist Creek was named for Nathaniel Gist, whose military surveys were located on the creek. Gist obtained patents for both surveys and later settled there, where he built a noted mansion called Canewood. The name of the creek was later changed to Stoner Creek in honor of pioneer Michael Stoner.

Bramblett's Lick

Bramblett's Lick was located near Wades Mill, about 1 mile southwest of the intersection of Wades Mill Road and White-Turley Road. This salt lick, which attracted deer and occasionally buffalo, was a hunting spot known from early times. The lick took its name from William Bramblett, a Baptist minister from Bedford County, Virginia, who came to Kentucky in the early spring of 1779.[14] (see procession #33)

Deposition of Benjamin Ashby [14]

Clarke County Sct.

We, William Sudduth, John Eliott, James Young and Dennis Dunham, being appointed Commissioners by the County Court of Clarke, pursuant to an act of assembly entitled an act for asertaining the boundries of Lands & for other purposes, being convened at a Spring at which there is some choping and marks Cald for in an entry of a preemption Claimed by William Ewestace, caused to come before us Benjamin Ashby, who after being Sworn deposeth and saith that some time in the summer of one Thousand seven Hundred and seventy five [1775] he the said deponant in Company with William Ewestace & others found said spring as described in the calls of said Entry & that the said William Ewestace made such improvements by choping Trees & making such other marks as was common to be made in them times & that the said Ewestace from that time claimed said Land by his improving the same.

That he the said deponant, Ewestace and others, after they had made the improvement above Mentioned, traveled nearly a north Course, as well as he can Recolect, about four miles. They Then came to a large Creek on which was a Lick, and from this deponants acquaintance with the Country since, is the Lick called *Bramblets Lick*. Further This deponant saith That when They came to the Creek above mentioned, they knew no name for it, but shortly after it was Known by the name of *Gists Creek*, by reason of Gist having land surveyed on it by one [James] Douglass & that he the said deponant verily believes the spring that he is now at to be the indenticle place called for by said Ewestace, and further This deponant saith not. [signed] Benjamin Ashby

The forgoing Deposition of Benjamin Ashby was taken before us, William Sudduth, John Eliot, James Young, Denis Dunham, this 13th day of July 1795, as commissioners apointed for that purpose at the place Known by the name of the cave spring & Ewestaces improvement, lying on the west side of Stoners fork, a Branch of Hinkston, in Clarke County and being intended for the senter of said Ewestaces Preemption of a thousand acres, as appears the said Ewestace has a Claim to by his entry with the Court of Commissioners and with the surveyor May 16th, 1783, and an amendment the 28th day of the same month in the presence of William Henry, Robert Higgins & Bennet Clark, Disinterested witnesses, as the Law directs.
Present also Jacob Smith, Micajah Clark, Jonas Haun [Hon], James Sudduth, Jesse Copher, Martin Judy, Nathaniel Lander, George Brooks, David Bullock, Alexander Ramsey & others & in order to perpetuate the place the said Spring comes out of some rocks.
Choping and marks are in a state of decay & which is deposed to in the foregoing Depositions, There onlay being a few marked trees and a lin tree marked EW, We caused a lin tree standing at the Head of said spring to be marked SEY & WSY. The first mentioned tree marked WE stands about 10 or 12 feet from the spring on the west side of the spring branch. Given under our own hands and seals this day & year above written.
William Sudduth
John Eliott
James Young
Dennis Dunham

Deposition of Hugh Forbes [17]

Clarke County Sct.
We, William Sudduth, John Eliott, James Young, Dennis Dunham, Commissioners appointed by the County Court of Clarke pursuant to an act of Assembly made and intitled an act for ascertaining the boundries of Lands and for other purposes, being Conveined at the spring and improvement called for in an Entry of William Ewestace of a thousand acres of Land, caused to come before us, Hugh Forbis, who after being duly sworn deposeth and saidth that some time in the summer one thousand seven Hundred & Eighty three [1783] he was in Company with Richard E. Beal in Lexington, and that said Beal informed him that said Ewestace had a preemption on the waters of Stoner including a large

Cave spring, at which spring said Ewestace name was Marked or the two first letters thereof.

That some time in the fall following he the said deponant being in company with Captain William Triplett had missed there way and accidently came to the spring above mentioned & that some short time after he fell in company with said Beal and informed him that he the said deponant had found an improvement with the first letters of Ewestace name marked at a Cave spring, which he the said deponant had reason to believe it was Ewestaces improvement & then the said Beal employed him the said deponant to come & show the improvement, which in order to find they Came up Gest Creek a considerable Distance & struck across to the spring & when they came to said spring, the said Beal imployed him the said Deponant to carry the chain to survey said Land. Further this Deponant saith not.
[signed] Hugh Forbis

The Foregoing Deposition of Hugh Forbises was taken before us, William Sudduth, John Eliott, James Young and Denis Dunham this 13th day of July 1795, as commissioners appointed for that purpose, at the place known by the name of cave spring and William Ewestaces improvement, lying on the west side of Stoners fork, a branch of Hinkston, in Clarke County, and being intended for the Center of said Ewestaces preemption of a Thousand Acres, as appears the said Ewestace has a Claim to by his Entry with the Court of Commissioners dated January 31st 1780, also by his Entry with surveyor May 16th 1783 & his amendment dated the 28 day of the same month, in the presence of Robert Higgins, Micajah Clarke and James Sudduth, Disintrested witnesses resident in the County of Clarke, as the Law directs.

Present also Nathaniel Lander, Martin Judy, Daniel Ohare, Jacob Smith, George Brooks, Bennet Clarke, David Bullock, Alexander Ramsey, David Kincaid, Jonas Haun [Hon] & others, and in order to perpetuate the place where the said spring comes out of the rocks, choping and marks are now in a state of Decay & which is deposed to in the forgoing Deposition, there only being a few choped trees & a lin tree, Marked WE, standing on the west side of the Spring branch about ten or twelve feet from the said spring. Given under our hands and seals this 13th day of July 1795.
William Sudduth
John Eliott
James Young
Denness Donham

3.

Elias Tolin for Martin Hammond

Martin Hammond

Martin Hammond may have been a brother of John Hammond, both of whom were in Kentucky early. John was born on the James River in Goochland County, Virginia. John and his widowed mother lived with John's grandfather, William, a Baptist minister, who fled to Surry

County, North Carolina to avoid persecution. There Martin's name appears on a list of militia compensated for "going against the Cherokee" in 1771. Martin was in Kentucky by November 1777, when he signed a petition stating that the inhabitants were destitute of salt and urging Virginia to "errect Salt Manufactories at the different Springs." The names of John Hammond and his wife Sarah and Martin Hammond are inscribed on the tablet at Bryan Station as defenders during the siege of 1782. Martin appears to have left the state before 1790. The surname is spelled Hammon and Hammond in the records.[15]

Hammond was awarded a 400-acre settlement and 1000-acre preemption by the Virginia land commission sitting at Harrodsburg on February 8, 1780. In his absence, Hammond's claim was entered by Nathaniel Henderson:

> Martin Hammond . . . this day claimed a settlement & preemption to a tract of
> land in the district of Kentucky on Account of residing in the Country 12 Month
> before the year 1778, lying on a small Creek that runs into licking Creek about 10
> or 12 Miles above the Upper Salt Spring Known by the Name of the Flat Creek,
> beginning about ¾ of a Mile above where a big Buffalo path crosses the Creek,
> including some improvements made by Colonel William Lynn &c.[16]

The processioning below took place prior to Hammond receiving his patent. He was not present when "a motion of Martin Hammond was entered by his agent, Jeremiah Poor," setting forth his claim" to 1400 acres on "Flatt creek." This land, located about 4 miles east of Sharpsburg in Bath County, was later the subject of a lawsuit. According to papers filed in the case, Hammond's tract was surveyed, but the surveyor was killed by Indians before he could return it to the land office, and a grant was not issued. Hammond had the land surveyed again, by William Sudduth in 1797, and finally received a Kentucky grant in 1799.[17] Hammond died soon after and his son, Martin Hammond of "the ninety six district of South Carolina," deeded the property to Mark Mitchell of Hawkins County, Tennessee, who in turn sold parcels to Peter Hanks, James Stewart, John Elliott, and others.[18]

The controversy leading to *James Berry, Peter Hanks et al. vs Robert Gunnell* arose because Robert Gunnell received a grant for an interfering tract in 1785, twelve years prior to Hammond's. However, Gunnell's claim to the land dated to his entry made in 1784, while Hammond's entries were made in 1780.[19]

Elias Tolin

Elias Tolin was born in 1755 in Culpeper County, Virginia, and enlisted in the Virginia Line in Stafford County in 1775. In the latter year, he went out with a company of locators in search of land in Kentucky. After the Revolutionary War, he moved to Kentucky and applied for a pension while living in Montgomery County in 1818. At that time Tolin, age 63, had a wife, age 46, four young daughters and four sons. He was called upon frequently to testify regarding lands claims on Hinkston, Slate and Flat creeks. Tolin died in 1824 and was buried in the Old Presbyterian Cemetery in Mt. Sterling.[20]

Upper Blue Licks

This lick, upstream on Licking River from the famous Lower Blue Licks, was known as a hunting spot from early times. The pioneers usually called it the "upper salt springs." In 1782, Upper Blue Licks was the site of John Holder's defeat by the Indians, the week before the more memorable battle at the Lower Blue Licks. Upper Blue Licks is located about 10 miles east of Carlisle, on KY 57 at the crossing of Licking River, the boundary between Fleming and Nicholas counties.[21]

Deposition of Elias Tolin [20]

Clarke County Sct.

We, William Sudduth, James McLHany [McElhaney] & John Eliott, Commissioners appointed by the County Court of Clarke, persuant to an act for assembly entitled an act for assertaining the Boundres of Lands & for other purposes, Being convenied at an Improvement about two Hundred yards above the mouth of the East fork of flat Creek and on the east side of the Creek, caused to come before us Elias Tolin, who after being sworn deposith and saith that some time in the month of September 1775, he the said Deponant was in Company with Colonel William Linn & Thomas Clarke & others, assisted in Making a Cabin at the place we are now assembled & that he the said deponant very well recollects to see Thomas Clarke girdle a red Oak tree and mark the Letters TC on the south side of said tree & that said Linn & Company marked & deadened sundry trees, as was Common for them to do in improving Lands in them times, which said tree marked TC stands on the East side of Flat [Creek] about two rods from the bank.

Question by Mr. [Valentine] Stone: Do you recolect the boffolo road Crossing the creek about 3/4 of a mile below the lower Improvement sworn to by you in your former Deposition?
Answer: I Can't recolect in particular the crossing at that Distance, tho remember that the road Crossed Frequently. And further this deponant saith not.

[signed] Elias Tolin

The foregoing Deposition taken by us the under subscribers at the Improvement mentioned, and the said improvement being in a state of decay, we caused to be marked a fresh a red oak tree, E, in the presence of John Morgan, Thomas Rogers, Josiah Fugate Junior, Eliott Hamilton and others, Disinterested witnesses in whose presence the said Deposition was taken. Given under our hands & seals this 7th day of September 1795.
William Sudduth
James McLHaney
John Eliott

Deposition of Elias Tolin [21]

Clarke County Sct.
        This day We, William Sudduth, James Mclhany [McElhaney] & John Eliot commissioners appointed by the court of Clarke County pursuant to an act of assembly entitled an act for assertaining Boudries of Lands and for other purposes, being convenied at an Improvement at the mouth of a small branch running in on the East side of Flat Creek, caused to come before us Elias Tolin, and after being duly sworn, Deposeth and saith that some time in the month of September 1775, he the said deponant was present at the mouth of the above mentioned branch on the East bank of flat Creek in Company with Colonel William Linn & Company & assisted in marking trees & raising a Cabin in such manner as was Custamary to raise in them times by Improvers in them days & also in his presence sundry other trees was marked and deadened & sundry trees marked with letters as follows: standing about one Hundred yards south of the above Cabin on a high red Clay bank, a sugar tree marked, thus, E, ajacent to which stands a large white Oak tree marked TC & sundry trees deadened which said marks, as above described, this deponant well remembers to of seen made,

except the large white Oak tree marked TC, tho has reason to believe said mark was made by Thomas Clarke who was in Company with this deponant & Company & Frequenly marked his name at any improvements the company made & this deponant well remembers the situation of the plaise said improvement now is on & that he does not recolect of any improvements made by Lin & Company lower down on Flat Creek then the one we now are at & that when Lin and Company had made the improvement they went from thence to the *uper blue Lick* & when they arive at the said Lick, some conversation arise about the distance they had travelled since they had made said improvements, to which it was generally agreed the distance to be about ten or twelve miles.

Question asked by Valentine Stone: Was Martin Hammond one of the Company of Linn?
Answer: He was not & and further this deponant saith not.

[signed] Elias Tolin

The Foregoing Deposition was taken by us the subscribing Commissioners at the Improvement above mentioned, and as the marks appeared In a state of decay, we caused to be marked a spanish oak tree, WS, and there is a white Oak tree marked RB, which said trees stands ajacint to said Cabin mentioned in said Deposition. We also marked afresh a large white Oak tree that stands about one Hundred yards south of said cabin with the letters PDB, and marked as a corner the said tree [that] has a old mark, TC, as desolved [described] in the above Deposition, which marks were made and deposition taken by us the commissioners on the 7th day of September 1795 in the presence of Thomas Rogers, John Morgan, Josiah Fugate Junior & Eliot Hamilton & others. Given under our hands & seals this day above mentioned.
William Sudduth
James Mclhany
John Eliott

4.

William Hays for Leonard Beall

Walter Chiles

Walter Chiles was listed on the tax rolls of Spotsylvania County, Virginia, where he was charged for eleven slaves for the year 1782. The name is found on the Shelby County, Kentucky tax list for 1800. Chiles received several patents in Kentucky: 500 acres on the waters of Slate Creek adjoining Walter Carr and 500 acres in Clark County. In 1811, Chiles' heirs had a tract in Montgomery County surveyed in his name but no patent was issued. The Chiles and Carr families were closely related in Spotsylvania County; however, no further effort was made to establish the genealogy of Walter Chiles in these Depositions.[22]
In February 1780, Thomas Jones, of Louisa County, Virginia, received military certificates entitling him to 150 acres of unsettled land for serving three enlistments as a private during the French and Indian War. Jones assigned his military warrants to Walter Chiles.[23] In April 1780,

Chiles obtained an entry for 150 acres on Licking River and had a survey made by William Hays in 1784. Chiles assigned the survey to Leonard Beall.

Leonard Beall

Leonard Beall obtained the patent for the tract processioned below. The patent was not issued until May 1796—twelve years after the survey—for reasons explained in Hays' deposition below. Beall was a Kentucky resident for a time. A Leonard Beall is listed in the records of Augusta County, Virginia, for 1782 and 1783. Beall was on the first roll of taxpayers in Clark County in 1793.[24]

The survey describes this tract as "lying on the Waters of Licking. Beginning one mile below Daniel Boones Settlement, on the same creek." Boone's settlement was located near Schollsville in Clark County, which would place Beall's land on Stoner Creek near the mouth of Georges Branch. Beall appeared before the county court in July 1795 and entered a motion for Walter Chiles to procession the 150-acre tract. In 1804, Beall's heirs—Zachariah, Edward, Rezin and Margaret—sold 107 acres of this tract to William Frame of Clark County.[25]

William Hays

William Hays married Daniel Boone's daughter Susannah. He taught Boone "to write with an improved hand" and kept Boone's accounts for a time in North Carolina. Newly married, William and Susannah came to Boonesborough in 1775. He was present during the siege of the fort in 1779, moved with Boone to Boone's Station in Fayette County and then to Marble Creek in Madison County. Hays engaged in surveying and remained in Kentucky until 1799, when he moved to the Boone enclave in Missouri. He reportedly was "a bad tempered, drinking man" and was killed in 1804 at the hand of his own son-in-law.[26]

Deposition of William Hays [24]

The Deposition of William Hays, of Lawfull age, Deposeth and saith that on April 26th 1780, I attended at the surveyors office at Wilson station where I offered to enter one Hundred & fifty acres of Military Land warrants for Walter Chiles. George May told me that I must make out the Location & put it in the warrants & he would Enter it when it come to its turn, which I did, and he strung it on a thread which I found afterwards was entered the next day, but not in the words of the Location that I put in the warrants Exactly. Instead of settlement, he put station, which was not what I had wrote. My view when I made the Entry was to begin one mile below Boon's settlement line, where I did survey it, which Creek at that time was called the middle fork of Licking by them that knew no better, Beginning at a Honey Locust & Hickory one mile Below Boon's settlement, since (as the Chain Carriers informed me) in the fork of a creek, thence North 45 [degrees] East 160 poles crossing a Creek to a Hickory, ash and white Oak, thence North 25 degrees West 150 poles to a Honey Locust and Buckeye, thence South 45 degrees West 160 poles crossing a Creek to three Linns, thence south 45 degrees East 150 poles crossing a creek to the Beginning. And further this [deponent] saith not.
[signed] William Hays
[attested] Original Young, John Young

Clarke County Sct.
We, Original Young and John Young, Commissioners appointed by the County Court aforesaid & pursuant to an act of assembly intitled an act for assertaining the Boundries of Lands and for other purposes, being convened on

the Land Claimed by Lenord Bell and at the Begining of the Same, at a Honey Lockest & Hickroy Trees, caused to come before us William Hays, witness, who after being sworn Deposeth and saith that [this] is the Identicle place he intended for the Begining of Walter Chiles, assignee of Thomas Jones, Entry of one Hundred and fifty acres, which are in the following words, To wit, as above mentioned in the said Depos[i]tion and signed by the said Deponant William Hayes.

The foregoing Deposition was taken before us, Original Young & John Young, Commissioners, and on the Land of Lenord Bell at the said Begining Corner as above mentioned, in the presents of Edmond Raglin [Ragland], William Frame & John Stephenson, Disentrusted witnesses, on the first day of September 1795, Witness our hands & seals the day and date above mentioned.
Original Young
John Young

N.B. We the commissioners also caused to be Marked afresh the said corner with the letter Y. Original Young, John Young

5.

Daniel Boone for William Watson

William Watson

William Watson gives a thorough biography of himself in his Revolutionary War pension application. He was born September 5, 1742, in Louisa County, Virginia, and was living in Pittsylvania County at the time of his enlistment in the Virginia Line. Watson lived in Clark County, when he bought land on Boone Creek from Charles Morgan in 1797, and in Madison County when he sold the tract to John McCall in 1814. He applied for a pension from Madison in 1832, stating that he had lived in Kentucky approximately 28 years. Watson moved to Posey County, Indiana, in 1833 and died there on September 2, 1846.[27]

Watson's 950-acre tract was entered on a treasury warrant in 1780, surveyed by Daniel Boone in 1785, and granted to Watson's heirs—John, Matthew and William Watson—in 1788.[28] The property is located on Flat Creek in Bath County, a 8 or 9 miles south of the Upper Blue Licks on Licking River.

Daniel Boone

Daniel Boone, the famous hunter-woodsman and frontier leader, was involved in all aspects of the land business in Kentucky. He speculated in land on his own, having entered nearly 30,000 acres in his own name. He located tracts of land for others and was often paid in acreage. Boone was also a surveyor and at various times held the appointment of deputy surveyor for Bourbon, Clark, Fayette, Lincoln, Madison and Mason counties. He made many surveys in Clark County, including the large holdings of William Bush on Lower Howard's Creek and Twomile Creek. Daniel Boone was criticized by his contemporaries as a careless surveyor, but according to recent historical analysis, his work was probably no better or worse than average.[29]

Boone's Old Camp

This tract is associated with one of the most famous episodes in the history of Kentucky: Boone's rescue of daughter Jemima and the Calloway girls after their capture by the Shawnee in July 1776.[30] Considerable controversy exists regarding the exact location of the rescue,[31] but this deposition in Boone's own words identifies the spot where the party spent the first night after the rescue. He returned 9 years later to make a survey for Watson that included the site, subsequently referred to as "Boons old Camp."

Upper Salt Spring

The term "Upper Salt Spring" was used interchangeably by the pioneers for the Upper Blue Licks on Licking River.

Deposition of Daniel Boone [26]

The Deposition of Daniel Boon in order to prove and Establish the entry of William Watson containing 955 acres, Begining six miles nearly South West of the *upper Salt Spring* on licken river. This Deponant deposeth and saith that on the 16 day of July 1776, on my the said Deponants return from retaking my Daughters from the Indians, we, the said Deponant & Company, lay all night on Flat Creek at the mouth of a Small Branch, a small Distance from a Cabin on the East Side of said Creek.

In the year 1780 on the 15 day of May, I the said Deponant Entered 955 acres of Land for William Watson as followeth, viz., William Wilson [Watson] entres 955 acres upon Treasury Warrants, Begining six miles nearly south west of the upper Salt Spring, at *Daniel Boons old Camp* at the forks of a branch on the war road, running up the Branch on both sides for Quantity, and in the year 1785 I, the said Deponant, Surveyed the said Land & the Cabin was then standing, & that we now stand on or near the spot where we the said Deponant & Company lay that night, viz., the 16th of July 1776 & that the said survey encluded the same ground called for & Eluded to in the entry.

Question: Colonel Boon, were you employed to make said entry?
Answer: To be sure I was.

Question: Were there any writings past between you & any persons trusting the
    said business?
Answer: I do not recollect that there were.

Question: Were you to receive anything for making these entries?
Answer: Yes, I was paid for it.

Question: Did you know this to be Flat Creek when you made the entry?
Answer: I think I did Certainly know, because of Hammons & Herdersons
    [Henderson's] Entries.

Question: Were you employed to show as well as to survey said Land?
Answer: I was not imployed nor received any thing but the Surveyors fees.

Question: Were you acquainted with the upper salt spring on lickin at that time?
Answer: I was.

Question: What course do you at this time suppose the said upper salt Spring to
    be?

Answer: I now Supose it to be nearly north.

Question: What distance do you suppose it be from here, viz., from this old camp to the upper Salt Spring?
Answer: I suppose 8 or 9 Miles, but at that time I did not think so much.

Question: Did you make or cause to be made any Special mark at this old Camp or place of beginning?
Answer: No, I did not.

The said Deponant then, according to request, proceded to find the place where a cabin stood near said beginning, but when we came there appeared nothing but some vestages of an old Camp where some Cutting had been, viz., one old stump which said Deponant supposed might have been cut for a cabin. We then proceded to assertain the distance from said old encampment to the beging of said survey and found it to be 24 poles, viz., to said Camp aluded to or first mentioned.
[signed] Daniel Boon Sr.
attested Robert Doughherty, William Calwell [Caldwell], David Hughs
October the 22nd 1795

Jonathan Landers This day deposed & saith that he was summoned to notify Thomas Montgomery, agreeable to Law, to attend at the place where William Watson entry & Begining were to be proven &c, which said diponant proceded to Execute & that he, the said deponant, met said Montgomery going from home & that said Montgomery did not attend. Certifyed by me.
William Caldwell

6.

John Halley for Richard Halley

Richard Halley

Richard Halley (c1750-1816) and his brothers—Francis, William and John—came to Kentucky from Fairfax County, Virginia. The surname is also spelled Holley in the records. Richard was listed on the payroll for Capt. John Wood's company stationed at Estill's Station in 1782. Brothers Francis and John settled in Madison and Richard in Clark. According to the Clark County Chronicles, Richard's homeplace was located "about two and a half miles north of Winchester, between the Anderson and Sphar tracts and fronting on the Old Hood's road, between Paris and Mt. Sterling pikes." In 1819, Richard's heirs began dividing his land. He was buried in a graveyard on his farm.[32]

Richard claimed 400 acres in now Clark County, where he resided. The survey, entered on a treasury warrant, described the tract as

lying on the waters of Stoners fork of licking about five miles from Strouds [Strode's] Station . . . Beginning on the top of a ridge about one mile from Thomas Winns Northeast corner.[33]

John South surveyed the tract for Halley in the spring of 1784, and it was granted to Halley in 1785. Halley lived on his tract.[34]

John Halley

John Halley was the marker for his brother Richard's 400-acre survey. According to a deposition John gave elsewhere:

> [I] first came to Kentucky on 21st March 1780. I landed at the Falls from thence I came to Boonesborough and stayed but a short time before I returned to the land office.[35]

John settled near Boonesborough, where he opened one of the first stores, farmed, planted one of the first orchards, and owned a gristmill with John Wilkerson on Otter Creek. In 1789 and 1791, he took a fleet of produce-laden flatboats to New Orleans; his journals of the trips survive. John died in Boonesborough in 1838 and was buried in his family cemetery.[36]

Deposition of John Halley [29]

The Deposition of John Halleys, of Lawful age, Deposeth and saith that on the twenty first day of May one Thousand seven Hundred and Eighty four [1784] he attended the surveyor at Richard Halleys Beginning, at a Cherry, Mulberry, walnut and white oak, and Marked the said Begining Corner and instructed the surveyor to run it procisely agreeable to Location, and when the Land was run I conceived it to Include the Land I entended by the entry. The creek now called Woodrough is the creek mentioned in the Entry & runs through said Land. The Location was made on the tenth day of may one Thousand seven Hundred and Eighty [1780], and further saith not.

Question asked the Deponant by William Bush: Whether the Begining corner mentioned in the Deposition was marked before the Day of the survey? Answer by the Deponant: Twas marked the same Day surveyed.

[signed] John Halley
[attested] Original Young, John Young

Clark County Sct.

We, Original Young & John Young, Commissioners appointed by the County Court of Clarke and pursuant to an act of asembly Intitled an act for assertaining the boundries of Lands and for other purposes, being Convened on the Land clamed by Richard Halley and at the Begining of the same, at a Cherry tree, Mulberry and white Oak, caused to come before us John Halley, witness, who after being sworn Deposeth & saith that the above mentioned trees are the begining Corner of Richard Halleys four Hundred acres entry, which he is well ashured is the place he intended for the begining of the said Richard Halleys entry, and signed by the said Deponant, John Halley.

The foregoing Deposition was taken before us, Original Young & John Young, Commissioners, and on the land at the said Begining Corner above mentioned, and in the presence of Robert Binnifee, Livi Stewart, William Win, and Evan Morgan, Disentrusted witnesses, on this second day of september 1795, as Witness our Hands and seals.
Original Young
John Young

7.

Daniel Boone for Leonard Hall

Benjamin Barton

Little is known about Benjamin Barton. He is reported to have been born in Chester County, Pennsylvania, in about 1720 and to have been a brother of Joshua Barton, who was killed by Indians near Boonesborough in about 1780.[37] On December 24, 1779, Joshua and Benjamin both presented their claims to the Virginia land commission at a session held at Boonesborough. Benjamin's claim, which was near Joshua's, was described as follows:

> It appearing to the Court by Testimony that the said Barton raised a Crop of Corn in the Country in the year 1775 & that he is intitled to a settlement & preemption lying on the branch of licking Creek about 3 Miles North West of Daniel Boons land & Israel Grant.[38]

Benjamin sold his settlement and preemption to Leonard Hall, and Hall paid the fees to the commissioners. No other record of Benjamin in Kentucky has been found.

Leonard Hall

Leonard Hall married Joanna Letton in Frederick County, Maryland, in about 1750, and moved to Bedford County, Virginia, in about 1751. Hall was in Kentucky in 1780, the year he entered claims on four tracts of land, but continued to reside in Virginia until 1792, when he sold his land there prior to moving to Kentucky. Hall settled in Barren County and served on the first grand jury. He died there in about 1809. The inventory of Hall's personal estate included ten slaves, plus various livestock, furniture and utensils with a total value of $3,606.75.[39]

Daniel Boone surveyed four tracts for Hall, two on North Elkhorn and two on Stoner, the latter of which were processioned in Clark County. Hall acquired Benjamin Barton's 400-acre settlement and 1000-acre preemption lying "on a branch of Stoner." The description given in Barton's claim before the land commission places the land on Little Stoner Creek, about 4½ miles northeast of Winchester.[40]

Deposition of Daniel Boone [30]

Agreeable to an order of the Court of Clarke County July 1795, this day Daniel Boon Came before us, Elisha Colins and Joseph Scholl, Commissioners appointed agreeable by the said Court, first Duly sworn and made Oath that he was then on the place aluded to in the Entries made by the said Boone for Leonard, assignee of Benjamin Barton, that this was the spring, the fork of the Creek, and Buffaloe trace.

Question by James Young: When the said place in the said Entries was Marked? Answer by the Deponant: Never was Marked, but Discovered and taken notice of in August 1776.

Question by James Young: What part of Daniel Boons and Israel Grants Land he aluded to when he the said Boon made the Entries for the said Leonard Hall?
Answer By the Deponant: That he aluded to the spring called for in the said Boons Entry as he supposed, as he had not at that time surveyed his Entries at the time he the said Boon called for Leonard Halls Entries.

Question By James Young: What sum of money he the said Boon Received of
Leonard Hall to Locate the said Halls Entries?
Answer By the Deponant: He doth not Remember what sum but was Satisfied
and at the time the said Entries was made for the said Hall.

Question by James Young: Whether he the said Boon is not to receive a certain
sum of money from Hall for shewing the said Land marks mentioned?
Answer by the Deponant: That he has not Received one Shilling nor was never
offered any sum by the said Hall, but that he the said Boon intended to
Charge the said Hall for His trouble, and Further this Deponant sayeth not.

[signed] Daniel Boon
[attested] Joseph Scholl, Elisha Collins

Clark County Sct.
    We, Joseph Scholl [and] Elisha Collins, Commissioners appointed by the
county Court of Clarke and pursuant to an act of assembly entitled an act for
assertaining the boundries of Lands and for other purposes, being convenied on
the Land claimed by Lenord Hall, assignee of Benjamin Barton, at the Spring,
Creek and Buffaloe road aluded to in said Entries, caused to come before us
Daniel Boon, Witness, who after being sworn, deposeth and sayeth the above
Mentioned Spring, Creek and Buffalo Road is the place aluded to in said Entries
made by Daniel Boone for Leonard Hall, assignee of Benjamin Barton, which he
is well assured is the place aluded to when he made Leonard Halls Entries, and
Signed by the Deponant, Daniel Boon.
    The foregoing Deposition was taken before us Josepph Scholl & Elisha
Collins, Commissioners, and on the Land at the spring, creek and Buffaloe Road
above Mentioned, and in the presens of John Hardwick [and] Septimus Davis,
disintrested witnesses, on this 8th Day of September 1795. And further have
caused to be Marked at the Spring two ash Trees JS. Also Marked a small sugar
tree and Hickry at the Northwest Corner of the settlement, as Witness our hands
and seals.
Joseph Scholl
Elisha Collins

8.

William Hancock for Joshua Barton

Joshua Barton

Joshua Barton Sr. (1718-1780) was a frontiersman from Pennsylvania who lived in
Maryland, Virginia and North Carolina, before coming to Boonesborough with his brother
Benjamin in 1776. Joshua narrowly escaped an ambush near the fort:

> Joshua Barton and Joseph Kennedy were out in the lane when they were
> discovered and pursued by some Indians. Kennedy kept in the open land;
> Barton went with the [fence]. Both got in safe.[41]

A few years later, Barton was slain near the fort. According to Nathaniel Hart:

Joshua Barton Sr. Account opened June 14, 1776 [with Henderson's Company].
Was killed in spring of 1780. Mr. Hart's father took the family into what is now
called Tennessee, then called "Holston settlement."[42]

Hart recalled that Joshua Barton was the brother of William Barton and father of the Barton in
Congress, called the "Little Red" (i.e., David Barton).[43]

Joshua Barton Jr. was born in Rowan County, North Carolina, in 1757, was wounded in
the Revolutionary War, and married Frances Grubbs in Virginia. He lived for a time in Madison
County, and later settled in Clark County where he was a taxpayer from 1794 to1800. Joshua Jr.
died in Boone County, Missouri.[44]

Joshua Barton obtained his 400-acre tract on a settlement certificate for raising a crop of
corn in 1776. His claim was described as "lying on the head of the 4 Mile run Waters of Kentucky
River on the North side thereof, about 15 Miles North East from this place" [Boonesborough]. He
had it surveyed by William Calk on May 31, 1784; William Hancock and John Harper were chain
carriers, Joshua Barton marker. Barton was issued a patent in 1786. Since no mention was
made of the grantee being the heir of Joshua Barton, deceased, we assume the tract was
claimed by, surveyed for and granted to Joshua Jr. The land was located about 3 miles east of
Winchester and interfered with the claim of Barthelomew Dupuy.[45]

William Hancock

William Hancock was born in 1738 in Goochland County, Virginia, and served on Col.
William Byrd's Cherokee expedition near the close of the French and Indian War. Hancock
visited Boonesborough in 1775, removed to Kentucky in 1777, and was captured with the saltmakers in January 1778 and escaped that same year. He was at Boonesborough during the
great siege, served is several of Gen. George Rogers Clark's campaigns and participated in the
Battle of Blue Licks. He settled in Madison County, where he remained until 1797, when he
moved to Missouri. He died there in 1821. Hancock had a 400-acre patent adjoining Barton.[46]

Deposition of William Hancock [32]

Clarke County Sct.

We, William Sudduth, Original Young & John Young, Commissioners
appointed by the County Court of Clarke County pursuant to an act of assembly
entitled an act for ascertaining the boundries of Land and for other purposes,
being convenied at an Elm Tree standing in the fork of a branch on the Waters of
four Mile Creek, caused to come before us William Hancock, who after being
sworn, deposeth and saith that he Laid in the Claim, Begining at the said Elm tree,
of 400 acres for Joshua Barton, also 1000 acres adjoining the said Settlement with
the Court of Commissioners.

That he the said Deponant, when the said Bartons Land was surveyed,
came with William Calk, Surveyor, and conducted him to the place he Entended
said Survey to Begin at & that the Land surveyed by the said Calk for Joshua
Barton is the Identicle Land he intended for Bartons Settlement & preemption,
when he Laid in the claim with the Commissioners & that the elm tree standing In
the fork of the branch above Mentioned is the Begining tree for said Settlement
[and] also a corner to the said preemption, & that it was marked as such at the
time they surveyed, & further this Deponant saith not.

Question by Joseph Depuy: Was you well acquainted with the waters of this
    Creek & by what did you know this to be the head of fore mile?
Answer: By a Familiar acquaintance in that Quarter as Hunter for the Support of
    my Family.

Question by same: Did you make any Marks or improvement previous to your
        Laying in said Bartons claim with the Commissioners?
Answer: I never made any improvement before or since, nor knew of any for said
        claim, as I recollect, on these Warters.

Question by same: By what means did you ascertain the course and distance from
        Boons borough to this place?
Answer: I had frequently Hunted from Boon borough heare & generally
        supposed it to be about 12 or 15 miles.

Question by same: How long was it before you Laid in Bartons claim with the
        Commissioners that you made the discovery of said Land?
Answer: I do not recolect.

Question by same: What did you receive from Mr. Barton as a reward for your
        services?
Answer: I never received fee nor reward from Mr. Barton for bussiness but laid
        in his Claim as a friendly turn for him without the expectation of any
        future reward.

Question by same: What was the reason you directed the survey to run across
        into stoner warters?
Answer: It was my entention when I laid in the Claim with the Commissioners to
        include both warters [Stoner and Fourmile].

[signed] William Hancock his mark

    The Foregoing Deposition taken at an Elm tree in the fork of a branch
marked as a corner & sworn to by the said Deponant as the Begining Corner of
said Settlement, & we the under subscribing Commissioners caused the letter V to
be put on the Bark of said tree, which said Deposition was taken in the presence
of Andrew Ray, Ambrose Bush Jr. & Samuel Morton, Disintrusted Witnesses.
Given under our hands and seals this 10th of December 1795.
William Sudduth
Original Young
John Young

9.

James French, Beal Kelly and John Harper for Edward Williams

Edward Williams

    The following three processions—for Edward Williams, Nicholas Anderson and John
Harper—relate to adjoining tracts situated about 3 miles south of what is now Mt. Sterling. The
location is distinguished by being on the headwaters of three creeks: Lulbegrud, Hinkston and
Spencer. Williams, Anderson and Harper all came to Boonesborough in 1779. In June of that

year, William Calk led a party of men to what is now Montgomery County for the purpose of marking and improving lands. For the most part, the men in this party were looking for land to settle on, as opposed to many locators at that time who were simply speculating in land. A brief biography is available for Williams:

> Edward Williams, of North Carolina, went to Kentucky with Daniel Boone and lived for some time at Boonesborough, where he married Jemima Anderson, daughter of Major Jack Anderson.[47]

Williams was living in Stafford County, Virginia, in 1767 when he was admitted to the Chopawamsic Baptist Church on the same day as his wife "Jemiah Williams" and "Niclos Antherson." Anderson's wife, "Barbery Anderson," was admitted six months later. Williams settled on his claim in Montgomery County. In 1803, he began disposing property to his sons on account of "being old and infirm . . . and being desirous to lessen my fatigue and labour."[48]

Williams' 400-acre preemption was surveyed by James French in 1783 and a grant was issued in 1784.[49] The depositions refer to Williams' "poor right," indicating that he qualified as an indigent and did not have to pay for his preemption.

James French

James French (1756-1835) was born in Prince William County, Virginia of Irish immigrant parents. He served in the Virginia line during the Revolutionary War and studied at William and Mary College. James was a deputy surveyor for the Virginia counties of Monongalia, Fayette and Madison. He married Keziah Calloway, daughter of Col. Richard Calloway, at Boonesborough in 1783. In 1803, he moved his family to Montgomery County, where he served for many years as a judge and an elder in the Lulbegrud Baptist Church.[50]

Beal Kelly

Beal Kelly was born in Maryland in 1750, moved to Prince William County, Virginia and came to Boonesborough in 1778. That fall he enlisted in John Holder's company and served for a number of years as a scout. He was at Strode's Station during the Indian attack in March 1781 and was in the battle known as Estill's Defeat. In 1798, Kelly lost a tract of land in a suit of ejectment filed by George Kilgore. He later moved to Warren County, Kentucky, where he received a Revolutionary War pension for his service on the frontier.[51]

The two similar depositions below by James French give conflicting dates for his survey of Williams' 400-acre tract. The survey was actually made January 15, 1783.

Deposition of James French [35]

The Deposition of James French, of full age, taken before us Subscribing Commissioners at the House of Edward Williams this 15th day of January 1796, being Duly sworn, Deposeth & saith that as well as he recollects some time in the Latter part of the winter of 1784 he, this Deponant, surveyed what is Commonly Called a poor Claim of 400 acres for Edward Williams, and he believes the Crooked Oak this Day shewn the Commissioners to be the same that said survey began at.
[signed] James French
attested James Magill, Nicholas Anderson

Deposition of James French [35]

The Deposition of James French, of Lawful age, taken before us Subscribing Commissioner at the House of Edward Williams this 15 day of January 1796, being duly sworn, Deposeth and saith that some time in the winter of 1783 as well as he recollects this Deponant Surveyed for Edward Williams his

premption of 400 acres, and believes the poplar this Day shewn the Commissioners to be a corner made at that time for his Premption aforesaid.
[signed] James French
attested James Magill, Nicholas Anderson

Deposition of Beal Kelly [36]

The Deposition of Beal Kely, of Lawful age, taken before us Subscribing Commissioners at the House of Edward Williams this 15th Day of January 1796, being first duly sworn, Deposeth and saith that he, this Deponant, was present when Edward Williams Built a Cabbin & fenced it in in the Month of June 1779, and that the place where a stone was this day planted by the Commissioner, Marked on one side EWC and 96 on the other, he this Deponant believes to be the place where the Cabbin stood, and this Deponant further saith that the branch that runs between the said Williams Cabbin & John Harpers was at that time agreed by the said Williams and Harper should be the line that should divide between the lands that they might obtain in Consequence of their improvements, which branch he, this Deponant, believes to be the same that now runs betwen the Houses of said Williams & Harper, and further this Deponant saith not.
[signed] Beal Kelly
attested James Megill, Nicholas Anderson

Deposition of John Harper [37]

The Deposition of John Harper, being of full age, Taken before us Subscribing Commissioners this 15th Day of January 1796, being first Duly sworn, Deposeth and saith That the very spot of ground on which a stone was planted in my presents, Marked with EWC 96, is the Identicle spot where Edward Williams Cabbin and Improvement was made, and that corn was planted and inclosed with a rail Fence.

And further the Deponant saith that the Poplar this Day marked by the Commissioners with JMM 1796 is the Begining Corner of said Edward Williams preemption of 400 acres, and further the Deponant saith that the said Improvement was made June 1779, and further saith that he is acquainted with the surveys and that it includes the very Land which the said Williams expected to obtain in Consequence of his making the said Improvement, and further the Deponant saith not.
[signed] John Harper
attested James Magill, Nicholas Anderson

Deposition of John Harper [37]

The Deposition of John Harper, being of full age, taken before us the Subscribing Commissioners this 15th Day of January 1796 at the house of Edward Williams, being first duly sworn, Deposith and saith that a Crooked ash shewn To the Commissioners this day on the East side of a branch of the north forke of Lulbegrud, marked with the Letter W, is the Begining of Edward Williams poor right of 400 acres, [and] further the Deponant sath not.

24

[signed] John Harper
attested James Magill, Nicholas Anderson

This [is] To certify that in obedience to an Commission to us Directed by the Court of Clarke County, we have met at the Begining of Edward Williams poor right of 400 Acres and have taken the Depositions of James French and John Harper, who attended us at the said Beginning, together with Jilson Payn and Abihu Anderson, two Disintrusted Inhabitants of said County, and have marked the ash tree [and] stone, proved by said witnesses as the Beginning, with the letters JMNA and 1796, and also marked a hickroy northward of said ash with the letters JM.

And we further Certify that we have also attended at the said Williams Beginning of his Preemption of 400 [acres] with the said witnesses and Disintrusted persons, and have taken the said witnesses Depositions, and the said Beginning is a poplar and we have Marked the said poplar JMNA and 1796, and also marked a Beach tree a Small Distance westward of said poplar with the letters JM.

And have also Taken the Deposition of Beal Kelly, who also attended us at the said calls, and have also set up on that spot of Ground this Day shewn to us, whereon the said Williams Cabbin and Improvement was made, a stone Marked [with] the letters EWC on one side and on the other side with the Figures 96, which stone stands North 7 degrees West 10 poles from the stone Chimney of said Williams present mansion House, and the aforesaid Poplar tree stands from the aforesaid stone Chimney North 64 degrees West 27 poles. As Witness our hands this 15 January 1796.
James Magill
Nicholas Anderson

10.

Edward Williams, Nicholas Anderson, James French and Beal Kelly for John Harper

John Harper

Two Harper brothers, John and Peter, came to Boonesborough in 1779. They may have been the sons of George and Elizabeth Harper of Prince William County, Virginia. John and Peter were out with William Calk's party in June 1779, and both marked and improved claims that month. Peter was killed by Indians, or accidentally by James McMillan, in December 1789. John frequently assisted surveyors and locators north of the Kentucky River. He lived on his claim at the headwaters of Greenbrier, Hinkston and Lulbegrud, neighbors of Ed Williams and Nicholas Anderson. He left a will in Montgomery County, probated in 1840, that named wife Mary and eight daughters. He was reportedly buried in the graveyard at Old Lulbegrud Church.[52]

Harpers' 400-acre preemption was surveyed by James French in 1783, the same day he surveyed for Edward Williams. French surveyed for Nicholas Anderson two weeks later. All three presented their claims before the land commission at Boonesborough on December 21, 1779. These men appear together repeatedly in the records. Harper's preemption, processioned below, was 3½ miles south of Mt. Sterling, lying along the Levee Road (KY 11).[53]

Deposition of Edward Williams [39]

The Deposition of Edward Williams, of full age, Taken before us Subscribing Commissioners 15th Day of January 1796, who being duly sworn, Deposeth and saith that in the year 1779 in the month of June, he, this Deponent, assisted John Harper to Build a Cabbin, and that said Harper planted Corn at the summer time, fenced it with rails and worked it at the place where he built the Cabbin, and that a poplar tree near the said Cabbin was Either marked with first letters of said Harpers name or his name in full, and this Deponant cannot now recollect which.

And the place where the Commissioners this Day planted a Stone, marked on one side with the letter JHC and the figures 96 on the other, is the place where the said Cabbin was built, and the poplar stump that stands a few paces westwardly from the said stone is the stump of the tree that was marked by said Harper as aforesaid, and this Deponant further saith that the said Harper and himself, at the time of building their Cabbins in the year 1779, did agree that the branch that runs between the Houses of said Harper and this Deponant should be the Dividing line between the lands they might obtain in consequence of their Improvements, and that the said Harper has included in his preemption survey of 400 acres the Land that he, this Deponant, understood from said Harper he entended to endeavor to hold by virtue of said Improvement.

And this Deponant further saith that he has Known the place of said Cabbin, branch, and poplar tree or stump ever since, and this Deponant further saith that the white Oak shewn the Commissioners this Day is the Begining of said Harpers preemption survey of 400 acres, and further saith not.
[signed] Edward Williams
attested Jilson Payn, James Magill

Deposition of Nicholas Anderson [41]

The Deposition of Nicholas Anderson, of full age, Taken before us Subscribing Commissioners this 15th day of January 1796, who being duly sworn, Deposeth and saith That in the year 1779 in the month of June, he, this Deponant, assisted John Harper to Build a Cabbin, and that said Harper planted Corn, fenced it in, and worked it at the place where he Built the cabbin, and that a poplar Tree near the said Cabbin was marked either with the two first letters of said Harper name or his name in full, and this Deponant Cannot now recolect which, and the place where the Commissioners this Day planted a Stone, marked on one side with the letters JHC and the figures 96 on the other, is the place where the Said Cabbin was Built, and the poplar Stump that stands a few paces westwardly from the said Stone is the Stump of the tree that was marked by Said Harper as aforesaid, and this deponant further saith that the said Harper & Edward Williams at the time of Building their Cabbins in the year 1779 did agree that the branch that runs between there present Houses Should be the Dividing line between the Lands they might obtain in consequence of their improvements, and that the said Harper has included in his preemption Survey of 400 acres of the Land that he, this Deponant, understood from said Harper he Intended to endeavor to hold by Virtue of said Improvement, and further this Deponant saith that he has

26

been well acquainted with the place where the Cabbin was Built ever since the year 1779 and with the before mentioned branch & poplar tree or stump. And further this Deponant saith not.
[signed] Nicholas Anderson
attested Jilson Payn, James Magill

Deposition of James French [42]

The Deposition of James French, of Lawful age, Taken before us the subscribing Commissioners this 15th Day of January 1796, who being duly sworn, Deposeth and saith that, as well as he recollects, some time in the winter of 1783 he, this Deponant, surveyed for John Harper his preemption of 400 acres and believes the white oak this Day shewn the Commissioners is a corner of said preemption survey, but whither the Begining of said survey or not, I cannot now recollect, [but] that will appear from the records, and further saith not.
[signed] James French
attested Jilson Payn, James Magill

Deposition of Beal Kelly [43]

The Deposition of Beal Kely, being of full age, Taken before us the Subscribing Commissioners this 15th Day of January 1796, being Duly sworn, Deposeth and saith that the place or near the place where the Stone was planted this Day by the said Commissioners is where John Harpers Cabbin and Improvement was made.

And further the Deponant sayth that he heard the said John Harper and Edward Williams agree that the branch which runs between their Improvements should be the Division between their Land which they expected to obtain by Making said Improvements, and that he Believes that the Branch which runs between the said Harpers and Williams Houses to be the same Branch, and further the Deponant saith not.
[signed] Beal Kelly
attested Jilson Payn, James Magill

This is to Certify that In obedience to a Commission to us directed by the Court of Clark County, we have met at the request of and attended by John Harper at the place of the Cabbin at the Poplar tree (or stump) and at the Begining of his, the said Harpers, preemption survey of 400 Acres, and Taken the Depositions of Nicholas Anderson, Edward Williams, Beal Kelly, and James French, who attended us at the said place together with Samuel Hardin and Abihu Anderson, two Disentrusted House Holders of the county, and have set up a Stone at the place where said Harpers Cabbin Stood, marked on the one side with the letters JHC and with the figures 96 on the other, which stone is set up South 80 degrees West 24 poles from the Stone Chimney of Edward Williams present mantion House, and the poplar stump before mentioned stands a few paces westwardly from the place where the said stone is Planted, near to which is a sugar tree which we have Marked JMM and 1796, and we have Marked the said John Harpers Begining of his preemption survey of 400 Acres with the letters JMM 1796, which Begining is a white oak that forks at about Eight feet from the ground and stands North 48 degrees West 56 poles from Edward Williams Begining of his Preemption Survey of 400 acres, a poplar, and also marked on a small white Oak a few paces westwardly from said Harpers Begining JM. As witness our hand this 16th Day of January 1796.

Jilson Payn

James Magill

11.

Edward Williams, John Harper, James French and Abihu Anderson for Nicholas Anderson

Nicholas Anderson

Nicholas Anderson lived in Prince William and Stafford counties in Virginia before coming out to Kentucky in the spring of 1779. Anderson, Edward Williams and John Harper all signed the "Corn Compact" at Boonesborough on April 15, 1779. Settlement of their adjoining claims was delayed by Indian hostilities until 1791, when the three families built a small station near the junction of KY 11 and 646, about 3 miles south of Mt. Sterling. Anderson died in 1809, leaving a will in Montgomery County.[54]

Anderson had his 400-acre preemption surveyed by James French in 1782; William Calk and Spencer Reid were chain carriers, Anderson was pilot and marker. The grant was issued by Governor Benjamin Harrison of Virginia in 1784.[55]

Abihu Anderson

Abihu was one of the sons of Nicholas Anderson and lived near him at the head of Hinkston Creek in Montgomery County. Abihu was the administistrator of his father's estate. In 1817, Abihu and his wife Jane, James Bradshaw and wife Asena, and Aletha Wilkerson, the heirs of Nicholas, sold 100 acres of Nicholas' preemption to Samuel Hadden.[56]

Deposition of Edward Williams [45]

The Deposition of Edward Williams, Taken before us Subscribing Commissioners this 15th Day of January 1796, being of full age, Deposeth and sayeth That in June 1779 Nicholas Anderson made an improvement, such as Building a Cabbin and planting of Corn, on that spot of ground where a stone was this Day Set up, marked with NAC 96, eight poles south 46 Degrees west from the spring said Nicholas Anderson now makes use of.

And further the Deponant sayeth that a large Poplar marked with NA is the Begining of said Andersons preemption of 400 acres, and further the Deponant sayeth that the Conditional line between him, the said Deponant, and said Anderson is run exactly right, and the Deponant further sayeth that as fare as he knows the Land is included in said Anderson Survey as was Intended. Further the Deponant sayeth not.

[signed] Edward Williams

attested Jilson Payn, James Poage

Deposition of John Harper [45]

The Deposition of John Harper, of full age, Taken before us the

Subscribing Commissioners this 15th day of January 1796, Being first sworn, Deposeth & sayeth that Nicholas Anderson Improvement was Mad in June 1779 & Corn planted and worked in the same year on that Spot of Ground where there was a stone set up this Day, Marked NAC 96, & that the Conditional Line between said Anderson and Edward Williams was at the same place where the line is now Run, & that said Anderson had told him he had found a good spring and made some Marks at it at the same time, & further sayeth not.
[signed] John Harper
attested Jilson Payn, James Poage

Deposition of James French [46]

The Deposition of James French, of full age, Taken before us Subscribing Commissioners this 15th Day of January 1796, Deposeth and saith that, as well as he recollects, some time in the winter in the year 1783 he this Deponant run the survey of Nicholas Andersons Preemption of 400 Acres of [land], and he believes the large poplar this Day shewn the Commissioners & marked NA is the tree the said survey was Begun at, and further saith that the said Anderson had a Treasury Warrant survey made by this Deponant at the same time the Preemption aforesaid was surveyed and that the said Treasury warrant survey aforesaid [joined] The preemption on the westward and Cornered with the same at the North westward and southward Corners.
[signed] James French
attested Jilson Payn, James Poage

Deposition of Abihu Anderson [47]

The Deposition of Abihu Anderson, of full age, Taken before us Subscribing Commissioners this 15th day of January 1796, Being first sworn, Deposteh & sayeth that his farther took him to a spring about the year 1790 or 1791 where there was a box Elder Marked NA 1779, which Deponant sayeth his farther told him that it was the said spring that was Called for in His Entry of His Preemption, and further sayeth not.
[signed] Abihu Anderson
attested James Poage, Jilson Payn

This To certify that in obedience to an Commission from the Court of Clarke County to us Directed, we have met at the House of Nicholas Anderson and have attended the said Anderson at his Beginning and Improvement and Spring Together with John Harper, Edward Williams, James French and Abihu Anderson, witnesses, and Daniel Williams and Dudley Curl, two Disentrusted Inhabitants of Said County, and have Taken the before mentioned witnesses Depositions and have Marked a Sugartree, near the Poplar mentioned by the Witnesses as the said Anderson Beginning, with the letters JP & 96, & have Marked an Elm at the above Mentioned Spring with the same Marks as the above mentioned sugartree, and have set up a stone, eight Poles South 46 Degrees West from said Andersons useing spring on that spot of ground where the Witnesses have this Day proved to be where the said Andersons Improvement was Made,

29

marked with NAC 96, which [we] will consider a part of our report to be admitted to record. As witness our hands this 15th Day of January 1796.

Jilson Payne

James Poage

12.

Enoch Smith, Peter Scholl, Thomas Lewis, Jilson Payne, William Payne and Henry Payne for Edward Payne

John Lane

John Lane was Enoch Smith's nephew, the son of his sister Mary Jane Smith and James Hardage Lane of Loudoun County, Virginia.[57] John Lane and Enoch Smith appeared before the land commission on the same day to present their claims. Lane was awarded a settlement and preemption

lying on the dividing ridge between the head of the North Fork Lulbel Grood & the head of Hinkstons Fork to include the Waters of Lulbul Grood & Hinkstons fork by the said Lanes raising a Crop of Corn in the Country in the year 1776.[58]

Lane sold his 1400-acre claim at the head of Lulbegrud and Somerset Creek to Edward Payne. Lane settled in Montgomery County. His brother, James Lane, helped Enoch Smith settle Smith's Station.[59]

Edward Payne

Edward Payne was born in 1727 and married Ann Holland Conyers in Stafford County, Virginia, in 1750. Most of their children were born in Fairfax County and migrated with the parents to Fayette County, including sons, Sanford, Edward, Henry, William, Jilson, Daniel McCarty and James. Payne served as a trustee of Transylvania University from 1789 through 1793. He was closely involved with his son-in-law, Thomas Lewis, in Lexington. They were proprietors of a store in 1788, they were trustees of the Baptist church in 1789, and both were magistrates in 1792.[60] Payne died four months after his wife passed away; they were married for fifty years. The following death notice appeared in the *Kentucky Gazette*:

Edward Payne, died Saturday evening May 17, 1806, aged 80 years.[61]

Payne acquired the 400-acre settlement and 1000-acre preemption of John Lane, the land being between the head of Lulbegrud Creek and Somerset Creek (the latter referred to as the Hinkston Fork of Licking in the entry). John Payne surveyed the two tracts for Edward in 1783; Peter and Abraham Scholl were chain carriers, Henry Payne, marker. Edward received a patent for the land in 1786.[62] These tracts are located close to the Clark-Montgomery line on Prewitt Pike (KY 1960), near the old C&O railroad station at Klondike.

Payne's tracts interfered with the preemptions of Ebenezer Corn and James Davis. Processions to establish Corn's and Davis' boundaries are #14 and #15 in these Depositions.

Jilson Payne

Jilson, son of Edward Payne, was born in Fairfax County, Virginia, in 1767. Jilson married Dulcinea Harrison in Kentucky in 1789, and married Mrs. Anna Stiles in Frankfort in 1822. He settled in what is now Montgomery County on land patented by his father. Jilson served as a justice of the Court of Quarter Sessions, was a member of the Second Constitutional Convention in 1799, and represented Montgomery County in the Kentucky legislature, serving in the House of Representatives 1799-1803 and the Senate 1804-1808.[63]

William Payne

William, second son of Edward Payne, was born in Fairfax County, Virginia, in 1755. He married first, Mary Grimes in 1775, and second, Mildred Harrison in 1791. William served as an officer in the Revolution. He became an ardent Baptist minister with a long record of service. William died in Mason County in 1829.[64]

Henry Payne

Henry, eldest son of Edward Payne, was born in Fairfax County, Virginia, in 1753 and married Annie Lane March in Loudoun County in 1775. Henry inherited his father's estate in Virginia. He sold it and moved to Fayette County in 1786, settling on his 200-acre patent on the Town Fork of Elkhorn, about 4 miles from Lexington, later known at Thorn Place. In 1805, Henry Payne was granted permission by the county court to erect a water gristmill on Town Fork. He died in 1828 and is buried in Lexington Cemetery.[65]

Notices [48]

Sir,

Take notice that pursuant to a order of the Court of the County of Clarke in October last appointing Commissioners for the purpose of taken the Depositions of sundry witnesses of Establishing certain calls in an entry of a settlement of four Hundred acres and a preemption of one thousand acres on the Dividing ridge between the Head Warters of the North fork of Lubulgrud and Hinksons fork of Licking, which Dividing is near the place where Jilson Payn now resides, and I am informed that you have Lands adjoining to or claims interfering with The said settlement and preemption. I therefore request you to attend at the place aforesaid on the 25th Instant [November] for the purposes aforesaid, agreeable to an act of assembly intitled an act to ascertain the Boundries of Land and for other purposes. I am yours &c.
[signed] Edward Payne
Fayette County
November 9th 1795
[sent to] Major John South

Fayette County Sct.

This day Personally appeared before me, a justice of the Peace for the county aforesaid, Fielding Lewis Turner, and made oath that on the tenth Day of November 1795 he Delivered to John South a notice, of which the foregoing is a true copy. Given under my hand this 10th Day of November 1795.
[signed] James Trotter

Clarke County, State of Kentucky, to wit,

Pursuant to an order of the Court of Clarke County aforesaid, made in October 1795, a Commission having issued in these Words, "Clarke County, October Court 1795, On the petition of Edward Payne Sr., [that] James Poag, Bennett Clarke, William Matier, and Nicholas Anderson are appointed Commissioners under the act of Assembly entitled an act to Ascertain the Boundaries of Lands and for other purposes, to take the Depositions of Witnesses to Establish the certain Calls in an Entry of a settlement of his [Edward Payne] made November 10th [11th] 1779, and a Preemption of one thousand acres adjoining made April 29, 1778 [1780], On the Dividing Ridge between the Heads of the north fork of Lulbegrud and Hinksons Fork and also the Beginning and Boundries of the Surveys of the same.

Ordered that the Clerk of the Court of this County issue a warrant Directed to the aforesaid Commissioners requiring them, or any two of them, to attend the said Payne at the said Calls in the aforesaid entries and to cause To come before them such witness or witnesses, as well without or within the County of Clarke, as the said Payne shall require, and that the said Commissioners, or any two of them, shall, at such time and times as the said Payn shall appoint, examine on oath the said Witness or Witnesses touching the said Calls in the aforesaid Entries, and take the same in writing, which shall be signed by the Deponant and tested by the said Commissioners, or any two of them, who shall make return thereof to the Clerk of this Court.

And the said Commissioners, if to them it appear necessary, shall cause the aforesaid calls to be Marked afresh and do whosoever thing or things as may be Deemed proper in their Judgment [to] perpetuate the Calls in the aforesaid entries in Conformity to the requisitions of the before recited act.
attested David Bullock, Clark County Clerk

Now on this day, to wit, on the 25th day of November 1795, We the Subscribing Commissioners pursuant thereto and Conformible to notice given us by the said Edward Payn Sr., Convened on the Lands aforesaid at the House of Jilson Payne, where was shewn to us the Kentucky Gazettes for the three Preceeding weeks, in each of which is an advertisement in these words,

"Pursuant to an act of Assembly intitled an act to ascertain the Boundries of Lands and for other purposes, I have procured a Commission from the Court of the County of Clarke to Perpetuate the testimony of sundry witness to establish certain calls in an entry of a Settlement of four Hundred acres made November 11th 1779 and a Preemption of one Thousand acres adjoining made April 29th 1780 on the dividing ridge between the head of the north fork of Lulbegrud and Hinkstons fork of Licking, which dividing ridge is near the Place where Jilson Payn now resides, and also the Begining and the said Boundries of the Surveys of the said entries.

The Commissioners for taking the Depositions are to meet on the Place on the 25 day of November in the present year [1795], of which proceedings, this is a notice to all who may have interfering Claims or land adjacent, that they may attend to the testimony of sundry Witnesses that may be called upon for the purposes aforesaid. Edward Payn Sr."

There was then to us also Produced a Coppy of notice Given by Edward Payn, the applicant, to John South & Ebenezer Corn, who it has been alledged has interfering or adjacent claims, [which together] with the depositions of Fielding Lewis Turner and Jilson Payne [are] to be Considered as a part of our Report and to be entred of record. There was also produced a Copy of the Certificate of Survey and Platt of the Land, which is refered to in the Deposition of Thomas Jones [*not found*] and thereto annexed.

That Enoch Smith, Peter Scholl, Henry Payne, William Payne & Thomas Lewis, whose depositions are herewith annexed, attended us over the Dividing Ridge called for in the entries and viseted the Corners of the outside Boundry of the said Lands, in Company with William Lock & Richard Griffin Jr., two Disentrusted Inhabitants of the County of Clarke, and marked a Honey Locust about 24 feet from the Beggining Corner with the Letters MMBCEP. Also Marked a forked Poplar with the letter EP, about 27 feet from the Linns & Elms Corner and a few steps West from the poplar, [also] Marked a Black ash with the same, one of the Lins now dead at the said Corner. Given under our hands and seals this 25th day of November 1795 at Johnson [Jilson] Payn.
Binnat Clarke
Nicholas Anderson
William Mateer

Deposition of Enoch Smith [53]

The Deposition of Enoch Smith, of Lawful age, Taken before the Subscribing Commissioners, appointed for this purpose, on the Lands of Edward Payne on the 25th of November 1795. This Deponant Being duly sworn, Deposeth and saith That he put in John Laines claim before the Commisioners for the District of Kentucky and obtained a certificate for Settlement & Preemption, which Claim was sold by the said Lane to Edward Payne, and the Deponant farther saith that he assisted to Enter the saim claim with the survey on the ridge between the North fork of Lulbegrud and the head of Hinkston.

And this Deponant farther saith that the north fork of Lulbergrud he has been acquainted with ever since the Year 1775, and has always looked upon it as the north fork of Lulbergrud, and has heard others distinguish it by that name, which fork heads Southward of Jilson Payns hous he now lives in.

And the Deponant farther saith that the Creek distinguished by the name of Summerset, which heads more South than any of the branches of Hingstons fork, he called the middle or main fork of hi[n]gstons, as it will appear by refering to the records of Fayette County, and to such Surveys and Entries that he made. And this Deponant farther saith that he believes that an Entry made In the name of Jeremiah Moore, joining William Barneyby Sears entry of 500 acres, will explain it, which Entry calls for lying between that creek and the creek the said Deponants Settlement & Preemption lies to the west of, which creek was distinguished by the name of small mountain (by the mount in Mount Sterling), and is nown by that name by many of the Inhabitants of Boonsburgh, and in Particular William Calk and Robert Whitledge, who explored the cuntry and found the little Mount in the year 1775.

And the Deponant farther saith that he is acquainted with the most west, North, and south Corners of said Claim, and that he knows that the survey includes the warters of Both Creeks, and lies on the ridge he Intended it should be when he Located it And assisted to Enter with the Surveyor. Farther this Deponant saith naught.
[signed] Enoch Smith
attested William Meteer

Deposition of Peter Scholl [54]

The Deposition of Peter Scholl, Taken before the Subscribing Commissioners appointed for the purpose, on the Land of Edward Payn on the 25th day of November 1795. The Deponant being duly sworn, Deposeth and saith that on the 7th Day of October 1783, he attended John Payne, a Deputy Surveyor of Fayette County, to assist in making two Surveys of Land for Edward Payn, one a Settlement of four Hundred acres, the other a Preemption one thousand acres adjoining, and when they came to the Head of the north fork of Lulbegrud, the said John Payne directted him, the Deponant, and Abraham Scholl, the other Chain man, to measure from the Head of Lulbergrud over to the Head warters of Hinkston fork, which measurment terminated at a Honey Locust on the head warters of Hinkston (now called Summerset), which Locust is the Beginning of the said Edward Payne Settlement, which was laid from the aforesaid Honey Locust over to the Head warters of Lulbegrud and down the Dividing ridge between the said warters, and also the Preemption adjoined the Settlement and Extended down the said Dividing ridge to include some of the warters of each Creek.

And this Deponant further saith that the survey he has attended and Examined (in presence of the Commissioners above cited) this day, by its meets and Bounds, is the same that was made by John Payne on the day and year above mentioned, and includes the warters of Each Creek, and Includes what this Deponant formerly thoutht, & now believes to be the Deviding ridge between the North fork of Lubergrud and the Head warters of Hinkston fork.
[signed] Peter Scholl
attested William Meteer, Nicholas Anderson, Benett Clark

Deposition of Thomas Lewis [56]

The Deposition of Thomas Lewis, Taken before the subscribers, Commissioners appointed for this Purpose, on the Lands of Edward Payne Sr. on the 25th November 1796. This Deponant being duly sworn, Deposeth and Saith that in October 1783 he went in the woods in Company with John Payne, surveyor, and several others, with an Intention to Survey a Settlement and Preemption for Edward Payne Sr., as Assignee of John Lain, and when the said Payne after riding some time through the woods untill he was fully satisfyed where the said the survey aught to be, he then made a begining at a Honey Locust, and this Deponant Cut the letters EP & 1783 on the said Honey Locust tree, [which] reference to the platt & certificate will more fully appear. And he proceeded on the said survey until he closed.

And this Deponant being called on, went in Company with the said Commissioners this day to the corners of said survey, which are all Standing, which he believes were made by the said Surveyor John Payne in 1783, and this Deponant further saith that he believes the aforesaid Survey includes the warters of Lulbegrud and Hinkston fork (but now called Summerset), which names this Deponant was told was the warter courses called for In the said Entry in which the said survey was made, and Dividing ridge, and further saith not.

[signed] Thomas Lewis
attested William Meteer, Nicholas Anderson, Bennett Clark

Deposition of Jilson Payne [57]

The Deposition of Jilson Payne, being of full age and Duly sworn, Deposeth and saith that he gave Ebenezer Corn Notice fifteen Days before the 25th Day of November 1795 that Edward Payne Senior would attend on the aforesaid 25th Day of November at the Boundries of his Settlement and Preemption in order to Perpetuate Testimony, and further the Deponant sayeth not.
[signed] Jilson Payne
November 25th 1795
attested William Meteer, Bennet Clarke, Nicholas Anderson

Deposition of William Payne [57]

The Deposition of William Payne Taken Before the subscribers, Commissioners appointed for this purpose, on the lands of Edward Payne on the 25th [November] 1795. This Deponant being duly sworn, Deposeth and saith that about the middle of April one thousand seven Hundred and Eighty [1780] that he carried the chain and Measured the ridge between the warters of Lulbergurd And the Head of Hingtons fork of Licking, now Called Summerset, for the purpose of Knowing how to enter the Settlement and Preemption of Edward Payne Sr., assignee of John Lane, and that the Boundry that was this day shewed includes the said ridge that the Deponant then Measured, and also the head warters of the north fork of Lulbergrub and Hingston was then shewed unto him, the Deponant, by Mr. Enoch Smith as the Land called for in the Commissioners Books, before the land was Entred with the County Surveyor of Kentucky, and this [deponent] further sayeth that the warter course that is now called Summerset was then called Hingston and shewed to him by that name, and this Deponant further Saith that he then Acted by the Instruction of Edward Payne Sr., Claiment to the said land, and this Deponant further saith not.
[signed] William Payne
attested William Meteer, Nicholas Anderson, Bennett Clark

Deposition of Henry Payne [58]

The Deposition of Henry Payne Taken [before] the subscribers, Commissioners appointed for this purpose, on the Lands of Edward Payne on the 25th of November 1795. This Deponant, being of full age and Duly sworn, Deposeth and Saith that some time in the month of October one thousand seven Hundred & Eighty three [1783] that he went in company with Thomas Lewis, Peter Scholl and Abraham Scholl and John Payne, surveyor, to survey Edward Payne Sr.'s, Settlement and Preemption, as assignee of John Lane, and after the said surveyor got satisfied that he was on the ground cald for in the said Payne Entrys, he, the said Surveyor, Proceeded to make the above mentioned Surveys.

This Deponant further says that the Corners he has attended this day in the

Presence of the above Mentioned Commissioners was made by the above named surveyor as Corners to the said Paynes Settlement and Preemption, and further this Deponant Saith not.

[signed] Henry Payne

Question by Edward Payn: Does the survey include the head warters of Hingston and Noth fork of Lulbergrud?

Answer: From the Information [above mentioned] and my own Knowledge, it does.

[signed] Henry Payne
attested Benett Clark, Nicholas Anderson, William Meteer

13.

Nicholas Anderson, Edward Williams and John Harper for Benjamin White

Benjamin White

Benjamin White was an early resident of Fort Boonesborough. In 1779, he was out with William Calk's company making improvements in the Montgomery County area. Others in the company included Nicholas Anderson, Edward Williams, John Harper, Peter Harper, William Mateer and James Poage. White claimed a tract adjoining Peter Harper's on Spencer Creek, a few miles from where Morgan's Station would later be built. The Virginia land commission awarded White a preemption for 400 acres located "about 3 Miles from Nicholas Andersons land by making Actual settlement 1st of June 1779." Anderson stated in an 1803 deposition, that White "was listed a soldier under Captain [John] Holder. We understood he was killed by the Indians."[66]

David Crews

Prior to his death, White sold his 400-acre tract to David Crews, who had it surveyed by James McMillan in 1784, and received a grant in 1786.[67] David Crews (1740-1821) came to Boonesborough in 1777 and began clearing land near Foxtown in now Madison County. Crews was named one of the trustees of Boonesborough, petitioned the Virginia Court to establish a ferry at Jack's Creek on the Kentucky River, and was appointed an inspector of tobacco at Collier's warehouse in 1789. Crews built one of the finest early mansion houses—Homelands— in Madison County in 1812. He is counted as one of the county's Revolutionary War veterans and is buried in the Crews Cemetery, 8 miles north of Richmond.[68]

Harper's Station

The land commission awarded Peter Harper a preemption of 400 acres "by making an Actual Settlement on the 1st June 1779." Harper's Station was established in 1789 on his claim adjoining Benjamin White's land. Harper, who was the brother of John Harper, was killed while out hunting that winter, either by Indians, or accidently by James McMillan. His station was a cabin located in now Montgomery County, several miles west of Morgan's Station on Harpers Creek, a branch of Spencer.[69]

Deposition of Nicholas Anderson, Edward Williams and John Harper [59]

The Deposition of Nicholas Anderson, Edward Williams & John Harper, of full age, Taken This 7th Day of December 1795, being first Duly sworn, Deposeth and saith that a large ash tree, Marked B White June 1779, on a ridge

about twenty poles from a branch & on the North Side of said branch & that said ash tree was Marked for the improvement of Benjamin White, & that Said branch was the Conditional Line Between Said White & Peter Harper & further sayth not.
[signed] Nicholas Anderson
    Edward Williams
    John Harper
attested Jilson Payn, James Poage

This [is] to certify that in Obedience to the within order of court, we the subscribing Commissioners have met at *Harpers station* on this 7th Day of December 1795, and have Taken the Depositions of Nicholas Anderson, Edward Williams and John Harper, for the purpose intended in said order, and they have attended with us at the ash Mentioned in their Depositions, and also Charles White and James Harper, two disentrusted Persons, and in our presents have marked a sugartree near the said ash with the letters JJP in order to Perpetuate Testimony, and we Consider it a part of our report and to be admitted to record, in witness whereof we have hereunto set our hands this Day above written.
Jilson Payne
James Poage

14.

Elizamond Basye for Ebenezer Corn

Ebenezer Corn

The following three sets of three processions—for Ebenezer Corn, James Davis, and James Hendricks—are related in that all three men made cabin improvements in what is now Clark County in early January 1776 while in company with Samuel Tomlinson. Each of the three had 1000-acre preemptions approved by the land commission on April 22, 1780. Each then assigned his claim to the great land trader and surveyor of Kentucky County, John May, who in turn assigned the tracts to a pair of speculators, John Craig and Robert Johnson. Craig and Johnson had the tracts surveyed by John Fleming on October 20, 1783; Samuel Strode and John Donaldson were chain carriers, John McIntire, marker. Craig and Johnson obtained the patents on all three tracts in 1785.

Ebenezer Corn (1755-1828) with his father George and brothers Timothy and others reportedly left Redstone Old Fort, Pennsylvania, for Kentucky in 1780. The surname is spelled Corn and Chorn in the records. Corn brought his family to the Big Stoner settlement in 1790 and resided in this neighborhood the remainder of his life. He achieved some notoriety for the bluegrass he cultivated on his plantation.[70] Ebenezer was later convicted of murdering one of his slaves.

Old George Corn that owned the station [Corn's Station near Harrodsburg] had a son, Ebenezer, that lived in Clark and who was sent to the penitentiary for killing a negro.[71]

Corn's 1000-acre preemption was located near the present Clark-Montgomery boundary. Corn assigned his claim to Craig and Johnson, who had it surveyed by Fleming, and they obtained the patent for the tract in 1785. Corn acquired 400 acres of this tract for his plantation. This appears to have been his payment for selling his preemption to Craig and Johnson. Craig and Johnson subsequently sold much of the tract to Simon Kenton.[72]

John Craig

John Craig and Robert Johnson formed one of the most prolific land speculation partnerships in pioneer Kentucky. Together they patented over 100,000 acres. They made a practice of purchasing preemption warrants claimed by early settlers, such as those of Ebenezer Corn, James Davis, and James Hendricks in these Depositions.

After the Bryan family left Bryan's Station and returned to North Carolina in 1780, the station was reoccupied by families from Virginia, including the Craigs and Johnsons. John Craig came to Kentucky from Spotsylvania County, Virginia, with the Traveling Church in 1779 and established a short-lived station on David's Fork in Fayette County, later called the Burnt Station. In the fall of 1780, Craig moved his family to Bryan's Station. John Craig was in command at the fort during the siege by the Indians in August 1782 that preceded the Battle of Blue Licks.[73]

Robert Johnson

Robert Johnson (1745-1815) was one of Kentucky's most illustrious early citizens. He and his brother Cave settled their families at Bryan's Station in 1780. Robert was back in Virginia during the famous siege of 1782, but his wife and son—Richard M. Johnson, who was a hero of the Battle of the Thames and later vice president of the United States—were there during the attack. Johnson was born in Orange County, Virginia; he married Jemima Suggett, and they raised eleven children. In 1783, he established his own station at Great Crossing in present-day Scott County. Johnson had a long list of military, political and civic honors. He was a delegate to the Virginia General Assembly in 1782, a trustee of Transylvania University, member of the first and second state constitutional conventions, representative from Scott County, 1796-1813, and a county justice. Robert Johnson is buried at the Great Crossing Baptist Church.[74]

Elizamond Basye

Elizamond Basye was born in Culpeper County, Virginia, c1752, the son of Edmond Basye. Elizamond married Nancy, daughter of Rev. William McClanahan, in 1773. Elizamond was still acquiring property in Culpeper County in 1800, when he was listed in a deed as residing in Bourbon County. There are numerous transactions of Elizamond recorded in Bourbon. In January 1825, a document was produced in court said to be his will but was not admitted. Elizamond left an extensive personal estate valued at nearly $6,500, including 24 slaves. His estate inventory included a pianoforte, 1 still and 11 still tubs, mill irons and stones, fan irons and mill gudgeon. The spelling here is adopted from the Basye family history; in the records, spelling of both his surname and given name varies widely.[75]

John Baker and Baker's Station

The commissioners and witnesses involved in the depositions below were to meet at Baker's Station. John Baker came to Kentucky from Frederick County, Virginia, settling for a time at Strode's Station before starting a station of his own near the present Clark-Montgomery line in the spring of 1790. According to pioneer Benjamin Allen, "John Baker, Lord Mayor of Winchester . . . bought a tract of land, where Judge [Richard] French now lives on the head of Somerset, of Simon Kenton." Baker's Station was located on Corn's preemption. Baker later provided the land for the town of Winchester.[76]

Notice [61]

Notice:
    That on the 19th of February next I will attend at my Improvement on the warters of Summerset near *Bakers Station* with the Commissioners appointed by the County Court of Clarke, then and there to Establish the said improvement and perpetuate other Testamony.
Ebenezer Corn
January 28th 1796
[notice served to] Mr. Edward Paine

Clark County Sct.

This day came Samuel McKee before us, William Sudduth [and] Original Young, Commissioners, and made oath that he the said McKee did serve Edward Payne, Gentleman, with a summons, of which this is a true coppy, on the 28th day January 1796, Sworn to this 20th day February 1796. Also that he the said Samuel McKee did serve and give notice timely unto Jacob Marche by his wife, also that I did give Johon [John] Jackson timely notice of the day and time as Certifyed in this notice.

Deposition of Elizamond Basye [61]

The Deposition of Elizemon Beasye, after being sworn, he Deposeth and Sayeth that some time about the month of January 1776 he was with Samuel Tumbleston, Ebenezer Corns & others & that they were improving lands & came and encamped near this Place and made this Improvement in the following manner, by Deadening some trees and raising a cabin.

They then went, as he believes, on the warters of Slate to improve Lands And that some time about the last of February 1776, the Company Parted & that he the said Deponant and Ebenezer Corns returned after Some time with an Intention to raise a crop of Corn and covered the cabin that we Built at this improvement.

Question by William Payne, agent for his farther Edward Payne: When you improved, did you know this fork by the name of the west branch of Licking?
Answer: No, we called it the warters of Licking at that time.

Question: When this improvement was made, was it made for Ebenezer Corns?
Answer: We made several improvements in this Quarter & then determined by lot who should have them, and this [one] fell to Ebenezer Corns.

Question: When you cast lots, did you mark boundries between each Improvement as a boundry for the claim to the same?
Answer: We mutally agreed that if we obtained Land by said improvement that we would Divide equally between each improvement.

Question: Whose improvement is that that stands at the Head of this branch?
Answer: I dont recollect whose it was.

Question: Whether was it Built by the Company?
Answer: I believe it was.

Question: Do you know where the improvement of Hendrix & Davises aluded to in Corns Entry are?
Answer: I knew of there having improvements in this Quarter & near the place, but cannot recollect Exactly where.

Question by Daniel Bryan: Did Mr. Corns draw any other improvement but this?

Answer: Not at this place for himself, but in the course of our improveing, he drew one not far from here. He said was for his Brother in law, which I think he called Stoker [Basil Stoker].

Question: Did Ebenezer Corns draw any other Improvements in the Country besides this for himself?

Answer: He did.

Question by William Payn: Do you recollect at what time you first Came to know these to be the warters of Hinkston?

Answer: I do not recollect at what time, as I never was in this Quarter from the time we improved until about two Years part last summer.

Question: Was Stoker in Company with you when you Improved?

Answer: He was not to my knowledge.

Question By Ebenezer Corns: Did you hear me say about the time of our Improveing that I intended to live on this place?

Answer: Yes, it was what we then concluded upon.

Question by William Payn: Do you know whether Ebenezer Corns was imployed by Stoker to Improve for him?

Answer: I do not.

Question By Samuel McKee: Did you hear Corns say that if he obtained but one claim in the Country, that he would lay it here?

Answer: He did. [And] further Saith not.

[signed] Elizemon Basye

Clark County Sct.

The foregoing Deposition taken before us William Sudduth & Original Young, commissioners appointed by the County Court of Clark for that Purpose, Pursuant to an act of assembly entitled an act for obtaining the Boundries & for other Purposes, & the improvement being in a state of decay, we caused to be Marked afresh a Lynn Tree standing about 25 feet Southeast from said improvement with the letter WS & OY in the presents of Edmund Raglin, James Walker & Robert Walker, Dinentrusted witnesses, & sundry others. The above Deposition [was] taken at the said improvement above mentioned. Given under our Hands & seals this 19th day February 1796.
Edmund Raglin
James Walker
Robert Walker
William Sudduth

15.

Ebenezer Corn and Elizamond Basye for James Davis

James Davis

James Davis was out with Samuel Tomlinson's company of locators in early 1776 and claimed a 1000-acre preemption "on the waters of Stoner and Somerset, branches of Licking." Joseph Tomlinson placed Davis' claim for a 1000-acre preemption before the land commission in April 1780. The tract was described as "lying . . . near the Land of James Hendricks." Davis assigned his claim to John May, who assigned it in turn to John Craig and Robert Johnson. Craig and Johnson had the tract surveyed by John Fleming in 1783 and received the patent in 1785. This tract was located immediately south of Ebenezer Corn's.[77]

Corn states in his deposition below that Davis planned to live on the tract, but there is no evidence that he did. It has not been possible to identify this James Davis, but he must have been older than the one from Mercer County, born 1763, whose procession (#18) appears elsewhere in these Depositions.

Sassafras Cabin

The cabin on Corn's tract was notable for being made of sassafras. William Calk referred to it in a deposition:

> Going from Boonesborough to my improvement [just south of Mt. Sterling] or through the woods, I have seen a Cabin near a branch, not far from this place, built of sassafras. It was often called Corn's Cabin, but usually the Sassafras Cabin.[78]

Elizamond Basye stated in his deposition that there was a "sasafras Grove" nearby.

Deposition of Ebenezer Corn [64]

The Deposition of Ebenezer Corns, he being sworn, deposeth & saith that James Davis was in Company with Tumbleston, this Deponent and others in January 1776 & assisted in Making these Improvements in the neighborhood & that when we had made a number of Cabbins, we drew lots for said cabins, as we Expected to hold a Claim to said cabbins & this Deponant saith that to the best of his knowledge this cabbin is the cabbin that fell to said Davis and is aluded to in his entry with the surveyor.

Question By William Payne for Edward Payn: Do you know if this is the cabin eluded to in Davis entry with the commissioners?
Answer: I do not, as I did not assist in Making the Entry.

Question: Do you know if this Cabin fell to Davis by lot?
Answer: I believe it did.

Question: Do you know this to be the warters of Hinkston?
Answer: I no it to be the warters of Stoner.

Question by Samuel McKee: Do you no whether Davis had any Cabin in these parts but the one?

Answer: I do not.

Question: Did you no these warters to be gist Creek at that time?
Answer: Yes, by reason of Gist Survey on that Creek.

Question by William Payne for Edward Payn Sr.: Do you no if Davis had any
  other improvements in this Country?
Answer: Yes, but none in these Parts.

Question: Where was them improvements?
Answer: He had one between Hinkston and the uper Blue Lick on little Summerst
  [Summerset], as now called, a branch of Hinkston, another on what is now
  called the sycamore fork.

Question by Samuel McKee: Are you Interested in Davis Lands?
Answer: I am not.

Question by Daniel Bryan: Does not your Location depend on James Davis
  improvement?
Answer: It does not.

Question by Samuel McKee: Did you prove Davis Claim before the
  commissioners?
Answer: I believe I did.

Question by William Payne, Esquire: Did you, when you Proved this Claim for
  Davis before the Commissioners, mention this as the cabbin intended for
  his claim?
Answer: I do not no that I did.

Question by Samuel McKee: Did you ever hear Davis say that he Intended to lay
  this Claim hear if he obtained but one?
Answer: I cannot say, only I heard him often say he intended to live hear.

Question: Did you assist in Making the Entry with the surveyor?
Answer: I did. And further This Deponant saith not.

[signed] Ebenezer Chorn

Clark County Sct.
  The foregoing Deposition taken before us William Sudduth & Original
Young, Commissioners appointed by the County Court of Clarke pursuant to an
act of assembly entitled an act for acertaining the Boundries of Land for other
purposes & the said improvement being in a state of Decay, we caused to be
Marked afresh a white walnut Tree standing about 3 feet from said improvement
with the letters WS & OY in the presents of Edward Raglin, James Walker &

Robert Walker, Disentrusted Witness, & sundry others. Given under our hands & seals this 19th of February 1796.
William Sudduth
Original Young

William Payn [and] Edward Payn objected to the Depositions of the above Deponant. Also Daniel Bryan objects to Corns as witness.

Clark County Sct.
This day came Paul Hulse before me, William Sudduth, a Justice of the Peace for the county aforesaid, & made oath that [he] heard Samuel McKee give James McMilion Notice the Depositions was to be taken on the 19th of February 1796 to perpetuate the calls in James Davis Preemption. Given under my [hand] this 20th of February 1796.
[signed] William Sudduth

Deposition of Elizamond Basye [67]

The Deposition of Elsemon Basey, after being of Sworn, Deposeth & sath that he does not know any thing of the cabbin & Improvement now claimed by James Davis, where we at this time are, nor whether it was made by the Company or not.

Question: Did the Company make any improvements when you were absent from them?
Answer: I believe they did, as I commonly Hunted for the Company.

Question by Samuel McKee: Do you know if James Davis had a cabbin in this Part of the Country?
Answer: I recollect at the lottery he drew one within the boundry of our Improvements on these warters.

Question: How far from the *sasafras cabbin* do you beleive your furthest cabbin that you made in these parts was?
Answer: I do not believe they exceeded three miles from this, the sasafras cabin, that is the cabins drew for when we drew for the sasafras Cabbin.

Question By Mr. McKee: Was it generally agreed by the Company that if they obtained only one claim whether they would lay it hear or not?
Answer: I do not no that it was, only by myself, Tombleson & Chorn, as we supposed this to be the best land we had improved in the country.

Question By William Payne for Edward Payn, Esquire: Do you know this to be Davis improvement?
Answer: I do not.

Question: Did you hear the Company say that they made a cabbin on a Warter

that run South?
Answer: I do not recollect.

Question: Did you make any cabins near the upper blue lick on the warters runing west?
Answer: We did, about 8 or 9 miles from the said lick on the warters I now believe to be Hinkston.

Question: Did Davis Draw one of the above cabbins near the Blue licks?
Answer: I believe he drew one in that Quarter.

Question: Where was Ebenezer Corns Improvement?
Answer: Where I swore to yesterday in my Deposition to Perpetuate Corns improvement.

Question by John Baker. Where was your improvement that fell to you by lot in this part of the country?
Answer: I do not no, only it was near a sasafras Grove and some fallen Timber near the dividing ridge. And further this Deponant saith not.

[signed] Elezamon Basey

The Foregoing Deposition taken before us this 20th of February 1796, at an Improvement Claimed by James Davis & included in his Preemption survey, in the presents of Edward Raglin, James Walker & Robert Walker, Disentrusted witnesses, and caused a white Walnut to be marked OY at the said Cabbin. Given under our hands & seals as Commissioners appointed by the County Court of Clark pursuant to an act of Assembly entitled as act for assertaining the Boundries of Land & for other Purposes.
Edward Raglin
James Walker
Robert Walker
William Suddith
Original Young

16.

James Galloway, Elizamond Basye and Ebenezer Corn for James Hendricks

James Hendricks

James Hendricks was in company with Samuel Tomlinson's party of locators on Somerset Creek in early 1776. James settled in Madison County. In October 1786 the county court ordered "James Hendrix," David Crews, John White and James Martin to view a road from the mouth of Tates Creek to near Boonesborough. In December 1786, he was appointed surveyor of the road from "Woodrooffs to Irvines Lick." In April 1787, he was nominated to serve as an ensign in Capt. Grubbs' company. In May 1794, he served on the jury that tried the slander case of *James Barnett vs Thomas Kennedy.*[79]

Hendricks' 1000-acre preemption was located immediately north of Corn's. Joseph Tomlinson placed a claim before the land commission in April 1780 for this tract "joining lands of Sam'l Tomleson, Ebenezer Coan & Lizmon Basey." Hendricks assigned his claim to John May, who assigned it in turn to John Craig and Robert Johnson. Craig and Johnson had the tract surveyed by John Fleming in 1783, and they received a patent in 1785. In 1802, they sold 500 acres of this tract to Nathaniel Tomlinson for 5 shillings. The land is in Montgomery County, lying on both sides of US 60 about 4 miles east and a little south of Mt. Sterling.[80]

James Galloway

James Galloway was out with Tomlinson's company in late 1775 and early 1776. He claimed a 1000-acre preemption on Stoner Creek, adjoining Michael Stoner's, and helped build the cabin on Hendricks' improvement.[81] Galloway married Rebecca Junkin in Cumberland County, Pennsylvania, in 1778, resided for a time in Bourbon County, and in about 1797 migrated to Ohio, where he was one of the pioneers of Greene County:

> The Galloways having been prominently represented here since the days of the very beginning of the Xenia settlement, or from the time that James Galloway Sr., a soldier of the Revolution and an Indian fighter, companion of Daniel Boone, came into the valley of the Little Miami with his family from Kentucky in 1797 and settled in the vicinity of the Indian village, or Chillicothe, now and for many years known as Oldtown, just north of the city of Xenia.[82]

His large log cabin home still stands in a city park in Xenia, Ohio.

Deposition of James Galloway [69]

> Clarke County, State of Kentucky
>
> The Deposition of James Galloway, being of full age, Deposeth and saith that some time in January of February 1776 That Moses Killpartrick and my self Built a Cabbin and made an Emprovement at this place, which we gave up to Samuel Tumbleston, James Hendricks & others in Company, for which they, the said Tumbleston and Company, was to build two other Cabbins or make Emprovements for us, and this Deponant further saith not.
> [signed] James Galloway
>
> Sworn to before us, William Sudduth and Original Young, commissioners, for the purpose of Perpetuating Testimony Concerning the call of an Entry made to Enclude the above mentioned improvement. Given under our hands this 19th of February 1796.
> [signed] James Galloway [sic]

Deposition of James Galloway [70]

> The Deposition of James Galloway, after being sworn, Deposeth and saith that he came down the Ohio with Tubbleston, Corn & Company in the year 1775 and landed at the mouth of salt lick Creek the 9th day of November. We then took our way through the woods to the upper Blue licks. We the[n] went to Hinkston & that this deponant and one other of the company parted from Tumbleston & Company & that some time in January 1776 this Deponant & his company came into this Quarter and found Tumbleston, Corns and others in a cabin about half a mile nearly a South Course from this place & in conversation

45

we Informed them we had seen this improvement and one other. They then said that we had encroached upon them & [they] proposed that if we would give up our claim to two Cabins we had built in this Quarter, that they would build us two more, to which we agreed & went and left them.

Question By William Payn for Edward Payn Sr.: Where was the two cabbins you Built on these warters?
Answer: The one about 50 or 60 poles up the first Branch that comes in on the west side of this Branch, below the place & on the north side thereof. The other I cannot recollect, but think it was on the East side of this Branch on the top of a ridge near a Small deer lick.

Question: Did you receive any compensation for the two Cabbins you gave up as Mentioned in your Deposition?
Answer: I did not.

Question: Did you give them cabbins up to any Individuals or to the Company at large?
Answer: To the Company at Large.

Question: Was Mr. Stoker within this Country at the time of your improveing?
Answer: Not to my knowledge.

Question by Daniel Bryan: Do you no where James Hendrix & James Davis improvements are?
Answer: I do not.

Question: Did Corn inform you that he had Built two Cabbins for you in lieu of these Cabins?
Answer: He did & I was satisfied with it. He told me at the Corn & Company aforesaid, and further this Deponant saith not.

[signed] James Galloway

Clarke County Sct.
        At the above mentioned improvement, The foregoing Deposition taken this 19th day of February 1796 by us, William Sudduth & Original Young, Commissioners appointed for that Purpose by the Court of Clarke County, Pursuant to an act of assembly entitled an act for assertaining the Boundries of lands & and for other purposes & the improvement being in a state of decay, we caused to be marked a fresh a lin Tree with the letters WS & OY, standing about 15 feet Southeast from Said Cabbin, in the presents of Edmond Raglin, Robert Walker & James Walker, Disentrusted witnesses & sundry others Present. Given under our hands and seals the day above Written.
Edmond Ragland
James Walker

Robert Walker
William Sudduth
Original Young

Deposition of Elizamond Basye [72]

The Deposition of Elismun Basey, after being sworn, deposeth and Saith that in the month of January or February 1776, James Galloway gave up his right and claim to two improvements to Tumbleston and Company.

Question by John Baker: Have you any knowledge what the company did with them Improvements or where they lay?
Answer: I do not know, but understood they was in this Neighbourhood, near some of our Improvements.

Question: Do you suppose that they were vested in the Company or not?
Answer: I conceived they were & that any one of the Company had a right to locate on them.

Question by William Payne for Edward Payn, Gentleman: Wheather the cabbin mentioned and the improvement was built & made by galloway?
Answer: I dont know that it was.

Question by the same: Where James Hendricks Emprovement is?
Answer: I do not [know], but beleve he had one some where near this place or in the Boundries of our Improveing on these warters, and this Deponant further saith not.

[signed] Elizemon Basey

Sworn to before us, the Commissioners, this 19 day of February 1796 & the Improvement being in [a] state of Decay, marked a Tree afresh with the letters WS & OY, in the presents of Edward Raglin, James Walker and Robert Walker, Disentrusted Witnesses. Given under our hands and seals.
William Sudduth
Original Young

Deposition of Ebenezer Corn [73]

The Deposition of Ebenezer Corns after being Sworn, Deposeth and saith that James Hendrick was in Company with Samuel Tumbleston, this Deponant & others & in the month of January 1776 & assisted in Making improvements & that when they made a lottery for the Cabins, James Hendrix did not Draw this cabin, but some time in the same year Said Hendrix informed him this Deponent that if the claims on two Cabbins made by James Galloway would not interfere with said Deponants Land at his improvement, that he the said Hendrix would Rathar have them, to which this Deponent said he had no Objections, & from that time I considered this improvement to be said Hendrix.

Question by William Payn for Edward Payn Sr.: Was this improvement made by James Hendrix or his Company?
Answer: It was not, but made by James Galloway.

Question: Where was the Improvement that was James Hendrix by lot?
Answer: I thought it was on the warters of Stoner until Mr. Beasey came up, but In Conversation with him am not certain where, but no that this improvement was Given to him in Lieu of his Lottery Cabbin.

Question: By who was that Cabbin given up to him?
Answer: By me.

Question: Was them cabins given to you by galloway?
Answer: It was not, but Given to the Company.

Question: Do you beleive that the branch this improvement is on heads East and runs west?
Answer: I do not.

Question: How far do you believe this cabbing is from the Mouth of this branch?
Answer: About Eighty poles.

Question: Whose improvement do you Believe this at the head of a branch of Stoner to be about 90 or 100 poles from corns improvement west?
Answer: I believe it to be one of Hendrixs lottery cabins, as he had Several.

Question by John Baker: Is this Cabbin the cabin that Hendrix Claim was laid on?
Answer: Yes. It is the one aluded to with the surveyor.

Question by Daniel Bryan: Was this Cabin ever given up by Tumbleston & Company to Hendrix?
Answer: It was by me & Hendrix was one of the Company.

Question: At what time did you & Hendrix agree that he should have this improvement?
Answer: Some time in the year 1776.

Question: Was any of the Company present at the time you gave up this improvement to Hendrix?
Answer: They were, but I do not recollect who of them, but no [know] there was no Objection made to his Having of it.

Question by William Payn for Edward Payn: Do you no if this improvement is the Improvement aluded in his Entry with Commissioners & included in

his survey?
Answer: I do not no as to the commissioners, but [it] is included in his survey.

Question by Samuel McKee: Where was Elizemon Baseys improvement?
Answer: Near the Head of Grassy Lick on the Dividing ridge betwen Summerset, Grassy lick & Stoner Warters & further this Deponant Saith not.

[signed] Ebenezer Corn

The foregoing Deposition was taken by us, William Sudduth & Original Young, Commissioners appointed by the County Court of Clarke for that Purpose Pursuant to an act of assembly entitled an act for assertaining the Boundries of Lands & and for other purposes & the Improvement being in a state of Decay, we Marked afresh a sugar Tree Standing about 20 feet Southeast from said improvement, in the presents of Edward Raglin, James Walker and Robert Walker, Disentrusted Witnesses, and Sundry others. Given under our hands this 19th of February 1796.
William Sudduth
Original Young
Edward Ragland
James Walker
Robert Walker

N.B. William Payne, for Edward Payne, objected to Ebenezer Corn being a Witness. Also the o[r]der of court was not present for perpetuating Testimony [in] Deposition. Also Daniel Bryan objected to his [Corn's] being a Witness.

17.

Nicholas Anderson, Edward Williams and John Harper for Mordecai Kelly

George Maden

George Maden (or Madin) made the improvement claimed by Mordecai Kelly and processioned below. Maden was at Boonesborough for a time and was mentioned in the residents' complaint against Richard Henderson and Company in a petition to the Virginia House of Burgesses in 1779:

> Without the least notice given for an election for trustees, the drum beat to arms, and these names read over by one of the trustees, to wit, Richard Calloway, Nathaniel Hart, George Maden, James Estill and Robert Cartright, and these questions was asked, "Gentlemen, has any of you any objections to these gentlemen to be trustees for this town?" to which little or no answer was made. Our silence taken for concent, they proceeded to business.[83]

The burgesses addressed the complaint when they established the town of Boonesborough in October 1779.

Mordecai Kelly

Mordecai Kelly was a long-time resident of Clark, and was living on or near the tract processioned below when the county was formed in 1792. Kelly purchased George Maden's 500-acre claim on Stoner Creek. Kelly had the tract surveyed on a treasury warrant in 1785 by James Morgan; John Harper was chain carrier and Belus [Beal] Kelly marker. A patent was issued in 1789.[84] Mordecai may have been related to John and Beal Kelly, both of whom also had land nearby Georges Branch.

Kelly's land was on Georges Branch of Stoner and interfered with a tract of Jeremiah Craig. As the result of a suit in Fayette circuit court—*Joseph Craig vs William Frame and John Waddle*—Kelly lost part of this land in 1805. He was still living in Clark County in 1810, when he deeded part of his patent to Joseph Craig of Franklin County. A survey map made in the lawsuit shows the location Kelly's tract in relation to Craig's, which adjoined Daniel Boone's preemption.[85]

Deposition of Nicholas Anderson [76]

The Deposition of Nicholas Anderson, of full age, after being Sworn, deposeth & saith that some time in the month of May 1779, he this deponant, William Caulk & others was improveing lands in this neighbourhood & that he this Deponant & a certain George Maden made this improvement by marking a sugartree MK 1779 and deadened trees and did such other things as was custamary in improving land in them times that he this said Deponant assisted in Making the said improvements For Mordecay Kelly & that it was Given up by the Company for said Kelly & further this Deponant saith not.
[signed] Nicholas Anderson

Clarke County Sct.

The foregoing Deposition taken before we, William Sudduth, Peter Scholl & Joseph Scholl, Commissioners appointed by the County Court of Clarke pursuant to an act of Asembly entitled an act for assertaining the Bundries of Lands & for other purposes & the improvement being in a state of Decay, we caused to be set up a stone with the letters MK engraven in it, in the presents of Alexander McGinty & Abram Shull, Disentrusted Witness. Given under our hands & seals this 14th of March 1796.
William Sudduth
Peter Scholl
Joseph Scholl
Alexander McGinty
Abraham School

N.B. The above Deposition taken at said improvement.

Deposition of Edward Williams [77]

The Deposition of Edward Williams, of full age, after being Sworn, deposeth and saith that subsequent to the year 1780 Nicholas Anderson frequently as they passed by this improvement informed him, this deponant, that he and others made this improvement in 1779 for Morduca Kelley & further this Deponant saith not.
[signed] Edward Williams

Clarke County Sct.

       The foregoing Deposition taken before us, William Sudduth, Peter Shull & Joseph Shull, Commissioners appointed by the County Court of Clarke, January 1796, pursuant to an act of assembly entitled an act for ascertaining the Boundries of Lands & for other purposes & the improvement being in a State of Decay, we caused to be set up a stone with the letters MK engraven in it, in the presents of Alexander McGinty & Joseph [Abraham] Shull, Disentrusted witnesses. Given under our hands & seals this 14 of March 1796.

William Sudduth

Peter Scholl

Joseph Scholl

Alexander McGinty

Abrahahm Scholl

Deposition of John Harper [78]

       The Deposition of John Harper, of full age, after being duly Sworn, Deposeth and saith that Subsequent to the year 1780, as they passed by this improvement, Nicholas Anderson frequently informed him this Deponant that He the said Anderson and others made this improvement in the year 1779 for Morduca Kelly & that when the surveyor Came to Survey said Morduca Kelly's entry of five Hundred acres, he the Said Deponant was applyed to by Bealus Kelly to show the Begining, which he acordingly did & that this was the Identicle place Showen by him this said Deponant and where Said Entry was Surveyed from & further this Deponant Saith not.

[signed] John Harper

Clarke County Sct.

       The foregoing Deposition taken before us, William Sudduth, Peter Shull & Joseph Shull, Commissioners appointed by the County Court of Clarke, January 1796, pursuant to an act of assembly Entitled an act for assertaining the boundries of Lands & for other purposes & the improvement being in a State of decay, we caused to be set up a stone with the letters MK engraven in the same, in the presence of Alexander McGinty & Abram Shull, Disentrusted witness. Given under our hands & seals this 14 of March 1796.

William Sudduth

Peter Scholl

Joseph Scholl

Alexander McGinty

Abraham Scholl

18.

Elias Tolin and John McIntire for James Davis

Thomas Clark

Thomas Clark made several early trips with his fellow Virginians locating land in the present-day Clark-Montgomery-Bath county area. Clark presented his claim for 1000 acres on Flat Creek to the land commission at the Falls of Ohio on November 20, 1779:

> Thomas Clark this day claimed a preemption of 1000 Acres of Land at the State price lying about 5 Miles North of Andrew Lynn's claim, on the head of a branch of Licking Creek by the said Clarks improving the same & building a Cabbin in the year 1775.[86]

Clark sold his claim to James Davis. Clark died before March 20, 1801, according to the deposition of Josiah Collins, who on that date referred to Clark as deceased.[87]

James Davis

James Davis was a taxpayer and slaveholder in Mercer County in 1789; he was living near the mouth of Dicks [Dix] River that year when he found a stray mare. In 1795, Davis advertised land for sale near Curd's Ferry. Davis was a neighbor of George Thompson and David Williams, mentioned elsewhere in these depositions. An 1800 Mercer County court order described a road leading from George Thompson's place to Harrodsburg, passing David Williams' and James Davis'. Davis' will was probated in Mercer County in 1821. His gravestone in the Davis-Johnson Cemetery on Munday's Landing Road reads "Rev. James Davis died 6 Dec 1820 aged 57 yrs."[88]

The tract processioned below was on Flat Creek in now Bath County. Davis, who purchased Thomas Clark's preemption, had the claim surveyed by Joshua Bennett in 1783; Michael Cassidy and John McIntire were chain carriers, William Clinkenbeard marker, and Thomas Clark, pilot. Davis received the patent in 1785. A Clark County deed helps identify this Davis: In 1794, "James Davis and Ann his wife of Mercer County" sold 100 acres of this tract to Robert McGary for 50 pounds.[89]

John McIntire

John McIntire came to Boonesborough from Berkeley County, Virginia, in 1779 and that fall helped erect Strode's Station, where he lived the next eight or nine years. He was an ensign in Capt. John Constant's company that participated in George Rogers Clark's expedition against the Ohio Indians in October 1782. McIntire later was appointed to the rank of major in the Bourbon County militia. He served as a deputy surveyor for Fayette, Bourbon, Montgomery, Mason and Fleming counties, the later being where he made his home for many years.[90]

Deposition of Elias Tolin [79]

The Deposition of Elias Tolin, after being sworn, Deposeth and saith that some time in the month of august or September in the year 1775, he this Deponant was in Company with Thomas Clarke and others and made this improvement by deadning Trees and building a cabin, as was usual by improvers in them times & that this deponant marked a Buckeye with the letter E cut left handed, and that there was a tree marked TB by Thomas Brazer who was also in Company.

Question by James Davis: Was this one of the Improvements that fell to Thomas Clark by lot?
Answer: It was.

Question by William Trimble: Had Thomas Clarke any Improvements by lot but this one?
Answer: Yes, he had seven.

Question: Was his Improvements all on Flat Creek?
Answer: I believe they were cheifly.

Question: Do you no where the others improvements that fell to Clarke by lot are?
Answer: There was two below this on Flat Creek & one above what is now called the East fork of Flat Creek.

Question: Do you know this to be the improvement called for & eluded to in Clarks entry with the Commissioners?
Answer: I do not & further this Deponent Saith not.

[signed] Elias Tolin

    The foregoing Deposition taken before us, William Sudduth and Thomas Gill, Commissioners appointed by the Clarke County, January Court, Pursuant to an act of Assembly entitled an act for assartaining the Boundries of Lands & for other Purposes, and the improvement being in a State of Decay, we caused to marked afresh a white Oak Tree with the letters WS & TG, in the presents of Edmond Tolbert, Daniel Deen & David Hughs, Disentrusted Witnesses. The above Deposition taken at the Improvement this 23rd of February 1796. Given under our hands & seals.
William Sudduth
Thomas Gill
Edmond Tolbott
Daniel Dean
David Hughs

Deposition of John McIntire [81]

    The Deposition of John McIntire, after being Sworn, deposeth and saith that in the month of may 1780, Thomas Clarke Described this improvement to this Deponant & that in the latter part of the Year 1783, Said Clarke came with this Deponant, Joshua Bennett and others & showed this Improvement & Directed the said Bennett to survey his preemption, including this improvement by James Davis, which was accordingly done & that the cabin at that time was about 4 or 5 logs high.

Question by James Davis: Was any other person with you & Clarke when he first showed you this cabin & informed you he had sold it to me?
Answer: There was George James & others that I do not Recollect their names, and further this Deponent saith not.

[signed] John McIntire

The foregoing Deposition taken at the improvement encluded in James Davis Survey of one Thousand acres, assignee of Thomas Clarke, by us, William Sudduth & Thomas Gill, Commissioners appointed by the County Court of Clarke at January Court 1796, pursuant to an act of asembly entitled an act for ascertaining the Boundries of lands & for other purposes, in the presence of Edmond Tolbert, Daniel Dean & David Hughs, Disentrusted Witnesses. Given under our hands & seals this 23rd of February 1795.

William Sudduth
Thomas Gill
Edmond Tolbot
Daniel Dean
David Hughs

19.

Daniel Boone and Michael Stoner for John Poindexter

John Poindexter

A single record in Clark County ties John Poindexter of Virginia to the land processioned below. In 1813, the administrator of Poindexter's estate in Campbell County, Virginia, sold 1700 acres of his land on Lulbegrud Creek to Gabriel Slaughter (7th governor of Kentucky) and Austin Slaughter of Mercer County at a public sale. John Poindexter Jr. is found in the 1810 census for Campbell County with a household of 1 male under 10, 1 male 26-45, 2 females under 10, and one female 26-45. According to a family history, there was a John Poindexter (1766-1819) the son of Thomas, who was a prosperous and respected planter of Louisa County. Thomas' will, probated in 1796, bequeathed over 1000 acres of land, many slaves and a large personal estate to his children, including son John. John was a high sheriff and clerk of Louisa County and a captain in the Revolution. He married three times and later became a Baptist minister. Kentucky pioneer Samuel Morris recalled that "John Poindexter, brother of George Poindexter the distinguished lawyer at Natchez, preached at the Roundabout Meeting House [Louisa County], a Baptist." Of John's son, John Poindexter Jr., it was said he "went to Kentucky."[91]

Daniel Boone entered two tracts for John Poindexter on treasury warrants in June of 1780, the first being 2000 acres on Lulbegrud at an old Buffalo Lick, and the second, 400 acres adjoining on the south side. Copies of the entries are found in Boone's survey book, but for some reason he did not return a survey to the land office. After a long delay, Enoch Smith surveyed the two tracts in 1793 and patents were issued to Poindexter the following year.[92]

In his interview with the Rev. John Dabney Shane, Jesse Daniel described his brother Beverly's involvement with this tract:

Boone proved an entry for John Poindexter, of Virginia, at a buffalo Lick on Lulbegrud. My brother Beverly got the half of it for attending to it. That was the first and last time I ever saw Boone. Mighty little land ever held under Boone.[93]

This land was in the area where the old ironworks road crossed Lulbegrud, which is probably close to where the Mountain Parkway and KY 15 cross the creek today.

Michael Stoner

Michael Stoner was born George Michael Holsteiner near Philadelphia 1748 and spoke with a heavy German accent his entire life. He joined Samuel Harrod on a "Long Hunt" to Kentucky in 1767. In 1774, Stoner joined Daniel Boone in an expedition to Kentucky to warn the surveyors of the Indian war. Stoner was part of Boone's 1775 expedition to Kentucky, serving as a hunter for the road cutters and later for Boonesborough. Stoner Creek took its name from his improvement on that creek about 5 miles south of Paris. He was wounded in an Indian attack on Boonesborough in 1777, was with George Rogers Clark at the taking of Vincennes in February 1779, and was wounded in the Battle of Blue Licks in 1782. Around 1786, Stoner married Frances Tribble, daughter of Rev. Andrew Tribble, and settled in what is now Clark County, five miles southeast of Winchester. In 1797, he moved to the Cumberland River area in Pulaski County, and later to Wayne County, near Monticello, where he died in 1815.[94]

Deposition of Daniel Boone and Michael Stoner [82]

We, William Eubank and Congrave Jackson, Commissioners appointed by the Court of Clarke, being Convened at the old Buffalow Lick on Lulbegrud called for in John Poindexters Entry of 2000 acres of land, which Entry says this May 16th 1780, John Poindexters Entries 2000 acres of Land upon a Treasury warrant on the East Side of Lulbegrud Creek, a Branch of red river, beginning on the west Side of the said Creek & at an Old Buflow Lick, to Run East & up and down Said Creek for Quantity (the word East interlined 28 June 1780), causes to come before us Colonel Daniel Boon & Mike Stoner, who after being sworn, deposeth and saith

Question ast Colonel Daniel Boone by Beverly Danniel: Is this the lick that you
        called for in the above Entry of John Poindexters?
Answer: It is the same Lick which I aluded to in the Entry.

Question: Did you consider it to be a buffalo Lick?
Answer: I knew it to be one.

Question: How far do you consider it from any part of this land to the old Indian
        town?
Answer: About Two miles.

Question Asked Mr. Michael Stoner by Beverly Daniel: Did you ever shoot a
        buffalo in this Lick?
Answer: I did.

Question Asked Colonel Daniel Boon by Cuthbert Combs: Was it Intended for as
        much land to ly Below an East line as above it?
Answer: I Expect from the nature of the Entry it was.

Question Asked Colonel Boone by Beverly Daniel: Did you Enter the [said]
        Poindexters four Hundred acres of State warrant adjoining this two
        Thousand [acre] Entry on the south Side of said Entry And run South for
        Quantity?
Answer: I did.

The foregoing Deposition Taken at The old Buffalo lick Called for in the above Entry before us, the subscribing Commissioners, the mark of the old Buffalo lick being so good, we think it not worth while to move the mark, which

Conclusion was done in the presence of Cuthbert Combs, Morduca Morgan, David Fraze[r], Jesse Daniel, William Frazer, John Combs, David Frazer, Joseph Scholl and James Frazer. Given under our hands and seals this 31st Day of December 1795.
[signed] Daniel Boon
[signed] Michael Stoner
attested Congrave Jackson, William Eubank

20.

William Hancock for Jesse Copher

Jesse Copher

Jesse Copher was born about 1756 in Virginia. He was living at Boonesborough in January 1778, when he accompanied Daniel Boone on a salt-making expedition to the Lower Blue Licks and was one of the twenty-seven men captured by the Shawnee. Copher was taken to Detroit with nine of the other prisoners, and he escaped with Nathaniel Bullock in June 1779. They made their way back to Kentucky in company with Simon Kenton, who had been captured by the Indians in 1778. Copher married Elizabeth Boone, a daughter of George Boone, Daniel's brother, and he lived in Madison, Fayette and Clark counties. In 1819, Copher moved to Boone County, Missouri, where he died sitting in his chair in 1822.[95] He was described as being

> about six feet in height, having blue eyes, a fair complexion, with a pleasing countenance; was worthy and patriotic and for many years a member of the Baptist church.[96]

Copher claimed a 400-acre settlement and 1000-acre preemption on Stoner Creek, which he was awarded for "actual settlement in the year 1777." His claim included the landmark known as Bramblett's lick, which his certificate mistakenly called "Bramlet's Station." These tracts were surveyed by William Hays in 1784, and grants issued to Copher in 1786.[97] Copher was residing here, about 6 miles northeast of Winchester, when this deposition was taken.

Deposition of William Hancock [83]

The Deposition of William Hancock, being of full age, after being duly Sworn, Deposeth and saith that he The said Deponant was Several times in Company with Jesse Cofair at a place called Brambletts Lick on Stoners fork, a Branch of Licking, and he the said Deponant often heard Jesse Copair say that he had fixed his Settlement & Preemption so as to enclude Brambletts Lick, and this Deponant further saith not.

Question by Jesse Copair: Do you no this to be Brambles Lick where we now are?
Answer: That this is Brambletts Lick, known by the Hunters in former times, that [they] used Hunting from Boonsbourrough to this place & also by myself.

Question by the same: Did you no me, being in Company with me at that time, offen to say my Settlement & preemption [was not] at any other place, only this?
Answer: No, I tried to influence you to lay it Else where, [so] we might be neighbours together, but you would not for some reason.

Question by same: Do you no that I made my settlement & preemption here at this place so as to include this Lick?

Answer: From repeatedly hearing you say that you had so done & that you entended to enclude the Lick on your Settlement & preemption, I have reason to believe it to be so.

Question by the same: Do you no any such a place as was called in them days by the name of Brambletts Station?

Answer: No.

Question by the same: Do you not believe that the word mentioned in the Certificate with the Court of saying Station is not a mistake?

Answer: I do suppose that its a mistake, because Bramblett had no place of residence in this Country, only as he raised a crop of Corn at Boons Bourough in the year 1779, and this Deponant further saith not.

[signed] William Handcock his mark

Clarke County Sct.

The foregoing Deposition being Taken before us, Original Young & John Young & James Guy, Commissioners appointed by the County aforesaid pursuant to an act of assembly entitled an act for assertaining the boundries of Lands & for other Purposes, in the presence of Isaac Ely, William Martin & Samuel Danaley, disentrusted Witnesses, and sworn to at this place, Brambletts lick, this 9th day of April 1796.

Original Young

John Young

James Guy

21.

John Halley for Thomas, George and Owen Winn

Thomas, George and Owen Winn

The three Winn brothers left their homes in Cameron Parish, Loudoun County, Virginia, and moved to Kentucky in about 1787. Thomas, George and Owen, sons of Thomas Winn Sr., settled near Athens in Fayette County, a neighborhood populated by other Loudoun Countians. Thomas died intestate in Clark County in about 1796. George died in 1801 and Owen in 1805, both leaving wills in Fayette County.[98]

The Winns' land claims preceded their removal to Kentucky. On May 19, 1780, the three brothers' entries were recorded on treasury warrants, as follows: 400 acres for Thomas, 1000 acres for George, and 500 acres for Owen. These adjoining tracts were surveyed in 1784 by John South, with John Halley acting as marker for the survey; grants were issued the following year.[99] This property is located on Stoner Creek about 2 miles north of Winchester, near the Mountain Parkway exit on I-64. Thomas' tract shared a common corner with Richard Halley's survey (procession #6 in these Depositions).

On May 7, 1796, the Winns placed a notice in the *Kentucky Gazette* to inform the public of their intention to take depositions at their beginning corner, "two red oaks and white oaks on the West side of the creek."[100]

Deposition of John Halley [85]

The Deposition of John Halley, of full age, after being duly Sworn, Deposeth and saith that he the said Halley marked this tree, being the Begining tree of Thomas Winn, George Winn & owen Winn, in April 1780, before the Land office opened & afterwards entered the same with the County Surveyor & attended at the Survey with the Debuty Survayer, and directed the said Surveyer to run it presisely to the Location. He further saith he then conceived the Land to be run out as he the Said Halley intended it when Entered & further saith not. [signed] John Halley

Clarke County Sct.

The foregoing Deposition was taken by us, the Subscribers, this 23rd day of May 1796, being Commissioners appointed by the County Court of Clarke, pursuant to an act of assembly entitled an act for assertaining the Boundries of Lands & for other purposes & we being convenied at a red Oak tree marked JH, being the place of Begining of Thomas, George & owen Wins entries, caused to come before us the said Deponant, who after being sworn, Deposed as above & the said marks being in a State of Decay, we caused to be marked afresh the said red Oak tree with the letters OY, in the presents of David Sutherlan & Frederick Sutherlan, Disintrusted Witness. Given under our hands & seals this date above written.
William Sudduth
Original Young
Richard Hickman
David Sutherland
Frederick Sutherland

22.

Enoch Smith for George Kilgore

George Kilgore

George Kilgore was a resident of Loudoun County, Virginia, where he was listed as a tithable and slaveholder in 1774 and afterwards. In 1800, he and Jeremiah Moore drew up resolutions for merging Difficult Church with the nearby Frying Pan Baptist Church. With the union of the two churches, Kilgore was appointed to keep the records, and he and his wife Martina joined the new congregation. Kilgore seems never to have been a resident of Kentucky, and this was his only land grant in the state. The surname is spelled Kilgore and Killgore in the records.[101]

In May 1780, George Kilgore entered 800 acres in Fayette County on a treasury warrant. Enoch Smith had located this land for Kilgore in late 1779 or early 1780, and in November 1783, Smith surveyed it in two tracts—300 acres and 500 acres. John Wilkerson and Richard Oldham were chain carriers, Richard Spurr, marker. Kilgore was issued the grant in 1785. The tracts were located on branches of Upper Howards Creek and began at "a white oak marked ES near a buffalow road on a ridge." KY 89 crosses this property, which lies about 1 mile southeast of

Ruckerville. The property is surrounded by surveys Enoch Smith made for Richard Spurr, John Wilkerson, John Thompkins, Tim Carrington, William Payne and Feebe Muse and a survey made by James French for Jeremiah Moore.[102]

In 1805, George Kilgore of Loudoun County, Virginia, began disposing of his Upper Howards Creek property through his agent, James Whaley of Fayette County, a former Loudoun County resident.[103]

Deposition of Enoch Smith [86]

Enoch Smith, of Lawful age, after being Sworn before us, commissioners appointed by the Court of Clarke County [for] perpetuateing of testimony of Certain Calls of an Entry made in the name of George Kilgore of 800 Acres, Entered on the warters of Howerds upper Creek near the Head of a West Branch of Said Creek, Deposeth and saith that in the winter before the Entry was made, he was in the woods with James French, and on his return to Boonsburgh, he marked the white Oak where he is now at, with an intent to make a Location from it, and in the year 1783 he then Located George Kilgores Land and fixed it as his Beginning and Sundry others Joining the same, and the Cabbin called for in the Entry is now to be seen on the point of a hill on the East side of the creek, and WB on a tree, which cabbin I almos expected was built by William Beasley, who was employed by Combs & Company in the Summer 1775. Further the Deponant Saith not.

Question by William Payn: Are you intrusted in Kilgores claim or in any of them you made joining the same?
Answer: I am not.

[signed] Enoch Smith
attested Cuthbert Combs, Peter Scholl

Clarke County, to wit
Agreeable to an order of the worshipful Court of Clarke County dated June Court 1796, We, Cuthburt Combs & Peter Scholl, Commissioners therein appoint, the advertisem being present of the notice of the day, [proceeded] to take the within Deposition of Enoch Smith on the premises at the Beginning of George Kilgores. Present William Cotton [and] Benjamin Combs, disintrusted persons. We there found the white oak marked ES & GK agreeable to the Entry, near a buffalo roade opposite to the head of a drain.
We then went to the cabbin discribed in the Entry, and there found the Bottom logs of Said Cabbin and a tree marked by it with the letters called for in the Entry, which appeared to anciently marked, which said Deponant made oath to before. We also marked fresh trees at the Beginning, which was two Sugartrees and black ash PS & three small chops on each, and also saw a white oak marked near the place of the Beginning with EW. Given under our hands this fifth day of August 1796.
Cuthbert Combs
Peter Scholl
attested Benjamin Combs, William Cotton

23.

Lucus Hood, William Sudduth and Thomas Harper for Philemon Thomas

Philemon Thomas

Philemon Thomas was born in Orange County, Virginia, in 1763. At age 14, he joined the Revolutionary Army and fought in the battles of King's Mountain, Eutaw Springs and Guilford Courthouse. After the war, he came to Kentucky, where he served in both houses of the legislature representing Mason County and in the Kentucky militia, achieving the rank of brigadier-general in 1799. Germantown in Mason County was founded on his land. In 1805, he moved to Baton Rouge, where he commanded the 2nd Division of the Louisiana militia in the War of 1812. Thomas served as a state senator and member of the U.S. House of Representatives from Louisiana. He died in 1847 and is buried in the Baton Rouge National Cemetery.[104]

The land processioned is Samuel Meredith's is 20,000-acre entry, located on the west side of Slate Creek in Montgomery County, beginning opposite the mouth of Little Slate Creek. Philemon Thomas made a motion for the procession below at the June term of Clark county court in 1796. These depositions precede the grant by ten years and were no doubt prompted by Jacob Myers' caveat (motion to postpone issuance of the grant) in 1789. Thomas' interest in Meredith's tract is uncertain.[105]

This tract was processioned again in November 1796 (see procession #41 in these Depositions).

Lucus Hood

Lucus Hood (1770-1843) was born in Berkeley County, Virginia, and died in Clark County, Kentucky. (His given name also appears in the records as Luke, Lukkus, etc.) In about 1785, his father, Andrew Hood, established Hood's Station several miles north of present day Winchester. Lucus married Frances, the daughter of Frederick Wills, in about 1790, and was the grandfather of Confederate Civil War general John Bell Hood. Lucus and Frances Hood are buried in a small graveyard near Stoner Creek, on the south side of Ecton Road, about 5 miles east of Winchester.[106]

William Sudduth

William Sudduth was born in 1765 in Fauquier County, Virginia, and came to Kentucky in 1783. He made his way to David McGee's Station and then to Strode's Station, where he kept a school during the winter of 1783-84. The following spring he went out surveying on Slate Creek with Ralph Morgan. In November, Sudduth returned to Virginia to help his father bring the family out to Kentucky. They settled at Andrew Hood's Station, a few miles northeast of Strode's. In the fall of 1786, Sudduth participated in a campaign against the Shawnee led by Benjamin Logan, one of numerous punitive expeditions against the Ohio Indians. After serving as a deputy surveyor for many years, Sudduth was appointed county surveyor for Clark in 1797. He held many local offices in Clark before moving to Bath County, where he died in 1845. He is buried beside his wife Eleanor—Andrew Hood's daughter—in the family graveyard near the head of Pretty Run on Wades Mill Road in Clark County.[107] According to one of the pioneers, Sudduth was

a monstrous bright man. He was long legged and slim. 'Twas said nobody could ever keep up with him.[108]

He left descendants in Clark, Bath and Menifee counties. The family name was adopted by the community of Sudith in Menifee County, 4 miles north of Frenchburg.

Thomas Harper

Thomas was a brother of John Harper who settled near Nicholas Anderson and Edward Williams at the head of Lulbegrud. Thomas states in his depositions (below and procession #56) that he was in Kentucky in 1784 and 1786. He was taxed in Clark County from 1793 until 1797, when Montgomery County was formed. In 1797, he was taxed in Montgomery County for seven horses, but no slaves or land. He reportedly died in Morgan County in 1830 and on his deathbed stated he wished his property to be divided between "his Brother John & Sons & Son in laws."[109]

Deposition of Lucus Hood [88]

Pursuant to an order from the worshipful Court of Clarke County to us directed, obtained by Philemon Thomas, [we] have met at the Mouth of little Slate [Creek] to parpetuate Testimony to Establish Samuel Merideths Begining of an entry of 2000[0] acres, agreeable to an act of assembly to assertain the Boundries of Lands and for other purposes, the 20th day of august 1796.

Luke Hood, of full age, who after being first duly sworn, Deposeth and sayth when I came here about seven years ago, there was the appearance of a road on the East Side of big Slate [Creek], but whether there is a road on the other Side I cannot tell, for I did not Cross the Creek, but the road went to the Creek at the mouth of little Slate at the Lower Side.

Question by Philemon Thomas: Was you ever at the mouth [of] Rose run where it emtyes into Slate?
Answer: Yes.

Question by the same: How Nigh did the Buffalo road cross Slate to the mouth of Said run?
Answer: I suppose the Distance from where I crossed to be about a Hundred and fifty yards from said run. I crossed at the Buffalow road.

Question by John Brackenridge [John Breckinridge, Meredith's brother-in-law]: What age are you?
Answer: I was born in the year 1770.

Question by the same: Is there not a large and well used Buffallow road at the mouth of Spencer [Creek]?
Answer: There was a plain road crossed there and appeared to be much used by something, but I know not what. It might be indians or Bares for what I know.

Question by the same: Was there not a large and much used Buffalow road which led by the pealed Black Oak toward the Mud lick?
Answer: There was a plain road there that led to the mud lick, as bigg as the common run of Buffalow roads through the woods at that time.

Question by the same: Was their not an other Buffalow road which crossed Slate between the pealed black Oak and this place?
Answer: Not that I know of, as I am unacquainted with the ground.

Question by the same: Did you observe two roads coming down little Slate, one on each Side, to its mouth?
Answer: No I did not.

Question by the same: Were not the Buffalow roads which Crossed at the mouth of Spencer and passed by the pealed Black Oak much larger then the road you say came Down Little Slate?
Answer: They appeared to be Larger and more resorted.

Question by the same: How do you know the road that you say led down Little Slate was a Buffalow road?
Answer: I supposed it to be used by Bufalow.

Question by Robert Johnston: Is little Slate a Branch of Slate Creek Running in on the East Side and Spencer on the West Side?
Answer: Yes.

[signed] Lukkus Hood
attested James Ward, James Poage, Joseph Simpson

Clarke County Sct.
We, the Subscribing Commissioners, being convianed at the mouth of Little Slate at Samuel Merideths 20 Thousand acres Survey, we begin on the 19th & 20 Instant [and] took the above Deposition in the presents of Patrick Goodin & Peter Forth [Fort], Disentrusted Persons. Given under Our hands and Seals this 20th Day of August 1796.
James Poge
James Ward
Joseph Simpson

Deposition of William Sudduth [90]

Pursuant to an Order from the County Court of Clarke to us Directted, we caused to come before us William Sudduth, of full age, who after being duly Sworn, deposeth and saith that he is acquainted with the Creek called Little Slate & that about four years past, he was Employed by William Shannon to survey 400 acres of Land on said Creek & that Elias Tolin was employed to show said improvement called for in said Entry of 400 acres & that he the Said Tolin Showed where there was a cabbin built, as he said, for William Linn, tho at that time none of the cabin appeared, but was other marks that appeared to of been made by improvers & that he this said Deponant knows of one cabin at the head of a Spring that makes into Little Slate about two or three Hundred yards from said Spring & that about the month April 1786, this Deponant came with John McIntire, William Kennedy & others to begin Samuel Meredithes Survey of 20,000 acres & that to the best of his recollection, there was a small Buffalow road on the upper side of Little Slate, near the mouth of said Creek & further this

Deponant sath not.

Question by Philemon Thomas: How nigh Did this Buffalow Road Cross Main
   Slate to the mouth of Little Slate?
Answer: I Dont know whether it crossed the Creek or not, as I never that I
   recollect was on the Opposite Side of main Slate untill yesterday, but
   recollect that it appeared to lead to the mouth of Little Slate.

Question by Philemon Thomas: Did you beleive the Road at that time was used
   by Buffalow?
Answer: I Did.

Question by John Brackenridge: Are there not three Large & Much used
   Buffalow Roads, One Crossing at the mouth of Spencer, another about a
   Mile below this Place & a third at the mouth of Stepstone [Creek], all
   Leading to the Mud lick?
Answer: There were Such Roads in 1786 & 1787.

Question by the same: Were there two Roads Leading Down Little Slate to the
   mouth?
Answer: Not that I know of, for I never traveled up from the mouth of the Creek
   to the Licks.

Question by the same: Are you well acquainted with the Lands Included in
   Samuel Merideths 20 Thousand acres Entry as now Surveyed & Does it
   Include, Either in one or More Places, a large quantity of falling timber?
Answer: I am Well acquainted With the Survey & know of no Pirticular Body of
   falling timber more than is common in the ajacent Lands.

[signed] William Sudduth
attested James Poage, James Ward, Joseph Simpson

Clarke County Sct.
   We the subscribing Commissioners, being Convenied at the place Samuel
Merediths Survey of 20,000 acres was began at, It being the mouth of Little Slate,
tooke the above Deposition in the presence of Patrick Goodin & Peter Fort,
Desentrested Witnesses. Given under our hands & seals the 19 & 20th days of
august 1796.
James Poage
James Ward
Joseph Simpson

Deposition of Thomas Harper [92]

   Pursuant to an Order of the Worshipful Court of Clarke County obtained
by Philemon Thomas, [we] have Met at the mouth of little Slate to perpetuate
Testimony to Establish Samuel Merideth Beggining, agreeable to act of Assembly

to ascertain the Boundries of Lands & for other purposes, the 19th day of August 1796.

Thomas Harper, of full age, Deposeth & Sayeth that in The year 1784 he & his Brother Crossed Slate at the Mouth of Little Slate & that there was a trace on Each side of the Mouth of Little Slate at that time.

Question by Philemon Thomas: Did the trace cross Main Slate at the Mouth of Little Slate?
Answer: Yes.

Question by the same: Do you see any appearance of the trace at this time at the Mouth of Little Slate that you then saw?
Answer: Yes.

Question by the same: Did that Trace, when you first saw it, appear to be plain?
Answer: So plain that we Could follow it up the Creek to the Licks.

Question by the Same: Did it appear to have been Made by Buffalow?
Answer: We supposed [it], at that time, to be made by the Buffalow coming out of the poor woods to the Cain.

Question by the same: Are you acquainted with the mouth of Rows [Rose] Run where it Emties into Slate?
Answer: I have Been there.

Question by the same: How far is it from the mouth of rowes Run where a Buffalow Road Crosses Slate?
Answer: There is a large Buffalow Road Crosses at the Head of the Bottom, about one Hundred & fifty or two Hundred yards.

Question by John Brackenridge: How Do you know the Difference Between Buffalow Road & a road Made by other game, Except by the sise?
Answer: I know by the Tracks.

Question by the same: Would you Call Every trace which Buffalow travel on to go to their food a Buffalow road?
Answer: Yes, Supposing they are coming from a lick going into their Range.

Question by the same: Where Did this trace End on the west Side of Big Slate, Whether one, two or five miles?
Answer: I know not.

Question by the same: In Making an Entry in 1784, would you have called that a Buffalow Road?
Answer: I would have supposed it to be a crossing place of Slate.

Question by the same: Which of the two traces coming Down Little Slate were the Largest & where Did Each cross Big Slate?
Answer: I do not know which was the Largest. One appeared to Cross Just above the mouth of Little Slate & the Other just Below.

Question by the same: Were not the woods, where Buffalow & Deer frequented, full of such traces as these two?
Answer: When Leading from any Lick Or Range, when Hills put in, they were.

Question by the same: Have you not seen as Large traces leading to Deer Licks & Does this trace lead to a Deer Lick?
Answer: It Leads to [a] Deer Lick & a Buffalow Lick both.

Question by the same: What Buffalow Lick Does it go to?
Answer: Little Slate Lick.

Question by the same: Was there opposite to the mouth of Little Slate, or any Where near to that Place a Large quantity of falling timber in the year 1784?
Answer: Not as I noticed.

Question by Robert Johnston: Have you seen Buffalow in any of those Licks Mentioned?
Answer: Yes, in one of them.

Question by the same: Were any of those Licks up Little Slate?
Answer: Several of them, in the bounds of 2 mile & a half.

Question by the same: Does both Roads at the mouth of Little Slate Lead up the branch toward the Licks on Little Slate?
Answer: Yes.

Question by the Same: Was there a Buffalow Road Leading from the Licks up Little Slate Leading toward the Great Mud lick?
Answer: Yes.

Question by the same: Does the tame Cattle use the Lick up Little Slate Since the Buffalow left the woods there?
Answer: I have seen them in it since.

Question by the same: Have you understood some person Intended To Make an Experiment at One of the Licks up Little Slate for Making Salt there?
Answer: Davis Hornsley had a notion of trying it.

Question by the same: Was such Roads as Crossed Slate at the Mouth of Little Slate in the year 1784 Called Buffalow Roads?

Answer: I should have Supposed it to be so.

Question by the same: What was your Meaning when you answered to [a] Road Crossing at the Mouth of Little Slate, One a little above & the other a little below? Did you Mean the two come together on the west Branch of Slate Creek?
Answer: I suppose the[y] Did.

Question by John Brackenridge: Did a large Buffalow Road Cross Slate about one Mile above this place?
Answer: There was a Road Crossed at the Mouth of Spencer.

Question by the same: Was not that a large & Much frequented Buffalow Road?
Answer: The Road was Pretty Much used, but I did not Measure the Bredth of any Buffalow Road.

Question by the same: Was there not a Large & Much frequented Buffalow Road about two Miles below the pealed Black Oak?
Answer: Yes.

Question by the same: Is there not another Large Buffalow Road Crossing big Slate about three quarters of a mile below this place?
Answer: There is a Crossing place about that Distance, not so large as the one below it.

Question by the same: Did you Ever see any Cabbins on Little Slate & how Many & where?
Answer: No, I never saw any as I recollect at Present.

[signed] Thomas Harper
attested [James] Poage, James Ward, Joseph Simpson

Clark County Sct.
     We the subscribing Commissioners, being Convenied at the Mouth of Little Slate at the place where Samuel Merediths 20 thousand acres survey was began at, took the above Deposition in the presence of Partrick Goodin & Peter Fourt, Disentrusted persons. Given under Our Hands & seals the 20th day of August 1796.
James Poage
James Ward
Joseph Simpson

24.

Lawrence Thompson and William Hays for Tilley Emerson

Tilley Emerson

Tilley Emerson settled in Clark County in about 1796, the year he had the tract below processioned. He appeared on the county tax list for the first time in 1797. Emerson settled on his claim of 750 acres near the mouth of Fourmile Creek. He had entered this tract years earlier, on December 3, 1782, to begin:

> on the dividing ridge between the Kentucky and the four mile creek about 6 miles East of Boonsborough at a hickory tree marked H.C., thence north 250 poles, thence northwest at right angles for quantity.[110]

At their June term, 1796, the county court appointed processioners to visit the land and take depositions of those knowledgeable about the claim:

> Benjamin Combs, Richard Jones & Richard Hickman are appointed Commissioners to meet on the Lands of Tilley Emmerson on the waters of the Four Mile creek to perpetuate Testimony of Witnesses for the purpose of Establishing the Beginning of the entry of said claim pursuant to an Act of Assembly for assertaining the Boundaries of Land and for other purposes.[111]

Emerson had the tract surveyed in January 1797, but a caveat was entered by Joseph Wright the following August. *Wright vs Emerson* was heard in the District Court at Lexington. In July 1798, the jury—with Christopher Greenup, Kentucky's third governor, as foreman—returned a verdict for the plaintiff based on technicalities, such as:

> We do not find the defendants Beginning . . . to be six miles from Boonsborough by any route then Traveled.[112]

Thus, no grant was issued to Emerson. His claim also interfered with the entries of Nathaniel Massie and Nathaniel Hart's heirs. Emerson then purchased 150 acres on Fourmile from James Brown and George Miller.[113]

Emerson died in 1816, leaving a will in Clark County that named four sons and five daughters. He left his home place to be divided equally between sons William, James and Francis: The tract of land "I now live on . . . 100 acres in [Nathaniel] Massie's survey and also 50 acres adjoining, purchased from Brown."[114]

Jonathan Bush, who owned the noted mill on Lower Howard's Creek, married Tilley's daughter Diana (listed in the will as Sue Bush) in 1814. She died in 1819 and was buried at the "Burying Ground at Old Jonathan Bush Mill."[115]

Deposition of Lawrence Thompson [97]

September The 7th 1796

We the Commissioners, appointed by the Court of Clarke County, has Caused to come before us Larence Thompson, who being of full age, Deposeth and saith, being first sworn, that he mad a location in the spring [of] Eighty two [1782], Begining at a White Oake marked HC on the Dividing Ridge Between the four mile Creek & the kentuckey river, which said location he Let Captain William Hays have, [and] being Brout to the tree, finds it much defaced, but Believes it to be the same Tree, to the best of his knolede, as shown to said Hays by me in the Year Eighty Three or Eighty four.

Question by Joseph Wright: Are you interested in said Claim?
Answer: No. The Deponant further saith not.

[signed] Laurance Thompson
attested Richard Hickman, Benjamin Combs

Deposition of William Hays [98]

      Also William Hays, being first sworn, Deposeth and saith that som time in November 1782, that he Received a Location from James McMallen, to Begin on the Dividing Ridge betwixt the 4 mile Creek & the Cantucky river, to Begin at a Hickory Tree Marked HC, but some time in 1784 passing by the place, Lawrance Thomson he shew me a White Oak, which he told Me was the Tree he gave me the Location for, which is the said Tree that we are now present at, which Location I got from said Thompson, but the copy from James McMillen. This Deponant further sayth not.
[signed] William Hays
attested Richard Hickman, Benjamin Combs

25.

James Duncan, Benedict Couchman, Edward Wilson and Frederick Couchman for John Strode

John Strode

      John Strode (1729-1805) came to Boonesborough in the spring of 1779 in company with the Swearingens, Morgans and others from Berkeley County, Virginia. Strode claimed a 1000-acre preemption at the site of his half-faced cabin built in 1776, located just west of present-day Winchester. There he set to work in the fall of 1779 building a station. Strode himself returned to Virginia for several years before permanently moving to Kentucky.[116] His death notice appeared in the *Kentucky Gazette*:

> John Strode, Sen., of Strode's Station. Died August 18, 1805. "As honest a man as ever God made."[117]

      On December 27, 1779, John Strode laid before the land commission his claim "lying on the South fork of licking near the head thereof, to include his Station on the premises . . . by marking & improving the same in April 1776." Benjamin Ashby surveyed the tract in 1782; James Duncan was marker, John Constant and Frederick Couchman, chain carriers. Strode received a patent in 1784.[118]

James Duncan

      James Duncan was born in Frederick County, Virginia, in 1750 and died in Bourbon County in 1817. He married John Strode's daughter Elizabeth.[119] He gave much biographical information in an 1805 deposition:

> James Duncan, aged 55 years, came to Kentucky, 1779, was at Boonesborough, returned to old settlement same year and came out to Kentucky again in the fall of that year and assisted Benedict Couchman and his brother to build the first house at Strode's Station, which was on a fork. That he was to and from Virginia several times and when in Kentucky he generally resided at Strode's Station, that he moved his family to Kentucky in the spring of 1784.[120]

Duncan settled on Kennedy's Creek, south of present-day Paris and represented Bourbon County at Kentucky's second constitutional convention in 1799.

Benedict and Frederick Couchman

      Frederick was a resident of Boonesborough in 1779; Frederick and Benedict were early inhabitants of Strode's Station. Benedict gave the following deposition in 1805:

> Benedict Couchman, aged 49 years, deposes . . . deponant lived at Stroud's

station in the year of 1780 and continued to live there until 1785.[121]

William Clinkenbeard said the brothers occupied a cabin on the east wall of Strode's Station, and went on to tell what became of the two men:

> Frederic Couchman died tother side of Winchester. Benedict Couchman moved off on the Ohio, towards Yellow Banks [Henderson].[122]

Frederick lived on Lower Howard's Creek and Benedict lived in Bourbon County. Benedict had a 1000-acre preemption just east of Winchester and a 500-acre tract adjoining the preemption on the south. The 500-acre tract was surveyed for "Bennedict Couchman" and granted to "Benjamin Couchman," which suggests that he used both names interchangeably. This is verified in a later deed dividing the 500-acre tract among his heirs in 1807; the same deed refers to the "heirs of Benjamin Couchman Deceased" and the "heirs benedic Couchman Deceased."[123]

Edward Wilson

Edward Wilson was a surveyor by trade. He patented a 1000-acre tract that encompassed most of the present downtown area of Winchester. John Baker purchased 319 acres from him and set aside 66 acres of that for the new county seat of Clark. Wilson came to Kentucky from Berkeley County, Virginia, "in the year 1776 and again in the fall of the year 1779." He may have been gone again in December 1779, when his friend John Strode placed Wilson's claim before the land commission, for which Wilson received a 1000-acre preemption "by marking and improving the same in 1776." Wilson lived for a time with Benedict Couchman at Strode's Station.[124] As a locator and surveyor, he was sometimes paid in land, as he stated in an 1805 deposition:

> Edward Wilson, aged 66 years, deposes . . . I received 300 acres out of every thousand of [Peter] Henry's claim, as locator, and have sold same.[125]

Wilson was residing in Bourbon County in 1794, and had moved to Knox County, Indiana, by 1808.[126]

Strode's Station

Strode's (often spelled Stroud's) Station was erected on John Strode's preemption in the fall and winter of 1779. The station was attacked by Indians in 1781, when Patrick Donaldson was killed and John Judy wounded. William Clinkenbeard's interview with Rev. John Shane gives a wealth of detail about this early Clark County fort. Strode's Station was one of the most important locations in the pioneer defense of central Kentucky. It was located on Strode Creek, about a quarter of a mile northwest of the intersection of US 60 and Van Meter Road.[127]

Deposition of James Duncan [98]

> Clarke County, to wit,
>
> Agreeable to an act of assembly for assertaining the Boundries of Lands, and for other purposes, and in Obedience to an order from the Worshipful Court of Clarke County appointing us Commissioners, and agreeable to a publication in the Kentucky Gazettes, We caused to come before us, at the time and place Described in said publication, James Duncan, aged forty six years, being Duly Sworn, Deposeth and saith that he was present when Mr. John Strode applyed for his Preemption Right, that he the said Strode Informed the Commissioners that he had Erected [Strode's] station, and that the Inhabitants of the station had there lots laid [so] that a Number of those Lots would be out [of] the Survey & beged Leave to move so fare Down the creek as would Enclude the fort growns [grounds], which the Commissioners said he should have Liberty to do.
>
> In the spring one Thousand Seven Hundred and Eighty [1780], said Strode called upon a number of the Inhabitants of said Station, and that he this Deponant

carried the compass, and [ran a] line north twenty Degrees East to a Buckeye Tree, NothEast corner, with a line showed this Deponant to be the line of James Strode, to a Buckeye where we made a Corner, and then rune at a Right angel till we Crossed the Creek, which Did but jest Include the Clear Land. When the Surveyor Benjamin Ashby went to survey, he this Deponant pilotted him the said surveyer to the aforesaid Buckeye to make his Begining, which is the same that we now are at.

[The above deposition was repeated almost word for word immediately following, on page 99. There is considerable variation in spelling between the two, and some variation in content in the last few sentences—an indication that the clerk did not make exact copies of depositions submitted to the court.]

Deposition of James Duncan [99]

Clark County, To wit,

Agreeable to an act of assembly for assertaining the Boundries of lands and for other Purposes, and in obedience to an Order from the Worshipfull Court of Clarke County appointing us Commissioners, and agreeable to a publication in the Kentucky Gazettes, we caused to come before us at the time and place Described in said publication, James Dunkan, aged 46 years, who being duly sworn, Deposeth and saith that he was present when Mr. John Strode applyed for his Preemption right, that he the said Strode informed the Commissioners that he had erected a station and that the Inhabitants of the station had their Lots laid off [so] that a number of those Lots would be out of the survey & begged Leave to move so far down the creek that would enclude the Fort Grounds, which the Commissioners Said he should have Liberty to do. In the spring 1780, said Strode called upon a number of the inhabitants of said station & that he this Deponant carried the cumpass and Began at a White Oak Tree, being the north East corner of James Strodes Preemption, as sworn to by Edward Wilson, and run a line from thence to a Buckeye, the north East corner of said John Strodes Preemption Survey, and run from thence at right angles to said line untill we crossed Strodes Creek, which did but Just enclude the clear land of said Station. And when Benjamin Ashby went to survey the said Preemption, he this Deponant Piloted him the said surveyor to the aforesaid Buckeye to make the Begining, which is this tree we are now are at & further this Deponant saith not.
[signed] James Dunkin

Clarke County Sct.

The foregoing Deposition taken before us, the Subscribing Commissioners appointed by the County Court of Clarke, Pursuant to an act of assembly in that case made and also Provided & that we the said Commissioners caused [a] Boxelder Tree [to be marked] V in the presents of James Duglass and William Lander, Disintruested Witnesses. Given under our Hands the 7th Day of November 1796.
Original Young
William Sudduth
John Young

James Douglass
William Lander

Deposition of Benedict Couchman [100]

The Deposition of Benedick Couchman, of full age, Taken at Strode Station, who after being Sworn, Deposeth and saith That he was present when John Strode laid in his Claim of 1000 acres & that the said Strode Mentioned to the Court of Commissioners that his former Survey as run would not include the Land cleared at his station, to which the Commissioners replyed that he might move it so as to include the said Station improvement & further this Deponant Saith not.
[signed] Benedict Coulmon

Clarke County Sct.

The foregoing Deposition Taken before us, the Subscribing Commissioners appointed by the County Court of Clarke Pursuant to an act of assembly in that case, made & provided in the presence of James Douglass & William Lander, Disentrusted Witness. Given under Our hand this 7th day of november 1796.
James Douglass
William Lander
Original Young
William Sudduth
John Young

Deposition of Edward Wilson [101]

The Deposition of Edward Wilson, of full age, Taken this 7th day of November 1796 at a White Oak Tre, who after being Sworn, Deposeth and saith that the above Mentioned Tree was marked on the Month of April 1776 for James Strodes Northwest corner of his Thousand acres survey, which he has since Obtained a Thousand Acres Preemption on, and further this Deponant Saith not.
[signed] Edward Wilson

Clark County Sct.

The Foregoing Deposition Taken before us, the Subscribing Commissioners appointed by the County Court of Clarke at the said Tree Mentioned (a White Oak) and have caused a little walnut to be marked with the letter W, pursuant to an act of assembly in that case, made & provided in the presence of James Douglass and William Lander, Disentrusted Witness. Given under our hands this 7th day of November 1796.
James Douglass
William Lander
Original Young
William Sudduth
John Young

Deposition of Frederick Couchman [102]

The Deposition of Frederick Coulman, of full age, who after being sworn, Deposeth and saith that in the month of December 1782, he was with Benjamin Ashby, Deputy Surveyor Fayette County & Begun at this Tree I have sworn to (a Buckeye) being the Begining Tree called for in John Strodes Preemption Survey & made said Survey of One Thousand Acres for the said John Strodes & that I carried the chain for the same & further this Deponant Saith not.
[signed] Frederick Coulman

Clark County Sct.

The foregoing Deposition Taken At the said Tree (a Buckeye) eluded [to] in the foregoing Deposition before us, the subscribing Commissioners Appointed by the County Court of Clarke, Pursuant to an act of assembly in that case, made & provided & we the said Commissioners marked a Boxelder V in the presents of James Douglass and William Lander, Disentrusted Witness. Given under our hands this 7th day November 1796.
James Douglass
William Lander
Original Young
William Sudduth
John Young

26.

Ebenezer Corn, Elizamond Basye, James Galloway and Enoch Smith for Basil Stoker

Basil Stoker

In 1780, Basil Stoker of Allen Township, Washington County, Pennsylvania, sold 361 acres near the Monongahela River to Jeremiah Riggs. According to the deposition of Elizamond Basye, below, Basil Stoker was the brother-in-law of Ebenezer Corn. An inventory of Stoker's personal estate in Washington County was recorded in March 1787. There is no indication that Stoker ever resided in Kentucky; however, he was out locating in 1783 and assisted John Fleming survey several tracts on Hinkston Creek.[128]

Ebenezer Corn obtained an improvement for Stoker while out with Samuel Tomlinson's company in 1776. Stoker was not present at that time, nor was he present when James Galloway placed the claim before the land commission in 1780. Stoker's 1000-acre preemption adjoined Corn's. The location given to the commissioners described the tract as

lying on a West branch of the East side of licking Creek, including a large sinking Deer [clear] lick, about ¼ of a mile from his cabbin, about 6 Miles from an old indian town.[129]

John Fleming surveyed the tract at 981 acres in December 1783. Basil Stoker was in Kentucky at the time and served as marker for the survey. That same month, he assisted Fleming as marker on several surveys on Hinkston Creek. Stoker received a patent for his tract in 1786. The land is just east of Corn's preemption and lies entirely in Montgomery County, just east of the Clark County line.[130]

Basil Stoker was deceased at the time of this processioning (June 1796). The required public notice was placed in the *Kentucky Gazette* by Abraham Stoker, and the deponents were questioned by Jonathan and Abraham Stoker. Stoker's tract interfered with several tracts of Edward Payne and was the subject of a lawsuit in Fayette circuit court in 1797: *Edward Payne, Plaintiff, by James Brown, attorney vs Abraham Stoker, James Hughes attorney, Basil Stoker codefendant.* The decision read, "Defendant could not 'gainsay the allegations' and plaintiff recovered."[131]

Indian Old Fields

Indian Old Fields was a well-known landmark in pioneer times, having been discovered by 1775. This site of a Shawnee village has also been suggested as the location of John Finley's trading post in 1767. Indian Old Fields occupies the large plain in Clark County, just before the Knobs, that lies north of where the Mountain Parkway crosses the Goffs Corner-Kiddville Road (KY 974).[132]

Deposition of Ebenezer Corn [103]

The Deposition of Ebennezer Corn, being of full age, and being first sworn at the Place called by a lick by Abraham Stoker, Deposeth and saith [that] he the said Corn doth no that this is the Lick we are now at, which the Entry Calls for Bassill Stoker with the Commissioners.

Question by Jilson Payne, Gentleman, for Edward Payne, Gentleman: Do you no if Basel Stokers Survey includes the Dividing ridge between Hinkstons fork and Licking?
Answer: It is betwen the warters of Hinkston & Lulbegrud, or between the said warters.

Question by the same: Did you Build any Cabbin within a Quarter of a mile of a large sinking clear Lick?
Answer: I did believe at that time the cabbin was within a Quarter of a mile of this Lick, but now believe it to be a greater distance.

Question by the same: Do you no if Basel Stokers survey encluded any Cabbin built in the year 1776?
Answer: I do not no any Cabbin that is Built at that time in it.

Question by the same: Was you Employed by Basell Stoker to Build a cabbin for him?
Answer: I Was.

Question by the same: Was Basell Stoker in this country in the year of 1776?
Answer: He was not.

Question by the same: What sum the said Stoker was to give you for Making the Improvement?
Answer: Five Pounds.

Question by Abraham Stoker: At what Distance do you suppose it is to the *Indian old fields*?
Answer: We supposed it to be six miles at that time & still belive it now to be

about the same Distance & further this Deponant Saith not.

[signed] Ebenezer Corn

Clark County Sct.
        The foregoing Deposition being Taken before us, Original Young, Samuel McKee & James Clarke, commissioners appointed by the County Court of Clarke, pursuant to an act of assembly entitled an act for assertaining the Boundries of Lands & other purposes, have met at a Lick & in the presence of Paul Hulce & Basell Meek, Disentrusted witness, and has caused the letter Y to be fixed on a small Honey Locust. Sworn to at the said mentioned Place, this first day June 1796.
Paul Hulce [Huls]
Basil Meek
Original Young
James Clark
Samuel McKee

Deposition of Elizamond Basye [105]

        The Deposition of Elizemon Beasye, being of full age, Deposeth and saith, being first sworn, I heard Ebenezer say that he was to make an Emprovement for his Brother in law Stoker, and after the said Basey & others drew lots for Cabbins [already] made, the said Corn took one for the said Stoker, which we had left out at the first. [The] lottery was made at the sassefac Cabbin.

Question by Jilson Payn, Gentleman, for Edward Payne, Gentleman: Was Mr. Basell Stoker in the country in the year 1776?
Answer: I dont no he was.

Question by the same: Do you no this Place where we are now at to be a lick in the time you were Making Emprovement here to be used by Bufalow or Deer?
Answer: I do not.

Question: Do you no if there was any Cabbin made by the Company at that time made within one Quarter of mile [a] large sinking clear Lick?
Answer: I do not.

Question by Jonathan Stoker: Did you, when all Together, make any Emprovements on the other side of Licking from this Place?
Answer: No.

Question by Payne: Where is the cabbin that was Layed in for Basell Stoker before the Commissioners then appoint[ed]?
Answer: I do not no & this Deponant further saith not.

74

[signed] Elizemon Basye

Clarke County Sct.

We, Original Young, Samuel McKee & James Clarke, Commissioners appointed by the county Court of Clarke, pursuant to an act of assembly for assertaining the Boundries of lands & for other Purposes, have caused Elizemon Basye to come before us, and Being first sworn at the Lick & Honey Locust, which we have caused afresh to be [marked] with the letter Y, the above being the Depossion of the said Basy taken before us & in the Presents of Paul Huls & Basell Meek, Disentrusted witness, this first day of June 1796.
Paul Hulse
Basel Meek
Original Young
James Clark
Samuel McKee

Deposition of James Galloway [106]

The Deposition for James Galloway, being of full age, after being first sworn, Deposeth and saith that in the year 1776 or about that time that he the said Deponent heard Ebenezer Corn say that he wood make Emprovements for his Brother in law & I think his name to be Basel Stoker, and that when he the said Deponent came to the Commissioners, he the said Corn informed the said Deponent that he had don it.

Question by Jilson Payne, Gentleman, for Edward Payne: Do you no if this Lick we are now at is the one called for in Basell Stokers Entry?
Answer: I do not.

Question by the same: Did you not agree to let Mr. Ebenezer Corn have a Cabbin that you Built for the said Stoker?
Answer: I and my company did make two Cabbins, which we gave up to Tumbleston, Ebenezer Corn & company on their making me two other Cabbins Elsewhere.

Question by the same: Do you no if Basel Stokers survey includes the cabbin and lick [called] for in his Entry?
Answer: I do not.

Question by the same: Did you not prove Basell Stokers claim of a Preemption of 1000 acres before the Commissioners in the year 1780?
Answer: I proved it then, no other way only that I seed Ebenezer Corn at work, and that he told me he had made the improvement at the time, or about the time, we met at the commissioners, which was what I proved there, as well as I now remember.

Question by the same: Do you no of any Emprovement or cabin made within one

75

Quarter of a mile of a large sinking clear lick?

Answer: I do not. Only one Cabin I & company Built near a lick on the top of a ridge, which place I do not no a[t] present.

Question by the same: When did you no this to be called a Lick?

Answer: This place we are now at I never knew untill this last winter to my knowledge to be called a lick.

Question by Abraham Stoker: Do you no where the Lick is that you Built your Cabbin at & what sort of a lick it was?

Answer: It was on a Ridge about Sixty or Seventy poles from a Branch, and near a lick on the rite hand sid Down the Branch, the Lick being of Round Ovell like a sink hole, as well as I now remember & small groath of walnut Timber round it.

Question Jilson Payn, Gentleman, for Edward Payn, Gentleman: Did you no a lick in the year 1780 called by the name of a large sinking Clear Lick?

Answer: I did not.

Question Abraham Stoker: Did you and your Company give up one of the Cabbins you had made unto Ebenezer Corn for Bisel Stoker?

Answer: I gave up to Tumbleston and Corn & Company two cabbins. And further this Deponant saith not.

[signed] James Galloway

Clark County Sct.

The foregoing Deposition Taken [before] us, Original Young, Samuel McKee, James Clark, Commissioners appointed by the county Court of Clarke, pursuant to an act of assembly entitled an act for assertaining the Boundries of land & for other Purposes, in the presents of Paul Huls & Basell meek, Disentrusted Witness, at a lick which we have caused to be fresh marked with the letter Y on a small Honey Locust. Sworn to at the said Lick & Honey locuss this first day June 1796.

Paul Huls
Bazel Meek
Original Young
James Clark
Samuel McKee

Deposition of Ebenezer Corn [108]

The Deposition of Ebenezer Corn, of full age, Taken at or near a Place which is now in the Corn field of Jilson Payne, now held by Richard Griffin Sr. & by leave from the said Payne to the said Griffin this first day of June 1796, and near to a cabbin which the said Payne has rented to the said Griffin, the said Corn, being first sworn, Deposeth and saith as followeth, that in the year 1776 he the said Deponent with others, Tumbleston & company, Built a Cabbin at or near the Place where we now are, which the said Deponant claimed for Basel Stoker.

Question by Jilson Payne, Gentleman, for Edward Payn, Gentleman: Did you Build the cabbin you make mention off your self?
Answer: I did not Build it my self, but it was Built by Tumbleston & company.

Question by the same: At the time this cabbin you now make Mention of, was it Built for Stoker or not?
Answer: No, it was Built for the company.

Question by the same: What persons were with you when you Drew this Cabbin for Stoker?
Answer: Samuel Tumbleston, Elizemon Basey, James Hendrix, James Davis, George Ward & myself.

Question by Mr. Stoker: Wheather did you prove this Cabbin before the Commissioners or not for Stoker?
Answer: This is the Cabbin that was Built here which was proved by me for Stoker & proved by me before the commissioners.

Question by Jilson Payne for Edward Payne, Gentleman: Did you prove this cabbin by your own Oath or by oath of others before the Commissioners?
Answer: I say that I built a Cabbin here with others for Basel Stoker & I answer it was by my own Oath before the Commissioners [that] he obtained the Certificate & further this Deponant saith not.

[signed] Ebenezer Chorn

Clark County Sct.
   We, Original Young, Samuel Mckee, & James Clarke, Commissioners appointed by the County Court of Clarke and Pursuant to an act of assembly for Establish[ing] the Boundries of Land & other purposes, have this first day of June 1796 caused Ebenezer Corn, witness, to come before us the subscribers, and being first sworn, which foregoing is the Deposition of him this Ebenezer Corn, being at or near a Cabbin in the corn field of Jilson Payne, Gentleman, which the said Corn says is near the place where the [cabin] was formerly Built, which Deposition was taken In the presence of Paul Huls & Basel Meek & William Kelsey, Disentrusted Witnesses, June the first day 1796.
Paul Huls
William Kelse
Bazel Meek
Original Young
James Clark
Samuel McKee

27.

Enoch Smith for Thomas Lewis

Thomas Lewis

Thomas Lewis was born in 1749 in Fairfax County, Virginia, and later lived in Fayette County west of Lexington. He served as an officer during the Revolution and in 1793 was married to Elizabeth "Betsey" Payne (1757-1827), daughter of Edward Payne Sr. Lewis served as a representative for Fayette County and was a member of the convention that framed the first Kentucky constitution in 1792. He had the distinction of swearing in Kentucky's first Governor, Isaac Shelby. Lewis purchased the south half of Nathaniel Gist's 6000-acre military survey in Clark County. He died at the Olympian Springs, while on his way to Virginia in 1809, and was buried near his home—Lewis Manor—on Viley Road, 4 miles west of Lexington. The executors of his Fayette County will were his wife Elizabeth, sons Asa and Hector, and brother-in-law Henry Payne.[133]

The processioning below involves a single deposition by Enoch Smith. This 500-acre tract was surveyed on a treasury warrant for Thomas Lewis by John Payne in December 1783. Lewis received a patent for the tract in 1785.[134] Insufficient data are given in the survey to precisely locate the tract, and little additional information is provided in the deposition below. The survey described the land as lying "on an east branch of stoners fork, where thear is an old Indian Camp." There are relatively few east branches of Stoner (the major ones being Donaldson Creek, Turkey Run and Georges Branch) and they all run easterly or southeasterly, while the branch shown in the survey plat runs northeasterly. The land is in Clark County, east or northeast of Winchester.

Deposition of Enoch Smith [110]

The Deposition of Enoch Smith, Gentleman, of full age, take before us, Original Young and James Guy, commissioners appointed by the county court of Clarke, being sworn, Deposeth & saith That in the year 1779 in the fall, I was at the spring we are now at, and south East of said spring there was a large Indian camp, and that he camped near the Spring in company with Richard Spur, Moses Thomas, Charles Beall, Cooper Chancellor and others. When the Land [Office] was opened in the year 1780, I gave a location to William Payne of five Hundred Acres for Thomas Jones. And the Deponant farther saith that he believes the spring is so remarkable that either of the above named persons, if they was brought forward, would know it. Further this Deponant saith naught.
[signed] Enoch Smith

The foregoing Deposition taken at a large spring that comes out of a rock, and now enclosed by William Hencely, as the place proved by the said above mentioned Deponant and Taken before us, Original Young and James Guy, Commissioners appointed by the County Court of Clarke, Pursuant to an act of Assembly entitled an act of assertaining the Boundries of Land and for other purposes & in the presents of Samuel [sic] Butcher & William Hancly, Disintrusted Witness, this 25th of August 1796.
Richard Butcher [his mark]
William Hancly
Original Young
James Guy

28.

John Donaldson for Thomas Swearingen

Thomas Swearingen

Thomas Swearingen was an early settler of Frederick County, Virginia, in the area that later became Berkeley County. Swearingen established a ferry across the Potomac at Shepherdstown in 1755, the same year he defeated George Washington for a seat in the House of Burgesses. Swearingen was also a surveyor, as was his brother Benoni. They came to Kentucky in 1779 with others from Berkeley County, including George Michael Bedinger, William and Ralph Morgan, and John Strode. The party arrived at Boonesborough in April and spent much of the summer locating lands. While most of the Berkeley men returned home in November, Thomas Swearingen stayed out in order to place their claims before the land commission and, subsequently, to survey their claims. Thomas died in 1786, leaving all his "lands and claims on the western waters" to be divided among his five children.[135]

Thomas Swearingen's 1000-acre tract was entered on a treasury warrant and surveyed by Swearingen in December 1783. The location was described as lying "on the dividing ridge including some of the heads of drains of Hingston fork on the north side thereof," and the beginning corner was at "two betty trees, one marked JF the other TS and buckeye marked V near small pond [Fleming's Pond] on the said ridge near head of Flemings branch, as per entry." Swearingen received a patent for the tract in 1785. This land is just south and east of the community of Sharpsburg in Bath County.[136]

Andrew Swearingen placed a legal notice in the *Kentucky Gazette* to announce the procession for Thomas Swearingen's heirs. The notice mentioned Jacob Myers, who had one of the tracts interfering with Swearingen.[137]

John Fleming

John Fleming (1735-1791) was born of Irish parents who came to Chester County, Pennsylvania, moved to Lancaster County and then settled in Frederick County, Virginia (later Berkeley County). He came to Kentucky in 1776 with his half-brother George Stockton and others locating lands. Fleming was among the defenders of Strode's Station when the fort was attacked in 1781, and in 1782 married Lucy Pettit, the widow of Patrick Donaldson, who was killed in the attack. Fleming was wounded in Holder's Defeat near the Upper Blue Licks in 1782, and later that year was appointed deputy surveyor of Fayette County. In 1788, he began building a station near what would become Flemingsburg. The cause of his death in 1791 is unknown. Fleming County was named in his honor.[138]

John Donaldson

John was the natural son of Patrick Donaldson, who was killed by Indians at Strode's Station in the spring of 1781, and the stepson of John Fleming. John Donaldson was a major in the 36th Regiment of Clark County and a colonel, commanding the Kentucky Mounted Volunteer Militia, in the War of 1812. He lived in the northeast section of Clark County and left a will, probated in 1829. A road and a creek in that area take their names from him.[139]

Fleming's Pond

This small pond in Sharpsburg, Bath County, is reputed to be the place where John Fleming camped the night after he was wounded in Holder's Defeat. Fleming later surveyed and patented 1000 acres around the pond. In 1851, excavation of the pond revealed bones, teeth and an 8-foot tusk thought to be part of the skeleton of a mastadon. The pond was on the east side of town near the water tower, about 100 feet east of the cemetery.[140]

Swearingen's tract, processioned below, adjoined Fleming's on the south side.

Deposition of John Donaldson [111]

Clark County Sct.

26 May 1796

      By virtue of an order from the Court of the above County held in July 1795 to us directed, we Commissioners for said County, to perpetuate The Beginging of an Entry of Thomas Sweringam at a pond Called *Fleming pond*, and marked on two Blue ash trees & a Buckeye JFTSV, and proved by John Danoldson as followeth, Viz., the said John Dannalson, being duly sworn before us, William Caldwell, David Hughs & James McLHeany, Commissioners, deposeth and sayeth that in the year 1782, at the time when General Clarke was gone to the Shawneetowns, that he the said Deponant in Company with John Fleming, Deceased, and Thomas Swearingham came to this above mentioned place, and that he seen the said Swearingem and Fleming mark the above mentioned Trees with the above described letters, as they now appear to us plain & Inteligible, and the said Deponant saith he seen no marks on the said Trees before that time & this Deposition was Taken on the same ground where the above Trees Stands, in the presents of the following disintrusted persons & Commissioners.

[signed] John Dannalson

attested James McIlhanny, William Caldwell, David Hughs

Clarke County, May 26th 1796

      We, Disintusted to the within mentioned Land and Entry, do afirm that we were on the ground where the within mentioned Trees stands and heard John Danalson declare the same as is herein mentioned. Given under our hand this day above mentioned.

William Caldwell

James McIlHenny

David Hughs

J[ohn] Blair

John McIntire

29.

Edward Wilson, John Jacob Judy and Michael Cassidy for Mathias Sphar

Mathias Sphar

    Mathias Sphar was one of many Virginia men from Berkeley County who settled at Strode's Station in the fall of 1779. He was killed by Indians in 1784 in what is now Bourbon County.[141]   The circumstances of "old man Spahr's" death were described by William Clinkenbeard: Michael Cassidy, Joshua Bennett (the surveyor) and Mathias Sphar

> had gone down Rockbridge pretty near to where it empties into Boone Creek, five or six miles the other side of North Middletown. . . . Had built their camp fire against the log. Indian just crept up behind it and shot over at them. Cassidy was a little chunk of an Irishman . . . lay right between Bennet and Spahr.[142]

Bennett and Sphar were killed, and Cassidy made his escape.

Mathias Sphar had a 400-acre claim on Green Creek in Bourbon County and a 500-acre claim on the middle branch of Strode's Creek, then called Taylor's Branch, in Clark County. Sphar entered the latter tract, processioned below, in 1780:

> Matthias Spear, assignee of James Duncan, enters 500 Acres upon a Treasury Warrant to include a white oak marked MS standing near Taylors branch of Licking about 2½ miles above said Taylors spring.[143]

Edward Wilson surveyed the tract in 1782; Mathias Sphar was marker, Michael Cassidy and John Jacob Judy, chain carriers. Sphar received a patent for the tract in 1784. The land is about 3½ miles north of Winchester.[144]

John Jacob Judy

Judy was wounded at Strode's Station when the fort was attacked by Indians in 1781. Daniel Sphar, son of Mathias, described the event:

> John Judy, a boy of about 16 and another boy was cutting some meat sticks, a little piece from the fort, when the firing commenced on the opposite side. The indians designed to take them prisoners, but they started to run, and Judy was shot in the back and out through by the left nipple. Both got in safe.[145]

In the spring of 1780, John Judy and his family went with Enoch Smith to settle Smith's Station just north of present-day Mt. Sterling. Judy obtained from Smith a choice tract, which became part of downtown Mt. Sterling. According to John Crawford:

> John Judy bought the 100 acres of Enoch Smith which I might have chosen, paid for it in sheep, cows, & stock, the currency of the country, &c. & laid it off, & sold it in different sized lots. This was after [Hugh] Forbes had come in & commenced a town.[146]

Judy lived in Montgomery County for some time. He was a resident of Jackson County, Indiana, in 1840, when he and wife Catherine sold a lot in Winchester to Thomas Burgess. The surname is sometimes spelled Juda or Judah in the records.[147]

Michael Cassidy

Michael Cassidy was born in Ireland and came to Virginia as an indentured servant. He lived at Strode's Station for a time before establishing his own station in what became Fleming County. William Clinkenbeard provided several assessments of Cassidy:

> Better soldier was never born . . . Cassedy loved liquor and got into two or three fights [while camped near Maysville] . . . Settled, or entered rather, a great deal of land as employed by others.[148]

Cassidy "was in upwards of thirty Indian fights, and so many was his 'hair breadth 'scapes,' that he was commonly said to have a charmed life." He served numerous terms in the legislature and died at his station in the year 1829.[149]

Deposition of Edward Wilson [112]

The Deposition of Edward Wilson, being of full age, after Being first sworn, at the mouth of a Branch runing into Taylors Branch from the North side, Deposeth & saith that in the year 1783 some time in the winter, Mathias Spar got me as surveyor & Brought me to a tree marked MS, which he then told me was his Emprovement, standing as well as I can remember between Eighty & a Hundred poles above John Woodruffs corner, a white Oak & shugar Tree, which survey I made at the request of the said Spar of 500 acres of land, which include the said marked Tree above mentioned, and at the same time the said Spar as well

a[s] I remember Emformed me that he had other Trees up the said Branch, which he intended to be taken in the said Survey, and this Deponant further saith not.
[signed] Edward Wilson

Clarke County Sct.

The foregoing Deposition being taken before us, Original Young [and] John Young, Commissioners appointed by the county court of Clarke, pursuant to an act of Assembly entitled an act for pepetuate and to assertain the Boundries of Land & for other peposes, In the presents of John Danolson & William Kelley, Disentursted Witness, and sworn to at the mouth of a small Branch running into a branch Called Taylor Branch & in a corn field and near a House where William Kelly now lives, which the above Deponant swears was the place or near the place called for in the survey. As the marked white oak is not to be found, we the said Commissioners has caused to be marked a Hickroy Tree stand[ing] in the said field with the letter Y. Sworn to this 27th day of June 1796.
John Donnalson
William Kelly
Original Young
John Young

Deposition of John Jacob Judy [113]

The Deposition of John Jacob Judy, being of full age, after being first sworn, Deposeth and saith that he thinks it was in the year 1783 that I came with Methias Spar at his request and he the said Spar Brot me to a tree, a white Oak, which was marked, but I do not Remember what letters the tree was marked with, but the said Tree was Standing near the Bank of Taylors Branch, which Creek he showed me for his Emprovement, and he the said Spar got me to be one of his chain carriers & [we] went from the said white Oak to John Woodroughs Corner trees, a large white Oak & a shugar Tree, and then began the said survey, and this Deponant further saith not.
[signed] John J. Judy

Clarke County Sct.

The foregoing Deposition being Taken before us, Original Young & John Young, Commissioners appointed by the County Court of [Clark], and pursuant to an Act of Assembly entitled an Act for assertaining the Boundries of land & for other purposes, In the presents of John Danalson & William Kelley, Disintrusted Witnesses, and Sworn to at the mouth of a small Branch runing into a Branch called Taylors Branch, and in a Corn Field and near a House where William Kelly now lives, which the above Deponant swears was the place or near the place called for in the survey, or where the marked Oak did formerly stand. We the said Commissioners have caused to be marked a Hickroy Tree Standing in the said field, and in the fork of the said Branches, with the letter Y. Sworn to this 27 day of June 1796.
John Danalson
William Kelly

Original Young
John Young

Deposition of Michael Cassidy [114]

The Deposition of Michal Casaday, being of full age, Taken this 27th day of June one Thousand seven Hundred & ninty six [1796] at a whit Oak called for in the Entry of Mathias Spar, assignee of James Duncan Entry for 500 acres of land near Taylors Branch of Licking, about 2½ miles above Taylors Spring, on June 16th 1780, after being first Duly sworn, Deposeth and saith, that in the year 1783 some time in the winter, I came as chain Carrier with Methias Spar wheare he took myself, Edward Wilson & John Judy to a white Oak marked MS Standing on the North side of the main Branch, then called woodroughfs Branch, which we then suposed to be between Eighty & a hundred pool [poles] from John Woodroufs south East Corner, a large white Oak & shugar Tree, which myself carryed the chain to run out the side[s of the] 500 acres mentioned in the said Entry, and this Deponant Further Saith not.
[signed] Michael Cassidy

Clark County Sct.

The foregoing Deposition being Taken before us, Original Young and John Young, Commissioners appointed by the County Court of Clarke, pursuant to an Act of Assembly intitled an Act for perpetuate and assertian the Boundries of Lands & for other purposes, In the presents of John Danaldson & William Kelly, Disintrusted witnesses, and sworn to at the mouth of a small Branch in a corn field, and near a House where William Kelly now lives, which the above Deponant swore was the place or near the place called for in the Survey. As the marked white Oak is not to be found, we the said Commissioners have caused to be marked [a] Hickory standing in the said field with the letter Y. Sworn to this 27th day of June 1796.
John Dannalson
William Kelly
Original Young
John Young

30.

William Foster and Leonard Hart for Anthony Buckner

Anthony Buckner

Anthony Buckner has not been positively identified, but he may be the Anthony Buckner Jr. who was mentioned in his father's will probated in Halifax County, Virginia. Anthony Sr. reportedly was born 1731 in Stafford County, where he married Amy Powell in 1755. They moved to Halifax County, where he died in 1780. His estate was appraised at nearly £13,000. His will lists his wife and 10 children, including Anthony Jr. Anthony Jr. was on the taxpayer rolls of Prince William County in 1787. There is no record of Buckner ever residing in Kentucky. The two tracts below are the only ones entered by Buckner in Kentucky. John Hedges placed the notice of Buckner's processioning in the *Kentucky Gazette*, and Original Young made a motion for the procession at the June term of Clark county court in 1796.[150]

Buckner was in Kentucky in January 1780, when he laid his claim and the claim of James French (also of Prince William County) before the land commission sitting at Bryan's Station. Buckner claimed a 400-acre settlement and 1000-acre preemption "lying on the North fork of the South fork of licking, to include his improvement, about 25 Miles from the Mouth of said North fork, by raising a crop of Corn in the year 1776." Apparently, Buckner had been out with John Crittenden and others in 1776 locating lands on branches of Licking River. The 1000-acre tract was surveyed on October 1, 1785 by John Peyton; James Duncan was marker, Leonard Hart and William Foster, chain carriers. The 400-acre tract was surveyed four days later by John's brother, Timothy Peyton. This land is on Somerset Creek in Montgomery County.[151]

William Foster

William Foster (1747-1824) was born in Prince William County, Virginia and died in Clark County. He enlisted in the Continental Army and fought at Monmouth, Ninety Six, Eutaw Springs and Yorktown. Foster received a pension and military warrants for 200 acres for his Revolutionary War service. He lived on Lulbegrud Creek on land purchased from John Rankin. In 1822, he appointed Levi Hart of Lexington as his attorney to sue for the return of a slave. Foster married Sarah Hart, daughter of Leonard Hart. The county court appointed three men to appraise Foster's estate in 1825.[152]

Leonard Hart

Leonard Hart was William Foster's father-in-law. He was on the 1800 tax list for Fayette County. His connection, if any, to the notable Hart families of Fayette County has not been established. Hart was in Kentucky by 1785, when he and William Foster served as chain carriers on the surveys of Buckner's settlement and preemption.[153]

Deposition of William Foster [115]

The Deposition of William Foster, of full age, after being sworn, Deposeth and saith that in the year 1785 that he this Deponant was Employed to carry chain at the surveying of anthony Buckners Settlement and preemption & that francis McDermerd [McDermid]was employed to show Anthony Buckners improvement & that said McDermerd Showed this identicle spot to be Buckners improvement & said he was ready to swere to the place, as he was one of the company that made the improvement & that it was Number 14. Further this Deponent Saith not. [signed] William Foster his mark

Clarke County Sct.

The foregoing Deposition taken at the Improvement above mentioned by us the subscribing Commissioners appointed by the county court of Clarke pursuant to an Act of Assembly entitled as Act for assertaining the Boundres of Land & for other purposes & the improvement being in a state of Decay, we caused to be marked afresh a Lin Tree with the Letters AB, in the presents of Coonrod See, John Graves and John Hedges Jr., Disintrused Witnesses. Sworn to before us the subscribing this 26th day of July 1796.
William Sudduth
John Young

Deposition of Leonard Hart [116]

The Deposition of Leonard Hart, of full age, Taken before us the Subscribing commissioners, who after being Sworn, Deposeth and saith that he was imployed as Chain man to survey Anthony Buckners Settlement and preemption & that Francis McDermerd was employed as a pilot to show Buckners improvement, who showed this as the place & said that this improvement was Number 14 & that the [one] next to [it] up the Creek, Claimed by [James] French, was No. 15, being the upermost improvement made by Cridenton [John Crittenden] & Company on said Creek & that the Number being 14 appeared plain at the time the survey was made & further this Deponant saith not. [signed] Leonard Hart

Clarke County Sct.

The Foregoing Deposition taken before us the subscribing Commissioners appointed by the county Court of Clarke pursuant to an Act of Assembly entitled as Act for assertaining the Boundries of Land & for other purposes & the improvement being in a state of Decay, we caused to be marked afresh a Lin Tree with the Letters AB, standing on the west bank of Summerset [Creek] near said improvement, in the presents off Coonrood See, John Groves [Graves] & John Hedges Jr., Disinturested Witness. Sworn to before us the subscribing Commissioners this 26th day of July 1796.
William Sudduth
John Young

31.

Enoch Smith for Jeremiah Moore

Jeremiah Moore

Jeremiah Moore (1746-1815) lived in Loudoun County and Fairfax County, Virginia. He was a Baptist minister, who founded numerous churches and whose preaching carried him far from home at times. One biographer wrote that "his person and voice are extremely advantageous; his style is strong and energetic . . . his ideas brilliant." Moore speculated extensively in Kentucky land—his claims amounting to 24,314 acres in Clark County alone; however, there is no indication he ever moved to Kentucky. In 1794, Moore deeded to James French a one-third share of his Clark County land, in payment to French for "surveying, Registering & clearing out of the several Offices" Moore's land claims. In 1805, John Adair, as Register of Kentucky, exposed to public auction a tract belonging to "Jeremiah Moore, a non-resident of the state." The land, 1271 acres on Slate and Flat creeks, was sold for $50.18, the back taxes owed on the property.[154]

The tract processioned below—1000 acres at Bramblett's Lick—was one of a number of overlapping claims near that lick on Stoner Creek. Enoch Smith states in his deposition below that Moore's original entry at Bramblett's Lick was later found to interfere with Gist's military survey, and he withdrew it. He used the warrant to enter a tract beginning at the mouth of a branch of Stoner on the east side—now known as Goose Creek. Smith surveyed this claim for Moore on a treasury warrant in 1784. William Said was the marker, John Wilkerson and Francis Jones, chain carriers. This land lies in the V formed by I-64 and US 60, about 6½ miles northeast of Winchester.[155]

Deposition of Enoch Smith [117]

The Deposition of Enoch Smith, of full age, Taken before us, the subscribing Commissioners appointed by the Court of Clarke County pursuant to an Act of Assembly entitled as Act for assertaining the Boundries of Lands & for other purposes, who after being Sworn, Deposeth and saith that in the year 1780 he passed by the Lick we are now at in Company with Jeremiah Moore, John Halley, William Payne & Moses Thomas. At the said lick he made marks and Entered an Entry for Jeremiah Moore of 1000 Acres, which Deponant afterwards found in Gists Military Survey and withdrew it. The said Halley I understood Entered at the same Lick, and Caled it by the name of the red Lick, which occasioned a dispute between Payn & himself, as Payn expected he was under obligation [not to] interfere with his Entry, which Controversy first made me Sensible that it was the Lick we are at, which now is Called Bramblets Lick & further the Deponant Saith Naught.

[signed] Enoch Smith

Clarke County Sct.

The foregoing Deposition Taken before us, Original Young, William Sudduth & James Guy, Commissioners apointed by the County Court of Clarke pursuant to an act of Assembly in that case, made & provided at the Lick Mentioned in the above Deposition, in the presents of John Hedges Jr. & Thomas Dickenson, Disintrusted Witnesses. Given under our hands this 5th day of September 1796.

John Hedges
Thomas Dickenson
Original Young
William Sudduth
James Guy

32.

Enoch Smith for John Wilkerson

John Wilkerson

John Wilkerson (1757-1834) was born in Fairfax County, Virginia, and died in Clay County, Missouri. He and his brother William and uncle, John Halley, signed a petition in 1787 to divide Fayette, Bourbon and Madison to form a new county with the seat at Boonesborough. From 1791 to 1796, John Wilkerson and John Halley were so closely associated in Madison County that their tax assessment was for "Halley and Wilkerson." They had a gristmill, sawmill and store on Otter Creek. In 1792 John Wilkerson was one of the subscribers who pledged a total of 18,550 acres of land and 2,630 pounds sterling to locate the Kentucky capital at Boonesborough. In 1799, he was appointed major in the 7th Regiment of the Kentucky militia and was elected to represent Madison County in the Kentucky General Assembly. The name was sometimes spelled Wilkinson.[156]

Wilkerson entered 3050 acres on a treasury warrant, the land lying "between the head of hingstons fork of licking and the uper Salt Spring, and about 6 miles Southward of said Spring." Enoch Smith surveyed the tract in 1784, with John Wilkerson, marker, Francis Jones and William Said, chainmen. This land lies on Flat Creek in Bath County, about 4 miles east of Sharpsburg.[157]

Deposition of Enoch Smith [118]

Enoch Smith, of full age, being sworn before us Commissioners, Deposeth and saith that he Surveyed James Whaleys Land of two Surveys, Containing

487½ Acres each, on the warters of Lickings, and after he had done the same, he Returned to [Thomas] Marshall Office and entered John Wilkerson entry of 3050 Acres, to begin 450 Poles South 85 degrees East of said Corner, and the Corner We are now at he knows to be Whaleys North Eastword Corner Called for in the Entry, and that he Measured [by] Actual Survey the distance Called for in said Entry of Wilkersons, and there marked his Begining Corners, which we have now examined, which is Four Hickories [and] sugar tree saplings, which the Deponant saith he knows to be John Wilkersons Beginning. Further this Deponent saith naught.

[signed] Enoch Smith

Question By Benjamin Berry: Are you in any way Interested in John Wilkerson
        Claim of 3050 Acres of Land?
Answer: I am not.

[signed] Enoch Smith

We the under Written Commissioners appoint[ed] by the Worshipful Court of Clarke County, agreeable to an order of said Court Dated June Court 1796, met at the Northeast Corner of James Waleys Survey of 487½ Acres, and there Enoch Smith made oath to said Corner, which is a Honey Locust marked JW & JM & Hickory & sugar tree, and then we went to John Wilkersons Begining, Four Hiccories and Sugartrees, and near to said Begining marked a Sugartree JW, which said Smith also made Oath to. Disentrusted persons present, Thomas Doggett & David England. Given under our hands this 15 day of September 1796.
David England
Thomas Doggett
William Caldwell
James McElhany

33.

Benjamin Dunaway for William Bramblett

William Bramblett

William Bramblett was a Baptist minister from Bedford County, Virginia. He was born in 1719, moved to Bedford County in 1747, served as a sergeant in the French and Indian War, and married Anna Ballard in about 1760. Bramblett was a member of the Goose Creek Church, where he may have been serving as minister when he came to Kentucky in 1779. He preached at Bryan's Station ("probably the first man who ever preached north of Kentucky River"), went out on Stoner Creek in search of land, and started back to Virginia in July 1779. He was killed by Aquilla White in a hunting accident along the Wilderness Road. Bramblett and White went out to hunt deer and became separated in the woods; hearing a noise, White shot Bramblett thinking him an Indian. Bramblett's grave was near where US 25E crosses the Cumberland River. His will was proven in Bedford County in August 1779.[158]

Richard Calloway placed Bramblett's claim before the land commission at Boonesborough on December 23, 1779:

The Heir[s] of William Bramblett, deceased, by Richard Calloway this day claimed a preemption of 400 Acres of land . . . lying on a branch of Stoners fork of licking Creek, joining Benjamin Duniways Claim to land by actual settlement made in the month of April 1779.[159]

The Calloway and Dunaway families were neighbors of the Brambletts in Bedford County, Virginia. The commissioners issued the heirs a certificate for 400 acres, but the tract was not surveyed until 1797—more than a year after the deposition below. William Sudduth was the surveyor, and William Bramblett Jr. was the pilot. The survey included Bramblett's "improvement" in Clark County. Kentucky issued a grant to Bramblett's heirs in 1798. The land is located in the Wades Mill area, near the landmark which bore his name: Bramblett's Lick.[160]

Benjamin Dunaway

Benjamin Dunaway was an early settler in Clark County. The Virginia land commission granted his claim for 400 acres on a branch of Stoner Creek by by proof of his "making an Actual settlement in April 1779." In 1795, he placed a notice in the *Kentucky Gazette* that he found a horse near his home on Upper Howard's Creek. There was a village named for the family—Dunaways—that was located in southeast Clark County, near present-day Trapp.[161]

Deposition of Benjamin Dunaway [119]

The Deposition of Benjamin Dunaway, of full age, after being sworn, Deposeth and saith that about the month of April or may 1779, he the said Deponant was in Company with William Bramblet & others and assisted in Making this improvement, as he believes from viewing and examining the Same at this time.

Question by James Buford: Did you and Company Plant corn at this place at the time you made the improvements?
Answer: We did.

Question by the same: Do you recollect of any peach stones being Planted at this Place?
Answer: I do not, nor [recollect] any being in Company.

Question: What Kind of Improvement did you make before you planted the Corn?
Answer: We Deadned some trees & cut the Bushes out of the way & further this Deponant Saith not.

[signed] Benjamin Dunaway his mark

Clarke County Sct.
The Forgoing Deposition being taken before William Sudduth and Original Young, Commissioners Appointed by the County Court of Clarke Pursuant to an Act of assembly entitled an act for assertaining the Boundries of Lands and for other purposes, in the presents of Jese Coffer & Henry Dooly, Disentrusted Witness & sworn to at the above mentioned improvement the 23rd March 1796.
William Sudduth
Original Young

34.

Elias Tolin and John Crittenden for Thornton Farrow

Thornton Farrow

Thornton Farrow was in Kentucky in 1775 viewing land on Grassy Lick and Somerset creeks. Farrow was a member of an illustrious company of locators that included George Rogers Clark, John Crittenden and William Lynn. He may have come out from Prince William County, Virginia, where his brother, William Farrow, lived at that time. John Crittenden placed Thornton's claim before the land commission in 1779. Farrow was in Lexington in December 1781, when he purchased a lot from the trustees. He placed an entry on his Grassy Lick claim in April 1783 but was deceased by November 1783, when his heirs had the tract surveyed.[162]

Thornton Farrow and several of the company returned in 1776 and built a cabin at Farrow's improvement. His entry gives a good description of the location:

> Thornton Farrow enters 1000 acres on a preemption warrant, No. 979, on Buck Lick Creek, waters of Hinkston's fork of Licking Creek, and to include his improvement and a buffalo lick at the forks of said creek of a square tract.[163]

The "forks" refers to the point where Somerset Creek branches off from Grassy Lick Creek. John Fleming conducted the survey in 1783, John Donaldson was the marker. The patent was issued to William Farrow in 1791. This land is on Grassy Lick Creek in present-day Montgomery County, about 6 miles north and west of Mt. Sterling.[164]

John Crittenden

John Crittenden was an officer in the Revolutionary War and migrated to Kentucky at the end of the war. He was one of the early settlers of Woodford County and a trustee of the town of Versailles. His residence is shown on John Filson's map of Kentucky, west of Lexington on South Elkhorn Creek. The Crittenden Cabin was built about 1783 and still stands just north of US 60, 2 miles east of Versailles. His son, John J. Crittenden, held many state and national offices and became governor of Kentucky in 1848; Crittenden County was named for him.[165]

Buck Lick or Grassy Lick

Buck Lick was the first name given to what later became known as the Grassy Lick, so called because of its famous stand of bluegrass, one of the first found in Kentucky. The place also was called Pasture Lick by some of the pioneers. Unrecognizeable today, the lick was located 5 miles northwest of Mt. Sterling near the present intersection of KY 713 and KY 2931, close to the base of the hill on which stands Grassy Lick Methodist Church.[166]

Deposition of Elias Tolin [120]

The Deposition of Elias Tolin, of full Age, Taken at a Lick Called *Grassy Lick*, who after being sworn, Deposeth & saith that in the year 1775 he this Deponent, Major John Cindenten [Crittenden] and others came on Summersett [Creek] & there encamped & in the course of a few days Thompton [Thornton] Farrow, John Cridinten, George Rogers Clarke [and] William Lynn went out from said camp & steered their course down Summerset & perhaps the ensuing Day came into camp as tho they came down the west fork of Summersett & gave an account of a Lick [they] Called *Buck Lick*. Next morning the said William Lyn, Andrew Lyn & this Deponent & others went down Summersett a Buffalo Hunting & this Deponent got lost from the Company & fell on a Trail of men which bore nearly Northwest.

Then he concluded it must of been the Company that was out the Day before by the number of Tracks & Followed down said Trail down a branch now

Called Yates branch to the mouth & then Come up this fork to the lick on the Trail aforesaid & found a fresh improvement at the Lick, that is to say a Cabbin & some Trees Deadned & found the following mark, F, which Confirmed to the said Deponant that it was the same Company that brought to Camp the account of Buck Lick, by knowing the mark to be Thornton Farrows usual Marks & he this Deponant then kept the Trail untill he came to Camp & Mentioned being at a Lick & improvement & the Company said from the Description it was Thornton Farrows improvement. Some few days after, William Lyn & this Deponant & others came to this place again & Lynn informed this Deponant Then that it was Thornton Farrow Improvement.

Question by Benjamin J. Taul: When you followed the Tract from this Place to
       Camp, did you Discover any other improvement on the Creek?
Answer: I do not recollect of any & further this Deponant Saith not.

[signed] Elias Tolin

Clarke County Sct.
       The foregoing Deposition Taken at the Lick aforesaid by us the Subscribing Commissioners, appointed by the County Court of Clarke Pursuant to an act of assembly in the Case, made & provided in the presents of Joshua Yates & Joseph Frakes, Disintrusted Witnesses. Given under our hands this 14th day of September 1796.
Original Young
William Sudduth
Henry Chiles

Deposition of John Crittenden [122]

       The Deposition of John Cridentin, Gentleman, being of full age, Taken at a Lick Called by the said Cridenton in the year 1775 Buck Lick, but now known by the Inhabitants by the name of Grassey lick, who after being Sworn, Deposeth and saith that to the best of his knowledge he the said Deponant, William Lyn & Thonton Farrow came to this Place in the summer 1775 & that they Called this place buck Lick & that some time in the year 1775 or 1776, he the Said Deponant, George Rogers Clarke, Thornton Farrow & John Clarke built a Cabbin at this Place for Thornton Farrow & intended it for his use.

Question by William Jackson: Did Thornton Farrow make any other
       improvements in Kentucky but this?
Answer: Yes.

Question: Where Did Thornton make any other improvements?
Answer: On this same branch above here, in conjunction with the Company
       above Mentioned, that is to say the left hand fork as We go up the Creek
       & further this Deponant saith not.

[signed] John Crittenten

Clarke County Sct.

     The foregoing Deposition Taken at the Lick aforesaid by us, the Subscribing Commissioners appointed by the County Court of Clarke pursuant to an act of assembly in that Case, made & provided & in the presents of Joseph Frakes & Joshua Yates Jr. this 19th day of September 1796.
Original Young
William Sudduth
Henry Chiles

35.

John Crittenden for William Farrow

William Farrow

     William Farrow was not present when the tract processioned below was located by Thornton Farrow's company. William resided in Prince William County, Virginia, where we find him on the tax list in 1782 and again in 1787. In 1796, William and wife Sarah, living in Prince William County, sold part of his preemption on Grassy Lick Creek. He was still there in 1803, when he sold more of his land on Grassy Lick, with William Farrow of Montgomery County acting as his attorney. The latter, referred to as William Jr. in the deposition below, is presumed to be William's son.[167] William Sr. moved to Kentucky in later life. His obituary appeared in the *Kentucky Reporter* and is quoted in full here to give an idea of the florid style of the times:

> Departed this life on the 17th of October last, Captain William Farrow, at the residence of Col. William Farrow, Fleming County, Ky., in the 80th year of his age. He was a native of Prince William County, Virginia, and among the first of that state that took up arms in opposing the tyranny of Britain in support of the independence of the United States. His friendship was warm and without deception. The needy and distressed were never turned away from his door; and a cordial and hearty welcome ever awaited the stranger. Alas! he is no more. In his last illness although lingering and painful, he bore it with fortitude nor ever was heard to murmur at providence. He retained his senses to the last and met death with manly firmness and died without a struggle.[168]

     William Farrow's 1000-acre tract was south of and adjoining Thornton Farrow's. John Crittenden laid William's claim before the land commission at St. Asaph's in April 1780. John Fleming surveyed the tract in 1783 on a preemption warrant and a patent was issued to Farrow in 1786. The land is on Grassy Lick Creek in Montgomery County, about 6 miles northwest of Mt. Sterling.[169]

William Farrow Jr.

     In 1798, William Farrow Jr. was residing on his father's claim in Montgomery County, when he was appointed captain of the county militia; he was promoted to major in 1802 and to lieutenant colonel in 1808. Farrow served as a state representative for Montgomery County 1801, 1810-1811 and as a state senator 1812-1815. Later in life, he moved his residence to Fleming County.[170]

     Thaddeus Dulin's patent overlapped William Farrow's. In 1809, William Jr. sued Dulin for a writ of injunction on behalf of William Sr., arguing that Dulin's entry was "vague and uncertain" and "interferes with your Orator." The Fayette circuit court found in Farrow's favor.[171]

Deposition of John Crittenden [123]

The Deposition of John Cridenton, Gentleman, Taken at the improvement Claimed by William Farrow & included in his preemption of 1000 acres & after being sworn, Deposeth saith that to the best of his knowledge, the improvements at the Place William Jaines now lives at was made the Day or day after the improvements made at buck lick for Thornton Farrow. Also the Improvement near the Creek & opposite to where William Farrow Jr. now lives were made about the same time, that is the in the same Rout & with respect to this improvement. The Said Deponent Says he is not so well Satisfied with it, but further says that to the best of his recolection they made two or three improvements by Building Cabins, marking Trees or Cutting Down Bushes, as was Customary for improvers to make, above that Buck Lick.

Question by Arthur T. Taul: Was William Farrow in this Country at the time of your Improveing?
Answer: No.

Question by William Jeans [Janes] Jr.: Did you expect to hold Land from each improvement you made?
Answer: We did Expect to hold by Each Improvement.

Question by Benjamin J. Taul: What was the cause of your Making Several Improvements?
Answer: For the Mutual Advantage of the Company, which were George Rogers Clarke, John Clarke, John Crittenton & Thornton Farrow & that there was no other in Company at the time we were here that I recolect of & further this Deponant Saith not.

[signed] John Crittenden

Clarke County Sct.

The foregoing Deposition Taken at this place, being the place Claimed by William Farrow & included in his survey of 1000 acres on preemption Warrant, being at the said improvement eluded to in the within Deposition, above the one at Buck Lick, before us the Subscribing Commissioners, appointed by the County Court of Clarke pursuant to an act of assembly in that Case, made & provided in the presents of Joshua Yates Jr. & William Higgins Jr., Disintrusted Witnesses. Given under our hands this 19th day of September 1796.
Original Young
William Sudduth
Henry Chiles

92

36.

John McIntire, Evangelist Hardin and Patrick Jordan for Enos Hardin

Enos Hardin

Enos Hardin was a native of Virginia. He married Martha Ann, a daughter of Benjamin Ashby, in 1793. Enos was a farmer and trader and the father of four children. He was listed as a taxpayer of Bourbon County in 1792, Clark from 1793 to 1796, and Franklin from 1802 to 1817. Hardin died in 1820. He was a slaveholder and owner of approximately 10,000 acres of Kentucky land.[172]

David Williams placed Hardin's claim for 1000 acres before the land commission in April 1780, Hardin claiming the benefit for

> improving the same in 1775, lying on the head of the main fork of Stoners fork of licking Creek, about 5 Miles above douglasses Survey on the said Creek.[173]

Hardin entered his preemption in Bourbon County in 1783, but the tract was not surveyed until 1789. As explained below, when Hardin took John McIntire out to make the survey in 1783, Hardin was not satisfied he had found the beginning trees that had been marked for him by his brother Evangelist, so no survey was made at that time. In 1789, Henry Martin surveyed the tract. He was assisted by Patrick Jordan, one of the chain carriers and marker, who had been with Evangelist when he made the improvement in 1775. A patent was issued to Hardin in 1793. The tract overlapped William Scholl's patents (Daniel Boone's settlement and preemption) and resulted in the Scholls losing a portion of their claim. The land was on Georges Branch of Stoner Creek, about 7 miles east of Winchester.[174]

Evangelist Hardin

Enos Hardin was a brother of Evangelist Hardin (sometimes called Vangelis). Evangelist was in Kentucky with the Fincastle surveyors in 1775. That summer he left Harrodsburg in company with James Douglass and others and made an improvement for his brother Enos on Stoner Creek. Evangelist received a preemption warrant from the land commission in February 1780, but it was revoked in 1780, when it was found that his 400-acre claim on the Ohio River near the Yellow Banks (present-day Henderson) was covered by the military survey of Leonard Price. Evangelist was a taxpayer in Franklin County from 1803 to 1815. During those years, he paid taxes on 200 acres of land but no slaves.[175]

Deposition of John McIntire [125]

The Deposition of John McIntire, being of full age, take this third day of October 1796 by us, the Subscribing Commissioners oppointed by the County Court of Clarke pursuant to an act of assembly made for the Establishing the Boundries of Lands & for other Purposes, after being first sworn at a Spring, which is now In the plantation of Peter Shull, Deposeth and Saith that in January 1786 or 1787 he met with Enes Hardin and John Severns at Strodes Station on there way to Hunt an Improvement.

That Said Hardin had Laid his preemption of 1000 acres on a branch of the East Side [of] Gists Creek, and at the same time Imployed this Deponant to go along and Survey the Land if they found the Improvement. And [we] Hunted up Stoner untill we struck the Branch where Peter Sull [Scholl] now lives Some Distance below, and said Severns said if this was the branch the Improvement was on, he marked a Sugartree with the two first letters of his name.

[We] kep up the Branch a Small Distance & found a Sugartree marked JS, and kap to the place where Peter Shull now lives and Hunted for an Improvement, but found none, but Saw the vestage of 2 or 3 old Stumps, and where Some person had Campt at a Spring. But Severns said he believed it was the place Enis Hardin preemption lay, and that before they made the improvement, they keep up Summerset and out at the head of the main Branch & Steared nearly a West Course until they struck the Head of a Branch [of] Gist Creek, and the first improvement they made was the place said Hardins preemption Eluded to.

And this Deponant told Hardin he had better hunt untill they were Satisfied before he Surveyed, as Colonel Daniel Boon had a Settlement & Preemption at this place, and Isrel Grant another Joining, and [deponent] saw a red Oak Tree marked SDB at said place.

And this Deponent further sayeth that before they came out to hunt for the improvement, that said Hardin & Severns described the place and asked me if I knew any place that answered the description. I told them that did not know any place that answered So well as the place where Boon or Grant had laid their settlement and preemptions.

Question by Peter Shull: Did you see any Cabbin when you Came with Enes
         Hardin to Survey at this spring, or any sign of any?
Answer: We could not make out that there [were] any at that time.

Question by the same: Did Enes Hardin ask you to survey at that time?
Answer: Not then at that time, as he was not Satisfied with the Emprovement,
         and he was not fully Convinced untill he Brot forward other men.

Question by the same: Did not you tell Hardin if [he] would Show you his
         Cabbin, you woud Survey for him?
Answer: There was such Conversation and further this Deponent Saith not.

[signed] John McIntire

Clarke County Sct.
         The forgoing Deposition Taken this third day of October 1796 before us, Original Young & Samuel McKee, Commissioners appointed by the County Court of Clarke, at a Spring in the Plantation of Peter Shull and pursuant to an act of Assembly entitled an act for assertaining the Boundries of Land & for other purposes, and in the presents of Benett Clarke & Josiah Collins, Disentrusted Witness. Given under our hands this Day & year above Writen.
Bennett Clark
Josiah Collins
Original Young
Samuel Mckee

Deposition of Evangelist Hardin [128]

         The Deposition of Vengelis Hardin, being of full age, Taken this third day

94

of October 1796 by us, Original Young and Samuel McKee, Commissioners appointed by the County Court of Clarke Pursuant to an act of Assembly entitled an act for assertaining the Boundries of Land & for other purposes, after being first Sworn at a Spring, which is now on the Plantation of Peter Shull, Deposeth & saith that some time in the month of July 1775, this Deponant Started from Harrods Burgh in Company with Patrick Jordan and others, and came to Stoner Warters, at Which Time myself and Patrick Jordan Made an Emprovement for Enos Harden at the Spring where Peter Shull now Lives, and Know it to be the place perfectly well, and [it was] about a half a mile below another Emprovement which was made for John Severns.

And the improvement made where Peter Shull now lives was made and intended for my Brother Enos Hardin. And that it was frequently talked over in the Company and well Known to be Enos Hardin Emprovement, nor do I know of no other being made for the said Enos Hardin.

Question by Peter Shull: Did you obtain a Settlement & Premption for the same years service in which you say you made this for Enos Harden?
Answer: Yes.

Question by the same: Are you any ways interested in this Survey if Gained or lost or ever was?
Answer: I am not Interested.

Question by the same: Did you not tell my farther William Shull that you Built a Cabbin here Seven or Eight loggs High and Cleared the Small Track out of the way of half an acre?
Answer: I did not tell your farther that I had put up the Cabbin Loggs Seven or Eight High.

Question by the same: Do you no Wheather them other persons in Company with you Obtained preemption for the same years service?
Answer: I dont no that they did & further this Deponsant Saith not.

[signed] Evangelis Hardin his mark

The foregoing Deposition this Third of October 1796 before us, Original Young & Samuel Mckee, Commissioners appointed by the County Court of Clarke, at a Spring in the Plantation of Peter Shull, and pursuant to an act of Assembly entitled an act for assertaining the Boundries of Land & for other purposes, in the presents of Benett Clarke & Josiah Collings, Disentrusted Witness. Given under our hands this day & year above written.
Bennett Clarke
Josiah Collins
Original Young
Samuel McKee

Deposition of Patrick Jordan [130]

The Deposition of Patrick Jordan, being of full age, taken this third day of October 1796 by us, the Subscribing Commissioners appointed by the County Court of Clarke pursuant to an act of assembly made for the Establishing the Boundries of Lands & for other Purposes & after being sworn at a Spring, which is now in the Plantation of Peter Shull, Deposeth & saith that some time in the month of July 1775, this Deponant Started from Harrods Burgh in Company with Vangelis Hardin and others and came to Stoner warters, at which time the Said Deponent and Vangelis made an Emprovement for Enos Hardin on one of the Head forks of Stoner where Peter Shull now lives, and the said Deponent & Vangelis Harden Laid the foundation of a Cabbin, and he believes Raised the Said Cabbin about three or four Loggs High.

And further the Said Deponent saith that he has Been at the said Spring since, in September he believes, but cant well Remember the Day & dates, but before Peter Shull had settled this place or any land Cleared, and also once since I have been at this place since Peter Shull has settled this Land, and [k]now it perfectly well to be the Land that was Emproved for Enos Hardin in the year 1775.

Question by Peter Shull: Do you Remember who was with you when you say you Emproved this place?
Answer: John Souvins, Garrat Jordan and Vangalis Hardin.

Question by the same: Did you Obtain a preimption for the same years servis?
Answer: Yes, and so did Garret Jordan & John Soverins.

Question by the same: Are you any ways interested in this Tract of Land if Gained or lost or ever was?
Answer: No.

Question by the same: Did you at the time you Came here to Show Enos Hardin his Emprovements see any of the loggs you say you Built or Laid up?
Answer: No.

Question by the same: Did not you understand that Daniel Boon had a survey & Emprovement here [when] you came here with Enis Hardin to show him his Emprovement?
Answer: I do not remember Daniel Boon had any survey or Emprovement here?

Question by the same: Did not you see no Marks about the Springs or Camp, or did you not see a Tree near a Spring Marked DB?
Answer: I do remember I seed letters on a Tree, but Dont no What they were at this present time & further this Deponant Saith not.

[signed] Patrick Jordan

The Foregoing Depositions taken this third day of October 1796 before us, Original Young & Samuel McKee, Commissioners appointed by the County Court of Clarke, at a Spring in the plantation of Peter Shull, and pursuant to an Act of Assembly made and Provided for the assertaining the Boundries of Lands & for other Purposes, and in the presents of Benett Clarke & Josiah Collings, Disentrusted Witness, as Witness our hands the day above Writen.

Benett Clark
Josiah Collins
Original Young
Samuel McKee

37.

John South, Lawrence Thompson and William Hays for Joel Lipscomb

Joel Lipscomb

This may be the Joel Lipscomb (1760-1836) who was born in Spotsylvania County, Virginia and died in Greene County, Alabama. No record was found of Lipscomb ever being a resident of Kentucky. He moved from Virginia to South Carolina before the revolution and from there, in 1821, to a part of the Mississippi Territory, which became Alabama. The tract processioned below appears to be the only land entered for Lipscomb in Kentucky. Lipscomb married Elizabeth Chiles. William and Walter Chiles, also of Spotsylvania County, had land near Lipscomb on the waters of Slate Creek.[176]

Joel Lipscomb entered a tract of 1000 acres in 1782 that was not surveyed until 1793. The survey by Enoch Smith states that the tract was on the waters of Slate, which on the entry had been "called by John South, though a mistake, waters of Hingston's." The following unsigned note appears at the bottom of the survey: "One half of the above Survey is Assigned to Laurence Young." The tract adjoined William Chiles, who had a survey of 850 acres on Greenbrier Creek, a tributary of Slate Creek. This would place the land in Montgomery County, southeast of Mt. Sterling.[177]

Lawrence Young

Lawrence Young, half owner of Lipscomb's claim, was on the tax rolls of Fayette County in 1789. In September 1796, Young made a motion in the Clark county court "to perpetuate . . . the entry of Joel Lipscomb"; in October, he placed a notice of the procession in the *Kentucky Gazette*; and in November depositions were taken on the property.[178]

Deposition of John South [133]

The Deposition of John South, being of lawful age, taken before us the Subscribing Commissioners this 8th Day of November 1796, after being sworn, Deposeth and sayth that in January or february in the year 1782, that I was at this pond and in company with Larrance Thomson and Valentine Starns and Marked this Large black Oke with the letters HC, which letters he Now see is on this Black oke, and [he] marked this tree in order to Make an Memorandon for to Locate or enter by. And the waters runing from this place he then thought to be the warters of Hingston forke of Licking and further the Deponent saith not.

[signed] John South
attested Jilson Payn, William Ellis

Deposition of Lawrence Thompson [133]

The Deposition of Larrance Thomson, being of lawfull age, taken before us the Subscribing Commissioners this 8th Day of November 1796, after being first Duly sworn, Deposeth and saith that sometime in January or February 1782 he was at this pond and in Company with John South and Volantine Starnes, and knows that this black Oke was Marked by said John South with the letters HC, and said letters was cut with a desire to Make an Entry from, and he let William Hays have said Location, and that he supposed at that time that the warters running from this place was the warters of Hingston forke of Licking, but now [knows to be] the warters of Slate, [and] further the Deponent sayth not.
[signed] Larrance Thomson
attested Jilson Payn, William Ellis, Commissioners

Deposition of William Hays [134]

The Deposition of William Hays, being of lawful age, taken before us the Subscribing Commissioners this 8th Day of November 1796, after being Duly sworn, Deposeth and sayth that sometime in November 1782 he obtained a number of Locations from Lawrence Thomson, which said Thomson informed him he had made in Company with John South and Valentine Starnes, and one of said Locations he Laid on to warrants Containing one Thousand acres in the name Joel Lipscomb, beginning at a large black Oke tree near a Pond, marked with the letters HC, and running across the branch and Down from the pond on both sides for Quantity, which entry from Every thing He has under stood and from what I now see, he believes this to be the place Called for in said Entry, [and] further Deponant sayth that he never made any other entry by Said Location, [and] further this Deponant saith not.
[signed] William Hays
attested Jilson Payn, William Ellis, Commissioners

This is to Certify that we have attended Larrance Young at a large pond [that] is now known by the name of the pond Lick, and at a Large Black Oke Tree marked with the letters HC, which letters was in said Tree when we came to this place, and the said tree stands near this pond, and near a Well which is now sunk at the head of the pond, and we have taken the Depositions of Larrance Thomson, John South and William Hays (which Depositions have inclosed in this Paper), and have caused a large white Oke Tree to be marked with the letters WY, a few steps Northward of the said Black Oke tree, and David Denton and John McCullough attend[ed] with us from Begining to the end of this business of Perpetuating Testimony on this Claim of 1000 Acres (entered in the name of Joel Lipscomb) which persons Declared themselves to be Disentrested Inhabitants of said County. Given under our hands this 8th Day of November 1796.
Jilson Payne
William Ellis, Commissioners

38.

William Hays, John South and Lawrence Thompson for John White

John White

John White lived in Madison County. In 1786, he was called on along with James Hendricks and David Crews to view a road from the mouth of Tates Creek to near Boonesborough. He served on a grand jury in 1789 and was appointed surveyor of the road from Archibald Woods' to John Carpenter's Mill in 1790. White died in 1825 and left a will in Madison County naming five sons and six daughters.[179] He may be the same John White who deposed in 1804 that

> he came to Kentucky in 1779 and settled at McGee's station and continued to live there about four years.[180]

Lawrence Thompson, John South and Valentine Starnes, who were all in Boonesborough by 1780, made a number of locations in the fall of 1782. One location of 1000 acres was entered for John White on a treasury warrant in 1782. The survey was delayed for many years. Enoch Smith ran the lines in 1793, with William Ellis and Abihu Anderson, chain carriers. The tract was described as "lying on a small branch of Licking at a large Lick." In 1794, White assigned the tract to Walter Chiles, who assigned half of it to Lawrence Thompson. The patent issued to Chiles and Thompson in 1795.[181]

In the procession, the "large Lick" was identified by the commissioners as Mud Lick in present-day Bath County, later site of the Olympian Springs. They identified Salt Lick Creek as the "small branch of Licking" where Mud Lick was located; however, Mud Lick is actually on Mud Lick Creek, a separate branch of Slate Creek. This survey would have interfered with Jacob Myers' 500-acre patent, which was made to include the Mud Lick. This land is in Bath County, 7 miles southeast of Owingsville.[182]

Lawrence Thompson

Lawrence Thompson (1753-1835) was a Revolutionary War soldier. He served in the North Carolina line after enlisting in Orange County. He made an early trip to Kentucky in 1775, then settled in Madison County after the war, where he married Keziah Hart, daughter of Nathaniel Hart, one of the proprietors of the Transylvania Company. Lawrence applied for a pension from Madison County in 1832.[183]

Walter Chiles assigned Lawrence Thompson half of John White's patent. The reason for the assignment was not stated.

Deposition of William Hays [136]

> The Deposition of William Hays, being of Lawful age, taken before us the subscribing Commissioners this 9th Day of November 1796, after being Duly sworn, Deposeth and sayth that some time in the Month of November 1782, that he got a Number of Locations from Captain Laurance Thompson, which said Locations was Marked in Company with John South and Valentine Starnes, one of which Locations he Entered 1000 Acres for John White on a Small branch of Licking, begining at a white Oak Tree marked HC at a large Lick, and Running across the branch and up on both sides for Quantity, and he believe [this] to be the place as far as he knows, and that he never Entered for any body Else by Virtue of That said Location, [and] the Deponent further Saith not.
> [signed] William Hays

attested Jilson Payn, William Ellis, Commissioners

Deposition of John South [137]

The Deposition of John South, being of Lawful age, Taken before us this 9th Day of November 1796, being first Duly Sworn, Deposeth and saith that some time in January or February 1782, that he came to this place in Company with Larrance Thomson, Volentine Starnes and marked this White Oke with these Letters HC. The warters Running from this Place we Called at that time a branch of Licking, and Called this Lick a large Lick, [and] further this Deponant Sayth not.
[signed] John South
attested Jilson Payne, William Ellis, Commissioners

Deposition of Lawrence Thompson [137]

The Deposition of Larrance Thomson, being of Lawful age, taken before us Commissioners this 9th Day of November 1796, being first Duly Sworn, Deposeth and Sayth that some time in January or February 1782, he in Company with John South and Volentine Starnes Came to this place and said South Marked this White Oke with the Letters HC, and the warters Running from this place we Called a branch of Licking, and this Lick we are now at we Called a large Lick, and that he let William Hays have this Location with a number of othe[r] Locations in the month of November 1782, [and] further this Deponant saith not.
[signed] Lurrence Thomson
attested Jilson Payne, William Elis, Commissioners

Clarke County Sct.

This is to Certify that we have attended Larrance Young at a large Lick now known by the name of the mud Lick, and at a White oke near the said Lick marked HC, which letters were on said tree when we came to this place, and have Taken the Deposition of John South, Larrance Thomson and William Hays (which Depositions we have enclosed in this paper), said tree is the begining of John Whites entry of 1000 acres, and said Lick is on a small branch of Licking now known by the name of Salt lick Creek, and the aforesaid white oke tree marked with the letters HC stands a few steps Northward of a well now sunk in said Lick, and David Denton and Charles Barns attended with us, who Declared themselves Disintrusted Inhabitants of said County, while this business was Closed of Perpetuating of Testimony of said claim of 1000 acres. Given under our hands this 9th Day of November 1796.
Jilson Payn
William Ellis, Commissioners

39.

John Harper, Edward Williams and Lawrence Thompson for John South

John South

John South and his son John Jr. were at Fort Boonesborough during the siege of 1778. During the engagement, all of their cattle, brought out from Virginia, were killed by the Indians. Nathaniel Hart left a vivid description of John Sr. at Boonesborough:

> General John South lived on Holston on Col. James Thompson's place . . . as a tenant. [He] spun tow on a little wheel, and kept what was called a tickler; that is, his cup was always sitting in the window and liquor was dealt out in it by the small. A great big, mulatto looking fellow, he was often seen, clad in hemp, in the shade of his cabin spinning tow. One of his daughters [Elizabeth] married Jacob Stearns, another [Sarah married] Aaron Lewis. His three sons, John the eldest, William and Samuel, all became generals.[184]

John Jr. was in the battle of Blue Licks in 1782 and rose through the ranks to general in the Kentucky militia. He was awarded a preemption by the Virginia land commission for his improvement on Otter Creek in Madison County. He was a deputy surveyor in Lincoln and Fayette counties. John Jr. lived in Fayette County and served a number of terms in the Kentucky legislature.[185]

John South Jr. acquired James Townsend's "Poor Wright" for 400 acres on the waters of Slate Creek, mistakenly entered in 1783 on the "waters of Hinkston's Fork." South surveyed the tract himself, with Ephraim Drake, marker, Samuel Drake and Samuel South, chain men. The tract was granted to South in 1786. The survey provides further information, indicating that the tract was about 5 miles southeast of William Calk's settlement and preemption. Calk adjoined the town of Mt. Sterling on the south. Using this direction places the land about where US 460 intersects Brush Creek, about 6 miles southeast of Mt. Sterling.[186]

James Townsend

Little is known of James Townsend after he filed for his poor right. Along with Garrett Townsend, he signed petitions to the Virginia General Assembly to create a new county out of Fayette, Bourbon and Madison (1787) and another to form a new county out of Fayette and Bourbon (1789). His name appears with Garrett's on the tax list for Fayette County in 1787, 1788 and 1790, and for Clark County in 1793. He died in 1794; his will named wife Rhoda and Markham Ware executors. Townsend's reputation as an old hunter is supported by his estate inventory, which included two buffalo hides, four deer skins and three possums.[187]

While poor rights were intended to help indigent settlers obtain land, nothing prevented them from selling their claims, as James Townsend did. Thus, to a limited degree, poor folk were able to join their rich brethren in that most popular Kentucky enterprise: land speculation.

Deposition of John Harper [139]

The Deposition of John Harper, being of Lawfull age, Taken before us the Subscribing Commissioners this 7th Day of November 1796, after being first Duly Sworn, Deposeth and sayth that some time in the year 1781 he saw this pond, and afterwards marked the place in his mind as Vacant Land for Lawrance Thomson and Nathaniel Harte to Locate their Lands on, agreeable to his article of agreement, and he heard Edward Williams say that John South had made an entry of a poor right of James Townsons [Townsend's] of 400 acres on this pond, and when he came to shew this Place to said men, there was a Tree marked with some

letters, but what [letters] he Knows not, [and] further he sayth not.
[signed] John Harper
attested Jilson Payne, William Ellis, Commissioners

Question by John South: At the time you found this pond, Did you not beleave
        the Warters Runing from this place to be the Warters of Hingston fork?
Answer: I thout so at that time and Called them there by that Name.

Deposition of Edward Williams [140]

      The Deposition of Edward Williams, being of lawful age, Taken before us
the subscribing Commissioners this 7th Day of November 1796, after being Duly
sworn, Deposeth and sayth that some time before the Land Office was Oppened,
on this side of North Kentucky he saw this Pond we are now at and Intended to
have Laid a Claim on it himself, only his bond was Given to Larrance Thomson
and Nathaniel Harte to show all the Vacant Land in this parte to them, and at
October Courte 1782 or about that time, John South informed him that if he did
not Lay his Clame on this pond that he woud lay a poor Clame of James
Townsons [Townsend's] of 400 acres on the same place, and that he has seen an
Elm Tree at the head of this pond marked VS, [and that he] beleaved that the
blazed elm that now Stands at the head of the pond to be the Tree which had the
said letters, on or one near the same place, and that ever since the said South Laid
in said Clame in with the Court, this pond has been Called Souths pond, [and]
further sayth not.
[signed] Edward Williams
attested Jilson Payne, William Ellis, Commissioners

At the request of John South the Commissioners ask the Deponant if he was
        Interested in the Claim if ground [gained] or lost?
Answer: Not one farthing.

Question by Joseph Turner: Was this or these warters known by the name of slate
        at that time the said Court set?
Answer: No, if I should have made any entry on this place at that time, he would
        have Called these warters Hingston, if he had Called for any warters.

      This is to certify that we have attended John South at A pond near Joseph
Turners House, and a part of said pond enclosed by said Turners fence, and have
taken the Deposition of Edward Williams and John Harper (and we have enclosed
Depositions in this Paper), and we have Caused an Elm Tree a few Steps South of
said pond to be marked with the letters JP, and David Denton and Nicholas
Anderson attended with us at the said pond and was present while this business
was Closed of Perpetuating of Testamony, who Declared themselves Disintrused
Inhabitants of said County. Given under our hands this 7th Day of November
1796.
Jilson Payne
William Ellis, Commissioners

Deposition of Lawrence Thompson [142]

The Deposition of Larrance Thomson, being of Lawful age, Taken before us the subscribing Commissioners this 8 Day of November 1796, after being first Duly Sworn, Deposeth and sayth that in the month of January or February 1782, I was in Company with John South and Volentine Starnes [and] came to this Place whare we now are at and marked this white Oke with the letters HC, and near this said Tree was a few forkes and poles Set up as well as he now recollects, and this said Tree was marked with an intention to locate or enter by, and well remembers that the lick in the Creek near said Tree, [and] further this Deponent Sayth not.
[signed] Laurence Thomson
attested Jilson Payne, William Ellis, Commissioners

This is to Certify that we have attended John South at a white Oke Marked HC on the warters of Slate Creek near a lick, and have Taken Larrance Thomsons Deposition and in this enclosed said Deposition, and Caused a White Oke to be marked with the [letters] JP, Standing a few steps from said white Oke marked HC, and David Denton and and Charles Barns, two Disintrusted Person of said County, attended with us on this Business of Perpetuating Testimony on a Claime of the said South, containing 400 Acres entered in the name of Crouch [South]. Given under our hands this 8 Day of November 1796.
Jilson Payn
William Ellis, Commissioners

40.

William Hays, Lawrence Thompson and John South for Walter Carr

Walter Carr

Walter Chiles Carr was one of the prominent members of an early Fayette County family. He represented the county in the Kentucky legislature in 1796, and again in 1798-1801, and was one of the delegates at the convention which met at Frankfort August 17, 1799, and framed the second constitution of the State of Kentucky. He was born in Fredericksburg, Virginia, in 1753. His mother was reported to be Elizabeth Chiles, the daughter of Henry Chiles and Susannah Dicken. Walter had a farm on East Hickman Creek in Fayette County.[188] His death notice was in the local newspaper:

> Capt. Walter Carr, of Fayette county, a member of the Convention that formed
> the Constitution of Kentucky. Died December 7, 1838, aged 86 years.[189]

In 1784, William Hays surveyed the 1000-acre tract processioned below on a treasury warrant. William Brooks and Larkin Sandridge were chainmen and Austin Sandridge, marker. The survey described the tract as "lying on the south side of and adjoining William Ellis and on the waters of Slate Creek, the waters of licking." A patent was issued to Carr in 1786, and in 1805, he and wife Elizabeth sold 200 acres of the patent to Joseph Simpson of Clark County. The tract was then described as lying on Greenbrier Creek, a tributary of Slate, which would place the land in present-day Montgomery County southeast of Mt. Sterling.[190]

Deposition of William Hays [143]

The Deposition of William Hays, he being of Lawful age, Taken before us the subscribing Commissioners this seventh Day of November 1796, after being first sworn, Deposeth and Saith [that] Sometime in the Month of November 1782, I got from Captain Larrance Thomson a Number of Locations, which he told me he made and Marked in Company with Major John South and Volentine Starnes, and that agreeable to one of the said locations, he entered with the surveyor for William Chiles 850 Acres on such a place as we are now at, Calling for a branch and Begining on said Creek where a Buffalo rode crosses, and running a cross the Creek and Down the Creek on both Sides so as to have equal Quantity of Land on each Side for Quantity, [and] further the Deponant sayth not.
[signed] William Hays
attested Jilson Payne, William Ellis, Commissioners

Deposition of Lawrence Thompson [144]

The Deposition Larrance Thomson, being of Lawful age, Taken before us the subscribing Commissioners this 7 Day of November 1796, after being first Sworn, he Deposeth and saith [that] In the Month of January or February 1782, John South, Volentine Starnes and myself Set out to Make locations. After Crossing Slate at a yellow banks [and] coming about two Miles, as we supposed, East from said yellow banks, [we] Made a begining where the buffallow road Crosses a branch, which Crossing I believe to be on now, and [we] let Captain William Hays have said Location, and further this Deponant say that the said yellow bankes he then thought to be on Hi[n]gston forke of Licking, but now finds them to be on Slate Creek, [and] further this Deponent Sayth not.
[signed] Larrance Thomson
attested Jilson Payne, William Ellis, Commissioners

Deposition of John South [145]

The Deposition of John South, being of lawfull age, taken before us the Subscribing Commissioners this 7 day of November 1796, after being first sworn, Deposeth and saith that in February or January 1782, as well as he now Recollect, that he in company with Larrance Thomson and Volentine Starnes set out from Boonsborrough in order to find out vacant Lands, we Came to a place Called the yellow banks (we then thought to be on Hingston forke of Licking but now find them to be on Slate Creek), and from said Bankes we came to this spot, where we made a Memorandom for to make an entry by Calling for this place whare this Buffalo Road Crosses, whare we now are at, [and] further the Deponant sayth not.
[signed] John South
attested Jilson Payne, William Ellis, Commissioners

41.

Wilson Maddox and Elias Tolin for Samuel Meredith

Samuel Meredith

Samuel Meredith Sr. of Amherst County, Virginia, fought in the French and Indian War. Captain Meredith was a company commander in William Byrd's 2nd Virginia Regiment. In 1774, John Floyd surveyed 2000 acres on North Elkhorn Creek for Meredith on a military warrant, the tract lying about 7 miles north of Lexington on what is now Newtown Pike.[191] In 1783, Meredith advertised this land for sale in the *Virginia Gazette*:

> This tract . . . is equal in quality to any . . . in that Country; is also free from the disadvantages that attend many rich tracts, having . . . several never failing springs and streams. . . . Cash, tobacco, hemp, or negroes will be received in payment.[192]

Samuel Sr. died in 1809 leaving a will in Amherst County.

Samuel Meredith Jr. came to Kentucky in 1775 with John Floyd to view his father's survey, as well as the surveys for Patrick Henry and others, but "Floyd could not shew the land owing to the situation [Indian hostilities] of the country." In 1786, Samuel Jr. married Elizabeth Breckinridge, a daughter of Robert and Letitia Breckinridge, in Virginia. They moved to Fayette County in 1790, where Samuel was active in business and politics. He was a long-time quartermaster for the 10th regiment of the Kentucky militia in Fayette County, and later appointed major. Samuel Jr. resided on his father's military tract on North Elkhorn, where he built his brick residence "Winton" in 1823.[193]

In 1782, Samuel Meredith (not clear whether Sr. or Jr.) entered 20,000 acres in Fayette County on treasury warrants, and John McIntire surveyed out 19,934 acres in 1786. The grant was delayed due to a caveat entered by Jacob Myers, but finally issued in 1806. The land is located on the west side of Slate Creek in Montgomery County, beginning opposite the mouth of Little Slate Creek and extending west nearly to Mt. Sterling.[194]

John Hawkins, a Clark County resident in 1796, placed the legal notice for Meredith's procession in the *Kentucky Gazette* and also appears to have served as Meredith's attorney in the taking of depositions.[195]

Wilson Maddox

Wilson Maddox was born in Charlotte County, Virginia, in 1757, and enlisted in the Virginia Line in Pittsylvania County in 1778. He served in George Rogers Clark's regiment, being stationed at Boonesborough and the Falls of Ohio, and participated in a number of expeditions against the Ohio tribes from 1779 to 1782. Pioneer Josiah Collins recalled Maddox being along on a trip to the Kaskaskia saltworks and a hunting adventure, both in 1778. After the war, he married Delilah Ruth in Bourbon County in 1785 and applied for a Revolutionary War pension from Shelby County in 1832. Maddox died in Bourbon County in 1834 and is buried in the Smithfield Cemetery.[196]

George Nicholas

One of the interrogators below is the distinguished George Nicholas, who was born in James City County, Virginia in about 1743. Nicholas graduated from William and Mary College, was a member of the Virginia House of Burgesses, served as a captain in the Revolutionary Army, and played a prominent role in the Virginia convention called to consider the U.S. Constitution. He has been called the "father of the Kentucky's First Constitution," having authored most of that document. He was Kentucky's first attorney general and served as trustee and professor of law at Transylvania. He died in Lexington in 1799.[197]

Arthur Fox

Arthur Fox was one of the founders of Washington, Mason County. He built a small log station there before the town was settled. Fox was a noted early Kentucky surveyor.[198]

Simon Kenton and Kenton's Station

Simon Kenton (1755-1836) was the famous pioneer who, at age sixteen after a fight in which he feared he killed his rival, ran away to Kentucky and assumed the name "Simon Butler." Kenton fought Indians on the frontier for many years and is credited with saving Daniel Boone's life during an attack at Boonesborough. He managed financial matters poorly, was jailed for debt in Kentucky and then moved to Ohio.[199]

Simon Kenton's Station was established in what is now Mason County in 1784. The station was located on Lawrence Creek near Washington, about 3 miles south of Limestone (now Maysville), and was a frequent stopping point of early Kentucky settlers who came down the Ohio River.[200]

Slate Creek

According to Elias Tolin's deposition below, Slate Creek was given its name in 1775 by Thomas Clark's company of locators. The name, one supposes, derives from the slate-like appearance of rock layers in the creek and its banks.

Deposition of Wilson Maddox [146]

The Deposition of Wilson Maddox at the Mouth of Little Slate Creek on Monday the 7th of November 1796 before Enoch Smith and Joseph Simpson, Gentlemen Commissioners appointed by the Court of Clarke County to receive Testimony respecting the Begining of Samuel Merediths entry of 20,000 acres of Land on Slate Creek. The Deponant Being sworn, Deposeth that in May 1785 Captain [Simon] Kenton brought him to this Place & informed him that it was the place which Merideths entry was to be begin at & Described the place so specially before he came to it that the Deponant looked upon it to be the place.

Further, the Deponant marked a Beach Tree with WK & SK, which are now visable on the tree, and the Deponant Saith that he was brought to this place in order to bring a surveyor to survey Merideths entry of 20,000 Acres, and the Deponant saith that he afterwards brought Aurther Fox to the place to survey the land, but being alarmed by Indians sign, did not survey.

Further, the Deponant saith that at that time there was a Buffalo Road that crossed at the Mouth of Little Slate on the lower side thereof. Farther the Deponant saith that at that time there was a good deal of fallen timber on the west side of Slate Creek, in view at the Mouth of Little Slate.

Further, the Deponant saith that the said Kenton informed him that he Crossed at this place when he was returning from going express, as he believes in the year 1781, and understood as well as he recollects that a certain George Hart was with him.

Question By John Hawkins: In coming [out], before you found the Place, did not Kenton inform you that there was a fallen Sycamore tree with the top towards the Begginning of said 20,000 Acres Entry?
Answer: He did, and I found the Tree answering the Description on getting to the place.

Question by the same: Did you understand by Kenton that he ever had been at the place since he Crossed it on his return as aforesaid on his jerney, until he came with the Deponant?
Answer: I understood from him he had not.

By being interogated by George Nicholas, he [Maddox] saith that they started from said *Kenton Station* near the Town of Washington when they come to hunt the Beginning, and crossed over Slate some distance below the mouth of Little Slate, and then went up Slate to the mouth of Little Slate, and went up little Slate about a mile and half and saw two Cabbins, one of them being on the head of a little branch which made into the Creek on the lower side, and about a half Mile from said creek. The other cabbin was on the opposite side of little Slate above the mouth of the Branch that the other was on the head of, and that they saw no other Cabbin on said Creek or its warters, and the last mentioned Cabbin Appeared more like a Hunters camp than a cabbin, but the greater part of the cabbin was fallen Down, and Deponant saith that they did not examine where the Buffalo Roade came from nor w[ent] to, and that there was an unusual Quantity of Fallen Timber on the west side of Big Slate, and that of a midling large groth, and at that time there was no part of the survey made by Fox, and he believes the Chain not streached.

And the Deponant saith that the Buffalo Road above Mentioned was as large as Buffalos generally make, except near large licks, and the Deponant saith that he understood by the said Kenton that he had made the Discovery of this place on his Jerney in the year 1781, as before Mentioned.

And the Deponant saith that on their Rout the said Kenton made no sarch for any other Lick but the one we are at, and at that time he understood by said Kenton that he [Kenton] was to have part of the land for Locating the same, and that he saw no appearance on either side of the creek but of the one Buffalow Road, the fallen timber being nearly opposite to the mouth of Little Slate, some being above and some below, and that he has this day seen fallen timber nearly about the same place that he saw it at that time, but does not now appear to him as thick as it did then.

And the Deponant saith that he understood that the Cabbin was on the creek that the Entry was to begin at & further the deponant saith not.
[signed] Wilson Maddox
attested William Owsley, William Ward

Clarke County, to wit,
The within Deposition was sworn before us, subscribing Commissioners, at the Begining of the 20,000 Acre entry, before the Deposition was attested [by] William Ward & William Owsley, disentrusted persons being present. Given under our hands this 7th day of November 1796.
Enoch Smith
Joseph Simpson

Deposition of Elias Tolin [150]

The Deposition of Elias Tolin, Taken by Virtue of an order of Clarke Court to perpetuate Testamony respecting the Begining of Samuel Merideths entry of 20,000 acres of Land on Slate Creek. The Deponant saith that in the year 1775 that the said Deponant and Company came on a branch of a large fork of

Licking, which branch the said Company named *slate Creek*, it emptying in on the east side of the said large fork of Licking, now known by the name of Big Slate, and on the east side of said Branch Built a Cabbin, and proceeded farther to a Rocky Spring emptying into the said branch, and built another Cabbin suppose to be betwixt a Quarter and half a mile from said Branch now known by the name of Little slate, and on the westward side of Little slate, they also built a Cabbin at a spring about a Quarter or half a mile from the mouth of said spring Branch Emptying into Little slate, and it is to be understood that the whole of the above cabbins are on Little Slate & its warters, and that he the said Deponant was at the place where the Cabbins was built at the two springs this summer past, and the appearance of them was then to be seen.

And there was a marked tree where they built the other cabin, but no appearance of a Cabbin at the place where the marked tree was. The woods has been burnt since the Cabbin was made, and at the place where the Cabbins was made, there is the Letters at the spring on the west side of Little Slate TC on a Walnut, by the Cabbin on the east side of the Creek a large Red oak marked with two WW, at the Rocky Spring near the Cabbin marked WL as he believes on a sugartree, and that those marks was made by the company at the time the Cabbins was built.

Being interogated by George Nicholas, [Tolin] saith that he believes it was about two miles from the mouth of Little Slate to all three of the Cabbins, but that he never traveled from the mouth of Little Slate to the Cabbins, or from them down, and that the Eastward and Westward cabbins is about half a mile or Three Quarters asunder, and the Cabbin on the creek rather higher up than either of the [other two] Cabbins.

And that he was not at the mouth of Little slate in the year 1775, and that he never was at the mouth of Little Slate untill August last. And the Deponant saith at that time there was a large Buffalow road at the mouth of spencer, leading cross Little slate to the Indian fields, and up Little slate to a Lick, and that there was a Large Buffalo Road from the Licks that crossed main Slate towards Flat Creek, and that he has not discovered any remarkable Quantity of fallen timber on the west side of Big Slate opposite to the mouth of Little slate.

And the Deponant further saith that he did not say in the presence of John McIntire & others that he did not know of three cabbins on Little slate and its warters, and that he refused to give testimony in August last at this place because from the extent of the claim he did not Know but it would interfere with his Claim, and that he has received no reward, nor no contract for one, for his Coming this Day to give his Deposition, neither has [he] had any promise for any[thing] except for the Legal Witness fee, and that he expects nothing more, but it will depend upon their honour whether they will give him any more or not.

And the Deponant further sayth that he avers he has formerly said he would not show Cabbins to any one without fee or reward, nor prove them.

Question By the Commissioners: Did not you and Tom Clarke Build Cabbins on
        other branches of Big slate emptying in on the East side?
Answer: We did, but he did not recollect any but one on each Branch, [and]

further the Deponant saith not.

[signed] Elias Tolin
attested William Owsley, William Ward

Clarke County, To wit,

The within Deponant was sworn before us, subscribing Commissioners, before this Deposition was wrote. Present at the time [were] William Owsley and William Ward, disintrusted persons. Given under our hands this 7th Day of December 1796.
Enoch Smith
Joseph Simpson

42.

Daniel Boone for George Smith

George Smith

This George Smith has not yet been identified, except as the owner of the tract processioned below. There are a number of men by that name in Kentucky in early times—twelve in 1800. The tax lists of Clark and Montgomery indicate that George Smith was not a resident of either county between 1792 and 1810. Nothing further has been learned of this George Smith.

George Smith's 1500-acre tract was located by Daniel Boone in 1770, entered by Smith on a treasury warrant in 1780, and surveyed by Boone in 1785. A patent issued to Smith in 1786. Locating this tract has proven difficult due to conflicting information provided by Boone.[201] The entry states that the land is

5 miles north east from Lulbrulgrud lick called the plumb lick to run north and East for quantity.[202]

The survey repeats and amplifies this information, stating that the tract is "in the County of Fayette [1785] and bounded as follows (Viz.)":

Beginning 5 miles northeast from Lulbergrud lick on a small branch of Slate Creek near a small lick called the Plumb lick.[203]

Daniel Boone's deposition below on September 16, 1796 was taken at Log Lick, which Boone says he called "Lulbegrud Lick" in the year 1770. Log Lick Creek is located in Clark County and flows into Red River from the north, about 12 miles southeast of Winchester. Going five miles northeast would place Plumb Lick near the head of Brush Creek, a tributary of Red River, in present-day Powell County. Neither of these streams is a branch of Slate Creek.

To get from Log Lick Creek to the waters of Slate, one must go northeast at least 10 miles, to the head of Spruce Creek. In this neighborhood is a small stream called Plum Tree Branch, a tributary of Upper Spruce Fork. If this is the location, Boone's distance was incorrect.

If Boone's direction was incorrect, however, five miles east of Log Lick Creek would be in the neighborhood of Plum Branch, a tributary of Red River in Powell County.

There is a fourth possible location to consider. Pioneer William Risk, who claimed that "all Boone's entries were mighty vague," told Rev. Shane that this tract caused Boone considerable embarrassment: "Boone swore that the Oil Springs was known as Lulbegrud." While this statement seems implausible at first, it does bring some consistency to Boone's description of Smith's Plumb Lick tract. Five miles northeast of Oil Springs would place the tract on the head of Brush Creek, the waters of Slate, a few miles south of Camargo in what is now Montgomery County. Evidence strongly supports this location. In July 1796, George Smith petitioned the Clark County court to procession "an entry of 1500 Acres made in his name on Brushy creek waters of Slate Creek."[204]

Whichever location is correct, we must agree with William Risk: At least some of Boone's entries were "mighty vague."

Alexander Neely

Alexander Neely came out with Daniel Boone in 1775 and lived at Boonesborough and McGee's Station. Neely was killed by Indians near his home in Sumner County, Tennessee, in 1796.[205]

William and Major Beasley

William and Major Beasley were at Boonesborough in 1775. They were hired by Marquis Calmes Jr. to stay in a little cabin on Lulbegrud and tend Calmes' corn that summer. According to Cuthbert Combs Jr., the Indians killed Major and took William captive in the year 1795. William "married an indian squaw, by whom he had three or four children" and eventually returned to Clark County.[206]

Plumb Lick

Boone's depositions refer to two Plumb Licks, one northwest of Lulbegrud Lick and the other northeast of the lick. The "northwest" Plumb Lick lies near Boone Creek in Bourbon County at the intersection of KY 57 and 537, about 12 miles east of Paris. The creek was named for a tragedy that occurred nearby in 1780, when Daniel's brother, Edward, was killed by the Shawnee.

The "northeast" Plumb Lick was named in 1770, when Boone was there hunting with his brother-in-law, John Stewart.[207] Boone's deposition gives a colorful account of the reason he gave it the name:

> Because we Brought Plumbs neare a mile in our hats and eat them while we watched this lick.

This Plumb Lick, the site of George Smith's entry, is not a known place name today.

Lulbegrud Creek

The depositions below are among the most valuable that Boone ever gave regarding Clark County, in which he describes the naming in 1770 of Lulbegrud Lick—which he said later came to be known as Log Lick—and how the name eventually became attached to the nearby creek. We learn that Boone carried a copy of Jonathan Swift's *Gulliver's Travels*, which he read aloud to the men in camp. He described an incident in the story where Mistress Glumdalclitch took Gulliver to the Brobdingnag capital, Lorbrulgrud. Boone carefully pointed out that he named the lick "Lulbegrud," not the creek. The creek has been known as Lulbegrud since 1776 but, according to Boone, "took its name from this lick."

Log Lick

The name Lulbegrud Lick did not gain wide usage. Boone recalled that in 1775, William and Major Beasley cut down a number of trees in order to trap buffalo at the lick, and soon after the place was given the name Log Lick. The lick has gone by that name ever since.

Deposition of Daniel Boone at Plumb Lick [154]

> The Deposition of Daniel Boon, being of lawfull age, Taken before us the subscribing Commissioners this 16th Day of September 1796, he being first Duly sworn, Deposeth and sayth That the Lick we are now at is the Lick aluded to in George Smith entry of 1500 Acres and Called the *Plumb lick* in the year 1770, which name I gave this Lick in the said year 1770, at which time John Staurt [Stewart] was with me.
> [signed] Daniel Boone

Question by Enoch Smith: Are you acquainted with the Plumb lick near the head of the Plumb lick Creek on the Old Trace leading from Strodes to the uper Blue lick?
Answer: I am very well acquainted.

Question by same: Did you ever know the said Plumb lick Distinguished [by] aney other name?
Answer: Not to my Remembrance.

Question by same: Why was this lick we now are at Distinguished by the [name] Plumb lick, as there is no plumb Trees about it?
Answer: Because we Brought Plumbs neare a mile in our hats and eat them while we watched this lick.

Question by same: Who Did you ever here call this Plumb lick but Yourself?
Answer: By no Persons except the persons who was with me, and I never heard it called by aney other name.

Question by same: As it appears by your Testimony that there was two plumb licks in this Country when you was locating George Smiths entry, why Did you not Distinguish which you meant to fix the Clame at?
Answer: Becaus this lick lais about 5 miles northeast of Lulbergrud, and the other Plumb lick about 15 miles northwest from Lulbergrud, which I thought a Sufficient Distinction. Further the Deponant sayth not.

[signed] Daniel Boon
attested Jilson Payne, Peter Shull

Clarke County Sct.
    This is To certify that we have Taken this above Deposition of Daniel Boone this 16th Day of September 1796 at this Lick, and have Marked a large beach Tree on the east side of the Branch in which the lick is in, thus, PS, in the Presents of two Disintrusted Inhabitants. We have Inclosed a news paper which has an advertisement in the name of George Smith, Informing all who it might Concern to meet at the Log Lick on the 15th of this Instant, which we Consider as a part of our Report and to be admitted to Record. Given under our hands this Day and year above Writen.
Jilson Payne
Peter Shull

Deposition of Daniel Boone at Log Lick [156]

    The Deposition of Daniel Boon, being of Lawfull age, taken before us the subscribing Commissioners this 15th Day of September 1796, being first Duly sworn, Deposeth and sayth that in the year 1770, I Incampt on Red River with five other men, and we had with us for our amusement the History of Lemuel Gulivers Travels, where in he gives a account of his young Mistress Glumdelclik carreing him on a Market Day for a show to a town Called Lulbergrud. A young man of our Company Called Alexander Neely came to Camp one Night and told us he had been that Day to *Lulbergrud* and had killed two Brobdenags in their Capotal [i.e., had been to the salt lick and killed two buffaloes].

Their was no place in this Country went by that name of the *log Lick* untill the year 1775, when William and Major Beezley cut a number of Trees Down in and about this Lick we are now at in order to ketch Buffalows, and from that time some people called this the Log Lick, but it was from the lick itself the name sprang from and not the Creek, that is to say Lulbegrud.

Question by George Smith: Is this lick we are now at Called Lulbergrud in my entry of 1500 acres which you made for me?
Answer: It is the very Lick.

Question by William Orear: Is it known to you that Lulbergrud [Creek] has been distinguished by that name ever since the year 1775 and 1776 by the Inhabitants of Boonsbough?
Answer: I believe in 1776 and 1777 it was Distinguished by that Name, but took its name from this lick.

Question by the same: Did you ever know Lulbergrud Creek Distinguished by any other name?
Answer: I did not.

Question by same: Is it know[n] to you that the log lick took its name from the logs fell about it, which Is said to be fell by the Beezleys in the year 1775?
Answer: I expect it was, for I never knew it called the log Lick untill afterwards.

Question by same: If this lick was known to you by the name of the log lick at the time you made this entry?
Answer: I believe it was, but it was not so well known as the name I gave it myself.

Question by the same: Will you be gainer or looser if the land claimed by this Entry is saved or Lost?
Answer: Not a farthing, [and] further the Deponant sayth not.

[signed] Daniel Boon
attested Jilson Payne, Peter Shull

Clark County Sct.
This is to certify that we have take[n] this above Deposition of Daniel Boon in Obedience to an order of Court of said County in the presents of William Ellice and Cuthburt Combs, Disentrusted Inhabitants of Said county, and we have marked a White Oke, thus, PS, about two poles from the Lick. Given under our hands this 15th Day of September 1796.

Jilson Payn
Peter Shull

43.

Hugh Forbes for William Brent

William Brent

William Brent left few traces in Kentucky. He may be the William Brent Esq. of Stafford County, Virginia, who was a colonel in the Revolutionary War and lived near the mouth of Aquia Creek on the Potomac River. According to his nephew, Nicholas Porter, Brent died about five years after the end of the war.[208]

In April 1780, Hugh Forbes appeared before the Virginia land commission sitting at St. Asaph's to present William Brent's claim for a settlement and preemption

> on the West fork of Licking Creek on a small branch that runs in on the East side above the lands claimed by Benjamin Harrison, to include his improvement.[209]

The commissioners issued Brent a certificate for 1400 acres on Stoner Creek. Brent's heirs had his claim surveyed by John McIntire in 1791, with Hugh Forbes, marker, Nicholas George and Cornelius Ringo, chain carriers. Brent's claim was judged defective—it interfered badly with other earlier patents—and a grant was never issued. This land was on a branch of Stoner, about 5 miles east of Winchester.[210]

Deposition of Hugh Forbes [159]

The Deposition of Hugh Forbes, after being sworn, Deposeth and saith that some time in the year 1776, he this Deponant & others made this improvement by Deadening trees and raising a Cabbin and Making such other marks as were customary for improvers to make in them times.

Question by Original Young for William Brent: Do you know how this improvement fell to Brent?
Answer: I do not, only John Cridenton Located it for him, as I believe.

Question: Have you generally known this to be called Brents improvements from the time it was first entered?
Answer: I have believed it was & further this Deponant saith not.

[signed] Hugh Forbes

The Foregoing Deposition was taken this 23rd Day of May 1796 by us, the subscribers, Commissioners appointed by the County Court of Clarke pursuant to an act of assembly entitled An Act for assertaining the Boundries of Lands & for other purposes, at the above mentioned improvement & the said improvement being in a state of Decay, We caused to be marked afresh a White Oak Tree, standing about four feet from said Cabbin, with the Letters WSIS, in the presents of [blank space], Disentrusted Witnesses. Given under our hands the date above Writen.
William Sudduth

44.

Enoch Smith for Isaac Davis Jr.

Isaac Davis Jr.

Little has been learned of Isaac Davis. From the depositions that follow, we discover that he was in Kentucky in 1775 and helped Enoch Smith make an improvement on a tract that later became part of Mt. Sterling. Smith and Davis then made another improvement, for Davis, just to the north and adjoining Smith's. In December 1779, Smith laid Davis' claim before the Virginia land commission, which granted a preemption for 1000 acres by "the said Davis building a Cabbin on the premises in the year 1775." Davis was not awarded a settlement, meaning he must not have resided long enough in Kentucky prior to 1779. The tract was surveyed by Enoch Smith in 1783 and patented to Isaac Davis Jr. in 1785. There was an Isaac Davis who resided in Montgomery County on Flat Creek for a time, but it is uncertain if this is the same man. Isaac Jr. was in the county in 1796, when he had his tract processioned and also gave a deposition for Enoch Smith's procession (#45).[211]

Deposition of Enoch Smith [160]

The Deposition of Enoch Smith, of full Age, taken before us the subscribing Commissioners Appointed by the County Court of Clarke, Deposeth and saith that in the fall 1775, he and Isaac Davis came from Clinch River into the Country together, and near Christmas they built a Cabbin near the head of the most north fork of the Deponants spring branch for Isaac Davis, which improvement is in the forks of said Branch. And the Deponant further saith that he Located the same Land before the Comitioners [commissioners of the Virginia land commission], and entered the preemption warrant with the surveyer, and also surveyed the land and that he knows that the improvement is included in the survey. Further the Deponant saith that he and the said Davis was Generally together in the County of Kentucky at that time, and he never knew of the said Davis ever making any other but the above described improvement, and never heard him set up any Claim to any other. Further the Deponant sayth nought. [signed] Enoch Smith

Clarke County Sct.

The Deposition of Enoch Smith, Gentleman, Taken before us the subscribing Commissioners this 24th day of October [1796], and in the presents of William Metear & Hugh Forbes, Disentrusted Witness, persuant to an act of assembly entitled a Act for Assertaining the Boundries of Lands & for other purposes, and at the said Isaac Davis Emprovement, and in the fork of a spring Branch, which the said Deponant says is the most North fork of this spring Branch, and at an Elm Tree at said Emprovement, which we have caused to be marked afresh with the letters, thus, D, as the Emprovement is in a decaying Condition. Given under hands at the said place the day & date above Written.
William Metear
Hugh Forbes
Original Young

James Poage

N.B. The [newspaper] advertisement of Notice were present.

45.

John Lane and Isaac Davis Jr. for Enoch Smith

Enoch Smith

Enoch Smith came to Boonesborough with William Calk in April 1775. At the land court at Harrodsburg in 1779, Smith was awarded a certificate for his 400-acre settlement and an adjoining 1000-acre preemption, both located on Hinkston Creek. He founded Smith's Station here in 1790. Much of Mt. Sterling would later be built on what was once his land. He was very active in the militia and was appointed to the rank of captain for Bourbon County in 1792. Smith married Nancy Belfield, widow of William Lane, in Virginia in 1778, and thereafter spent part of his time at Boonesborough and part back in Stafford County. He did not bring his family out until he was prepared to settle on his land claims in Montgomery County. Smith brought his four small children to Kentucky in 1789 and settled in a home he built on his station. The homesite was a few hundred feet east of Maysville Street on Hinkston Road (Ky 1991) in Mt. Sterling.[212]

Smith was deputy surveyor for Fayette County and was appointed the first county surveyor when Clark was formed. He surveyed extensively on Hinkston, Lulbegrud and Slate creeks, often receiving land in exchange for his services. The tracts processioned below were Smith's settlement and preemption where he lived on Hinkston Creek. The Virginia land commission awarded Smith 1400 acres on "Small Mountain Creek," as Hinkston was then called, for "improving the same & raising a Crop of Corn in the year 1775 & 1776." Smith had the tract surveyed by his nephew Henry Lane in 1783, with himself as marker, John Coppage and John Gass, chain carriers. Henry was killed by Indians later that year while surveying on Fourmile Creek.[213]

Deposition of John Lane [162]

The Deposition of John Layne, being of full age, and Taken this 24th day of October [1796] before us, the subscribing Commissioners Appointed by the County Court of Clarke, after being first sworn, Deposeth and saith that in the year one Thousand seven Hundred & seventy six [1776], he the said John Lane and Enoch Smith came to small Mountain and to the spring where the said Smith now lives, and about Twenty poles near[ly] a west Course from said spring he & said Smith covered a Cabbin, Built as said Smith informed him by himself and Isaac Davis in the year one Thousand seven Hundred and Seventy five [1775].

Further the Deponant saith that in the forks of the Branch, near where a certain John Ramy now lives, by us at that time supposed to be near a half mile from the above Mentioned Cabbin near a Southwestward Course, he and said Smith Cleared a small Corn field, where they in the Year one Thousand seven Hundred and Seventy six [1776] Planted Corn.

The Deponant further saith that he and said Smith resided together all that term of time he lived in the Country, which [was] near one Year, and [he] knew of said Smith making no other Improvement or Clearing any other piece of Land by Improvement in the Country. And further this Deponant saith not.
[signed] John Lane

Clark County Sct.

   The Deposition of John Lane, Taken by us the subscribing Commissioners this 24th day of October [1796], and in the presents of William Metear & Hugh Forbes, Disintrusted Witnesses, pursuant to an Act of Assembly entitled an act for Assertaining the Boundries of Lands and for other Purposes & at the said Enoch Smiths Emprovement, the said place now to be seen in the Garden of said Smiths, and also the said Deponant proves the said Corn field at a Rotted old Cherre Tree which is now standing, which we have caused to be marked with the letters, thus, ES. Given under our hands this day above Writen at the said Emprovement.

Hugh Forbes
William Metear
James Poag
Original Young

N.B. The advertisement were present.

Deposition of Isaac Davis Jr. [164]

   The Deposition of Isaac Davis, Gentleman, being of full age & taken this 24th day of October [1796] before us, the subscribing Commissioners Appointed by the County Court of Clarke, after being first sworn, Deposeth & saith that in the Month of December one Thousand seven Hundred and seventy five [1775], he the said Davis and Enoch Smith came to small Mountain and to The spring where the said Smith now lives, and about twenty poles near[ly] a West course from the said spring, he and the said Smith Built a Cabbin for the use of the said Smith.

Question by Enoch Smith: Do you no that I made any other Cabbin [or] only this which you have now proved?
Answer by the Deponent: No. And further this Deponant saith not.

[signed] Isaac Davis Jr.

Clarke County Sct.

   The Deposition of Isaac Davis, Gentleman, taken before us the subscribing Commissioners this 24th day of October [1796], and in the presents of William Metear & Hugh Forbes, Disentrusted Witness, pursuant to an Act of assembly entitled an Act for assertaining the Boundries of Land and for other purposes & at the said Enoch Smith Emprovement, the said place now to be seen in the Garden of the said Smith. Given under our hands at the said Emprovement this day and at date above Writen.

Hugh Forbes
William Metear
Original Young
James Poag

N.B. The advertisement were present.

46.

Patrick Jordan for Charles Morgan

John Morgan

John Morgan was the son of Simon Morgan and Mary Darnall of Fauquier County, Virginia. John reportedly served in the Virginia Line during the Revolutionary War. In 1776, he came to Kentucky with a group of men in search of land. His improvement on Stoner Creek was widely known in pioneer times as "Morgan's cabin." John must have died prior to January 1780, when his heir, brother Charles, petitioned the Virginia land commission for the rights to John's claim.[214]

Charles Morgan

There were two different Charles Morgans, cousins, who claimed land on Stoner Creek in early times. The Charles Morgan (c1736-1810), whose land is processioned below, was the brother of John Morgan. Charles was born in Prince William County, Virginia, and settled near Pittsburgh in Allegheny County. He accompanied George Washington on his western tour in search of land in 1770. Morgan surveyed land for Washington and managed his Pennsylvania property from about 1785 until Washington's death in 1799. One of Washington's letters to Morgan has been published in the *Filson Club History Quarterly*. Charles died in Allegheny County leaving a wife, Frances, five sons and four daughters. This Charles Morgan never lived in Kentucky.[215]

Charles' petition for his brother John's claim was presented to the Virginia land commission sitting at Harrodsburg. In Charles' absence, John Bradford presented the petition for a 1000-acre preemption on Stoner Creek, which was described as

> lying on the Most Easterly branch of Stoners fork of licking Creek near the head thereof, including a Spring Known by the Name of John Morgans spring & a Cabbin.[216]

John Bradford surveyed the tract in 1784; Charles Morgan was the chopper. This is one of the few times Charles is known to have been in Kentucky, the other time being in 1802, when he had the same tract processioned again (#78). The patent issued to Charles Morgan in 1785. This land is located on Stoner Creek, about 6 miles northeast of Winchester.[217]

(For a biography of the other Charles Morgan, who moved to Kentucky and died in Muhlenburg County, see procession #60.)

Morgan's Cabin

John Morgan's cabin on Stoner Creek in Clark County was a well-known landmark of early Kentucky surveyors and settlers. The deposition below indicates that Morgan built the cabin for his brother Simon; however, it was John's brother, Charles Morgan, who eventually entered and patented the claim. Patrick Jordan's date of 1775 for the cabin contradicts Thomas Moore's date of 1776 in his testimony for procession #76 and given in other depositions elsewhere. The location of Morgan's cabin and spring are shown on several contemporary surveys.[218]

Deposition of Patrick Jordan [165]

Clark County Sct.

This day came Partrick Jorden, of full age, before us the subscribing Commissioners & after being duly sworn, Deposeth and saith that in the year 1775 about the Month of July or August, he this Deponant was in Company with John Morgan and assisted the said *John Morgan* to build a *Cabbin* and make such other Marks as was Custamary to be made by improveers in them times, and that said John Morgan, at the time he and this Deponant made this improvement, informed him this said Deponant it was for his Brother Simon Morgan.

Question by Simon Morgan: Was any other person with you at the time this
        improvement was made [or] only John Morgan?
Answer: Yes, Garrat Jordan & Thomas Clarke.

Question: Did John Morgan inform you that he was under any Obligation to
        Simon Morgan to make said improvement?
Answer: He did, in Consequence of some exchange in Lands in the Mongahala
        [Monongahela] Country, which he had received of the said Simon Morgan
        & promised to Make an improvement as a Compensation for the same in
        Kentucky.

Question: Do you recolect the marks on a large Ash tree about 50 or 60 yards
        from the place down the Creek?
Answer: Yes, I marked it myself at the time I assisted in making said
        improvement & further this Deponant saith not.

[signed] Partrick Jordan

The foregoing Deposition taken at the above mentioned improvement before us, the subscribing Commissioners appointed by the County Court of Clarke pursuant to an Act of Assembly entitled as Act for the assertaining the boundries of lands & further purposes, in the presents of John Young, Price Key & John Barr, Disentrusted Witness, this 25 day of July 1796, sworn to before to before the subscribers.
William Sudduth
Original Young

47.

Hughes Forbes for Peter Ringo

Peter Ringo

Peter Ringo (1751-1829) was one of seven sons of Henry Ringo of Hunterdon County, New Jersey. Henry moved his family to Virginia, to Loudoun County in 1768 and to Prince William County in 1772. Peter came to Kentucky with John Hinkston's party of settlers in 1776. That summer Peter raised a crop of corn at his claim on South Elkhorn Creek, for which he was awarded a 1400-acre settlement and preemption by the Virginia land commission. He continued in Prince William County until moving to Kentucky in 1789, settling on another of his claims, the one processioned below in present Montgomery County. In 1819, "being rendered by age and infirmity incapable of transacting ordinary business," Peter appointed his brothers Major and Joseph his agents to oversee his plantation. The following year he died. His name is also spelled Ringoe and Ringold in the county records.[219]
    Peter Ringo patented a 1000-acre preemption on Hinkston Creek where he lived. The land had a complicated history. John Sovereigns had a claim there for 187½ acres, and Daniel Whalen had an adjoining claim for 812½ acres. Sovereigns and Whalen both appeared before the Virginia land commission and were awarded rights to 1400 acres on the waters of Licking—a settlement certificate and preemption to each. Whalen acquired Sovereigns' 187½-acre claim

and sold his interest to Peter King, along with his 812½-acre claim. King entered the claims in 1784 on part of a preemption warrant and had them surveyed in two parcels in 1786. William Calk was the surveyor, Hugh Forbes, pilot, Nicholas Anderson, marker, Edward Williams and Cornelius Ringo, chain men. King then sold his interest to Peter Ringo in whose name the patent issued in 1790. The land processioned below was the 812½-acre parcel, which badly interfered with a 1000-acre claim of Thomas Jameson. Jameson and Ringo subsequently signed an agreement on the division of this land, which was about 1 mile north of Mt. Sterling on Hinkston Pike (KY 1991).[220]

Deposition of Hugh Forbes [167]

Clarke County, to wit,

The Deposition of Hugh Forbes, of full age, duly sworn before James Ward and Enoch Smith, Commissioners appointed by the Worshipful Court of the County aforesaid by Order bearing date October Court 1796, Who being first duly sworn, Deposeth and saith that in the year 1776 that he was in Company with Daniel Whalen and others, and helped them to make sundry improvements on a Creek Called by them Buck lick Creek, but now known by the name of Hingston Creek, and that the Improvement we are now at was made for said Whailen, and that it is the same Improvement which Peter Ringo now Claims his preemption by. Further the Deponant saith the Honey Locust that the said Ringos 812½ Acres Begin at did stand [at] Enoch Smiths North East corner of his settlement, near Cornelious Ringoes House, the said tree being down. Further the Deponant saith not.

[signed] Hugh Forbes
attested Enoch Smith, James Ward

Clarke County, to wit,

We the subscribers, Commissioners, met on the Land of Peter Ringoe, where we found two fresh sugartrees & Hickory that had been lettered ES & marked a White Oak EM on Wednesday the fourteenth day of December 1796, the advertisement being present to show that it was legally advertised, and then and there Hugh Forbes made oath to the within Deposition. Disentrusted persons present [were] John McCroy & Duncan Camble. Given under our hands the Day and month and year above Writen.

John McCroy [McCreery]
Enoch Smith
James Ward

48.

Peter Ringo and Elias Oldfield for Hugh Forbes

Hugh Forbes

Hugh Forbes was in Kentucky by 1776, when he was out locating land on Stoner and Grassy Lick. Mt. Sterling was laid out on part of Forbes' land, and according to one witness Forbes gave the town its name.

Enoch Smith proposed it should be Little Mountain Town. But Forbes said no, it should be Mount Stirling. He had come from a town in Scotland named Stirling.

Forbes ruled.[221]

Forbes died in Montgomery County in 1806 and was buried in the Old Presbyterian Cemetery in Mt. Sterling.[222]

The claim processioned below is the 1000-acre preemption on Stoner Creek awarded to "Hugh Forbis" for "raising a crop of corn in the Country in the year 1776." The tract was surveyed by William Triplett in 1783, with Forbes the marker, Benjamin and Frederick Couchman, chain men. The tract, which adjoined Gist's southernmost military survey on the south side and was a little downstream from Bramblett's Lick, interfered with Jesse Copher's settlement. The land is about 6 miles northeast of Winchester.[223]

Elias Oldfield

Elias Oldfield may not have been in Kentucky much before 1791, the date which he testified to in his deposition below. He appeared for a few years on the Clark County tax rolls (1794-1796) and married Rue Biggs there in 1796; William Keeton was his witness and James Wills his surety, both of whom lived in the eastern end of the county. Oldfield was in Montgomery County from 1797 to1800 and in 1810 was listed in the census for Floyd County.[224]

Calk's Cabin

William Calk's cabin on Hinkston Creek was another landmark during pioneer times. William Calk built the cabin on his claim, south of present-day Mt. Sterling, in 1779 but did not live there until much later. His cabin was often used by hunters and locators passing through the area. (see William Calk, procession #59)

Bull Lick

In his deposition below, Peter Ringo states that a lick on Stoner Creek they called Bull Lick was later known as Bramblett's Lick.

Deposition of Peter Ringo [169]

Clark County, to wit,

The Deposition of Peter Ringoe, of full age, sworn before us, James Ward & Enoch Smith, Commissioners appointed by the Worshipful Court of Clarke County, Order bearing date October Court 1796, who being first sworn, deposeth and saith that in the year 1776 he assisted in Company with others to improve and made sundry improvements on the Creek that is now Called Hingston, but then at that time was Called Buck lick creek by that company, and the Deponant saith that they made improvements as high as *Calks cabbin*. And the Deponant saith that the place we are now at they made an improvement for Charles William Cross, by which he claims his settlement and preemption. Further the Deponant saith not.

[signed] Peter Ringoe
attested Enoch Smith, James Ward

Clarke County, To wit,

We the subscribers, Commissioners, met on the Land of Hugh Forbes, where we marked a Red Oke, H, on the west side of the Creek on wednesday the fourteenth day of December 1796. The Advertisement being present to show that it was legally advertised, and then and there Peter Ri[n]goe made Oath to the within Deposition. Disentrusted persons present John McCroy [McCreery] & Duncan Camble. Given under our hands the day month and year above written.
Enoch Smith

120

James Ward

Deposition of Elias Oldfield [170]

The Deposition of Elias Oldfield, of full age, taken this 30th day March 1797 before us, the subscribing Commissioners appointed by the County of Clarke, after being first sworn, Deposeth & saith that he the said Deponant came to a Red Oak where there was appearance of an old improvement in the year one Thousand seven hundred and ninety one [1791], which place is now in the field of Mr. Jese Copher.

Question by Jese Copher: What appearance were there of an improvement?
Answer: There was the foundation of a Cabbin and some Clearing.

Question by the same: What reason have you to believe there was a Cabbin?
Answer: Because there was Logs laid in the form of a Cabbin as a foundation when I came there, and also it appeared there was a place about the same cleared.

Question: Did you see any sign of any Choping made by an ax at the said place when you came there in the year 1791?
Answer: I do not know whether there was or not, and further this Deponant saith not.

[signed] Elias Oldfield

30th March 1797, Clarke County

The foregoing Deposition taken before us Original Young & John Young, Commissioners appointed by the County Court of Clark, and in pursuance to an Order of said Court to us Directed, and have Caused Elias Oldfield to come before us, and after being first sworn, at an Old red oake stump now standing in the field of Jesse Copher, which he saith on Oath to be near the place where the said Cabbin & Clearing was, and about 70 yards from the red Oak stump to a Double sugartree which we have Caused to be marked with the letters JH, and done in the presents of Martin Judah & John Hargis, Disentrusted Witness, and the same time the advertisement which the Law Directs of the notice was produced. Witnesses out hands the day above written.
Martin Juday
John Hargis
Original Young
John Young

Deposition of Peter Ringo [172]

The Deposition of Peter Ringo, of full age, taken this 30th day of March 1797 before us, Original Young & John Young, Commissioners appointed by the Court of Clarke County, after being sworn, Deposeth & saith that in the year 1776 & about the month of July that he the said Ringo Came in Company with Hugh

Forbes, John Cretin [Crittenden], William Bennett, Luke Cannon, Francis McDermed & others to a lick then Called *Bull Lick*, Which is now Called Bramblets Lick, and tarried all Night and the next day as a Company went to work & improving by Building Cabbins, as was Customary in them times, which said Building & Emprovements was for Hugh Forbes & Company on the waters of stoner, which I always understood that the said Hugh Forbes was to have the three Lowermost Cabbins & Emprovements made by him & the said Company on stoner (which One of them is now in the plantation of Jesse Copher), which he this Deponant saith he believes to be where the Cabbin was made, and now in the plantation of Jesse Cofer, and further this Deponant saith not.
[signed] Peter Ringo

Question by Jesse Copher: Did you and the Company make any improvement on any other Warter Course but what is now called stoner?
Answer: Yes, We did.

Question by the same: Did you hear Hugh Forbes lay Claim to any other improvement but those above Mentioned?
·Answer: No, I did not.

Question by the same: Did you make improvements any lower Down the said Creek than Bramblets Lick?
Answer: We did not, to the best of my recollection.

Question by same: What improvement was there made at this place by Forbes & Company?
Answer: There was a Cabin built and some deadning [of trees].

30th March 1797, Clarke County
        The foregoing Deposition taken before us, Original Young & John Young, Commissioners appointed by the County Court of Clarke & in pursuance to an Order of Court to us Directed, and have cause Peter Ringo to come before us, and after being first sworn at an Old red Oak stump now standing in the field of Jesse Copher, which he saith on Oath to be near the place where the said Cabbin & Clearing was, and about seventy one yards from the red Oak stump to a Double sugartree, which we have caused to be marked with the letters JH, and done in the presence of Martin Judy & John Harges, Distrusted Witnesses, and at the same time the advertisement which the Law directs, the Notice were produced.
Witnessed our Hands the day above writen.
Martin Judah
John Harges
Original Young
John Young

<h1 style="text-align:center">49.</h1>

<h1 style="text-align:center">Enoch Smith for Robert Fryer</h1>

Robert Fryer

Robert Fryer settled in the Boone Creek area of Fayette County. He was an original member of the Boone Creek Baptist Church, established there in 1785. Fryer was a member of Kentucky's first constitutional convention in 1792 and the following year was elected to the state legislature. His will, probated in Fayette County in 1818, named wife Jane, sons Robert, James and David, and daughters Nancy Arnold, Elizabeth Arnold, Polly Welch, Peggy Vallandingham, Parthena Easton, Leah Miller, and Jane Reed.[225]

Fryer had two adjoining 500-acre claims entered on treasury warrants and surveyed by Enoch Smith in January 1784. The southernmost tract, processioned below, was described as "lying on Stoner fork of licking creek about 1½ mile above a sand lick, Including a cabin where there is a cherry Tree marked DC." The land was on a branch of Georges Branch, about 7 miles east and a little north of Winchester. In 1813, Robert Fryer and wife Jane of Fayette County sold 104 acres of this land at the mouth of Georges Branch to William Sudduth and Henry Chiles.[226]

The deposition below was taken on Fryer's claim "at the house of David Fryer." Although Robert Fryer never lived on his claim, this provides evidence that his son David did. Robert did not give David a deed for the property, but David did appear briefly on the tax rolls for Clark County, from 1795 to 1797.

Downey's Sawmill

In May 1801, William Downey and David Brandenburg petitioned Clark County court for a water gristmill, "where their sawmill now stands." Their mill was located on Stoner Creek, "near where the old Greenbrier trace [now the Mt. Sterling Road] crosses the creek." After 1810, the mill was referred to simply as Brandenburg's Mill.[227]

Deposition of Enoch Smith [175]

The Deposition of Enoch Smith, of lawful age, Take[n] before us the subscribers, Commissioners, at the house of David Fryer, this 5th day of February 1796, being duly Sworn, Deposeth and saith that in the year 1779, he was employed by a Company known by the name of Difficult company in Order to enter lands for them, and that he was in this Country in the fall 1779 and Continued here untill the Office was Opened for Entering Land Office Treasury warrants, and during that fall and winter made sundry marks and took memoranden of places, as well as attended the Commissioners that was appointed for proving the Claims for settlement & preemptions, and had reason to believe that there was no Preemption laid on a improvement that was made near the fork of stoner, which fork is now known by the name of Georges Creek, and the improvement was a Cabbin and deadening where there was a Cherry tree marked DC with [gun]powder, and thought the Cherry tree and Cabbin is gone, yet there is sundry trees that was deadened at the place to be seen eastward of the forks of the Creek.

The Deponant farther Saith that he entered Fryers 500 Acre entry at the above improvement, and was careful when he made the first survey for to include the Cherry tree and Cabbin Called for in the entry. And the Deponant further saith that the same Lick mentioned in the Entry is the Lick below *Downey sawmill* on stoner, and has been know[n] by the name of the Elk Lick, and also by the name of the gravley Lick.

The Deponant further saith that the five sycamores [at] the Beggining of the upper survey is about six poles below the forks of the Creek, and that the Two stumps that now appears is the stumps of two of the trees called for as the beginning of the survey, which has been cut down, and on some of the other trees is the first letters of Robert Fryers name formerly cut with the tomehawk, and [on] which is the letters WP & JP now cut.

And the Deponant further saith that a Hickory on the ridge in the forks of the Creek marked formerly RF and three sugartrees is the South west Corner of the upper survey of Robert Fryer, and that the south east corner of said survey is a Walnut & Hickory on the East side of Georges Creek, on a hill where the letters RF was formerly marked, and now the letters WP is made. Further the Deponant saith not.

[signed] Enoch Smith

Question asked the said Deponant by Robert Fryer: Which of the forks of Licking in the year 1780 was called stoners fork?
Answer: That one that now runs between Leonard Bealls House and the Begining of Robert Fryers upper survey.

Question: Whither at that time did you Know any place within two miles of the above mentioned fork of stoner known by the name of Boons station?
Answer: I did not.

[signed] Enoch Smith
attested William Payne, Jilson Payne

In Obedience to an Order of the Court of Clarke County, we attented with Robert Fryer at the noted Calls in his entry, and have taken the Deposition of Enoch Smith, and have marked at the said begining, two sycamores, one with JP 96, and another WP, and at the second corner have marked a Hickory RF, the third corner a Walnut marked RF and WP, and at the Lick Called for in said entry we have marked a forked sycamore with WP on one fork and PS on the other fork, and said tree stands on the Bank of stoner near the said Lick and six poles from a Large Elm form[er]ly marked with DWB. As Witness our hands this 5th Day of February 1796.
William Payne
Jilson Payne

N.B. The Day which said Fryer was to meet agreeable to his Advertisement was a snowey Day, which prevented our attendance untill the Day Following, as witness our hand this Day above writen.
William Payne
Jilson Payne

50.

Flanders Calloway and Samuel Boone for Peter Scholl

Daniel Boone

The tracts at issue in this processioning were surveyed for Daniel Boone and are referred to in other entries and surveys as "Boone's settlement." Boone assigned the tracts to William Scholl, whose two sons married into the Boone family. Boone's claim, which lay on Georges Branch of Stoner Creek, was laid before the Virginia land commission on December 24, 1779:

> Daniel Boone this day claimed a settlement & preemption to a tract of land . . . including a small spring on the North East side of a small branch, a Camp & some Bushes Cut down at the same, about 20 Miles east of Boonesborough, by said Boons settling & raising a Crop of Corn in the Country in the year 1775 & 1776.[228]

Boone selected the location on account of its rich soil, ample streams and a noted spring. The spring was located near the Schollsville-Kiddville Road (KY 1960). William Hays surveyed the two tracts in 1783; William Scholl was marker. Boone assigned the surveys to Scholl "for value received" in 1784, and the patents issued to Scholl in 1785.[229]

William Scholl

William Scholl, a native of the Shenandoah Valley of Virginia, moved to Rowan County, North Carolina, then in 1779 brought his family to Kentucky, arriving on Christmas Day. He stopped at Boonesborough first, but soon after settled at Boone's Station (near present-day Athens). William later made his home on Marble Creek in Madison County.[230] Daniel Boone's settlement and preemption was patented in William's name and was the site of Scholl's Station (later Schollsville) in Clark County. William's three sons, Peter, Abraham and Joseph, settled there and established the station.

Peter, Abraham and Joseph Scholl

Peter Scholl (c1754-1821) married Mary Boone, daughter of Daniel Boone's brother Edward, in about 1782. Abraham (1765-1851) married first Nellie Humble and following her death, married Tabitha Noe in Clark County (1803). It was said that Abraham "refused to own slaves and would not work two that belonged to his wife." Joseph Scholl (1755-1835) married Lavina Boone, daughter of Daniel Boone. All three brothers fought in the battle of Blue Licks in 1782. They began Scholl's Station sometime in the mid 1780s, and each raised large families in the neighborhood: Peter had fourteen children, Abraham eighteen and Joseph seven. In 1810, Peter sold to the trustees of the "Church of Bethlehem" one acre of land, site of the Bethlehem Meetinghouse. The brothers' 1400-acre tract was plagued by numerous conflicting claims, and the Scholls lost much of their land in court: 200 acres to Enos Hardin (procession #36), 296 acres to Ephraim Drake, and 91 acres to John Price (procession #51). In 1826, Abraham Scholl, perhaps discouraged by these losses and other financial misfortunes, moved to Pike County, Illinois.[231]

Flanders Calloway

Flanders Calloway was the son James Calloway, who was a brother of Colonel Richard Calloway, the noted Boonesborough pioneer. Flanders was in the party that rescued Jemima Boone and the Calloway girls captured by the Shawnee in July 1776. He married Jemima, Daniel Boone's daughter, the following spring. Two of Flanders' brothers—James and Micajah—were captured by the Shawnee with Boone's saltmakers in 1778; James escaped from Detroit and Micajah was later exchanged. Flanders and Jemima moved to Missouri with Boone's extended family in 1799. Boone's funeral in 1820 was held at Flanders' house on Charette Creek.[232]

Samuel Boone Jr.

Samuel Boone Jr., the son of Daniel Boone's brother Samuel, was born in 1758 on the Yadkin River in Rowan County, North Carolina. He served in the militia during the Revolutionary War, including several tours as a substitute for his father. He moved to Kentucky in the fall of 1779 and resided at Boone's Station. Samuel Jr. served in several campaigns against the Indians, including Holder's defeat at the Upper Blue Licks in August 1782. A few days after Holder's defeat, in the battle at Lower Blue Licks, his brother Squire was badly wounded and his brother Thomas was killed. Samuel Jr. moved to Clark County in 1829 and died there in 1843.[233] The deposition below could have been made by either Samuel Sr. or Samuel Jr.

Deposition of Flanders Calloway [178]

The Deposition of Flanders Calloway, of full age, taken before the Commissioners Appointed by the Worshipful Court of Clarke Count for the purpose of perpetuating Testomony on an improvement made at a spring on the North East side of a branch by Colonel Daniel Boone, and now belonging to Peter Scholl, Deposeth and saith that in the latter End [of] the month of November 1779, he the Deponant came in company with Colonel Daniel Boone to this spring and encamted within two rod of said spring, and the next morning the said Boone and myself turned out for to hunt, and about nine Oclock he returned to the Camp [and] found said Boone there.

And this Deponant further saith that he prosed to the said Boon, as there appeared to be a quantity of good land, for them to make some marks and divide the land between them, on which this Deponant saith he took his Tomnahawk to make some marks, and the said Boone told him that he was two late.

And this Deponant further saith that on Boons telling him that he was too late, he then examined to see if there was any Choping or marks to be seen, and when he the Deponant had Examined he Could not disern that there was any, and on this the said Boone told this deponant for to look on the lower side of a spanish Oak that stands about two Rod above the Head of the said spring. And when I examined the said tree, I found it to be marked with the two first letters of Boons name [made in 1775].

And this Deponant further saith that he & said Boone at that time had some Conversation about the Distance from this spring to Boonsborough, and we concluded it to [be] about twenty miles from the course we Came. And further this Deponant saith not.

Question by Peter Scholl: Did you at the time that you and Boone came to this spring Discover any Stumps or improvement of any kind?
Answer: I did not.

Question by the same: Did it appear as if there had been any encamping or burnt logs by Hunters or others when you Came here with Boone?
Answer: It did not appear.

Question by the same: Do you know this to be the spring and place of encampment called for in Daniel Boones Entry with the Commissioners?
Answer: I do.

Question by the same: Were you intrusted in this Claim, whether gained or lost?
Answer: I am not.

[signed] Flanders Callaway

Clarke County Sct.
    The foregoin Deposition of Flanders Callaway, being Duly sworn before us the subscribing Commissioners, at a spring on the North East side of a small branch and a red Oak ancently marked B, Called for in Daniel Boons Entry, in the presents of Paul Huls & Micajah Callaway, Disintrusted Witnesses, and have caused a red Oak Tree to be marked with the letter Y. Given under our hands this 18th of November 1996.
Paul Hulse
Micajah Callaway his mark
William Payne
Abraham Miller

Deposition of Samuel Boone [181]

    The Deposition of Samuel Boone, of full age, taken before the Commissioners Appointed by the Worshipful Court of Clarke County for the purpose of Perpetuating Testimony on an improvement made by Colonel Daniel Boone, and now belonging to Peter Scholl, Deposeth and saith that in the month of August 1783, I came to this place in Company with Daniel Boon, William Scholl, William Hays, Robert Boogs [Boggs], Samuel Shortridge, Peter Shull & Abraham Scholl and Killis Morrice in order to survey a settlement and preemption for said Daniel Boone, and I tarried at this place and near about here one Day by my self whilst the others went a surve[y]ing, and to amuse myself walked about looking for nothing particular but to pass the time away (being alone), and I saw no old Improvement of any kind but some old Camp poles, which said Daniel Boone said were his old Camp poles, nor no stumps nor Chopt trees nor Bushes but the red Oak near the spring marked, thus, B. And further this Deponant saith not.

Question by Peter Scholl: Are you intrusted in this claim, whether it is gained or
        lost?
Answer: I am not.

Question by the same: Are you sure that this is the place where we lest [left] you
        when we went to make the survey of Daniel Boons settlement and
        preemption?
Answer: I am sure that it is.

Question by the same: Did you discover any marks of fire or logs burnt that
        might destroy any former improvement made at this place?
Answer: I did not.

[signed] Samuel Boone

Clarke County Sct.

     The foregoing Deposition taken before us, the Commissioners Appointed by the County Court of Clark, at a spring on the North East side of a small Branch Called for in Daniel Boons Entry, in the presence of Paul Huls [and] Micajah Callaway, Disintrusted Witnesses, and have caused a red Oak to be marked with the letter Y. Given under our hands this 18th November 1796.

Paul Huls
Micajah Callaway his mark
William Payn
Abraham Miller

51.

Enoch Smith for John Price

John Price

     There were so many John Prices in Kentucky (twelve in 1800) that it is difficult to positively identify the one who processioned this tract, except where he is tied to the land. He most likely was John Price and wife Sarah of Jessamine County, and not John Price and wife Anna of Clark County, who lived in the area between Lower Howard's Creek and Boone Creek.[234] Price was referred to in another deposition of Enoch Smith, given in 1806 at a lick on nearby Hinkston Creek:

> In the spring, after breaking up of the winter in 1780, I marked this sycamore tree with the letters "ES," that we are now at on this lick and after it was marked I brought several people to this place to see it, where I told them I should make a claim of entries for Moses Thomas, John Halley, William Payne, John Price, Jeremiah Moore, and others which saw the place.[235]

Price represented Jessamine County at Kentucky's second constitutional convention in 1799. In 1813, he sold 48 acres of his tract on the waters of Stoner to James M. Daniel of Clark County.[236] Price's death notice appeared in the *Kentucky Reporter*:

> Reverend John Price, of Jessamine county. An early settler of Kentucky. Died September 10, 1822, aged 77 years.[237]

     John Price placed an entry on a treasury warrant for a 500-acre tract "lying on the head of Stoners fork" in 1780. Enoch Smith surveyed the land in 1784, assisted by John Wilkerson and William Said, chain carriers. Price received the patent in 1785. His patent interfered with William Scholl's preemption, the land Scholl obtained from Daniel Boone on Georges Branch. Price and his wife Sarah sold part of his tract—91 acres that interfered with Scholl's preemption—to Mordecai Morgan in 1806. The processioned land was in Clark County, about 7 miles east of Winchester.[238]

Deposition of Enoch Smith [183]

     The Deposition of Enoch Smith, of full age, taken before the Commissioners appointed by the Worshipful Court of Clarke County for the purpose of Perpetuating and Establishing certain calls in an Entry of 500 Acres of Land made for John Price. The Deponant saith that in the spring 1780 before the

[Land] Office was opened for Entering Treasury warrant[s], he went into the woods in Company with the said John Price, William Shortridge & their marked the poplar we are now at with an intent to make a Location on account of the spring that was near to said Poplar.

And when the Office was Opened he had a Land warrant of said Prices which he entered on the place, to Begin on the Branch 80 poles Below the spring, and he afterwards surveyed the Land and measured down the Branch nearly as the Branch runs, and made the Begining at a Buckey and some other trees, the buckeye being marked JP where he made the survey. Farther the Deponant saith that he gave John Price this Location and never did, nor never expects, nor never desires anything for said Location.

Farther the Deponant saith that he was deceved in the Course of the Branch. The Entry calls for runing southward & Eastward and when he went to survey was reduced to the necessity of runing southward or not include the spring. Farther the Deponant saith not.

[signed] Enoch Smith

Clarke County Sct.

The foregoing Deposition of Enoch Smith, being duly sworn, was taken before us the subscribing Commissioners at a spring and Poplar ancently marked ES, called for in the Entry of John Price, which we have caused to be fresh marked with the letters WP, in the presence of Micajah Calaway and William Stephenson, Disintrusted Witnesses. Given under our hands this 19 day of November 1796.

Micajah Callaway his mark
William Stevenson
William Payn
Abraham Miller

52.

Job Glover, Alexander McClure and Enoch Smith for Bartholomew Dupuy

Bartholomew Dupuy

Bartholomew Dupuy was of French Huguenot heritage. He came out to Kentucky with the Trabue family and others from Amelia County, Virginia, in the spring of 1780. In about 1785, he moved to Kentucky with his brother, Rev. John Dupuy. Bartholomew lived only a few years after settling in Woodford County, where he died in 1790, leaving a will. On July 29, 1797, Joseph and Joel Dupuy, executors of the estate of Bartholomew Dupuy, deceased, placed a notice in the *Kentucky Gazette* regarding the procession of Bartholomew's land in Clark County. James, another son of Bartholomew, was present to question the deponents.[239]

In 1780, Bartholomew Dupuy entered two tracts on Stoner Creek on treasury warrants, one for 950 acres, the other for 2000 acres. Enoch Smith surveyed both tracts in December 1783; John Wilkerson, William Said and James Dupuy were chain carriers, Richard Spurr, marker. Grants were issued in 1785. Dupuy's land was about 1½ miles east of Winchester. In 1810, George and Elizabeth Smith of Franklin County, Kentucky, sold 150 acres out of the 950-acre tract to Jacob Wilson Jr. and George Martin, both of Clark County. The deed stated that "said Elizabeth holds [the land] as heir at law to her father Bartholomew Dupuy, deceased" and went on to explain that she received the land at the division of Dupuy's estate in Woodford County.[240]

Job Glover

Job Glover was listed as a private in Capt. James Brown's company of mounted volunteers in the campaign against the Wiaw Indians led by Gen. Charles Scott in 1791. Based on his deposition below, Glover probably arrived in Clark County about the time the county was formed in 1792. He was listed on the county's tax rolls from 1793 through 1800 (absent in 1801). He and his wife Alice purchased a small tract of land on Stoner Creek from John McGee in 1799 and sold it the following year to Henry Welch. In 1810, Job Glover of Barren County sold a slave to John Glover of Franklin County.[241]

Alexander McClure

Alexander McClure of Woodford County married Nancy Ann Dupuy, a daughter of Bartholomew Dupuy. Dupuy's widow, Mary, died at Alexander's home in Woodford in 1831 at the age of 90. Between 1807 and 1815, Alexander and his wife sold off 340 acres from Dupuy's 950-acre tract in Clark County.[242] The commissioners' report, below, states that the parties convened "at the spring where Alexander McClure now lives." It is uncertain if this was Alexander, the son-in-law of Bartholomew Dupuy, or Alexander Jr.

Deposition of Job Glover [185]

The Deposition of Job Glover, of full age, taken before us, the subscribing Commissioners, who after being sworn, Deposeth & saith that he has been well acquainted with this Place for about five years & that at the time of his first Acquaintance here, there was Old Plantations at this place & that He then Discovered an old improvement or Deadening at the Head of this spring, which he believes Contained about a half an Acre & that this said Deponant there Discovered this Elm tree marked ES, which letters now Appears, and [was] Antient at that time & further this Deponant saith not.
[signed] Job Glover

Clarke County Sct.

We the subscribing Commissioners being appointed by the County Court of Clarke and pursuant to an order from the Court afforesaid to us directed, bearing date July Court 1797, we being convenied at the spring eluded to in Bartholemew Depeys [entry] of 950 Acres on the first day of september 1797, caused to come before us the above Named Job Grover, who Deposed as above, which said Deposition was taken in the presents of Disentrusted Witness. Given under our hands & seals the date above Writen.
Robert Clark
William Sudduth
Dillard Collin[s]
James Sudduth

Clarke County Sct.

James Suddeth, one of the above Commissioners, not being a Justice of the peace for said County, to[ok] an Oath to Act impartially as a Commissioner in said Business. Given under my hand this 1st day of september 1797.
William Sudduth

Deposition of Alexander McClure [187]

      The Deposition of Alexander McClure, of full age, taken before us the subscribing Commissioners, after being duly sworn, Deposeth and saith that he has been acquainted with this place for about five years, at which time there was no plantation made at this place & he the said Deponant recolects to of seen the appearance of an old improvement & that there was two trees then Standing that had been deadened by chops & that he also recolects to have seen an Elm tree with some marks made on it, tho [the marks] appeared to be not long done.
[signed] Alexander McClure

Question Abraham Owings: How much Land appeared to of Been deadened or
      improved?
Answer: About half an acre at the head of the spring.

Question: How large did the letters appear to of been made that you saw?
Answer: About one inch long.

Question: Do you recolect that this Elm tree standing by the Spring was at that
      time marked ES, which letters now appear [and] that the letters appeared
      much older than the letters abbove Described?
Answer: I do.

Question: Did the letters first mentioned appear to of been cut in the tree with a
      knife after the bark had been taken off?
Answer: They did, as the tree appeared to of Been barked for some time & it was
      dead [and] in some measure decayed & further the Deponant saith not.

[signed] Alexander McClure

Clarke County Sct.
      We the subscribing Commissioners being appointed by the County Court of Clarke in & pursuant to an order from the Court aforesaid, to us Directed as Commissioners, being Duly qualifyed, bearing Date July Court 1797. We convened at the Spring eluded to in Bartholomew Dupues Entry of 950 Acres on the first day of september 1797 [and] Ca[u]sed to come before us above named Alexander McClure, who Deposed as above. Said Deposition was taken in the presents of John Young & Barnet Fields, Disintrusted Witnesses. Given under our hands & seals the date above Writen.
Robert Clark
William Sudduth
James Sudduth
Dillard Collins

Clarke County Sct.
      All the above Commissioners being Justices of the Peace for said County except James Sudduth, [who] took an Oath to Act impartially in taking such

Depositions as may required to perpetuate such Testamony as may be produced respecting the Claims of Bartholomew Dupue, one of 950 Acres, the other of 2000 Acres on Stoners fork. Given under my hand this 1st day of september 1797.
William Sudduth

Deposition of Enoch Smith [190]

The Deposition of Enoch Smith, of full age, taken to perpetuate the Calls in two Entrys made in the name of Bartholemew Dupey, who after being Sworn, Deposeth and Saith that in the month of May 1780, he the said Deponant [was] engaged for a Certain Consideration to Locate for the said Dupey a Treasury Warrant, Number 1322, amounting to two Thousand nine Hundred & fifty [2950] Acres in Certain Conditions, that should the Land be taken by any prior Claim, that the said Deponant should refund the consideration money or remove said Warrant on[to] Land of equal quality with said consideration. The said Deponant appears to be released from as, by Records of Woodford County, will at large appear.

And this Deponant further saith that in the big snow in 1780, he the said Deponant encamted at the spring we are at & that then marked a tree on the uper [side] of this spring with the letters ES & which were the spring, tree and & letters eluded to by him in the following Entry, To wit, May the 18th 1780, Bartholmew Dupey enters 950 Acres upon a Treasury Warrant on a west branch of stoners fork of Licking that head Opposites to 4 mile Creek Warters of Kentucky, to include a Spring at a small deadening with a tree marked at the Spring ES, to begin on the Creek about forty poles below the springs & extending up the Creek on both sides for Quantity. Also 2000 Acres Joining the above Entry on the South West above on the Creek & extending Southward & Westward for Quantity.

And this Deponant further saith that when he came in order to make said Survey on the above waters, that the tree he marked as above was in a state of Decay, which he supposed to of Been Occationed by Elks eating the Bark of the same & that he this Deponant then marked this Elm that now is standing, on which the letters ES now appear & further this Deponant saith that now by examining the Trunk of the tree that was Originally marked, [he] has Discovered the marks he first made.
[signed] Enoch Smith

Question by James Young: Do you know who made the improvement you eluded to in Dupuys entry?
Answer: I do not.

Question: Was the improvement made before you marked the tree?
Answer: Yes & further this Deponant saith not.

[signed] Enoch Smith

Clarke County Sct.

The within Deposition was this day taken before us, the subscribing Commissioners being appointed by the County Court of Clarke as by their warrant to us directed, bearing Date July Court 1797, who being Convenied at the spring where Alexander McClure now lives, being the spring eluded to in Bartholomew Dupey Entry of 950 Acres [as] by the within Deposition will appear, who caused to come before us Enoch Smith, of full age, who Deposed as within Inserted. Said Deposition was taken in the presents John Young & Barnett Fields, Disintrusted Witnesses. Given under our hands and seals this first Day of September 1797.
Robert Clark Jr.
William Sudduth
Dillard Collins
James Sudduth

Clarke County Sct.

James Sudduth, one of the above Commissioners, not being a Justice of the peace for said County, took an Oath for that purpose to Act impartially in said Business. Given under my hand this 1st Day of september 1797.
William Sudduth

W[e] the subscribing Commissioners hearby Certify that by the Advertisement to us produced, satisfactory proof was Given to us that the time of taking these Depositions was duly advertised, also that the letters on the trunk of the tree eluded to by Captain Smith in his Deposition still appear. Given under our hands this first day of September 1797.
Robert Clark Jr.
William Sudduth
Dillard Collins
James Sudduth

53.

George Balla, John Six, Thomas Cartmill and David Hughes for William Smith

William Smith

William Smith may be related of the Smiths of Stafford County, Virginia, one of whom (Weathers Smith) also had land on Flat Creek. A William Smith of Stafford County was the brother of Enoch Smith, surveyor and one of the founders of Mt. Sterling. William's will was probated in 1817 in Montgomery County naming his wife Frances, sons Daniel, Robert, Elkanah, Enoch, John, William, Henry and George, and daughters Sarah Crump, Elizabeth McClenny, Nancy Smith and Lydia Smith.[243]

William Smith entered the 977-acre tract processioned below in June 1780. His entry identified the tract as lying

> on the head of a small branch running in on the west side of flat Creek where a large buffaloe road leaves said creek, being the waters of licking Creek, to include an improvement made by Joshua Hughes in the year 1776.[244]

The motion for Smith's procession was approved at the July term of Clark county court in 1796. Smith's tract was not surveyed until August 1796, when William Sudduth ran the lines, assisted by William Smith, marker, George Balla, pilot, William Cracraft and Jonas Fugate, chain carriers. The depositions below inform that the "small branch" referred to in the entry is ¾ of a mile above the mouth of Maux Branch. This places the land in Bath County, about 4½ miles northeast of Sharpsburg.[245]

John Six

According to his deposition below, John Six was out on Flat Creek in 1776 and later settled there. The area was part of Montgomery County in 1797, when Six was taxed for 330 acres of second-rate land on Flat Creek, two horses and no slaves. He still was listed as a resident of Bath County in the 1820 census. John Six and John Cockey Owings—early owner of Bourbon Furnace, the first iron furnace in Kentucky—jointly patented 1000 acres on Mud Lick Branch, located between the furnace and the famed Olympian Springs. The tract overlapped others and was the subject of a lawsuit in the 1840s.[246]

Thomas Cartmill

Thomas Cartmill was a long-time resident in what is now Bath County. In an 1802 deposition he stated that

in the year 1793 Thomas Clark came to his house where he now lives on Flat creek in search of Forrester Webb's land.[247]

He was still living there in 1827, when he paid John Cartmill $2,245 for land on Hinkston Creek and Flat Creek.[248]

David Hughes

From his deposition below, we learn that David Hughes was on Flat Creek in 1784, when Thomas Clark Jr. showed him an improvement made for Joshua Hughes (relationship unknown). Hughes lived in Montgomery County, where he was one of the first justices. He was assessed for one slave, twelve horses and 250 acres on Hinkston Creek in the year 1797. He married Lydia Swearingen, a daughter of Andrew Swearingen (see biography in procession #56). In 1837, Hughes was living in Clark County on a 500-acre tract patented to Thomas Swearingen, pioneer and father of Andrew. The tract was located on the south side of Colby Road, about 3 miles west of Winchester.[249]

Deposition of George Balla [194]

The Deposition of George Balla, of full age, taken before us the subscribing Commissioners, who after being Sworn, Deposeth and Saith that in the year 1776 in the month of June that he the said Deponant in Company with John Six, Thomas Clarke Jr. & Thomas Clarke Sr., Hugh Sidwell, Lewis Barnett, Thomas French & Joshua Hughes were in this part of the Country improving Lands & that they built eight Cabbins & after they had finished said Cabbins, they drew lots for said Cabbins & that the above mentioned Joshua Hughs drew in said allotment a Cabbin we had built on this Branch, which to the best of said Deponants knowledge was at the place we are at.

Question by Original Young, agent for William Smith: What reason have you for saying this was the branch that the Cabbin was on that was drew by Joshua Hughs at the allotment of Cabbins in the year 1776?
Answer: From our being incamped at the mouth of a large branch that now is known by the name of monks [Maux] run, which empty into the flatt Creek about ¾ of a mile below the mouth of this branch & by my

134

frequently travelling up the creek to the mouth of this branch. And another Reason why I perfectly recolet this to be the branch, [we] built a Cabbin at the forks of said branch about a quarter of a mile below this place, which by the Company was known by the cross road & Tavern.

Question: What was the reason you & Company called the cabbin below this the cross road and Tavern?

Answer: There was a Buffalo road Came up this branch out of the bottom of Flatt Creek & another left flatt Creek, near to where Thomas Cartmill now lives, leading towards the upper blue Licks, which two Buffalo road[s] crost each other at or near the Cabbin Called the cross road and Tavern.

Question: Was this one of the first Cabbins that was built & allotted among the Company or did the Company draw lotts for any other Cabbins in this part of the County in 1776?

Answer: This was one of the first eight Cabins that the Company built & [it] fell to Joshua Hughs by lott & no other allotment ever took place in the Company, as from the time of the first allotment we Continued to build Cabbins & afterward divided them by Choice.

Question by Volentine Stone: Do you recolect [how] many Cabins each man of that Company claimed?

Answer: Five.

Question: Do you recolect If Joshua Hughs claimed any Cabins on the East side of Flatt Creek?

Answer: I do not.

Question: Where was the five cabins claimed by Joshua Hughs?

Answer: One at this place, one on what is now called Mocks run about a mile from the mouth of the same & on this side of said run & one on the East side of slate [and] the other two I cannot recollect where they stood.

Question: Do you recolect If there was a large Buffalo road left flatt Creek at the mouth of mocks run?

Answer: There was.

Question: Was the Buffalo road that came from Flat Creek up this branch or the road that leaves Flatt Creek near Thomas Cartmill the largest?

Answer: The one that left the Creek near Thomas Cartmill was the largest of the two.

Question: Have you or any other friend of yours to receive any Compensation for your showing or proving this place?

Answer: There was a relation of mine by marage to receive one Hundred Acres of this Land for my showing the Cabbin of Joshua Hughes at this place.

Question by Original Young: Are you Gainer or Looser, let it stand or fall?
Answer: I do not no that I am a penny gainer or looser, let it stand or fall.

Question by same: Was there a Buffalo road left flat creek at or near the mouth of
    this branch?
Answer: There did & further this Deponant Saith not.

[signed] George Balla

Montgomery County Sct.
        The Foregoing Deposition was taken before us, the subscribing
Commissioners appointed by the County Court of Clark, as by their Order bearing
Date July Court 1796, being convenied at the Cabbin called for in the entry of
William Smith of 977 Acres. [We] caused to come before us George Balla, who
deposed as above & we the Commissioners further certify that is was sufficiently
proved [th]at the time of this meeting was duly Advertised in the Kentucky
Gazeette, and the Improvement being in a state of Decay, we caused to be marked
a Honey Locust & white Walnut with the Letters RY, in the presence of Samuel
Burcham & William Craycraft Jr., as Disintrusted witnesses. Given under our
hands this 4th Day of September 1797.
William Sudduth
James McEhany
Josiah Fuget

Deposition of John Six [199]

        The Deposition of John Six, of full age, taken before us the Subscribing
Commissioners, who after being duly sworn, deposeth and saith in the year 1776
he the said Deponant was in company with George Balla, Thomas Clark Jr.,
Thomas Clark Sr., Hugh Sidwell, Thomas French & Lewis Barnett & Joshua
Hughes improveing lands in this part of the Country & that they incamped at the
mouth of a run about ¾ of a mile below the mouth of this branch & that to the
best of his recolection they built eight cabins, one of which was to the best of said
Deponants knowledge was at the place we are now at, and after they had built said
Cabins they determined who should have said Cabbins by lot, at which alotment
this Cabin fell to Joshua Hughes.

Question by Original Young, agent for William Suddeth: Do you know this to be
    the branch that the cabbin built by the company that fell to Joshua Hughes
    was on?
Answer: I believe it was, as it is the first branch of any size emptying in on the
    West side of Flatt Creek above Our encampment.

Question: Do you recolect If there was a large Buffalo road that left flatt Creek at
    or near the mouth of this Branch?
Answer: There was.

Question [by] Volentine Stone: Do you recolect if there was a Buffalo road left the Creek at the mouth of what is now called mock run?
Answer: I do & further this Deponant saith not.

[signed] John Six

Montgomery County Sct.
        The Foregoing Deposition taken before us, the subscribing Commissioners being appointed by the County Court of Clarke, as by their order to us directed bearing date July Court 1796, being convenied at the improvement Called for in an entry of William Smith of 977 acres. [We] caused to come before us the above Deponant, who deposed as above, and we the commissioners further Certify that it was proved to our satisfaction that the time of our meeting at this place has been duly advertised in the Kentucky Gazeete & the improvement being in a state of Decay, we Caused to be marked a Honey Locust & White Walnut with the letters RY, in the presents of Samuel Burchum & William Cracraft Jr., Disintrusted Witnesses. Given under Our Hands and seals this 4th day of September 1797.
William Sudduth
James McElhany
Josiah Fuget

Deposition of Thomas Cartmill [201]

        The Deposition of Thomas Cartmil, of full age, taken before us the subscribing Commissioners, who being sworn, Deposeth and saith that he has been acquainted in these parts about five years & that [he] recolects a plain Buffalo road to of Left flat Creek at the mouth of mocks run, and another near where this Deponant lives, and one at the mouth of a branch called minors run.

Question by Volentine Stone: Do you recolect any Buffalo road leaving flat Creek at the mouth of this Branch?
Answer: I do not.

Question: Do you ever recolect to off seen this Cabin?
Answer: Yes, but took it to be a Hunters Camp & further this Deponant Saith Not.

[signed] Thomas Cartmill

Montgomery County Sct.
        The foregoing Deposition was this Day taken before us, the subscribing Commissioners appointed by the County Court of Clarke, as by their order to us Directed bearing date July Court 1796, being Convenied at the Cabbin called for in the entry of William Smith of 977 Acres. [We] caused to come before us Thomas Cartmill, who Deposed as above, and we the Commissioners further Certify that it was sufficiently proved that the time of this meeting was duly

advertised in the Kentucky Gazeete, and the improvement being in a state of Decay, we caused to be marked a Honey Locust and White Walnut with the letters RY, In the presents Samuel Burchum & William Cracraft Jr., as Disentrusted Witness. Given under our hands & seals this 4th Day September 1797.
William Sudduth
James McElhany
Josiah Fugate

Deposition of David Hughes [203]

The Deposition of David Hughs, of full age, taken before us the Subscribing Commissioners, who after being Sworn, Deposeth & saith that in the forepart of the summer 1784, that he the said Deponant came thro these parts in Company with Thomas Clark Jr. & came up this Branch to the fork & to one improvement above the forks on a right hand fork & came by this place & said Clarke turned himself round pointing to this place & said that [this] was Joshua Hughs improvement & further this Deponant saith not.
[signed] David Hughes

Montgomery County Sct.

The foregoing Deposition was this day taken before us, the subscribing Commissioners appointed by the County Court of Clarke, as by their order to us directed bearing date July Court 1796, being convenied at the Cabin Called for in the Entry of William Smith of 977 Acres. [We] caused to come before us David Hughs, who deposed as above & we the Commissioners further Certify that it was satisfactory proved that the time of this meeting was duly advertised in the Kentucky Gazzette & the improvements being in a state of Decay, we caused to be marked a Honey Locust & White Walnut with the letters RY, in the presents of Samuel Burcham & William Creacraft Jr., Disentrusted Witnesses. Given under our hands & seals this 4th of September 1797.
William Sudduth
James McElhany
Josiah Fugate

54.

John Strode and John Hart for Thomas Hart

Thomas Hart

Thomas Hart was a resident of Berkeley County, Virginia. (Not to be confused with the Thomas Hart of North Carolina who was one of the trustees of the Transylvania Company.) Thomas' 800-acre claim was a notable one, as a portion of it became part of Winchester. The southern line of his survey runs roughly along what is now Washington Street. The tract was surveyed on a treasury warrant by Benjamin Ashby in 1783, with Thomas Swearingen, marker, Benjamin Couchman and Isaac Clinkenbeard, chain men. In 1796, while still residing in Berkeley County, Thomas and Sarah (Morgan) Hart sold the entire preemption to son Josiah, with Robert Daugherty serving as Thomas' attorney.[250]

Josiah Hart

Josiah Hart (1764-1845), the son of Thomas, was one of the first trustees of Winchester and a deputy surveyor of Clark County. In 1789, he was one of the men who established Ralph Morgan's Station in Montgomery County. Part of the town was laid out on the tract where Josiah lived, which he acquired from his father. Josiah married Judith Tanner, and they eventually moved onto land that had been owned by her father, Archelaus Tanner. The couple became the parents of Joel Tanner Hart, an internationally acclaimed sculptor, and Thomas Hart, who became the surveyor of Clark County. Josiah and his wife were buried in the Tanner family graveyard. Joel T. carved elaborate gravestones for them from Carrara marble he brought from Italy.[251]

John Hart

John Hart, another son of Thomas, also lived in Clark County. He signed a petition to the Virginia General Assembly in 1790 asking for the removal of obstructions on Licking River all the way up to Bramblett's Lick on Stoner Creek. John lived on a tract he obtained from his brother Josiah, part of Thomas Hart's claim. In 1795, John sold this land to John Hendrick of Berkeley County. John and his wife Catherine were living in Warren County, Kentucky, in 1808, when he sold additional Clark County land to John Hampton.[252]

Deposition of John Strode [205]

Clarke County Sct.

The Deposition of John Strode Sr., aged between Sixty and Seventy years, who after being duly Sworn, Deposeth & saith that he this Deponant was personally present at the time of the line of Edward Wilsons preemption was run, [and] that Thomas Harts Survey adjoins, which was on the 20th day of April 1776, which line still remains the line of Wilsons Preemption & has never been altered & further this Deponant Saith not.
[signed] John Strode Sr.

December 1st 1797

We the subscribing Commissioners having met & taken the above Deposition, the other Witness that were summoned failing to appear, we therefore adjurned untill tomorrow 12 Oclock.
Samuel Ritchie
Benjamin Turner
Richard M. Tanner
William Sudduth
John Young

Deposition of John Hart [206]

We the Commissioners having met agreeable to adjirnment, proceeded to take the Deposition of John Hart, who after being Sworn, Deposeth & saith that he this Deponant marked the ash tree JH, as eluded to in Thomas Harts Entry of 800 Acres, some time prior to said Entry being made, [and] that this tree standing at the spring where Josiah Hart now lives is the said tree meant & called for in the said Thomas Harts Entry as aforesaid & further this Deponant Saith not.
[signed] John Hart

Clarke County Sct.

We the subscribing Commissioners proceeded to take the above Depositions, convened at the said tree marked JH, in the presents of Samuel Ritchie, Richard M. Tanner & John Taylor, Disentrested Witnesses. Given under our hands & seals this 2nd day of December 1797.
Richard M. Tanner
John Taylor
William Sudduth
John Young

55.

Daniel Boone and Elias Tolin for Philip Drake

Philip Drake

Philip Drake was born in Middlesex County, New Jersey, in 1742, married Ann Larue, and was in Kentucky by 1779. He may be the Philip Drake who came out to Kentucky in 1775 with William Calk, Enoch Smith and Abraham Hanks; Drake turned back before reaching Boonesborough. Calk mentioned Drake a number of times in his journal:

> [March 13] abrams Dogs leg got Broke By Drakes Dog. [March 30] made a turrabel flustration amongst the Reast of the horses. Drakes mair Ran against a sapling & noct it down. we cacht them all again. [April 11] Mr. Drake Bakes Bread with out Washing his hands. [April 12] Abram & Drake is afraid to go aney further. [April 13 at Richland Creek] Abram & Drake turn Back, we go on & git to loral River.[253]

Frances Faulconer stated that she came out in the fall of 1779 and on the way met Drake, who went on to Lexington. Drake was a Baptist minister. He was one of the founders of the Bracken Baptist Church in Minerva, Mason County, in 1793. As a pioneer minister of the Bracken Association, he preached at a number of their churches and annual meetings of the association. He died in 1824, leaving a will in Mason County.[254]

Daniel Boone located and surveyed Drake's 1500-acre tract on Somerset Creek in 1784. The survey stated that the beginning corner was "between 3 & 4 miles North West of Corks [Calk's] Cabbin." William Calk's cabin stood about 1 mile south of Mt. Sterling. A grant was issued by Virginia in 1785, and in 1796 Drake of Mason County sold two-thirds of the tract to Robert Johnson of Scott County and one-third to William Payne of Clark County.[255]

Deposition of Daniel Boone [207]

The Deposition of Daniel Boone, of full age, taken in Clarke County the 30th Day of May 1796, near the mouth of the west Fork of summerset, where the lower line of a survey made in the name of Philip Drake for 1500 acres crosses said west fork & near four miles from the head of summerset. This Deponant sayth that in December 1779, he crossed The small Creek called for in Drakes Entry (at the Begining corner of said Drakes survey), which is now caled summersett, near the mouth of a small Branch runing in on the East side, [and] that he proceeded on Westwardly a Small distance from where he left the said small Creek, [and] he came on the west fork of said Creek & Camped on the same, which is the fork he is now on at Drakes lower line.

And this Deponant further sayeth that He the said Deponant Located the said Drakes Claim & is not Interested in said Claim, nor any other that Depends on it, and that the west fork Called for in the Entry, which he Intended to include, is the one he is now at, where Drakes Lower Line crosses the same, and that he surveyed the said Drakes Claim so as to take the land he Intended to include in the Entry.

Question by Henry More for James More: Is this the small creek at Drakes Begining, which is now Called summersett, the small creek Called for in Drakes entry?
Answer: It is.

Question by same: Which is the West fork you Included in Drakes Entry?
Answer: The same that we're now on.

Question by same: Did you Intend to Include the mouth of this fork?
Answer: I did not.

Question by same: Did you Intend to make your Begining of Drakes survey when you crossed summersett at the mouth of a small Branch coming in on the East Side?
Answer: I did, within one Hundred Yards. Further this Deponant saith nought.

[signed] Daniel Boone
attested Enoch Smith, James Ward, Bennett Clark

Clarke County, To wit,
        Agreeable to an order of the Worshipful Court of Clarke County, dated January Court 1796, wherein we was appointed Commissioners for the perpetuating of Testamony of the Calls of a certain Entry of Land made in the name of Philip Drake of 1500 Acres, we met agreeable to advertisement, where there was three papers produced of its being advertised agreeable to Law, it being at the said Drakes begining, where there was a Hackberry marked PD, and where we marked on a Buckeye JW.
        We then went to a west branch of Summerset, which the Deponant made oath was the one called for in said Drakes Entry, where said Drakes lower line crosses the same, and there marked an Elm JW & a sugartree ESE & DB, also a small walnut ES, and then and there the within Deponant made Oath to what is Contained in the within Deposition. Given under our hands this 30th Day of May 1796. Present Disentrusted Persons Robert Rowland [and] William Norton.
Enoch Smith
James Ward
Bennett Clark

Deposition of Elias Tolin [210]

        The Deposition of Elias Tolin, of full age, taken the 30th of May 1796 on the west fork of Summersett, where a line Crosses the same, and [an] E cut on a tree. The Deponant sayth that the west fork of summerset, which he is now at, where E is cut on a sugartree, is the most notable west fork of Summerset Creek,

and this Deponant further saith not.
[signed] Elias Tolin
attested Enoch Smith, James Ward, Bennett Clarke

Clarke County, To wit,

Agreeable to an order of the Worshipful Court of Clarke County, dated January Court 1796, wherein we was appointed Commissioners for the perpetuating Testamony of the call of a certain Entry of Land made in the name of Philip Drake of 1500 Acres. We met agreeable to Advertisement, present Disintrusted persons, Robert Rowland [and] William Norton, where there was three papers produced of its being advertised agreeable to Law, it being at the said Drakes Begining, where there was a Hackberry marked PD, [and] where we marked on a Buckeye JM.

We then went to a west branch of summerset, which the within Deponant made Oath was the most notable west branch of said summersett Creek. We there marked an Elm JW and a Sugartree ESE and DB, also a Walnut ES, and then and there the within mentioned Deponant made Oath to what is Contained in the within Deposition.
Enoch Smith
James Ward
Bennett Clark

56.

Thomas Harper, Thomas Montgomery Sr., John McIntire and Elias Tolin for Andrew Swearingen

Jacob Myers

Jacob Myers was reported to be an immigrant of Jewish and German ancestry, and to have settled in Frederick County, Maryland, prior to the Revolutionary War. He may be the Jacob Myers there whose wire manufactory made him a substantial fortune. He came out to Kentucky in 1779 to John Bowman's newly-formed station near Harrodsburg and stayed during the "hard winter" of 1779-1780. In February, appearing before the land commission at Harrodsburg, he received a certificate for his 400-acre settlement claim on Hanging Fork of Dicks (Dix) River in Lincoln County, where he later settled. Myers speculated in Kentucky lands on a grand scale and with extraordinary success. One pioneer described "an enterprising Dutchman named Myers, a land agent and general locator in whose name more land has been entered than in that of almost any other man in the west." Between 1782 and 1800 Myers patented nearly 185,000 acres—an area slightly larger than Fayette County. While he acquired land all across Kentucky, he held over 40,000 acres on Slate Creek, which contained extensive reserves of iron ore and timber. Here Myers erected the first iron furnace in Kentucky, which went into blast in 1793. The Bourbon Furnace still stands beside Slate Creek, about 2 miles south of Owingsville.[256]

The land processioned below is a 5,000-acre tract entered by Myers in 1780, surveyed by Thomas Swearingen in 1783, and patented by Myers in 1785. Ralph Morgan acquired the property from Myers and built a station there.[257]

Ralph Morgan

Ralph Morgan was the son of William Morgan and Drusilla Swearingen, she the daughter of Thomas Swearingen. William raised a company of volunteers during the Revolutionary War, eventually reaching the rank of colonel. Ralph, the eldest child, lived with near Shepherdstown until he moved to Kentucky in 1779. He came out that summer with a party from Berkeley County headed by his father and included Thomas Swearingen, George Michael Bedinger, John Strode and others. Ralph was listed as a private in Capt. John Holder's company at Boonesborough in 1779. He took up locating and surveying land, eventually entering over 30,000 acres in his name. In the spring of 1789, a company of men he recruited established a small station on Slate Creek, about 7 miles southeast of present-day Mt. Sterling. On April 1, 1793, Morgan's Station was burned and nineteen captives taken in what has been called "the last Indian raid in Kentucky." The station was located on land referred to in deeds for years afterwards as "the 5000-acre Morgan Station tract originally granted to Jacob Myers."[258]

Andrew Swearingen

Andrew Swearingen was a son of Thomas Swearingen of Berkeley County. Thomas died in 1786, leaving his Kentucky property to be divided among his five children. Andrew's brother, Capt. Van Swearingen, was killed in St. Clair's defeat in November 1791. Andrew rose to the rank of major in the first battalion of the Montgomery County militia in 1798. Like their father, Andrew and Van were both surveyors. Andrew was appointed deputy surveyor of Clark County in 1793. He later acquired the tract in Montgomery County where his cousin, Ralph Morgan, had established Morgan's Station in 1789. The stone house he built on the site (c1793) still stands today.[259]

Thomas Montgomery

Thomas Montgomery helped build Morgan's Station in 1789. In the fall of 1791, Montgomery established his own station at the head of Stepstone Creek and moved there with his wife and eight children. Montgomery was born in Botetourt County, Virginia in 1745 and married Martha Crockett—first-cousin of Davy Crockett—in 1767. Montgomery served in George Rogers Clark's expedition against the Shawnee towns following the battle of Blue Licks in 1782. Lieutenant Montgomery earned the nickname "Purty Old Tom." Montgomery's Station was probably located in the Ewington area, near the junction of Stepstone and Howards Mill roads in Montgomery County.[260]

Abraham Becraft and Becraft's Cabin

Abraham Becraft was one of the early residents of Morgan's Station. Becraft's house, mentioned in the depostion below, was a cabin located at the edge of a cornfield, about ¼ mile northeast of the station. The cabin was burned during the Indian raid in 1793. Becraft's wife and five children were killed; one son, Benjamin, and one daughter, Betsy, were captured but survived.[261]

Deposition of Thomas Harper & Thomas Montgomery [211]

The Deposition of Thomas Harper & Thomas Montgomery Sr., Both of full age, Taken before us Subscribers, Commissioners appointed by the Worshipful Court of Clarke County for perpetuating Testimony of the Calls of an Entry made in the name of Jacob Myers of 5,000 Acres, Deposeth and Saith that some time in the fall 1786, they saw a spring where Abraham Becrafts House was Afterwards burnt, and about forty or fifty yards North East from the head of said Spring, the[y] saw an old Cabbin which appeared to have been built a Considerable time before. These Deponants further Saith not.
[signed] Thomas Harper
[signed] Thomas Montgomery
attested Enoch Smith, James Poge [Poage], James Ward

Deposition of John McIntire [212]

The Deposition of John McIntire, of full age, taken before us

Commissioners for Perpetuating testimony to the Calls of an Entry Made in the Name of Jacob Myers of 5000 Acres, Deposeth and sayth that he came Out from Stroads Station Early in the fall 1783 & down Spencers branch & passed a Cabbin on the foot of an hill about 30 or 40 poles from the mouth of said Creek, in Company with Thomas Clark, which Cabbin our Deponant sayth Said Clark then informed him was one of the Cabbins aluded to in the Calls of a 5000 Acres Entry of Jacob Myers & that the Creeks now Called Spencer & Harper was the Warters of a Large fork of Licking alluded to in Said Entry & said Clarke Informed our Deponant that the[y] had Made other improvements on Said Warters, but none up the large fork now Called Slate & further sayth not.
[signed] John McIntire
attested Enoch Smith, James Poage, James Ward, Commissioners

In Pursuant of a Warrant to us directed from the Worshipful Court of Clarke County on the application of Andrew Swearingen, Assignee of Ralph Morgan, who was Assignee of Jacob Myers, we have attended him on the Land described in the following Entry, to Wit, "Jacob Myers enters 5000 Acres on the warters of a large fork of Licking runing Parrellel with the mountains, and empties in the branch about 30 miles above the upper blue lick, including 4 or 5 Cabbins made by Clark & Company in the year 1775."

On the twentieth day of June 1796, agreeable to the advertisement, one paper being present, also attended by William Ward, Thomas Harper & Peter Fort, disinterested persons, and Caused to Come before us Elias Tolin, Thomas Harper, Thomas Montgomery, and John McIntire, who was duly sworn before us, [and] whose Depositions are attested by us.

Also that we made sundry marks. At the first Cabbin at the mouth of the Long branch, we marked a Red Oak ESN, also a White Oak JPH. And below said cabbin about 100 poles was a Sugartree marked WJ, supposed by Elias Tolin to be made by William Lynn in the year 1775. And about 30 or 40 poles from the mouth of spencers Creek, swore to another Cabbin where the letters of his name was on a dead Sugar Tree, E. And about Twenty poles from said Cabbin [we] found a Sugartree marked WL. And about Ten poles from said Cabbin, [we] found another Sugartree marked TC that was dead, and there marked a small poplar ESJPTCJWTMH. And near the Cabbin marked an ash ESJPH and a poplar JWTMH. And the third cabbin that the Deponent Elias Tolin made oath to on the North side of Harpers Creek we marked a Red Oak ESJWTJLP and Number 3. The 4th Cabbin the Deponant Elias Tolin made oath that he believed was near the spring where *Beecrafts House* was burnt, which marks we Consider as part of our report. Given under our hands this 20th June 1796.
Enoch Smith
James Poage
James Ward

Deposition of Elias Tolin [215]

The Deposition of Elias Tolin, of Lawfull age, being sworn before us, Commissioners for perpetuating Testimony to the Calls of an entry made in the

144

name of Jacob Myers for 5,000 Acres, Deposeth and saith that in the year 1795 [1775], he was in Company with Thomas Clarke, William Lynn, Andrew Lynn & Thomas Brazier, a Cabbin building on a large fork of Licking which is now Called slate Creek, which they conceived ran parrellel with the mountains, on which they built sundry Cabbins, which is as follows. One at the mouth of a Branch now Called the long branch of Spencer Creek, and another about thirty or forty poles from the mouth of a Creek now known by the name of Spencers Creek, and another on the North Side of a Creek now known by the name of Harper Creek, and another near a spring where Becrafts House was burnt by the Indians, all which cabins the Deponant saith he knows was built in the year one Thousand seven Hundred and seventy five [1775] by Clark and Company, and that there was none built higher up on the large fork (now called slate Creek) at the time & further the Deponant saith Naught.
[signed] Elias Tolin
attested Enoch Smith, James Poage, James Ward, Commissioners

57.

Flanders Calloway for William Collinsworth and Reuben Searcy

William Collinsworth

Ephraim Drake appeared at a court of the Virginia land commission at Boonesborough in December 1779 and presented the claim of William Collinsworth to 400 acres

lying on the North fork of Howards [Lower] Creek where the trace of the Salt Spring crosses the said Creek after passing the indian Camp.[262]

The court awarded Collinsworth a preemption of 400 acres for "making an actual Settlement in the Month of April 1778." No other information has been found on this Collinsworth. He did not receive a patent for his preemption, nor did Reuben Searcy on whose behalf the tract was processioned.

From the calls of adjoining patents, Collinsworth's claim can be placed on the waters of Lower Howard's Creek. The patents of John Patrick, Richard Searcy and Robert Burton met at a "hickory and sugartree" that the surveyors referred to as "Searcy and Collins conditional corner." Searcy's and Burton's all surveys were run by Bartlett Searcy, brother of Richard. The conditional corner was near where McClure Road crosses the North Fork of Lower Howard's Creek, about 4 miles southwest of Winchester.[263]

Reuben, Bartlett and Richard Searcy

Reuben, Bartlett and Richard Searcy were brothers who came to Kentucky early from Granville County, North Carolina. Reuben and Bartlett were privates in Capt. John Holder's company at Boonesborough in June 1779. Bartlett was a surveyor in Fayette County (1782-1787) who was killed by Indians, and left a will recorded in Madison in 1795. Richard had a gristmill in Woodford County, where his wife was killed by Indians in 1788. Reuben also lived in Woodford. In December 1779, Bartlett Searcy presented a claim for his brother Richard Searcy for 1400 acres, the tract adjoining "the lands of William Cothenworth on the Western side." The next claim presented was by Reuben Searcy for his 1400-acre settlement and preemption on Stoner Creek.[264]

The depositions below were taken for Reuben Searcy, who made the motion in county court to procession the "400 acre claim of William Collinsworth." Searcy placed a legal notice regarding the claim in the *Kentucky Gazette* in July 1796. The commissioners stated that the purpose was "for assertaining the old trace leading from boonsborough to the salt spring on licking, where the said trace crosses the North fork of Howards Creek, for Establishing the Claim of William Callingworth for four Hundred Acres of land." Reuben had no land in Clark County, and it is uncertain what interest, if any, he had in this matter. The procession may have been to help establish his brother Richard's adjoining claim, which depended on Collinsworth's "conditional corner."[265]

Deposition of Flanders Calloway [217]

State of Kentucky, Clarke County Sct., July the 25th 1796

Agreeable to an order of the aforesaid County Court of Clarke appointing us, Jacob Fishback & Edmond Hockaday, Commissioners to take Depositions in behalf of Reuben Searcy for assertaining the old trace leading from boonsborough to the salt spring on licking, where the said trace crosses the North fork of Howards Creek, for Establishing the Claim of William Callingworth for four Hundred Acres of land.

We have caused Flanders Callaway to come before us at Mr. William McMillions Dwelling House, and after duly qualifying the said Callaway, he this Deponant Deposeth and saith that in the year of Christ 1779, he was well acquainted with the then trace leading from boonsborough to the salt springs On Licking, and that after passing the Indian Camp, the said Trace crossed the North fork of Howards Creek within one Hundred Yards of the now dwelling house of Mr. William McMillan, to the best of his knowledge.

He this Deponant further saith that he this day followed the said Trace from near the said Indian Camp to near the plantation of the said McMillan, and further this Deponant saith not.

Also Jesse Hedges, being duly qualifyed, Deposeth & saith that he verily believes the above deposition of Flanders Callaway to be Just & true to the best of his knowledge & further Saith Not.
[signed] Flanders Callaway
[signed] Jesse Hedges

Sworn to before us, the aforesaid Commissioners & in presence of William Hayse [and] William McMillan.
Edmund Hockaday
Jacob Fishback, Commissioners

58.

Edward Williams and John Harper for James Garrard

James Garrard

James Garrard (1748-1822) was the second governor of Kentucky. Garrard County was named in his honor. Born in Stafford County, Virginia, he married Elizabeth Montjoy, served in the Revolutionary War and the Virginia legislature before migrating to Kentucky in 1783. He settled in Bourbon County, where he farmed, opened a lumber mill, made whiskey and preached at Baptist churches. Garrard participated in the state conventions of 1787 and 1788 and the constitutional convention of 1792. He was elected governor in 1796 and reelected in 1800. Garrard died at his home in Bourbon County. His three-story stone house—Mount Lebanon—still stands on Peacock Pike about 3 miles north of Paris.[266]

James McMillan

James McMillian was one of five brothers from Frederick County, Virginia, who were in Kentucky in early times, the sons of James McMillan Sr. James Sr. was born in Scotland, educated at the University of Edinburgh, and immigrated to Virginia, where he married Margaret White. James Sr. followed his sons to Kentucky and settled on Lower Howard's Creek. He died leaving a will in Clark County, probated in 1799, that named sons Robert, James and William and daughters Mary and Elizabeth.[267]

James' brother John was killed by Indians near Cumberland Gap, and another brother, Jonathan, was killed at the battle of Blue Licks. Brothers William and Robert and brother-in-law William Trimble would live on lands surveyed by James on Lower Howard Creek. James stated that he first came to Boonesborough on March 3, 1776, and he lived there and at Boone's Station for a number of years. He was along on the famous rescue of the Boone-Calloway girls. James fought in numerous campaigns on the frontier and was a major in the militia. According to one of the pioneers, "McMullen was a fine soldier; would fight like a horse." He was one of the first justices of Clark County and a representative in the Kentucky legislature. James married Ellen McClure and later lived in Montgomery.[268]

James was a prolific surveyor in the area that became Clark County. He surveyed the 4000 acres processioned below in the year 1784, assisted by Elijah Gadey, marker, and Aaron Horn and John Long, chain carriers. He divided this land "on the waters of Lulbergrud" into three tracts, two of 1000 acres and one of 2000 acres. The patents were issued to Garrard and McMillan as partners, the latter though not identified was probably James Jr. James Sr. did patent a 316-acre tract on Lulbegrud, which he willed to sons Robert and James, but there is no other evidence for a land partnership between James Sr. and Garrard. This large tract began, according to the deposition below, on the west bank of the North Fork of Lulbegrud Creek, which places this land about 11 miles east of Winchester, partly in Clark and partly in Montgomery.[269]

Deposition of Edward Williams [218]

> Clarke County Sct.
>
> The Deposition of Edward Williams, aged fifty eight years, being duly sworn, Deposeth & Saith that Early in the fall of the year 1782, this Deponant in Company with Colonel James Mc[Mi]lion, Laurance Thomson and John Harper came to the spot where we now stand, and to the best of his recollection, Laurance Thomson marked the cherry tree, which the Deponant understands is the Beggining Corner of a four thousand acres Survey made in the name of James Garrard & James McMillian, the same being marked with the letter N, thus, and being on the west bank of the North fork of Lulbergrud & understood at the time the same was marked, that it was intended as the Begining of two Entrys to be made, for whom this Deponant does not know & further Saith not.
>
> Question by Elisha Collins: Are you interested in Establishing James Garrard & James McMilion Beginning [of] their 4000 Acres survey?
> Answer: No.
>
> Question by Commissioners: Did you understand that Cherry Tree, when it was marked, was for the Beginning of an Entry of any of your Company?
> Answer: Yes I did.
>
> [signed] Edward Williams
> attested Jilson Payne, John Hardwick Jr., Commissioners

Deposition of John Harper [220]

Clarke Sct.

The Deposition of John Harper, aged 49 years, being Duly Sworn, Deposeth & saith that Early in the fall of the year 1782, This Deponant in Company with James McMilion, Laurance Thomson & Edward Williams came to the spot where we now stand to the best of his recollection. Laurance Thomson marked the Cherry Tree, which this Deponant understands is the Begining Corner of James Garrard & James McMilion survey of 4000 Acres, which Said Corner is on the West Bank of the North fork of Lulbergrud, and is marked with the Letter N, thus.

And this Deponant understood at the time said tree was marked, that it was intended as the Begining of two Entries then to be made, but for whom this Deponant did not understand, but was for one of the Company & further this Deponant Saith Not.
August 29th 1796
[signed] John Harper
attested Jilson Payne, John Hardwick Jr., Commissioners

Question by Commissioners: Are you interested in establishing the Beginning of
        James Garrard & James McMilion 4000 acre Entry?
Answer: No.

Clarke County Sct.

We the Subscribers, Housekeepers of said County, do hearby Certify that we were present on the 29th day of August 1796, where the above Commissioners took the Depositions of the above subscribing Edward Williams & John Harper, who were sworn & said Depositions were legally taken & that two sugartrees [were marked], the one about one pole to the north of the Cherry tree marked with the letter N, which is mentioned in the above Deposition, the one of which is marked with the letters JG & the other sugartree marked JMC. August 29th 1796.
[attested] Joseph Colvill[e], James Fowler

Clarke County Sct.

We the subscribers being appointed Commissioners, under the Act of Assembly entitled An Act To asertain the boundries of Land & for other purposes, by the County Court of Clarke, having met on the 29th day of August at the Beginning of a 4000 Acre survey made in the name of James Garrard & James Mcmilion, agreeable to a publication, Do hereby Certify that at the time & place above mentioned, we caused Edward Williams & John Harper to Come before us, who being duly sworn agreeable to Law, and subscribe the above Depositions & at the same time in the presence of Joseph Colville [and] James Fowler, two Housekeepers of the County aforesaid. We caused two sugartrees, standing near to the Cherry marked with the Letter N as above described in the Depositions of the two subscribing Deponants, to be marked, the one with the letter MC & the other JG.
Jilson Payne

59.

David Frazier, Nicholas Anderson, William Calk and John Harper for Cuthbert Combs

Cuthbert Combs

Cuthbert Combs was one of two brothers—sons of John Combs of Stafford County, Virginia—who came to Kentucky in 1775 in search of land.[270] The company consisted of Cuthbert and Benjamin Combs, Marquis Calmes, Marquis Calmes Jr. and Benjamin Berry. Their arrival at Boonesborough was noted in Richard Henderson's journal entry for May 3:

> The day before this, one Capt. Calames and Mr. Berry, with five other men arrived, here from Frederick or somewhere in the north-west frontiers of Virginia. They had heard nothing of our purchase when they left home, but merely set off to view the country, and etc. Hearing of us and our pretensions they thought it proper to come, though they seemed not very conversable; and I thought I could discover, in our first intercourse, a kind of sullen dissatisfaction and reserve, which plainly indicated a selfish opinion to our disadvantage. This, after some time, wore off. . . .[271]

According to tradition, while out searching for land, the company climbed to the top of Pilot Knob to get their bearings. From there they viewed the broad valley that encompassed Indian Old Fields, where they immediately proceeded in order to establish their claims. Cuthbert's claim was a little south and west of the Indian Old Fields.[272] After making their improvements, the men went back to Boonesborough where there return was recorded in Henderson's journal:

> Sunday 21st. Capt. Callomees men returned. Had been lost. Gave great pleasure.[273]

At a court of the Virginia land commission in October 1779 at St. Asaph's, Cuthbert Combs presented his claim to 1400 "lying at an Indian Town on the North side of Kentucky between Lulbegrud Creek & Howards Creek to include both side of the said Howards Creek for quantity." The commission accepted his claim by virtue of Combs "making Corn in the Country in the year 1775." Cuthbert eventually settled on his tract and died in 1815, leaving a will in Clark County.[274]

David, William and James Frazier

According to Cuthbert Combs Jr., there were several Fraziers living on his father's place when he moved to Kentucky in the fall of 1795. (In the records the name is also spelled Frazer, Frasure, etc.) The Fraziers had a station on Combs' preemption, as described by Cuthbert Jr.:

> Frazier's Station was about 8 miles from the mouth of Howard's Upper Creek, on that Creek, on Cuthbert Combs' place. My brother Joseph had settled two or three families of that name on the place about twelve months before we came. The station was close by the side of the road as you come from the factory (Kiddsville P.O.) down this way, where Mrs. Watkins lives. There were two or three families of the Fraziers living there, all of them gone from the country now.[275]

William Risk recalled, "Cud Combs came to Frazier's, I think, the year after I came. The Fraziers then left." William Frazier was the one most often named in depositions and court records, and he is the only Frazier who owned land in early Clark County. He purchased 100 acres of John Holder's land on the waters of Lulbegrud, sold at auction in 1803. Clark County taxpayers in the year 1794 included several Fraziers: David, David Jr., James and William. David gave a deposition for Combs' procession; William and James appeared as "disintrusted witnesses" from the neighborhood. Only William remained in Clark County after 1800.[276]

William Calk

William Calk (1740-1823) was born and educated in Prince William County, Virginia. In March 1775, Calk set out for Kentucky with four companions—Enoch Smith, Abraham Hanks, Philip Drake and Robert Whitledge. Along the way Calk kept a journal, one of the most remarkable documents to be preserved from those early days on the frontier. (In 2004—229 years later—Calk's descendants donated the original journal to the Kentucky Historical Society.) Calk resided for many years at Boonesborough, while he plied his trade: land surveying. He eventually settled on his 1400-acre plantation just south of Mt. Sterling. His homeplace is still owned by his descendants.[277]

Old Indian Town

What the pioneers called the "old Indian town" was located at the Indian Old Fields in eastern Clark County. The settlers recognized the place as a place that had been inhabited by the Indians—most likely the Shawnee. The "town" contained several landmarks, including the gate posts referred to in the deposition. The Old Indian Town was included in the patent of Marquis Calmes Jr.

Beasley's Cabin

William and Major Beasley were hired by Marquis Calmes Jr. to tend Calmes' corn on his claim in 1775. Enoch Smith recalled seeing the Beasley's cabin on Upper Howard's Creek

> on East side of the creek, and WB on a tree, which cabbin I almos expected was built by William Beasley, who was employed by Combs & Company in the Summer 1775.[278]

William Calk was also familiar with the cabin, which was on Cuthbert Combs' land: "[Calk] deposeth and sayth that this was Called Beazleys Cabbin in the year 1779. [Their] Christian names was Major and William." The cabin is shown on a map of the Indian Old Fields area prepared in a lawsuit, *Cuthbert Combs Sr. vs Thomas Porter's heirs*.[279]

Deposition of David Frazier [223]

The Deposition of David Frazer, being of Lawfull age, Taken before us subscribing Commissioners this 3rd Day of March 1796, being first Duly sworn, Deposeth that I have seen and is now to be seen in the survey of Curthbert Combs, works Done by Indians or other Humans. And further the Deponant saith that he Dos not know but what these workes was Called the *old Indian Town*, where as I believe two posts now stands in Marquis Callomeas Jr. survey I suppose.

And further the Deponant sayth that their is in this survey of Curthburt Combes an appearance of a fort, which is now to be seen, and further the Deponant sayth not.

[signed] David E. Fraizer his mark
attested Jilson Payne, Elisha Collins

Deposition of Nicholas Anderson [223]

The Deposition of Nicholas Anderson, being of Lawful age, being first Duly sworn, Deposeth and saith that in May 1779 I was with William Calk and others and Marked a tree for Jeremiah Storkes [Starke], and said Calk Informed me that it was not worth while, for it was in the Combeses or Callemeses Land.

150

And on the same rout, we came to this Cabbin which William Calk told me was beasleys.

And further the Deponent Saith that when ever he Came to *Beasleys Cabbin*, he supposed to be on the Land which was Called the old Indian Town. And further the Deponant sayth that he never has known it to be Called by any other name but Beasley Cabbin.

And further the Deponant sayth that this red Oak is a Corner of Marques Callomeas Jr. survey of a preemption of one Thousand Acres, and further the Deponant sayth not.

[signed] Nicholas Anderson
attested Jilson Payne, Elisha Collins

Deposition of William Calk [225]

The Deposition of William Calk, being of Lawfull age, Taken before us subscribing Commissioners this 3rd Day of March 1796, being first Duly sworn, Deposeth and sayth that this was Called Beazleys Cabbin in the year 1779. [Their] Christian names was Major and William.

Further the Deponant sayth that Enoch Smith, Robert Whitledge, Marquis Callomese Sr., Markes Callomeas Jr., Benjamin Berry, Benjamin Combs, John Combs, Eenes [Enos] Combs, Joseph Combs and Cuthbert Combs, together with myself agreed to improve this Land round about this place, as I was afterwards Informed to be the Place. And that Cuthbert Combs with others agreed to give me fifty shilling to relinquish my Claim to this place, to which I agreed.

Further the Deponant sayth that I believe this red Oak is the Begining Corner of Cuthbert Combs settlement of 400 acres and is the south West corner to marquis Callomeas Jr. Preemption. And further the Deponant sayth that all about this Place was Called the old Indian Town in the year 1775. And further the Deponant saith not.

[signed] William Calk
attested Jilson Payne, Elisha Collins

Deposition of John Harper [226]

The Deposition of John Harper, being of Lawfull age, Taken before us subscribing Commissioners this 3rd Day of March 1796, being first Duly sworn, Deposeth and Sayth that in the year 1782 or 1783, I know this to be called Beasley Cabbin. And further the Deponant sayth that when ever he came to this Cabbin, he supposed [it] to be a part of the old Indian Town on the place so Called. And further the Deponant sayth not.

[signed] John Harper
attested Jilson Payne, Elisha Collins

Clarke County Sct.

This is to certify that in Obedience to an order of the Court of said County, we have attended Curthbert Combs on this 3rd Day of March 1796, and have Taken The Deposition of William Calk, John Harper, Nicholas Anderson and David Frazer, and have taken the Course and Distance from an Indian improvement or town, and find it to be south 36 degrees West 65 poles to Beasleys Cabbin, which was this Day shown to us by the Witnesses, which Cabbin also stands about 7 poles East from Howards upper Creek, whare we have this Day marked a plumb and Cherry tree, to wit, thus, CC. And also marked a White Oak near the Cabbin, thus, CCCJC. And we have also attended at the Beggining of said Combses settlement of 400 Acres, and find his corner standing, Where we have marked a red Oke about Two poles East of south from the said beggining, thus, JC. One mark more we have seen near the said Cabbin, which appears to be made about the time the Cabbin was built, which is a red Oak marked thus, WB. And James Frazer and William Frazer, two Disintrusted Inhabitants of said County, who have attended with us at all the aforesaid places. As Witness our hands this Day and year above writen.

Jilson Payne

Elisha Collins

60.

Presley Anderson, Joseph Proctor and Edward Williams for Charles Morgan

---

Charles Morgan

Charles Morgan was born in Prince William County, Virginia, and was in Kentucky by 1784, the year John Filson published his map of Kentucke, showing Morgan's gristmill on Boone Creek in Fayette County. Morgan's main business activity seems to have been buying and selling land. In 1788, he placed the following notice in the *Kentucky Gazette*:

> I want to purchase . . . land within the county of Fayette, to be of the first quality, well watered and timbered and conveniently situated. For payment I will give my bond and good security that any person applying with my order to my Father William Morgan in Faquier county, Virginia, whom said land will be for, shall receive the cash on sight. Charles Morgan[280]

Morgan was soon acquiring land in his own name, and over the next twenty years bought and sold more than 200,000 acres in Kentucky. In 1795, he put his Fayette County property, including the gristmill, up for sale. Soon thereafter he moved to Campbell County and then, in 1804, to Muhlenberg County. Morgan died in there in 1822. His will named three sons and four daughters, to whom he devised nine slaves and a substantial quantity of land.[281]

(There was another Charles Morgan in Kentucky during this period. Both owned land in Clark County. They were first cousins; their fathers—William and Simon—were brothers. The other Charles Morgan had land processioned in 1796 and 1802. #46 and #78)

The land processioned below is a 975-acre tract on the Sycamore Fork of Slate Creek, which was entered by Charles Morgan on a treasury warrant in 1783, surveyed by James Morgan in 1785, and granted to Charles in 1786. This land is located near Jeffersonville in Montgomery County. Morgan later petitioned the Montgomery county court to procession this same tract in 1809.[282]

Presley Anderson

Presley Anderson was one of the earliest inhabitants of Strode's Station. Pioneer William Clinkenbeard recalled that

> Old Pressly Anderson, I think, lived on the one side of that gate in the north [wall] till he got afraid & went back to McGee's. [There were] 3 Andersons, 1 at McGee's, 1 at Boonsborough, & this [Strode's], cousins, I think.[283]

Presley must have been a close relation of Nicholas Anderson of Stafford County, Virginia, as they are frequently found together in court records. For example, both gave depositions at Edward Williams' place in the case of *James McMillion vs John Miller and Charles Gilkey*. Presley was residing in Clark County when he purchased several tracts on Lower Howard's Creek, and was living in Montgomery when he sold the land.[284]

Joseph Proctor

Joseph Proctor (c1755-1844) enlisted in the Virginia line, and his company was sent to Boonesborough in 1778 to protect against the Indians. Joseph and his brother Reuben were listed as privates in John Holder's company at Boonesborough in 1779. Joseph and Reuben both fought in the battle of Little Mountain, or Estill's defeat, in 1782. When he went back to bury the dead, he "took out of Capt. Estill's pocket a small line and plumb and pair of silver knee buckles out of Adam Carpenter's [Caperton's] breeches, and took them to their wives." Joseph was a Methodist minister; he founded Proctor's Chapel in Madison County. The town of Proctor in Lee County was named for him.[285]

The Glade

According to Presley Anderson's deposition, Charles Morgan's company of locators discovered the Glade in 1783 on a branch—Glade Branch—of Sycamore Fork. Webster's dictionary defines "glade" as an open space in the forest. The commissioners met at a corner white oak tree, "standing between Phillip Hammonds House & the Glade branch." One of Rev. Shane's pioneer interviews reveals that Hammond lived at Jeffersonville. Thus, the Glade must have been located at or near present-day Jeffersonville in southeastern Montgomery County.[286]

Sycamore Fork

Sycamore Fork of Slate Creek was mistakenly thought at first to be a fork of Hinkston. Charles Morgan gave it the name in 1783, presumably for the large sycamore tree he marked as the beginning of his claim near the mouth of Glade Branch. The fork, near Jeffersonville, is known as Sycamore Creek today.

Deposition of Presley Anderson [228]

Montgomery County June 5th 1798

We the subscribing Commissioners having met agreeable to adjornment, Caused to come before us Presley Anderson, of full age, who after being sworn Deposeth and saith that in the month of January 1783, he this Deponant, Charles Morgan & Joseph Proctor came into this Quarter in pursuit of Vacant Land. We found *the Glade*, and from thence came down this branch from said Glade and incamped near this place & after we had Encamped, Charles Morgan left us & went down near the mouth of this branch and marked a large forked sicamore with the letters of his name and the date, as he informed us on his return.

Question by William Sudduth: Did Charles Morgan inform [you] of the situation that the sicamore Tree stood on [that] he had marked at that time as you find it now you have been at the place?
Answer: I think he did.

Question: Did Charles Morgan Inform you at that time you was out that he intended to locate this land?
Answer: He did.

Question: What warters did you suppose these [lands] to be [on] from the best information you at that time Acquired?

Answer: The best information we at that time had was from Joseph Proctor, who allowed them to be Hingston Warters.

Question by Thomas Stephens: Have you any other reason to believe that the sicamore tree [was] marked, but from the bare information of Morgan?

Answer: Only from finding the tree [that] agree[s] with the description Given of it on his return to Camp.

Question: How long after was it that you saw the tree & how was it marked?

Answer: I have not seen it untill this Day. The letters are Cheifly grown out or Picked out.

Question by Stephens: Was there any agreement between you & the Company that Came with you (that is, you, Morgan and Proctor) respecting vacant Land?

Answer: Not on my side. With Proctor & Morgan I believe there was.

Question: Who gave the Creek the name of the *sicamore fork* of Hingston?
Answer: Charles Morgan, from Procters information of its being Hingstons Warters.

Question: Had you ever heard it called so by any other person besides Morgan before then or since?

Answer: Yes, I heard Colonel James McMillian say that he dit not know himself whether it was Hinkstons Waters or not & that he beleived there was a Number did not no to the Contrary in them days.

Question: Is this Creek a Warter of Hingston?
Answer: I believe not. It doent pass for that now.

Question: How far is it from here to the nearest warters of Hingston?
Answer: I believe it is counted about 6 miles.

Question: Is there any creek between this creek and the warters of Hingston?
Answer: There is.

Question: Does that Creek ly between this & Williams Cabbin?
Answer: This is the first Creek we fell on as we came out.

Question: Do you know of any large Creek that is between this and Williams Cabin?

Answer: To come [by] the state road there is.

Question: Did you ever hear that large Creek that lies between this and Williams Cabbin Called Hinkston by Morgan or any body elce?

Answer: At that time we took all these to be Hinkston Warters.

Question: Was there any Buffaloe road crossing this creek at the mouth of this
          Branch you Called the *Glade branch*?
Answer: I cannot say whether there was or not.

Question: Was there any lick on this Branch?
Answer: Not that I know off.

Question by Philip Hammond: Are you Interested in any surveys that Depend on
          this Beggining?
Answer: I am not.

Question by Francis Pyatte [Wyatt]: What are you to have for Coming forward to
          prove this Beggining?
Answer: I have received nothing, nor expects nothing & further this Deponant
          saith not.

[signed] Presley Anderson

Montgomery County June 5th 1798
          The above Deposition taken on the above date before us the Subscribing
Commissioners on what is now Called the Glade branch & said by said Deponant
to be near the place where the said Deponant, Charles Morgan & said Procter
encamped at the time they first came out here & we caused to be marked a White
Oak Tree with the letter V, standing between Phillip Hammonds House & the
Glade branch near the bank of the same, in the presents of Nicholas Ander[son],
William Procter & Asa Massee, Disentrusted witness. Given under our hands the
date above.
Nicholas Anderson
William Procter
Asa Massie
Francis Wyatt
Phillip Haman

          Mr. James French was requested by William Sudduth in behalf of Charles
Morgan to give Testimony respecting the said Entry of Charles Morgan that lys at
this place & refused, and said he was intrusted person. Given under out hands as
Commissioners at the place within Mentioned.
Francis Wiatt
Philip Haman

Deposition of Joseph Proctor [234]

          The Deposition of Joseph Proctor, being of lawful age, taken before us the
subscribing Commissioners this fourth Day of June 1798, after being Duly Sworn,
Deposeth and saith that I and Charles Morgan and Presley Anderson came out

into this Quarter in order to hunt vacant Land, and we come into this branch some Distance above here and incamped there and called this Branch the glade Branch.

Question by William Sudduth: When your [party] enca[m]pted on this branch as above described, did Charles Morgan leave you and come down this branch?
Answer: He did.

Question by the same: Did he inform you of marking this forked sycamore tree, which we are now at, on his return to Camp that evening?
Answer: He did.

Question by the same: Do you recollect if you, Morgan and Anderson discovered this glade at the head of this branch at the time you was first here?
Answer: I did.

Question by the same: Did Charles Morgan inform you in your rout that he Intended to Locate this Land that we are now at?
Answer: He did.

Question by Francis Wiatt: Do you consider that you are Intusted in the Establishing of this Claim of morgans or not?
Answer: I do.

[signed] Joseph Procter

Deposition of Edward Williams [236]

Also the Deposition of Edward Williams, being of full age, after being duly sworn, deposeth and Saith some time about the 16th of January 1783, Charles Morgan, Joseph Proctor and Presley Anderson left the said Deponant cabbin, as they said, to explore land.

Question by William Sudduth: What was these warters called when Morgon, Proctor and Anderson left your cabbin?
Answer: This Warters I knew not, but the waters thot runs eastword from said Deponants Land was Called by said Deponant and others that was with him called hingstons warters & further this Deponant saith not.

[signed] Edward Williams

Montgomery County, June 1798
Pursuant to an order from the Worshipful Court of Clarke County bearing date January Clarke court 1797 To us Directed, we being convened at the mouth of what is now Called the Glade branch, caused to come before us the within named Joseph Proctor & Edward Williams, who after being duly sworn, deposeth and saith as within inserted, which Depositions were taken in the presence of

William Ellis, Nicholas Anderson and James Bradshaw Jr., Disintrusted Witness & the letters Called for in said Morgans entry of 975 Acres, being the Claim the above Depositions are taken to Establish, being in a state of Decay, we marked said sicamore with the letters CM, in the presents of the witnesses afforesaid & adjorn untill Tomorrow 12 Oclock.

William Elis

Nicholas Anderson

James Bradshaw

Francis Wiatt

Philip Haman

61.

George Rogers Clark and John Crittenden for William Davis

William Davis

William Davis purchased an enormous tract of 10,000 acres on Virginia treasury warrants. He entered his claim—adjoining George Rogers Clark's 15,360 acres—in 1782 and had it surveyed by John McIntire in 1788; William Anderson was the marker, William Clinkenbeard and Absalom Hanks, chain carriers. This land lies between present-day Mt. Sterling and Owingsville, partly in Montgomery County and partly in Bath.[287]

William may have been related to the James Davis who also had a tract on Flat Creek processioned (#18). There is no evidence that William resided in Kentucky. When he sold 2000 acres of this tract to William Anderson of Bourbon County in 1795, Davis was living in the "Town of Petersburg & County of Prince George" in Virginia. Enoch Smith signed the deed as attorney for the absentee owner. The following year, Davis sold the balance of the tract to Thomas Bedford of Mecklenburg County, Virginia.[288]

George Rogers Clark

George Rogers Clark was born and educated in Albemarle County, Virginia. At age twenty, he took up surveying, but his career was interrupted by the Revolutionary War. After participating in Dunmore's War (1774), Clark came to Kentucky where he helped Hancock Lee lay out Leestown—now part of Frankfort. That summer (1775) Clark went out with a company of locators seeking land in present-day Clark, Montgomery and Bath counties. He returned the following year with 500 pounds of gunpowder for the defense of newly-formed Kentucky County. Clark subsequently led an expedition that succeeded against all odds in capturing the British-held territory in the Northwest. Largely overlooked after the war, he spent some years in Clarksville, Indiana, followed by nine years at his sister's home (Locust Grove) in Louisville, where he died in 1818. Clark County was named in his honor.[289]

Deposition of George Rogers Clark [238]

Montgomery County, to wit,

The Depos[it]ion of General George Roges Clarke taken this 16th day of November 1797 to perpetuate the Begining corner of an Entry made in the name of William Davis the 21st day of December 1782 for 10,000 Acres in the followings Words.

"William Davis Enters 10,000 acres of Land on the sothern Warters of Licking, begining a south eastwardsly corner of a private survey of 15360 [acres] made by George Roges Clarke in 1775, runing East 1000 poles, thence north from the Begining & from the Termination there of at right angles for Quantity of waste Land."

We the subscribing, being the Commissioners appointed by the Court of Clarke to take Depositions respecting said Entry, have this day met at the most Sutherlandly corner of the said private survey of 15,360, being a large shellbark Hickory standing in a drain on the side of a Hill, having first sworn the said [George Rogers] Clarke on the holy evangelis [bible], he Deposeth and saith That in the summer 1775, major John Cridenton, Thomas Clarke, Luke Cannon, Thornton Farrow, William Linn, Andrew Linn, Eli Toland & some others set out from Boonsborough with the design on the part of said Rogers Clarke & Criddenton to make a survey, which they intended at a future day to make use of in securing said Land, and surveyed not knowing upon what terms or principles the titles to land in this Country should afterwards be granted.

That after exploring the country, they began to make said survey on a red Oak Tree standing on the East branch of summerset & due west Course and about 6 miles from this place. But from the said Begining, he saw a line due East to the corner where we now stand & marked the Large shellbark Hickroy, the marks wherein are still very plain.

That he then changed his course and run to the north and made a corner & then due West & quit. This Deponant says that the lines & corners of said survey were well marked & that it is the only survey he ever did make on the Warters of Licking. That he recollects That after making said surveys, the party made sundry improvements & then returned to Boonsborough.

This Deponant further saith that he has a perfect recollection of the said survey & after having examined said Begining corner on summersett & the corner where this Deponant now stands, he can positively say it is the same survey of 15360 Acres which he made as aforesaid in 1775. This Deponant says that the said private survey was never of any use to him, [he] having made no advantage thereof & [he] is in no manner whatever Interested in the Establishment of the said Davis Entry, or in any entry or Claim Dependant on the said private survey, and this Deponant further saith not.
[signed] George Rogers Clarke
attested Enoch Smith, James Poage, Commissioners

Deposition of John Crittenden [239]

The Deposition of Major John Credinton taken at the aforesaid time & place & in order to perpetuate the aforesaid Claim, who Deposeth that in summer 1775 General George Rogers Clarke & himself, with the party whose names are mentioned in the above & foregoing Deposition of said Clarke left Boonsborough with the purpose on the part of said George R. Clarke & this Deponent of making a survey wich at a future Day should be of use to them in obtaining Land under it.

That after exploring, the Country the said Clarke (who was the surveyer) made the Begining at a red Oak on the East bank of summersett & Run thence a straight line due East & made a Corner on the large shellbark Hickory, where this Deponant now stands, that then he Changed the Course & run North & cornered again, then changed the course & run West, but what distant, thus, does not recolect & then quit.

This Deponant has been twice at the Beggining Corner of the said private survey & once at this present corner since the same were made & prior to this day & does not hesitate to say Possitively that they are the corners of aforesaid private survey of 15360 made by George R. Clarke in 1775 & that the said survey was the only one the said Clarke ever made on Licking or its warters to this Deponants knowledge. This Deponant saith that the aforesaid party after making sundry improvements returned to Boonsborough, and further saith not.
[signed] John Crittendon
attested Enoch Smith, James Poage

The two foregoing deposition of George Rogers Clarke & John Cretindon contained in this sheet were taken this 16th day of November 1797. Because of the badness of the weather, it could not be taken yesterday. We certify that the same were taken [at the] southeastwardly corner of the aforesaid Private survey of 15360 Acres, sworn to above by the said Clarke & Credinton, being a large shellbark Hickory standing in a Drain on the side of a ridge. Present [were] Joseph Montgomery & John Story, disintrusted residents of the County, according to law.

And in order to perpetuate the said southeaswardly Corner, we have Caused [to be marked] a sugartree & hickory, standing on the west side of the said drain and about one pole below the said Corner, which were marked Yesterday by the Commissioners who perpetuated Testamony at this place for Abraham Buford, to be noted in this Certificate. And we Certify also that we have annexed hereto three sundry newspapers published by James Stuart Containing advertisement notifying the time and place of taking these Depositions. Given under our hands the Day & year aforesaid.
Enoch Smith
James Poage

62.

George Balla and John McIntire for Forrest Webb

Forrest Webb

Forrest Webb was in Kentucky by 1789, when he first appeared on the Fayette County tax rolls. (His given name is also found as Forest and Forrester.) Webb was living in Boone County, when he was recorded on the 1800 tax list and the 1810 census; he was not recorded in Kentucky on the 1820 census. There was a Forrest Webb (1743-1823) who was born in Spotsylvania County, Virginia, and died in Fayette County, Indiana, but it is not known if this is the same man. His mother reportedly was Mary Crittenden, a possible connection to John Crittenden of Kentucky. Webb only entered one claim in Kentucky. He was living in Boone County when he sold 99½ acres of his Flat Creek claim to Josiah Collins for 5 shillings.[290]

Webb's 500-acre claim was established on an improvement made on Flat Creek by Thomas Clark's company of locators in 1776, was entered for Webb on a treasury warrant in 1780, and surveyed by James Parker in 1785. The marker was John Clark, with Josiah Collins and Benjamin Berry chain carriers. The tract was surveyed and patented to Forrester Webb. William Webb placed a notice in the Kentucky Gazette in August 1796 regarding processioning of the tract. The land is on two unnamed branches of Flat Creek in Bath County, north of Ky 36 and about 5 miles east of Sharpsburg.[291]

Webb's land interfered badly with a 3050-acre survey of John Wilkerson (procession #32). Part of Webb's tract was acquired by Thomas Brown and became the subject of a lawsuit in Fayette circuit court in 1804, *Thomas Brown vs George Nicholas' heirs and John Wilkerson*. John McIntire's deposition gives a little background on Webb's claim:

> Thomas Clark came to Strode's in fall of 1783 and he set out with said Clark, Joshua Bennet and others to Flat Creek, in order to survey lands. . . . This deponent enquired of said Clark where and how far Forrester Webb's land lay from that place, and if he intended to survey the same at that time, and Clark made answer that he did not, nor never would until they gave him a part of the land for entering the same.[292]

A survey made for the suit shows Webb's and Wilkerson's tracts, as well as the Big Elm Spring and cabin, all on the east side of Flat Creek. Webb's claim did not hold, and Brown's complaint was dismissed.[293]

Deposition of George Balla [241]

Clarke County, October 28th 1796

Personally came before us, the underwritten Commissioners, George Balla, a person of full age, and after being duly sworn, Deposeth and saith that he was in Company with a Certain Thomas Clarke and others in the year 1776, and helped to build a Cabbin at a spring on a branch of Flat Creek, which to the best of his knowledge he this Deponant believes to the spring where he now stands at. [signed] George Balla

Question by John Wilkerson: Do you recolect that the above mentioned spring was Entered fo[r] Forest Webb?
Answer: No.

Question: Was this said spring Known by the name of Elm spring by Clark and Company?
Answer: It was.

Question: Did they, Clark and Company, consent that you the said Deponant should have said Elm spring?
Answer: Yes.

Question By William Webb: Do you the said Deponant hold any Claim to said Elm spring?
Answer: No.

Question by John Wilkerson: Do you know of any Cabins on south [side] of the Elm Spring Improvement made by Thomas Clark and Company?
Answer: I Know of one above the Elm spring on the most South fork.

Question by John Wilkerson: Was there any Cabbins Built by said Clark and Company on the north side of Elm Spring?
Answer: Yes, two partly Builte on the ne[x]t Run north of Elm spring.

[signed] George Balla

This foregoing Deposition was taken at the above Described spring by us, William Robertson and James McLHany, Commissioners appointed by Clarke Court In order to Establish Forrest Webbs Entry, and in the presents of John Bayley and Samuel Jackson, we have Marked a sugartree with the following letter JBJ. Given under our hands this Day above mentioned. John Bailey, Samuel Jackson, Disinterested Witnesses.

attested William Robertson, James McElhanny

Deposition of John McIntire [243]

Clarke County, October 28th 1796

Personally came before us, the underwriten Commissioners, John McIntire, a person of ful age, and after being Duly sworn, deposeth and saith he was in Company with a Certain Thomas Clark in the year 1780 some time In the month of May, and said Clarke Informed him the said Deponant that he had made an Entry for Forrest Webb on a Branch Running in flat [Creek] on the East side above William Scotts Land.

And this Deponant further saith that he came out from strodes Station to Flat Creek In Company with said Clark and others on the fifth of November 1783. And further saith that on their way down said Flat Creek, said Clarke pointed to a branch of said Creek, and told him the said Deponant that on said branch he had Entered 500 acres of Land for said Forrest Webb.

And sometime afterwards he the said Deponant came and found on the above described Branch a spring and Cabin, which answered said Clarks Descriptions. And this Deponant further saith that about the time of the opening of Thomas Marshalls [Land] Office, he the said Deponant got a copy of said Webbs Entry.

Question by John Wilkerson: Do you know anything of Forrest Webb Entry only by Information of Thomas Clark?
Answer: No.

Question by John Wilkerson: Do you know Thomas Clark['s] reason for not Describing the Elm spring in Forrest Webbs Entry, as he knew its name before the Entry was made?
Answer: He gave me reason, but I cannot Remember it.

[signed] John McIntire

The above Deposition was taken at the above Described spring By us Commissioners in order to Establish Forrest Webbs Entry. Given under our hands this Day above Mentioned.
James McElhanny
William Robertson

63.

James Swinney, Josiah Collins and John Williams for Stephen Collins

Stephen Collins

The Collins brothers—Josiah, Stephen, Joel and Elisha—came to Kentucky from Halifax County, Virginia. Brother Stephen was the entrepreneur of the family. He helped build the fort at Lexington in 1781, purchased one of the original lots laid out for the town, and later kept a hotel and tavern on Main Street. Willard Rouse Jillson credited Stephen with moving to Red River in 1787 and building an iron forge there. However, Collins appears to have been active in Lexington long after that date. For example, in 1791 he was listed as a trustee of a new school opened in Lexington and was still buying land in the town in 1797. He began divesting his property there in 1799, the deed then listing the sellers as "Stephen Collins and Catharine Collins, his wife, of Fayette County." On the next deeds, executed in 1801 and 1803, he and Catharine were listed as residents of Clark County.[294]

In the winter of 1785, John McKinney surveyed six tracts for the Collins brothers—three for Stephen on Red River, two for Joel on Red River, and one for Elisha on Brush Creek, which he assigned to Aquilla White. The 200-acre tract processioned below lay on the west side of Red River in the area of present-day Waltersville in Powell County.[295]

James Swinney

James Swinney had a brief yet memorable career in central Kentucky. He was married to Sally Haff, daughter of Paul Haff. In about 1795, Swinney laid off a town on Indian Creek in Bourbon County that he called "Swinneytown" and later became North Middletown. He built a gristmill there in 1797, then soon after removed his operations to Red River. At present-day Clay City, on land patented by Stephen and Joel Collins, Swinney built a gristmill, sawmill and "powermill," established Swinney's Warehouse on Red River and went into boat building for the New Orleans trade.[296] In 1800, Swinney had this land processioned by the Montgomery county court:

> Take notice that I shall attend with the Commissioners of Montgomery County, on Red River on the 22nd day of August, at a place known by the name of Fife lick, in order to perpetuate testimony respecting . . . land entered in the name of Joseph Collins . . . containing four hundred acres, beginning at said lick. James Sweny[297]

In March 1804, for the loan of 2,000 pounds, Swinney mortgaged his Red River land and mills to Robert Clark Jr. and William Smith, the future proprietors of the Red River Ironworks at Clay City. At the November 1804 term of Clark county court, "Sally Swinney, widow of James Swinney, deceased," was appointed administrator of his estate. Security was provided by Stephen Collins and Joseph Clark.[298]

Josiah Collins

Josiah Collins (1757-1845) came to Boonesborough by way of the Wilderness Road in 1778. The following spring, he was in company with Robert Patterson and others who built the blockhouse at Lexington. Collins claimed he cut down the first tree, a bur oak "about two feet across at the butt." He was involved in a number of campaigns against the Indians. In 1791, Collins married Jannette Bohannon in Woodford County and subsequently moved to Bath County, where he served as sheriff and county justice. Josiah Collins is best known today for his detailed interview—at age 84—with Rev. John Shane wherein he described early events at Fort Boonesborough, Harrodsburg and Lexington.[299]

John Williams

This deponent has not been positively identified. He may be the John Williams of Nicholas County who deposed in a lawsuit styled *John Henry et al vs Daniel Sturgis et al* that he "first came to Kentucky in year of 1781." John Williams appeared on the Nicholas County tax list in 1800 and in the census of the county in 1810 and 1820.[300]

Copperas Creek or Copperas Bank Creek

These names, appearing in the depositions below, were first used for what is known today as Brush Creek, a tributary of Red River. The creeks were named by Aquilla White, who found copperas along the bank of the creek in the year 1782. Copperas is another name for the beautiful blue-green iron mineral known as melanterite (hydrated ferrous sulfate). There is Copperas Creek in Powell County today; it flows into Lulbegrud Creek near the Oil Springs.

Deposition of James Swinney [244]

The Deposition of James Swinney, of Lawfull age, Deposeth and sayth that on the twenty fifth of December, one Thousand seven hundred and ninety Eight [1798], that Steven Collins notified Killis Ewband [Achilles Eubank] that he the said Collins Should proceede to and prove his Beginning of two hundred acres of Land Below the Mouth of *Copras Creek* upon red river, also an Entry of five hundred [acres] above the mouth of said creek, upon the nineteenth day of February, one Thousand and seven Hundred and ninety Nine [1799]. Sworn to before me the date above mentioned.
[signed] Joseph Combs

Deposition of Josiah Collins [244]

The Deposition of Josiah Collins, being of Lawfull age, Deposeth and saith That he hath no Interest in this land, and that he the said Collins nows this to be the Land alewded to in this entry, and in December the 26th day one Thousand seven hundred and eighty Two [1782] that Isaac Collins and Quiller [Aquilla] White was here on this Ground, and said White then Called this Creek *copras Bank Creek* and copras Creek, and it was then agreed betwixt Quiler White and myself that he the said White should Locate the warrant of Two hundred acres in the name of Steven Collins, assignee of John Sims Trible, to begin [t]wenty poles below the mouth of this Creek.
[signed] Josiah Collins
attested Beverly Daniel, Joseph Combs, Benjamin Combs

Deposition of John Williams [245]

The Deposition of John Williams, of Lawfull age, deposeth and saith that Quiller White told me that this Creek, which now bares the name of Bresh [Brush] Creek, formerly bore the name of Copras Creek, as well as I Remember.
[signed] John Williams his mark
attested Beverly Daniel, Joseph Combs, Benjamin Combs

Clarke County Sct.

This is to sertify [that] in obedience to an order of the Cort of said County we have attended Steven Collins on the nintenth of February 1799, and have Taken the Deposition of Josiah Collins and John Williams, which sheweth this day by the witnesses which Creek that now bares the name of Bresh Creek, formally bore the name of Copras Bank and Copras Creek. James Swinny and

Andrew Harrison, Two disintrusted inhabitants of this County, who have attended with us at all the aforesaid places of. Witness our hands [the day] and year above written.
Beverly Daniel
Benjamin Combs
Joseph Combs

64.

Patrick Jordan for George Caldwell

George Caldwell

George Caldwell was a prominent resident of Mercer County, where he resided for many years. He was in Kentucky by 1783, when he was one of the signers of a petition to the Virginia General Assembly. In 1789, he was one of the trustees of the Concord Congregation who purchased 2 acres on the west side of Danville from John Crow. In 1792, Caldwell's daughter Isabell married David Knox; the marriage bond was witnessed by another Mercer County notable, James Speed. Caldwell is listed in the 1810 census with eleven persons in his household.[301]

Van Swearingen surveyed two adjoining 1000-acre tracts for Caldwell on Stoner Creek, referred to as Gasses [Gist's] Creek in the survey. His first survey was on the east side of Nathaniel Gist's southern patent of 3000 acres. His second survey, the one processioned below, was east of the first one, and about 10 miles northeast of Winchester. He was issued a patent in 1781.[302]

In 1799, George Caldwell of Mercer County sold the processioned tract to Landie Richardson of Clark County for the sum of 350 pounds.[303] In 1804, Richardson sued Thomas Buck, whose tract interfered with this land. John Caldwell's deposition for that case provides considerable additional information on his father's claims:

> That some time in the year 1782, him in company with a certain John Severns [or Sovereigns], Van Swearingen, his father George Caldwell and two other men from Stroud's station, went to survey the two tracts of land entered in the name of George Caldwell, Sen. on Stoner's fork of Licking, near a lick in the bank called Bramblett's lick. When this deponent in company with the above named men arrived at the above lick the said Severns, who said he was the locator of the said entries, mentioned to the said Swearingen and George Caldwell that he thought he was near the beginning called for in said entries, being as he said, a corner to an old military survey which this deponent thinks was in the name of Ges [Gist]. If so, that he, the said deponent, and his company did at the time they were viewing the country and about to make the aforesaid entries, put into a hollow tree a quantity of bullets and that they also put an axe under a large log near the same place. The said Severns looked about a few minutes and fixed his eye on a black walnut which stood in the bottom near the Lick on the opposite side of the creek and said that must be the tree. The company all gathered round the tree and appeared to be of the opinion that he must be mistaken. Severns however, began to chop with a tomahawk at a place near the root of said tree, which had but a small appearance of being hollow, but at length cut through and made the hole large enough to put in his hand and after feeling about in the rotten wood inside of the tree, he brought a number of bullets. . . .

> After the bullets were taken out, this deponent with the rest of the company before mentioned proceeded on to find the aforesaid begining of said Caldwell's entry, which Severns said was on a ridge not far from said Bramblett's

lick. Accordingly Severns started before and went some distance on the ridge, I think one mile at least, through the cain which was very thick, When severns came to a large black or Red oak which had the appearance of a corner to some survey, having on it old chops. Severns said it was the begining of Caldwell's entry. Severns then directed Van Swearengen to [start] the survey at that point which he did, and we then proceeded to make both surveys for said Caldwell.[304]

The Fayette circuit court dismissed the complaintant's bill. Caldwell's was another of the many overlapping claims near Bramblett's Lick on Stoner Creek.

Deposition of Patrick Jordan [246]

The Deposition of Patrick Jordan, age about 50 years, taken to establish the calls of an Entry made May the 16th, 1780 for 1000 acres in the name of George Caldwell, who after being sworn, deposeth and saith that he this Deponant came to this place in the year 1775 with James Douglass, who made Gists survey that corners on this red or spanish Oak & Hickory, in order to know of said Douglas where the Military survey was, that this deponant might improve lands & be clear of said survey.

Question by Micajah Clarke: Do you know if this was the tree eluded to in George Caldwells entry of 1000 acres?
Answer: I assisted John Soverns to make out said Location & this red or Spanish Oak was the tree we aluded to.

Question by James Stewart: Do you recolect when Douglas showed you this corner that you Discovered any letters cut on the tree we aluded to?
Answer: I do not & further this Deponant saith not.

[signed] Patrick Jordan

This above Deposition taken on the 16th day of December 1799 before us the Subscribing Commissioners at the corner above mentioned in the presents of Stephen Dooly, Ephraim Doolly and Ezekiel Rogers, Disinterested Witnesses & the said corner not being in a state of Decay, we made no additional marks. The aforesaid Depositions was taken pursuant to an order from the County Court of Clarke at their October term 1799. Given under our hands the date above mentioned.
Benjamin J. Taul
William Sudduth
Henry Chiles

65.

Samuel Shelton, William Bush, Robert McMillan and Jacob Starnes for David Shelton

David Shelton

David Shelton and his brother Samuel came from Virginia to Kentucky in search of land after the Revolutionary War. David claimed a 1658-acre tract entered on a treasury warrant in 1780, the location being

> on a branch of Wolf Creek that Heads near the North forks of Howards lower Creek, being the first branch of Licking that the trace from BoonsBorough to lower Blue licks crosses, to Begin about one half mile above where the trace first strikes said Creek, to run upon both sides of the creek for quantity.[305]

William Hays surveyed the tract in 1785, with David Shelton, marker, Thomas Brooks, pilot, Samuel Shelton and John McGuire, chain men. Hays surveyed a 1000-acre tract for Shelton on the same day. Shelton was living in Caswell County, North Carolina in 1796, when he sold part of his 1658-acre tract. That same year he gave brother Samuel power of attorney to sell his land in Madison County. He had died by 1809, when a copy of his will was recorded in Madison County listing his wife Susannah and five children: Elizabeth, James, David, Nancy and Henry. That year, his heirs sold off 100 acres of his Clark County land.[306] An approximate location of this land is about 5 miles west of Winchester.

Samuel Shelton

Samuel Shelton (c1758-1833) grew up in Louisa County, Virginia. In about 1775 he enlisted in the Virginia line and served as a sergeant major. He married Jane Henderson in Hanover County in 1781, and moved to Mercer County, Kentucky, where he applied for a Revolutionary War pension. After his death, his wife applied for his pension.[307]

William Bush

"Captain Billy Bush," a close companion of Daniel Boone, was a noted pioneer and Indian fighter. He was among the earliest settlers of Boonesborough and Clark County. William Bush was born in 1746 in Orange County, Virginia, and married Frances Tandy Burrus, daughter of Thomas Burrus. He came to Kentucky with Daniel Boone's road cutters in the spring of 1775. With Boone's assistance, Bush located and had surveyed nearly 10,000 acres for himself and others. Most of this land was on the waters of Lower Howard's Creek and Twomile Creek and was the site of a diffuse community of Baptist immigrants often referred to as the "Bush Settlement." Four of his brothers—John, Philip, Ambrose and Francis—and his sister Mary Bush Richards settled in this area. The Providence Baptist Church held its first meeting in Clark County at the cabin of Brother William Bush on November 27, 1784. Bush was "about 5 feet 8 inches in height, rather heavily formed, possessing great energy, perserverance and benevolence with little or no avarice or show of ostentation." His grave stands on his home place on the Old Boonesborough Road.[308]

Robert McMillan

Robert was the oldest son of James McMillan Sr., whose five sons were early settlers of Kentucky. Robert was in Kentucky by 1776 and lived at Boonesborough and Bush's settlement, before settling on a 900-acre plantation on Lower Howard's Creek, located in the area of what is now Stoney Brook subdivision. He died in 1811, leaving a will in Clark County that named wife Mary and nine children: James, John, Nancy, Susanna, Robert Jr. and Ellender McMillan, Polly Robertson, Peggy Brice, Elizabeth Lott. His widow, the former Mary Strode, married John Parrish in 1815.[309]

Jacob Starnes

Jacob was one of several Starneses who came to Kentucky in 1775. His father, Frederick Starnes, was killed by Indians near Boonesborough in 1779. Jacob made an improvement on a branch of Strodes Creek, and his brother, Valentine Starnes, had an improvement on Strodes "about Two miles above his Fathers Improvement." Frederick's improvement was near the mouth of Strodes. Jacob, Valentine and Frederick each received certificates for a 1000-acre preemption from the Virginia land commission for "improving in the year 1775." The eldest brother, John, was awarded the land of their deceased father. Jacob married Elizabeth South, a daughter of John South Sr. of Boonesborough. Jacob served in John Holder's company during the campaign against the Ohio Indians in 1779 and was appointed one of the captains in the Lincoln County militia in 1785. He later resided in Clark County. Mary Starnes, widow of Frederick, and Valentine conveyed one-half of their preemptions to Aaron Lewis, as Lewis' fee for clearing the tracts out of the land office. Mary and Valentine were then (1802) living in Washington County, Virginia.[310]

Wolf Creek

According to the deposition of Jacob Starnes below, Wolf Creek was the early name for Johnson Creek, a fork of Strodes Creek. Robert McMillan states in his deposition that the name was in use from 1775 to 1780. A number of early surveys refer to Wolf Creek. The stream was called Johnson Creek in the 1784 survey of Samuel Henderson's 1000-acre preemption.[311]

Deposition of Samuel Shelton [247]

The Deposition of Samuel Shelton, of full age, after being Duly sworn, deposeth & saith that about fourteen years ago he was employed by David Shilton to Carry the chain. I proceeded with the surveyor from Strouds station on a trace within a few steps of a branch. The direction of the trace appeared as if it would cross the branch, but turned down said branch on a steep bank, whence we measured one half mile up the said branch, and made a corner on a sugar tree marked DS, which place we are now at, for the begining of 1658 acres of land.

Question by the Defendant: Do you know the said branch to be *wolf Creek*?
Answer: I do not of my own knowledge, but Thomas Brooks told me it was, and
    further this Deponant saith not.

[signed] Samuel Shilton

Deposition of William Bush [248]

The Deposition of William Bush, of full age, after being duly sworn, deposeth & Saith that in the year 1775, I knew that the branch alewded to In the above deposition was called wolf Creek till it emptied into strouds Creek, that this Creek was the first water course of the licking waters [that] the trace cross[ed] leading from Boonsborough to the lower blue lick.

Question by the Defendant: Do you know whither said trace did Cross some
    branches of said Creek before it came to this place?
Answer: I do not Recollect it did, but probibly it might.

Question by the Defendant: How far did the trace Cross the Creek below this
    place?

Answer: Within less than a mile of the *Syccamore forrest* [see procession #89] above said forrest being a grove of syccamore trees, and further this Deponant saith not.

[signed] William Bush

Deposition of Robert McMillan [248]

The Deposition of Robert McMillion, of full age, Deposeth and saith that the trace leading from Boonsborough to the lower blue lick came down this branch, being a branch of wolf Creek, which Creek bore that name from 1775 to 1780, that said trace crossed & recrossed the first branch it came to before it came to this place & did not cross, as I recollect, any more until it came witin about thre Quarters of a mile of the Grove of Syccamores called the syccamore forrest, and further this deponant says not.
[signed] Robert McMillion

Deposition of Jacob Starnes [249]

The Deposition of Jacob Starns, of full age, being first duly sworn, deposeth and saith that the trace l[e]ading from Boonsborough to the lower blue licks came down this Branch, that it crossed and recrossed the first branch that hit came to of this branch, before it came to this place. And that it did not cross said Branch until it came within half a mile or three Quarters of the Grove of sycamores called the sycamore Forrest. And that in 1778 this branch was called the long branch of the fallen Timber fork, and further that the Creek now called Jonston was then known by the name of Wolf Creek. That he supposed that [the branch] which he came down of this branch to be main one of this branch, and further this Deponant sayth not.
[signed] Jacob Starns

Clark County Sct.

We the subscribers, being appointed Commissioners by the County court of Clarke Pursuant to an act of Assembly intitteled an act for the ascertaining the Bounderys of land and for other purposes, being conveined at the Begining Corner Called for in the said survey of 1658 Acres Entered with the surveyor of Kentucky, caused to come Before us Samuel Shelton, William Bush, Robert McMillion and Jacob Starns, who after being Duly sworn, Deposeth as above anexed, and the said corner being like to fail and Decay, we caused two white Oaks about Twenty yards off to be Marked as Corners and with the letters DS Engraved on the Bark of said trees, in the presents of us. Given under our hands this 24 Day of January 1800.
Thomas Berry
Daniel Harrison
Matthew Patton

Deposition of Samuel Shelton [250]

[We] Removed from a begining Corner of 1658 acres of David Shilton to begining Corner of 1000 acres Survey of said Shilton and Twoo Hickoryry Saplins. There took the deposition of Samuel Shilton, being of full age, and first Dewly sworn, Deposeth and saith that the two Hickorys above mentioned is the begining Corner of said Shiltons 1000 acres Survey & that he saw the same corner made for said Shilton.

[signed] Samuel Shilton

Clarke County, to wit,

We the Subscribers, being appointed Commissioners by the county Court of Clarke pursuant to an act of assembly Intitled an act for the ascertaining the boundries of land and for other purposes, being convened at the Beginning corner called for in said survey of 1000 [acres] Entered with a surveyor of Kentucky, Caused to come before us Samuel Shilton, who after been duly sworn, deposeth and saith as above anexed. Given under our [hands] this 4th day of January 1800.

Thomas Berry
Daniel Harrison
Matthew Patton

66.

James McMillan for Archibald Woods

Archibald Woods

Archibald Woods of Albemarle County, Virginia, was a captain in the Virginia militia during the Revolutionary War, and his name is on the monument at Boonesborough, erected in memory of Kentucky pioneers. Woods was a prominent lawyer of Madison, one of the first justices and sheriff of the county. In later life, he lost most of his land and received a pension for his military service.[312] In 1800 the Madison circuit court established a road that ran

> from the Town of Richmond to A. Woods Esquire mill, beginning at the muddy creek road near the Tan yard.[313]

Woods entered 1500 acres on a treasury warrant in 1783, obtaining his right as the assignee of William Hoy, who in turn obtained his right as the assignee of Samuel Ewing. Woods had the land surveyed in 1798 by Philip Detherage; John Willson Sr. was "Pilot, Marker & Director of survey," Patrick and Samuel Willson, chain carriers. Woods, in a statement added to the survey, assigned the tract to Robert Craddock and John Wilson, who received the patent in 1799. The deposition of James McMillan, who located the tract for Woods, places the beginning corner at the mouth of Combs Creek. This land lies on Lulbegrud Creek partly in Clark County and partly in Montgomery, about 6 miles south of Mt. Sterling.[314]

No deeds of sale for this land by Robert Craddock or John Wilson have been found in Clark County, and John Wilson is not further identified. The tract may have been lost to them, as it badly interfered with the land of others, including Benjamin Combs and Marquis Calmes Jr.

Robert Craddock

Robert Craddock was a notable early citizen of Kentucky. He had a 325-acre patent just south of Winchester, between Two Mile Road and Muddy Creek Road. The tract was surveyed by James McMillan in 1785, who assigned it to Craddock. Craddock was one of the original lot owners in Danville, member of The Political Club, trustee of the Danville Library and one of the solicitors for the Bank of Kentucky, incorporated in 1806 with capital stock of $1;000,000. He moved from Danville to Bowling Green, where he acquired much property and many slaves. He died there in 1837.[315]

Deposition of James McMillan [250]

The Deposition of James McMillan, being of full age, taken the 24th day of December 1797, being first duly Sworn, depose and saith that some time in the month of May or June in the year 1782, he marked a black Walnut tree with the letters WH on the South East side of Lulbegrud, opposit or nearly opposit to the Mouth of the fork now called Combs Creek, with an intention of entering Land beginning at the said tree, and afterwards did locate 1,500 Acres for Archibald Woods, to begin at the said tree and to run South and up the Creek for quantity.

Question By Cuthbert Combs: Was the Walnut tree you marked a living tree when you marked it and not the bark taken off?
Answer: It was.

Question By the Same: Was you interested in the Said entry when it was made?
Answer: I was at that time.

Question By John Wilson: Do you believe that Walnut tree which we are now at to be the tree called for in Archibald Woods entry?
Answer: I do and am positive the tree I marked stood not more than fifty or Sixty yards from this spot.

Question By the Same: Are you now Interested in establishing the beginning of Archibald Woods entry of 1500 Acres on Lulbegrud?
Answer: I have not been Interested in the said Land for twelve years past, nor am I at this time.

Question By the Same: Is the Land contained in said Woods Survey the Same you located for him?
Answer: That part of the Survey which lies on the North East Side of Lulbegrud is the same which I located for Said Woods, which Land we are now on.

[signed] James McMillan

We, Absalom Hanks & Original Young, as Commissioners chosen &c, do certifie that the above mentioned Deposition was taken the day mentioned at the Walnut mentioned & the said Walnut being In a decaying condition, we have caused to be marked a bowing Shugar tree and a small Iron wood Sapling with the letters on each HY, near the said Walnut, and in the presence of James Wills & James Dunlap, disinterested persons. Witness our hand this 24th December 1799.
James Wills
James Dunlap
Original Young
Absalom Hanks

67.

Cuthbert Combs, Benjamin Combs and William Calk for Joseph Combs

Joseph Combs

Though not mentioned in traditional accounts, Joseph Combs was one of four Combs brothers, who came to Kentucky in 1775 from Stafford County, Virginia in search of land—Joseph, Enos, Cuthbert and Benjamin. There were a total of eleven in their company. Five of the company—Cuthbert and Benjamin Combs, Marquis Calmes, Marquis Calmes Jr. and Benjamin Berry—had a special agreement regarding their division of the land between Lulbegrud and Upper Howard's Creek. Joseph's claim was at the mouth of Upper Howard's Creek.[316]

At a court of the Virginia land commission in October 1779 at St. Asaph's, Joseph Combs presented his claim to 1400 acres

> lying on Combs [Creek] since called Howards Creek about eight Miles above Boonesborough on both sides of the Creek and about three or four Miles from the Mouth.[317]

The commission accepted his claim due to Combs "improving the said Land by building a Cabbin on the premises in the month of May 1775." It appears that Joseph did not move to Kentucky with his brothers Benjamin and Cuthbert, but stayed behind in Stafford County, where he was living in 1794 when he gave his brother Benjamin power of attorney to dispose of his Clark County lands.[318]

Combs received a patent for his 1000-acre preemption but not for his 400-acre settlement. He had the preemption surveyed for him by William Calk in 1783. Calk ran the survey in two tracts of 500 acres each, one at the mouth of Upper Howard's Creek and the other adjoining it and following the creek. Both tracts interfered with others. Thomas Maxwell had a 200-acre tract at the mouth of Upper Howard's Creek, surveyed on a military warrant by John Floyd in 1775. John Howard had a 1000 acre claim in the same location, surveyed by Jesse Cartwright in 1785. Howard eventually obtained the land covered by Combs' lower tract. Howard had made a deal with John Holder, giving Holder rights to 1000 acres at the mouth of Lower Howard's Creek, in exchange for Holder clearing out the title for Howard at the mouth of Upper Howard's Creek. In 1795, Holder bought out Maxwell's and Combs' claims and had the deeds issue to Howard.[319]

Combs' northern 500-acre tract, the subject of this procession, ran up the creek to the mouth of Dry Fork, where he had built his cabin. This tract was also interfered with Thomas Maxwell, who had another military survey made there by John Floyd, and also with Jeremiah Moore, who had a 5600-acre survey made by James French.[320]

Benjamin Combs

Benjamin Combs was a son of John Combs of Stafford County, Virginia. He was a member of the company who came to Kentucky in 1775 in search of land. Benjamin claimed a 1000-acre preemption north of the Indian Old Fields, which lies partly in Clark County and partly in Montgomery. He lived on his patent for a number of years before moving to the headwaters of the West Fork of Lower Howard's Creek. The Kentucky General Assembly named Benjamin one of the first trustees of Winchester in 1794. His death notice in the newspaper reads:

> Col. Benjamin Combs of Clark county. A soldier in the American Revolution. Died December 10, 1838, aged 89 years.[321]

His gravestone in the family cemetery on Becknerville Road states: "Captain Benjamin Combs. A Revolutionary officer and hunter of Kentucky. Died December 1839 [sic]. Aged 89 years." His wife, Sarah Richardson Combs, died in 1816 and is buried beside him. One of their sons, Samuel Richardson, married John Holder's daughter Theodocia. Another son, Leslie, a hero of the War of 1812, moved to Lexington where he had a long, illustrious career in the military and politics.[322]

John Howard

John Howard (1731-1834) was born in Goochland County, Virginia, served in the Revolutionary War, and after the war settled in Fayette County, on a large plantation a few miles north of Lexington, now part of Gainesway Farm between Paris Pike and Bryan Station Road. He led a long and remarkable life, dying at his home at the age of 103.[323]

Howard's Creek

There are two Howard's Creeks in Clark County. The mouth of Lower Howard's Creek is about one mile below Boonesborough; the mouth of Upper Howard's Creek is a little over 8 miles above Boonesborough. Upper Howard's Creek is so called because it is "upstream" from Lower Howard's Creek. Both were named for John Howard, and the names were in use by the year 1779.[324]

Deposition of Cuthbert Combs [252]

Clarke County Sct.

The deposition of Curthbert Combs, of full age, taken before us subscribing Commissioner this 13th day of September 1799, Being first duly sworn, deposeth and sayeth that in the year 1775 in May, he the said Deponant with Marques Callamese Sr., Marques Callames Jr., Benjamin Berry, Benjamin Combs & Ennes Combs went from boonsborough up howards upper creek to take land, and after being at an old Indian Town some days up the Creek, Joseph Combs & Ennes Combs left the rest of the company to take their land Down the said Creek. And sometime in June the said Deponant with the Company that was left with him went down the said Howards upper Creek and came to a Small cabbin. The said Deponant saw Joseph Combs & Ennes Combs names rote in the Cabbin and when they got to Boonsboroug, Joseph Combs told the said Deponant that he the said Joseph had built it. The said Deponant saith he neaver herd or know of Joseph Combs Claiming or having any other [cabin] on the said Howards upper Creek, and the said Cabbin stood on the east side of the dry fork, about 50 yards from the dry fork, and about 200 [yards] from whare it emtyes in the main Creek at or near the spot that stands some Cabbins built by Colonel John Holder. [signed] Curthbert Combs.

Deposition of Benjamin Combs [253]

The Deposition of Benjamin Combs, of full age, taken before us subscribing commissioners this 13th day of September 1799, being first duly sworn, Deposeth and sayth that in the year 1775 in May, he the said Deponant with Marga Callemese Sr., Margas Callemese Jr., Benjamin Berry, Cuthbert Combs, Joseph Combs & Ennes Combs went from boonsboroug up howards upper Creek to take land, and after being at an old Indian town some days up the Creek, Joseph Combs & Ennes Combs left the rest of The Company to take their land down said Creek, and sometime in June the said Deponant with the rest of the Company that was left with him went Down the said Howards Upper Creek and came to a small Cabbin, and when we got to Boonsbouroug I was informed that the said Joseph Combs made his improvement on said howards upper Creek, which Cabbin I took to be his, and I never knew nor heard of said Joseph Combs

Claiming or having any other on the said Howards Upper Creek. And said cabbin Stood on the east side of the dry fork, about 50 yards from the dry fork, and about 200 yards from where it Emtys in the main Creek at or near the spot where some Cabbins is built by Colonel Holder Stands.
[signed] Benjamin Combs

The over and above Deposition was taken before We the Commissioners with two disinterested Persons present, which is Thomas Halsell & Rezen Halsell.
John Duncan
William Edwards Sr.

This taken At the Place appointed in the advertisement, the advertisements being Present.
Thomas Halsell
Rezen Halsell

Deposition of William Calk [254]

Some time in may or June 1775, Joseph Combs Jr. came to our camp near the mouth of Oatter [Otter] Creek and borrowed some tools, he said to make an Improvement on a large Creek some Considerable distance above that place. He got some tools and set of[f] up the river, and in a few day[s] Returned and told us he had built a cabbin. Some time in June 1775, my self with some others went out a rout in the Woods and came on the Creek now Called howards upper Creek, and on a small rise near the mouth of the dry fork of said Creek and near the bank of said fork, I saw a small Cabbin that we supposed to be the same which said Combs had built, and it went by the name of Combs Cabbin, and I dont Remember ever hearing it called by any other persons, or do I know of the said Combs having aney other Cabbin in the Country at that time. And the Place shewn to the Commissioner this Day, I believe to be the Place or near the place the said Cabbin stood, and further saith not.
[signed] William Calk

The above Deposition was taken before we the Commissioners with two disinterested persons present, which is Thomas Halsell and Rezen Halsell.
John Duncan
William Edwards Sr.

At the Place appointed in the advertisement, the takers [of] the advertisements being present.

68.

Nicholas Anderson for Green Clay

James Estill

James Estill was a native of Augusta County, Virginia. He was at Boonesborough in 1775 and settled on Muddy Creek in present-day Madison County, where he built a station. He was injured at the station in a skirmish with the Indians in 1781. In 1782, Captain Estill was killed, just north of Mt. Sterling, in a battle with the Wyandots known as Estill's Defeat. Estill County was named in his honor.[325]

The tract processioned below involved numerous individuals. Nicholas Anderson testified in his deposition that he and others made the improvement for John White. However, it was John Kelly to whom the Virginia land commission awarded a 400-acre preemption for "his actual settlement in the month of May 1779." Kelly assigned the claim to James Estill. Green Clay surveyed the tract in 1785, with Nicholas Anderson as pilot, Francis Halley and Ashor Anderson, chain carriers. Estill's heirs received a patent in 1788. This land is located on Georges Branch of Stoner Creek, near Beal Kelly's claim.[326] One of the interested parties attending the procession was John Price, who also owned a tract on Georges Branch. (see procession #51)

Green Clay

Gen. Green Clay, surveyor, soldier and farmer, was born in Powhatan County, Virginia, in 1757. He married Sally Lewis, daughter of Thomas Lewis and Betsy Payne. Clay accumulated a large landed estate in Kentucky by locating and surveying land on shares. He represented Kentucky in the Virginia legislature, sat in the Virginia convention that ratified the U.S. Constitution in 1789, and was a member of the second constitutional convention in Kentucky in 1799. He was promoted to brigadier-general of the militia in 1813 and led 2,000 Kentucky volunteers to the relief of Fort Meigs. He devoted his remaining years to agricultural pursuits on his plantation in Madison County, dying there in 1826. Green Clay, a large slave holder, was the father of emancipationist Cassius Marcellus Clay. Green's home—White Hall—much modified by Cassius, is a state landmark in Madison County.[327]

Green Clay, who acquired Estill's 400-acre preemption, placed a legal notice for the procession in the *Kentucky Gazette*. In 1815, Clay sold his interest in the land for "love and affection" to John Speed Smith and wife Elizabeth, who was Clay's daughter.[328]

The "Bill of expence" at the end of the depositions indicates that commissioners received a little over 4 shillings each day for attending the procession.

Deposition of Nicholas Anderson [256]

We the subscribers, Commissioners appointed by the County Court of Clarke at the May term 1801 for the Purpose of taken Depositions to Perpetuate testimony respecting the calls & other Specialties contained in an entry for 400 acres of land entered in the name of James Estill, assignee of John Kelley, on a preemption warrant, lying on the west side of a branch of licking, including a spring and small improvement made for John White, and runing up said branch for Quantity, have according to notice published three times in John Bradfords Kentucky Gazette, to wit, on the 15th, 22nd, and 29th of Past June, met agreeable to said notice James Green & George Cleveland, being Called on as two disinterested house Keepers living and resident within said County.

Nicholas Anderson, aged about Sixty three years, a resident of Montgomery County, being Called on and sworn as a witness, deposeth and saith that as well as he recollects, on the 6th day of May 1779 he this deponant was there in Company with William Calk, George Maden & others, and that he this deponant and George Maden made the Improvement we are now at for John White, and that about the Month of December in the same year when the Commissioners were about to sett, the Kellys were without improvements & he this deponant gave this Improvement to John Kelley & one other to Beal Kelly.

Question by John Price: Were the Kelleys with you here?
Answer: No, but they were in the Country.

Question: Where is the spring?
Answer: Just down there (pointing between South Southeast to the head of a hollow).

Question by same: Where is the branch eluded to in the entry?
Answer: The one that the branch leads into from the spring described in the answer last above.

Question: Is not the branch between this and Beal Kellys entry the one eluded to?
Answer: It is not.

Question: How far do you suppose it to be from this improvement to the branch eluded to by you?
Answer: About 2 or 3 hundred yards. I have never measured, [so] I cannot tell exactly.

Question: Did you mark no other trees for John White?
Answer: Not at that time in these woods.

Question: Did you make this entry for John Kelley with the Commissioners?
Answer: I went to the Commissioners with Kelley & made or directed the entry.

Question: Was these waters in the year 1779 known by the waters of Stoner?
Answer: We did not know them by that name & Called it the waters of Licking.

Question: Were they not Generally known by other People to be the waters of Stoner?
Answer: I do not know. I was neither acquainted with the People nor the Waters, as I had but just came out.

Question: Which of these claims did you make first, Harpers or this?
Answer: This.

Question: How did you Know how far the branch was off that you eluded to in the entery?
Answer: After we made this improvement, we went and made the other & came

back and went down to the branch.

Question: Do you know who were the others with you besides Calk and Maden?
Answer: I disremember, except Lewis Reno was.

Question: Have you at any time received any reward for showing this place?
Answer: I was paid for my Days work for coming here one day.

Question by same: Where was John Harpers Claim that is said to be on the east side of the branch?
Answer: The claim that was called John Harpers claim is the one down here on the little branch Pointing northwardly, but further says John Harper never had a claim here, for I gave it to Beal Kelly.

Question by John Price: Did you make any other improvement on the waters of licking for John White besides this?
Answer: I did not.

Question: Do you know where John Kelley made an actual settlement in May 1779?
Answer: I knew of no other but this.

Question: Did he make this?
Answer: He did not.

Question By Joseph Craig: Does the entry with the Commissioners & the entry with the surveyor both ly on this place?
Answer: I know not exactly.

Question by Green Clay: Is this the improvement you assisted to make for John White & on which you located or directed the location with the Commissioners for John Kelleys Preemption of 400 acres?
Answer: It is the very spot.

Question: In Answer to a Question by John Price, you have said you were paid for a days work coming here. Were you employed By Samuel Estill merely as a pilot to conduct the survey into these woods to Survey a Preemption in the name of James Estill, assignee of John Kelly?
Answer: I was.

Question: Did you ever receive from any person whatever any Compensation for showing the improvements made for John White more than a reasonable Price for the time you lost the trouble & Danger attending the Journey?
Answer: I never did, except I received a dollar from Mr. Price, which I dont remember I ever did.

Question: Did you receive a greater Compensation from Samuel Estill for Piloting the surveyor and his Company out in making the survey of James Estill, assignee of John Kelley, then you would have charged him or any other Person at that day for showing the blue licks or any other place at which a survey was to begin?

Answer: I did not, for if I had of shewn the blue licks, I should have charged more for it.

Question By John Price: What was the amount of the Compensation given you by Samuel Estill?

Answer: As well as recollect, twenty five shillings.

[signed] Nicholas Anderson

Clarke County Sct.

The foregoing depositions taken before us the subscribing Commissioners on the 27th day of July 1801, where John Price & Joseph Craig came foreword as persons interested against the establishment of James Estills Clame assignee of John Kelley, who asked Questions in opposition to the Same. Sworn to before us
William Sudduth
Joseph Combs
Jonathan Morton

Bill of expence
To Nicholas a witness for traveling 6 miles & 1 Day attendance ...... £ 0:4:?
To William Sudduth, as commissioner 1 Day .... 4:?
To Joseph Combs, as commissioner 1 Day .... 4:?
To Jonathan Morton, as commissioner 1 Day .... 4:?
[total] .... £ 0:17:7

69.

Benjamin Ashby for John McCreery

Thomas Marshall

Col. Thomas Marshall (1730-1809) of Westmoreland County, Virginia, was a friend and neighbor of George Washington. Marshall commanded the Third Virginia Regiment in the Revolutionary War and has been called the hero of the battle of Brandywine. After being captured and paroled by the British in 1780, he came to Kentucky and acquired a number of sizeable tracts of land. He moved to Kentucky after the war and built his home—Buck Pond—about two miles east of Versailles. Marshall was the surveyor of Fayette County during the early years of the settlement period.[329]

Marshall assigned his interest in the procession below to his son John.

John Marshall

John Marshall (1755-1835) of Virginia, the first chief justice of the U.S. Supreme Court, owned a 1640-acre tract of land just north of Winchester.

John Marshall was born near Germantown in Fauquier County and remained in Virginia. After serving with distinction in the Revolutionary War, he became one of the leaders of the

Federalist Party. John was appointed ambassador to France by Washington in 1797, elected to Congress in 1799, appointed Secretary of State by John Adams in 1800, and appointed chief justice of the U.S. Supreme Court by Adams in 1801. Marshall County, Kentucky, was named in his honor. Marshall never lived in Kentucky.[330]

The land processioned below has a somewhat confusing history. It was entered on a treasury warrant, dated June 24, 1780, assigned to John from his father. The entry is one of the longest in the entry book:

> John Marshall Jr., assignee of Thomas Marshall, enters 5000 Acres with in the following surveyed & marked lines. Beginning at a white oak and two young buckeyes & a hickory standing upon the north side of one of the head branches of the north fork of Elkhorn, thence South 69 degrees East crossing the said branch several times and several drains and branches of the south fork of licking, 3200 poles to a red oak, two young hickories and a cherry tree standing near a drain, thence South 21 degrees West 540 poles to a large walnut and two sugar trees on the south side of the top of a ridge, thence North 69 degrees West crossing several drains of licking, 2640 poles to an elm, a forked elm & a hickory on the East side of a drain of Elkhorn, thence North 23 degrees West 820 poles to the Beginning, excluding or allowing for the deduction of the several prior entries made within the said lines. One of the trees at each of the corners of this survey are marked "Ohio Company."[331]

(Col. Thomas Marshall had a younger brother, also named John, who reportedly came to Kentucky and died in Bourbon County in about 1800. John Marshall, the chief justice, may have been designated John Jr. to distinguish him from the elder John Marshall, brother of Colonel Thomas.[332]) The lengthy entry was for a 5000-acre tract that came from a private, unauthorized survey run by Benjamin Ashby in 1775, prior to the entry. Thomas Marshall obtained the location from Ashby and assigned it to John Marshall, for whom it was entered in 1780. In 1783, Ashby surveyed 1640 acres out of the west end of the entry for John Marshall, and in 1784, Thomas Swearingen surveyed an adjoining 1300 acres for Marshall out of the east end. John Marshall assigned the 1300-acre parcel to Thomas Marshall. Grants for these two tracts were issued in 1784 and 1785. On June 24, 1796, John Marshall of Richmond, Virginia, deeded the 1640-acre tract to John McCreery of Clark County. The tract interfered with the grants of George, Thomas and Owen Winn. This land is situated immediately north and adjoining the city of Winchester.[333]

John McCreery

John McCreery was born in Virginia in 1765 and lived in Augusta County, where he served as county coroner and as a colonel in the militia during the Revolutionary War. He married Margaret Black and moved to Clark County by 1796, when he purchased 1640 acres from John Marshall, the tract whose corners McCreery sought to establish in the depositions below. In about 1816, McCreery moved to the Illinois Country and settled in what would become Franklin County. Then in 1818, as opposition to slavery grew in Illinois, he moved to Missouri, where he died in 1821. John's son, Robert McCreery freed the slaves he inherited from his father and started "Africa," a colony for free blacks in Franklin County, Illinois.[334]

The procession below was for McCreery, who purchased Marshall's 1640-acre claim "near Strouds Station" in 1796. Clark County Deed Book 4 records the sale from John Marshall of the City of Richmond in Virginia to John McCreery of the County of Clark in Kentucky for the price of two dollars per acre.[335]

Ebenezer Platt

Ebenezer Platt purchased an entry adjoining Marshall's, which is referred to in Ashby's deposition. According to Daniel Boone's son Nathan, Platt was a scoundrel who borrowed heavily from Boone and then absconded to New Orleans:

> At Limestone [Maysville] my father gave security for Captain Ebenezer S. Platt for £500 which he [Boone] had to pay off. He [then] loaned this man a Negro, a horse, a saddle and a bridle, supposedly to go to Louisville on business, but he

never heard of him but once afterwards. Captain Platt was in New Orleans, so my father never got his property or its worth again.[336]

Benjamin Ashby located a 403-acre tract (adjoining Marshall's 5000 acres), which we learn from his deposition, he entered in his name and sold to Platt for $100.

Deposition of Benjamin Ashby [263]

We the subscribing commissioners being convianed at a red oak, two hickories & a cherry tree said to be the North East corner of an entry of 5000 acres made in the name of John Marshall on the 24th Day of June 1780, for the purpose of establishing the said corner, also the beginning of an entry of 403 acres made the 28th Day of February 1783, which appeared to us to have been published in John Bradfords Kentucky Gazette first on the 12th of February 1802, 2nd on the 19th same month, 3rd on the 26th of the same Month, only a mistake appears in the Date of said 5000 acres entry, it being in said papers Dated the 24th of May instead of June 24th.

We caused to come before us Benjamin Ashby, who after being duly sworn, deposeth and saith that in the year 1775 he this deponant made a survey adjoining the Ohio Company Survey, which is the survey that John Marshalls entry of 5000 acres was laid in & that he believes this to be the second corner of said survey, as mentioned in said entry.

Question By Edward Bradley: Was this the corner that the entry of 403 acres in your own name was intended to begin at?
Answer: I do not Know anything more then the entry specifice its self.

Question by same: Are you not interested in establishing this corner?
Answer: I am Not.

Question by same: Did you not make this entry of 403 acres in your own name?
Answer: I believe I did.

Question by same: Did you not sell this entry of 403 acres?
Answer: I did, to E[benezer] S. Platt before it was surveyed & assigned it.

Question by same: Are you not interested in a 1300 acres survey of Thomas Marshalls that Joins this corner?
Answer: I am.

Question by same: Did not this entry begin in the head of the north fork of Elkhorn, that is the 5000 acres entry?
Answer: The entry determines that & I believe it did.

Question by same: Was the intent of the entry to allow for the deductions of the several prior claims within the boundary descr[i]bed?
Answer: I can say nothing as to that more then what the entry expresses.

Question by same: Are you interested in any lands that ly within the bounds

described in said 5000 acres entry?
Answer: I do not know that I am.

Question by same: Was this land surveyed & measured before the entry was
        made?
Answer: The lines were run in the year 1775, as referred to in said entry.

Question by same: Who by?
Answer: By myself.

Question by Daniel Winn: Has it been surveyed since?
Answer: Yes, I surveyed I think 1640 acres & returned a platt for the same [after]
        said entry was made.

Question by John McCreery: Was that 1640 acres on this end of the entry?
Answer: Yes. It lay betwixt this & Strodes [Creek].

Question by Edward Bradley: Was there any subsequent location made that
        described the beginning to have a cherry tree, at it as disc[r]ibed in the
        pattent of said 1640 acres survey as its beginning?
Answer: I know nothing about that, whether there was or was not.

Question by Edward Bradley: What compensations did you receive for your
        services respecting this 5000 acres?
Answer: I received a common Surveyors fee for the 1640 acres & nothing else.

Question by same: What compensation did you receive for the entry of 403
        acres?
Answer: I sold it to Platt for one hundred Dollars.

Question by same: Had you ever any interest within the bounds of said 5000
        acres entry?
Answer: I never had & further saith not.

[signed] Benjamin Ashby

        The above Deposition taken on the 9th Day of March 1802 Pursuant to an
order from the County Court of Clarke at the place aforesaid in the presents of
William Petty & Richard Bean, disinterested housekeepers. Given under our
hand the date above.
William Petty
Original Young
Richard Bean
William Sudduth

70.

William Bush for Joseph Forbes

John and Richard Embry

The tracts referred to in the procession below were entered and surveyed for John and Richard Embry. (The surname was spelled Embray in the survey.) The entries were made in 1780 but not surveyed until 1797; patents were issued on each in 1800. No deeds for the tracts are found in Clark County, and apparently neither of the men lived in the county. William Bush's deposition states that a company of locators including Bush, Thomas Burrus and John Embry were out in 1780. Bush and Burrus came from Orange County, Virginia, which may provide a possible association for the Embries.

William Sudduth surveyed the two tracts, with Lewis Sudduth, marker, James Hockaday and John Piersall, chain carriers. Both tracts were said to be on the waters of Licking but no other locational clues were given in the surveys. The entries states that the tracts are within 2 or 3 miles east of Daniel Boone's settlement at Schollsville. The tracts were actually west of Boone's settlement. This places the Embries' land on Little Stoner Creek in Clark County, about 3 or 4 miles from Winchester. The spring referred to in Richard Embry's entry was on Radford McCargo's plantation (1801).[337]

Joseph Forbes

Joseph Forbes first shows up as a taxpayer in Clark County in the year 1796. (The name also is spelled Forbis or Forbush in the records.) He bought land lying on Cabin Creek and Little Stoner. In 1806, he was taxed for 219½ acres of first-rate land, three slaves and twelve horses. Forbes sold most of his land to Jonathan Clinkenbeard in 1835.[338]

Forbes placed a legal notice for the procession in the *Kentucky Gazette*. Embry's land, also on Little Stoner, joined a tract that was patented by Menoah Clarkson. Forbes lived on part of Clarkson patent. Clarkson's beginning corner was "a walnut, northeast corner of Richard Embrays 400 Acre survey." Since Clarkson's location was dependent on Embry's, Forbes had the tract processioned to establish Embry's location.[339]

Deposition of William Bush [266]

The deposition of William Bush, about fifty two years, who after being sworn, deposeth and saith that in the year 1780, some time before the [land] office was oppened to locate Treasury warrants, this deponant came to this spring in Company with John Embray, Thomas Burrase & others & the said John Embray marked a red or spanish oak tree at or near the head of this spring with the letters JE & some time after this deponant Received from said Embray two warrants of 400 acres each, to locate one in the name of said John Embray & one in the name of Richard Embree, which this deponant entered with the surveyor of Kentucky on the 30th day of May 1780. The one in the name of Richard Embray to include this Spring and marked tree, the other in the name of John Embray to adjoin the said Richard Embrys location on the south side of the same.

Question by John Allen: Have you been frequently at this place since John Embray marked said tree?
Answer: Yes, several times.

Question: Did you see the tree with the marks on it?
Answer: Yes.

Question: At the time you made this location was you well acquainted with Boons settlement?
Answer: Yes.

Question: Can you account for the call in the entry that calls to be East of Boons Settlement?
Answer: It must of been in [William] May, the surveyor of Kentucky, in making the location, or in my giving him the information, as my intention was that Boons Settlement should be East of said location of Richard Embrays.

Question: At the time you received these warrants from John Embray, did you consider yourself authorized to locate either of them warrants on this spring?
Answer: I did & further I am not intersted in these claims, nor more [claims] that depend on them, as I did this [as] friends to them & further this deponant saith not.

[signed] William Bush

The foregoing deposition taken at a spring in the plantation of Radford McCargo, southwestwardly from his dwelling house, before us the Subsc[ri]bers, Commissioners appointed by the County Court of Clarke at their March Term 1801 To perpetuate the Calls in an entry of 400 acres made in the following words & figures, "May 30th, 1780 Richard Embray enters 400 acres of Land on a Treasury Warrant on the waters of Licking, 2 or 3 miles from Boons Settlement, an East course including a Sinking Spring & a tree marked JE above the Spring and runing up and down the ridge for quantity. It appearing to us that it was duly advertised & notifyed as the law directs. Given under our hands this first day of May 1801.
William Sudduth
John Donnaldson
Henry Chiles
Edward K. Bradley

We Certify as disinterested witnesses that we were present at the taking of the above Deposition.
Jonathan Bryan
Jonathan Morton

71.

Benjamin Ashby for James Ware

James Ware

A brief biography for James Ware of Woodford County appears in a genealogical history of that county:

James Ware was a citizen of Gloucester County, Virginia, and Agnes, his wife, was born and reared in the same county. His birth was in November 1714, and she was born in December 1714. He rendered service in the Revolution, as did several of his sons, and he and his wife, accompanied by the families of their sons and daughters came to Kentucky soon after hostilities incident to the Revolution had subsided. They settled in what was then Fayette County, but that section became a part of Woodford when the county was established in 1788.[340]

Ware lived on the Versailles-Frankfort Pike, his farm partly in Franklin and partly in Woodford. He died in about 1795. His son, James Ware Jr., a physician, married Catharine Todd in 1764. They settled in Fayette County, where he died in 1820, leaving a large estate. Thompson Ware was a son of James Jr. It is uncertain whether the tract below originally belonged to the father or son.[341]

Ware's 1500-acre tract was located by Benjamin Ashby in 1775, entered on a treasury warrant by Ware in 1780, surveyed by Joshua Bennett in 1783, and patented to Ware in 1786. The tract was described as lying on the dividing ridge between Stoner and Hinkston. This land is on the Clark-Montgomery line in northeast Clark County, near the junction of KY 1961 and 713.[342]

Deposition of Benjamin Ashby [269]

We the subsc[r]ibing Commissioners appointed by the County Court of Clarke being convened at a walnut & 2 Buckeye, the beginning corner of James Wares 1500 acres Survey, Daniel Morgans beginning corner of an entry of 2000 acres, John Ashbys entry of 1000 acres & Francis Ashes entry of 600 acres. It appearing to us that the said claims had been duly advertised that said Beginning were this day to be established in Bradfords Kentucky Gazette, to wit, 1st on the 29th day of January 1802, 2nd on the 5th of February 1802 & 3rd on the 12th of February 1802, said four claims all being included in said Advertisement, we the said commissioners being first duly sworn proceeded to examine Benjamin Ashby, who after being duly sworn, deposith and saith that the corner we now are at was marked by himself or some of the company in his presents in the year 1775 & that he this Deponant in the year 1780 made the Locations above mentioned to begin at these trees, a Walnut & 2 Buckeyes, which are James Wares, Daniel Morgans, John Ashbys & Francis Ashes.

Question By Thompson Ware: Did you at the time you made the above locations know of any other line crossing the South and middle fork of Licking that runs in the same direction of this, North 35 degrees East?
Answer: I did not.

Question By same: Did you know of any other corner made on this line that were of the same kind of trees of these?
Answer: I do not recolect that I do.

Question By Benjamin J. Taul: At whose request did you travel from Virginia to establish these beginnings of James Ware & others who Depends on this corner, and what compensation do you receive for proving these Corners?
Answer: I was not requested to come by any person & do not know that I am to receive a farthing for doing the same.

Question By same: What part of these claims or other compensation did you receive for Locating these claims that depends on this corner?

Answer: For James Wares, John Ashbys & Francis Ashes, I have been satisfied for making them. Daniel Morgan promised to Give some small compensation for Locating his, but never did it. Ann Churchwells I made her a present of Locating hers & I received some small trifle for locating Thomas Randsdalls, the amount I have forgot.

Question By same: Are you not interested in establishing the Ohio Company Line?

Answer: Not that I know of.

Question: Are you not interested in claims that depends on the establishing this corner?

Answer: I am not. I have a claim that Joins Gists millitary Claims & depends on it & also Joins John Ashbys Survey.

Question: When you run this line in the year 1775, did not you make other corners in it besides this?

Answer: Yes.

Question by Thompson Ware: Does the pay that you may possibly receive from Daniel Morgan depend on your establishing him this corner?

Answer: It does not.

Question By same: Did you mark any other corner on this line on the ridge between Stoner & the midle fork of Licking?

Answer: Only one that I recolect, of which I believe was a Locust Standing South 35 degrees West 260 poles from this place.

Question: Did you make any other location at corners of this line?

Answer: Not that I recollect of.

Question: At the time you made those entrys, did not you know of prior entrys on the Land?

Answer: No.

Clarke County Sct.

The within depositions taken before us the subscribed Commissioners on the 4th day of March 1802 between the hours of Ten in the morning & 7 Oclock in the afternoon at the corner within mentioned, where we marked a Buckeye, being one of the Corner trees, with the letters WY, sworn to before us the subscribers in the presents of James Wren & Samuel Marell, two disinterested house keepers.

James Wren

Samuel Merell

Original Young

72.

Jacob Starnes and John Harper for Aaron Lewis

Aaron Lewis

Aaron Lewis (1750-1821) was the son of Robert Lewis of Louisa County, a member of the Virginia House of Burgesses. Aaron Lewis was appointed surveyor of Washington County, Virginia, in 1779, coroner and county commissioner in 1780, and lieutenant colonel commanding the county militia in 1782. After extensive service in the Revolutionary War, he came to Kentucky and was made a trustee of Boonesborough when the town was incorporated by the legislature in 1787. The following year he was a delegate to the Kentucky statehood convention at Danville. He served in the Kentucky legislature representing Madison County. His wife Sarah was the daughter of John South. Lewis died in Christian County.[343]

Lewis' 1000 acres on Stoner Creek, processioned below, was entered on a treasury warrant in 1782 and surveyed by Lewis in 1798, assisted by Thomas Lewis and Samuel Stone, chain bearers. The tract was patented to Lewis in 1799. Lewis was living in Christian County when he sold 360 acres of this tract to Mayberry Evans for $100. The survey description places this tract on the headwaters of Stoner and Howard's Upper Creek, about 5 miles east and a little south of Winchester.[344]

Deposition of Jacob Starnes [273]

The Deposition of Jacob Starns, of Lawfull age, being first Sworn, Deposeth and Saith that some time in the year 1781 he the said Deponant in Company with John South and others came down this creek, being a Branch of Licking so called by us, and Camped here, which is the place we are now at, and the next morning I saw John South renewing an old Improvement, and at the same time he Told me he intended to lay a Warrant on that Improvement, and at that time said South lived with me [at Boonesborough], and when he went to the [land] office to enter some lands & returned Home & said South told me he entered a Warrant of 1000 acres of Land for Aron Lewis uppon this Improvement & further this Deponant saith Not.

Question By Thomas Lewis: Are you any ways Interested in any part or parsell of the said Lands mentioned?
Answer: No, I am not.

[signed] Jacob Starns
[attested] Original Young, Dillard Collins

We the Subscribers, Commissioners, agreeable to Warrant to us directed by thee County Court of Clarke, have met according to appointment this 24th day of February 1802, and at the Honey locust tree and red or Black oak tree, and the red or Black Oak tree being cut down. We have caused Jacob Starns to come before us, who was first sworn to the above deposition in the presence of Joseph Shull and Leonard Bell Sr., disintrusted House Keepers, and we have caused the Honey Locas to be marked with the letters CY. Given under our hand the day above Written.

Joseph Scholl
Leonard Bell
Original Young
Dillard Collins

Deposition of John Harper [274]

     The Deposition of John Harper, being of Lawfull age, deposeth and saith that the said deponant in the year 1781 passed by this place where we now are and saw [an] old improvement, four loggs laid at right angles [and] supposing it was inten[d]ed for a Cabbin, and also discovered a red or Black oak Belted around which was not dead, and near it stood a honey locust, which trees stood a little above the mouth of a small branch which emptied into the main branch of Stoner, and further this deponant saith not.

Question by Thomas Lewis: Wheather did you, Mr. Harper, ever hear Mr. John
       South Jr. say that he had an entry at this place?
Answer By the said deponant Harper: At this place I saw first marks in the year
       1782, and that same person had been freshening up their old Claim, and at
       my return to Boonsborough I happened in company with John South, who
       informed me that he had made them marks in order to locate lands, and
       further this Deponant saith not.

[signed] John Harper
attested Original Young, Dillard Collins

     We the subscribers, Commissioners agreeable to a Warrant to us Directed by the County Court of Clarke, have met according to appointment this 24th day of February 1802, and at the honey locust tree and a red or Black oak tree, and the red or black oak tree being cutt Down, and near the Small branch mentioned, and have caused John Harper to come before us, who was first sworn to the above Deposition in the presence of Joseph Shull and Leonard Bell Sr., Disintrested House Keepers, and we have caused the said Honey locust to be marked with the letters CY. Given under our hands the day above written.
Joseph Scholl
Lenard Bell
Original Young
Dillard Collins

73.

Benjamin Ashby for William Kennedy

William Kennedy

    William Kennedy (1728-1799) was born in Scotland and married there, came to Virginia in 1765, where he was a surveyor and served as a captain during the Revolutionary War. After his first wife died, he married a widow, Mary C. Lindsey, in Charlotte County in 1778. He came to Kentucky and became involved in politics and land speculation. He was one of the original trustees of Harrodsburg, established in 1785, and Danville, established in 1787; a captain of the Lincoln County militia in 1785; a member of the statehood convention in 1785 and again in 1787; an elector for the senate in 1792; a justice of the peace for Lincoln County, and a member of the prestigious "Political Club" in Danville. He and his son-in-law, Benjamin Beall, moved to Campbell County, where they surveyed thousands of acres of land.[345] His obituary appeared in the *Kentucky Gazette*:

> Departed this life in the 16th instant Captain William Kennedy of Campbell County. His many virtues were generally known to stand in need of no newspaper panegyrizes. He was amongst the first adventurers to Kentucky.[346]

The tract below on Stoner Creek is identified in a motion filed by William Sudduth to have the land processioned, it being

> 1000 acres entered in the name of William Kennedy on Treasury warrant 8589 lying about 3 miles west of John Morgans cabbin and near a line run for the Ohio Company in the year 1775 to include a sinking spring near some cain where Betts Collier cut down some trees and made a small improvement in the year 1776.[347]

This land is about 6 miles northeast of Winchester. In 1805, the administrator of Kennedy's estate, Benjamin Beall, began disposing of Kennedy's Clark County property. The deeds were made on behalf of "William Kennedy, deceased, late of Campbell County, Kentucky."[348]

In 1806, Benjamin Beall gave William Sudduth power of attorney to sell William Kennedy's Clark County lands. Sudduth placed the legal notice of Kennedy's procession in the newspaper and served as attorney for Kennedy's heirs during the procession.[349]

Deposition of Benjamin Ashby [276]

We the subscribing commissioners being convened on an old line South 74 degrees East 46 poles from the Spring now used by Elizabeth Pearcale [Piersall], in order to establish the same, an order from the County Court of Clarke being produced to us for that purpose & it appearing to us that the time of proving the Same was duly Advertised, as the Law directs, in Bradfords Kentucky Gazette on January 15th 1802.

[We] caused to come before us Benjamin Ashby, who after being sworn, deposeth and saith that he run this line we now are at in the year 1775 from the North Easte corner of an entry of 5000 acres in the name of John Marshall, which entry since the time of running said line made, to wit, in the year 1780, which is the corner we this day started from & run this line to this place, said Corner being a red oak, 2 Hickories & a Cherry tree.

Question By William Sudduth, attorney for William Kenndy Heirs: What course was the line eluded to by you that you are now about proving run?
Answer: North 20 degrees East.

Question By same: How far did you continue this line on this course North 20 degrees East?
Answer: To Stoners fork, a little above Brambletts lick.

Question By same: Was this a line run for the Ohio Company in the year 1775?
Answer: Yes.

Mr. Jacob Dawson, being applyed, made answer he had not.

Question By Cornelus Skinner: Have you any interest in Claims that depend on
    this line?
Answer: I have not.

Question By same: What compensation are you to receive for establishing this
    line?
Answer: Nothing that I know of, further saith not.

[signed] Benjamin Ashby

The within deposition was taken before us the subscribing Commissioners at two small Hickory Saplins about 40 steps north of a branch running from the affore mentioned Spring, said Hickories being antiently marked as a line & one of them with the letter Y, in the presents of Enos Harden, Patrick Goodwin, John McCreery, Edmund Raglin & Charles Tracy, disinterested House Keepers. Given under our hands this 8th day of March 1802.
Enos Harden
Charles Tracy
Edmund Ragland
Patrick Goodwin
John McCreery
Original Young
Henry Chiles

74.

Robert McMillan and William McMillan for John Wilson

John Wilson

A few details concerning John Wilson may be gleaned from the case of *James Wilson vs David McGee* in Fayette circuit court in 1803. In July 1780, John Wilson, as assignee of Robert King, made an entry on a treasury warrant for 500 acres on Jouett Creek. Wilson was killed at the Battle of Upper Blue Licks (Holder's Defeat) in August 1782 and left James Wilson, his eldest son, as heir-at-law. James Wilson had 178 acres of this entry surveyed in 1784 by James McMillan, assisted by James Ledgerwood, marker, Samuel Wilson and Robert McMillan, chain men. In September 1780, David McGee made an entry of 100 acres, which the plaintiff argued interfered with Wilson's prior entry. David McGee won an earlier suit against James Wilson that resulted in Wilson's ejectment from the claim. Presumably, Wilson had had a change of heart in 1806, when he sued McGee to recover his interest; however, he lost again. This land is about 6½ miles southwest of Winchester, between Jouett Creek and the West Fork of Lower Howard's Creek along present-day Combs Ferry Road.[350]

Samuel Ledgerwood

Samuel Ledgerwood acted as attorney for John Wilson's procession. Samuel was a son of William Ledgerwood who lived on his 500-acre preemption on Lower Howard's Creek, in the area of the present resevoir. William and his brother James Ledgerwood were at the siege of Bryan's Station in 1782. William died in 1794, leaving his land to wife Rebecca. At her death,

Samuel was to receive the home place, the remainder to be divided among son James and daughters Isabel and Margret.[351]

William McMillan

William was one of the distinguished sons of James McMillan Sr. He had a long military career as a militia officer on the frontier and as a lieutenant colonel of the 17th infantry regiment in the War of 1812. A pioneer recalled that McMillan was "one of three brothers [with James and Robert], all good hands with a gun." William served in the state legislature for Clark County for many years, both as a representative and a senator. He lived on a plantation adjoining his brother Robert on Lower Howard's Creek. William died on February 3, 1836 and was reportedly buried in the family graveyard on present-day McClure Road.[352]

David McGee

David McGee, a native of Botetourt County, Virginia, claimed several tracts on Jouett Creek, on one of which he established McGee's Station in 1779. According to Aquilla White, "there was above 130 people, old and young, who lived at McGee's station in 1780."[353]

Deposition of Robert McMillan [278]

Clark County, To Wit,

In obedience to an order of the County Court [of] the County aforesaid, we, Edmund Hacokeday, Isaac Hacokeday and James Morrow Jr., Commissioners appointed for the purpose of taking Depositions to Establish the special calls of an entry made in the name of John Wilson in the following words and figures, to wit, "July 5th 1780 John Wilson, assignee of Robert King, enters 500 acres upon a Treasury Warrant on a Branch of Jouits Creek, at a Spring known by the name of McMullins Spring, Waters of Kentucky [River], Joining David McGees Land on the east side towards the fork of Howards creek, and we the said commissioners having met at a spring, said to be the Spring called for in the above Entry. David McGee, a person claiming Land adjoining, and though not Legally Notified, attended and Gave consent to the taking of the said Deposition.

[We] have caused to come before us Robert McMullin, of Sound mind, aged about forty 5 or 6 years, who being Duly Sworn, Deposith and sayeth that some time in May or June 1780 he Gave a written direction to James Ledgerwood for John Wilson to make an entry of five hundred acres of Land, ajoining David Magees Settelment he supposed, and to include a spring known by the name of McMillians Spring, which spring he believed we are now at. That he went with the Survayer and directed the survey of said Land.

Question by David McGee: Which of the McMillians did the Spring take its name from?
Answer: I do not know.

Question by Samuel Ledgerwood: At what time did you first know the said spring by the name of McMillins spring?
Answer: Sometime in the year 1776.

Question by David McGee: Did you Know of any other spring westward of Howards Creek at that time by the name of McMillens spring?
Answer: Yes, I knew of one on the waters of Boons Creek near a place called the

Dog pond.

Question by Samuel Ledgerwood: Is the land on which the Spring is that we are
now at the same that you Intended in the written Directions sent to John
Wilson?
Answer: Yes.

Question by David McGee: Did you receive any compensation for your services
respecting the said Land?
Answer: No.

Question by same: Did you Know of any other person or persons that Knew the
spring we are now at in the year 1776 by the name of McMullins spring or
was it Generally Known by that name?
Answer: I Know there was some that Lived where I did that Knew it by that
name at that time, but do not Know whether it was Generally Known by
that name or not.

Question by the Commissioners: Are you any way Interest[ed] in the
Establishment of the Claim now in question?
Answer: I am not, and further this Deponant saith not.

[signed] Robert McMillion

Deposition of William McMillan [281]

Also The Deposition of William McMillen, of full age, taken in the same
case, Deposeth and saith that he was in company with James McMillan some time
in the year 1784, he believes, making a survey for William Dryden, which line
passed near to the spring we are now at. That he heard it then called McMillens
Spring, and that it was mentioned to said Dryden that his survey would cover the
entry above mentioned, or at least part of it.

Question by the Commissioners: Are you any way Interested in the
Establishment of Corner now in question?
Answer: I am not.

Question by same: How far Do you thing the Spring is from the present Dwelling
house of John Alexander?
Answer: Between eighty & one hundred yards, and about twelve or fourteen
[yards] from David McGees line, and further this Deponant saith not.

[signed] William McMillan

We the above named commissioners do certify that the above deposition
was taken before us this 22nd day of June one thousand eight Hundred and two
[1802].

Edmund Hockaday
Isaac Hockaday
James Morrow Jr., Commissioners

75.

Nicholas George for Timothy Peyton

Timothy Peyton

Timothy Peyton (c1746-c1787) came from a distinguished Virginia family; his parents were Col. Henry Peyton and Anne Thornton of Stafford County. Timothy was born in Prince William County, married Sarah Matson and was in Kentucky by 1776, when he made an improvement on the tract processioned below. He was appointed deputy surveyor for Fayette County and lived near John Grant's station in Bourbon County. Peyton was said to "a man about 5 feet 11 [inches], very large and heavy, one of the greatest bullies in Kentucky."[354] He was killed by Indians in ambush, an event remembered by the pioneers for many years. John Rankin, who "knew Peyton well," described what happened:

> Tim Peyton & one James Starks had been to Lexington. Peyton was a very wild, rattling, drinking sort of fellow. Had bought a fine bay horse at Lexington. Coming home, he would whoop & hollow and ride away from Starks out of sight & then wait till he came up . . . The last time he rode on, after he had crossed David's fork [of Elkhorn], Starks heard the gun fire . . . Starks came riding up and inquired, Why Peyton! what are you doing? Ah, said Peyton, the damned Indians have killed me at last.[355]

Peyton was shot very near where Bryan Station Road (KY 1970) crosses the Fayette-Bourbon line. He left a will in Bourbon County, probated in 1788.[356]

The Virginia land commission awarded Peyton a 1000-acre preemption "lying on the head waters of licking Creek about 4 Miles nearly South West from the Lands of John Cannon" for "improving the same in the year 1776." He surveyed the tract himself in August 1786, and his widow Sarah was awarded the patent in 1790. Sarah sold 100 acres of this tract "on Stoners fork of Licking" to William Said in 1793, and in 1803 Timothy Peyton's heirs sold another 100 acres of the preemption that adjoined the land of William Haynie. Said had a gristmill on Stoner north of the present Winchester-Mt. Sterling Road (US 60), and Haynie owned land on Stoner south of the road. This places Peyton's land in Clark County where Stoner Creek crosses US 60, about 6½ miles northeast of Winchester.[357]

Nicholas George

Nicholas George, the son on Nicholas Sr. and Margaret Whitson, came to Kentucky from Stafford County, Virginia. The Virginia land commission awarded him a settlement certificate for his 400-acre claim based on improvements made in May 1779. The tract was surveyed in 1783 by James French; Nicholas' son, Whitson George, served as one of the chainmen on the survey. The tract was located on Georges Branch of Stoner Creek.[358] According to Rev. Shane:

> George's fork heads at Schollsville, at Quisenberry's spring. Nicholas George gave name to George's fork of Stoner, once lived on it. Afterwards removed down to mouth of Boones? Creek neighborhood.[359]

George actually moved to Twomile Creek, where he lived on a 178½-acre tract he purchased from William Bush. George was a member of Providence Baptist Church. He died in Clark County in 1818.[360]

Deposition of Nicholas George [282]

The Deposition of Nicholas George, of lawfull age, taken to establish the

corners of a Survey of 1000 Acres for Timothy Payton, bearing date August 7th 1786, In conformity to an order from the County Court of Clarke at their September Court 1802, previous legal notice being given in Bradfords Kentucky Gazette of the 5th, 12th & 19th of October 1802, who being first sworn, deposeth and saith that a red oak noted as the Beginning Corner of Timothy Paytons Survey was made by this deponant or in his presents at the time the Survey was made, from thence South 10 degrees East 414 poles to a Coffeenut Tree & White oak Sapling & Walnut Supposed to be cutt down. This corner was Sworn to by this deponant as being made by this deponant or in his presence for the use of Timothy Payton at the Same time this Survey was made, [and] a hickory and white thorn now marked C, thence South 80 degrees West 436 poles to two Sugar Trees & hackberry, Sworn to by this deponant to have been marked by him in his presence at the time the Survey was made, thence North 10 degrees West 406 poles to a Scaly and White hickory, sworn to by this deponant as being either made by this deponant or in his presence for Timothy Payton at the same time that the Survey was made [by] Benjamin J. Taul, Deputy Surveyor of Clark County & further this deponant Saith not.
[signed] Nicholas George

The above Deposition was taken before us the Subscribing commissioners at the corners above luded to on the 30th day of October 1802 agreeble to adjournment on the 29th of October 1802. Given under our hands this date as above.
Henry Chiles
George Cleveland

76.

John McIntire, Jesse Copher, John Pleak and Stalver and Thomas Moore for James Speed

James Speed

James Speed was born in Virginia in 1739. His father was John Speed of Mecklenberg County. James was one of six brothers who served in the Revolutionary War. One brother was killed at Guilford Courthouse, where James received serious wounds that affected him for the rest of his life. At the close of the war, he brought his family from Botetourt County to Kentucky and settled near where Danville was later established. In 1784 he was appointed one of the first judges of the Supreme Court for the district of Kentucky. He was a member of the Kentucky statehood conventions in 1785 and 1787, long-time trustee of Transylvania University and one of the illustrious members of the Danville "Political Club." Speed owned much land, including the site of present-day Lancaster.[361] His death notice appeared in the *Kentucky Gazette*:

> Capt. James Speed, of near Danville. Died October 3, 1811. He was an early settler of that vicinity.[362]

The tract processioned below is not clearly identified but is probably Speed's 8200-acre survey lying on the northeast side of Gist's Creek (Stoner). Speed entered this and an adjoining 4000 acres on a treasury warrant in 1782. Both tracts were surveyed by Arthur Fox in 1784, with Joseph Duncan, marker, Martin Elliott and Isaac Clinkenbeard, chain carriers. The 8200-acre tract ran up Stoner Creek, beginning about one-half mile upstream from John Morgan's cabin.

Speed made these huge patents, covering 19 square miles, with the intention of securing any vacant, unclaimed land within the bounds. This land began on Stoner, about 6½ miles northeast of Winchester, and extended into Montgomery County, ending about 3 miles northwest of Mt. Sterling.[363]

In 1796, James Speed of Mercer County conveyed 232 acres of this land to Ezekiel Rogers of Clark County in consideration of "Natural love and affection." Then in 1799, Speed deeded 675 acres to the estate of William Kennedy in consideration of "said Kennedy's locating Fourteen Thousand acres of Land on the northeast side of Gists creek."[364]

In 1804, Speed sued Thomas Lewis, who was the assignee of Jeremiah Moore, to recover acreage from a conflict of patents. He claimed that Moore's 1000-acre entry was "vague and uncertain" and was not surveyed according to the entry. The Fayette circuit court disagreed and dismissed Speed's case. A valuable map made during the suit shows the location of the plaintiff's and defendant's patents, a number of other patents on Stoner and Grassy Lick, as well as several landmarks: Bramblett's Lick, John Morgan's cabin, Benjamin Harrison's springs, and a clay lick on James Moore's claim.[365]

John Pleak and Stalver

John Pleak and Stalver's original surname may have been Pleakenstalver, which he anglicized by spelling "Pleak and Stalver." His name also appears in records as Pleak, Plake or Plick. He came to Boonesborough in 1777 and participated in numerous campaigns in defense of the frontier: served as an ensign in George Rogers Clark's Illinois campaign of 1778 and led a company to the defense of Bryan's Station in 1781. He married Esther Wade, a daughter of Dawson Wade. Pleak and Stalver moved to Morgan's Station in present-day Montgomery County in February of 1791; he was living in the neighborhood when the station was attacked and burned by Indians in 1793. He was called upon to testify in numerous land cases and on several occasions refused to take an oath, saying it was "forbidden by scripture." In 1794, the Clark County court determined that John Pleak, though only thirty-nine years old at the time, was "an infirm" and exempted him from paying taxes. At his death in 1817, he left a widow and ten children.[366]

Thomas Moore

Insufficient information is available to positively identify this Thomas Moore. It is not the well-known Thomas Ransdall Moore (1785-1844) of Clark County, as he was born after the time referred to in the deposition below. Most of what we know about Thomas comes from his deposition below. He was out with a company of locators in the year 1776. He was 56 years old at the time he gave his deposition (1802), making his birth date about 1746. He lived about 32 miles from James Patton's house (in present-day Wades Mill area), which means he resided outside of Clark County. One Thomas Moore signed a petition in 1785 to the Virginia General Assembly requesting establishment of the town of Harrodsburg. In 1790, the only Thomas Moore listed on the county tax lists was in Woodford County (Versailles is about 32 miles from Wades Mill.)[367]

Cabin Creek

Cabin Creek takes its name from John Morgan's improvement: his cabin was located just below the mouth of the Cabin Creek, on the west side of Stoner. The location of Morgan's cabin and Cabin Creek is shown on map made by William Sudduth during a lawsuit in 1802.[368]

Hinkston's Station

John Hinkston's Station was established in 1775 but soon abandoned. The site was enlarged and fortified by Isaac Ruddell in 1779 and subquently called Ruddell's Station. Ruddell's and Martin's stations were captured by British-led Indians in 1780 and not reoccupied. The station was located on the South Fork of Licking River in present-day Harrison County.[369]

Deposition of John McIntire [284]

We, Original Young and Thomas Pickett, being appointed commissioners by the court of Clarke County for the purpose of taking Depositions to perpetuate Testimony in behalf of James Speed, have on pursuance of a warrant from the Clerk of the said court to us directed, and of the said Speeds notice advertised in the Kentucky Herald, met this 20th day of November 1802 at the house of James Patton on Stoner fork, and from thence proceeded to the place said to be known by the name of Morgans Cabbin on the West side of the Creek, near the mouth of *Cabbin Creek.*

There taken the Deposition of John McIntire, who being sworn, deposeth and saith that late in December 1779 he came in company with John Taylor and others from Strouds Station to this place, at which time John Taylor informed him that this was called Morgans Cabbin. John Crittington [Crittenden], Benjamin Ashby and Captain John Flemming and Hugh Forbis and many others informed me since that this was Morgans Cabbin, which has since been destroyed. The Deponant further sayeth that he never knew the Cabbin that was here to be called by any other name than that of Morgans Cabbin, and that he knew of no other covered Cabbin at that time on the waters of this Creek.

The Deponant further saith that it was generally known at Strodes Station by the name of John Morgans Cabbin, and that this Creek was Called in early days by the name of Stoner, from Michael Stoners improvement, and by the name of Gist Creek from Gist Military claim.

Question by James Speed: Whether or not do you believe that this improvement was as well known as any improvement on this creek?
Answer: From his own acquaintance and from the information of others, he believes it was as well known, further this Deponant Sayth not.

[signed] John McIntire

Given under our hands this 20th day of November 1802.
Original Young
Thomas Pickett [Commissioners]
Daniel Harrison
Matthew Thomson, Disinterested House Keepers

Deposition of Jesse Copher [285]

We, Thomas Pickett and Original Young, being appointed Commissioners by the County Court of Clarke for the purpose of Taking Depositions to perpetuate Testimony in behalf of James Speed, have in pursuance of a warrant from the Clerk of the said Court to us directed, and of the said Speeds notice advertised in the Kentucky Herald, met this twentieth day of November 1802, at the house of James Patton on Stoners fork, and from thence proceeded to the place said to be known by the name of Morgans Cabbin.

There taken the Deposition of Jessee Coffer, aged about forty seven Years, who Deposeth and sayeth that in 1779 he came to this place or very near hear and found a Cabbin, which he was told by the Company then with him was Morgans Cabbin, and that he had always heard it called by that name by the Hunters who commonly frequented these grounds, and [by] the people of Boonsborough, at which place he then resided. The Company which was with this Deponant were Benjamin Dunnoway and a man by the name of Proctor, as he believes. This Deponant sayeth the Cabbin was well covered, and that he knew of no other covered Cabbin on these waters at that time.

Question By James Higgins: Do you know that this Cabbin was built for John Morgan?
Answer: I do not.

[signed] Jesse Copher

Given under [our] hands this day and date above mentioned.
Thomas Pickett
Original Young

Deposition of John Pleak and Stalver [286]

We, Thomas Pickett and Original Young, being appointed Commissioners by the County Court of Clarke for the purpose of taking Deposition to perpetuate Testimony in behalf of James Speed, have in pursuance of a Warrant of the Clerk of the said Court to us directed, and of the said Speeds notice advertised in the Kentucky Herald, met this 20th day of November 1802 at the house of James Patton on Stoners fork, and from thence proceeded to the place known by the name of Morgans Cabbin, and there taken the deposition of John Pleak and Slaver, of lawful age, who deposeth and Sayeth that he had often heard the hunters of Boonsborough call this Morgans improvement, and always understood there was a cabbin here. He had never been here untill about the year 1780 or 1781.

Question by James Higgans: Do you know of your own Knowledge that Morgan Built a cabbin here or had one built?
Answer: I dont know as to my own Knowledge.

[signed] John PleakandStalver

The Deponant being called upon to Swear or affirm to the truth of this deposition, refused to do so alledging that he considered an oath and affirmation with an uplifted hand were the Same and were forbidden by Scripture, [but] that he did aver that what he had said was the truth, beleving himself to be under a Great obligation to tell the truth in this way, as if he had Sworn or affirmed with uplifted hand.

We the commissioners do certify that the above was take before us. Given under our hands this 20th day of November 1802.
Thomas Pickett
Original Young [Commissioners]
Matthew Thompson

Deposition of Thomas Moore [288]

We, Thomas Pickett and Original Young, being appointed Commissioners by the County Court of Clarke for the purpose of taking Depositions to perpetuate Testimony in behalf of James Speed, have in persueance of a warrant from the Clerk of the Said Court to us directed, and of the said Speeds Notice advertised in the Kentucky Herald, met this 20th day of November 1802 at the house of James Patton on Stoners fork, and from thence proceeded to the place said to be known by the name of Morgans Cabbin on the west side of the Creek, near the mouth of Cabbin Creek.

There taken the Deposition of Thomas Moore, aged fifty six years, who being first Sworn, deposeth and Saith that early in the Spring of the year 1776, the said Deponant in company with Benjamin Harrison, John Morgan, Betts Collier and one Keene came down the Ohio River to the mouth of Licking River, from thence proceeded up Licking to *Hinkstons Station*, and from thence we proceeded up this Stream now called Stoners fork, being piloted by John Morgan, who had been in this country the year before, till he informed us we were above Gists Military Survey.

And Sometime as this Deponant thinks in the month of April, we built a Cabbin, covered it and made it fit for habitation. At this Spot we cleared about half an acre or three quarters of Land & planted it in corn. This Improvement we made for John Morgan, and after making Several other Improvement on a right hand fork of this Creek, which puts in about three hundred [yards] above this Place, Harrison and this Deponant returned up the river, leaving Morgan & Collier at Morgans Cabbin, who were to remain there & endeavour to prevent others from making Improvements to interfere with ours & we were to return the ensueing fall and bring to Morgan and Collier Such necessaries as they had sent for.

This Deponant further Sayeth that the Spring near this Spot had the appearance of a lasting one, at which Several trees are marked with the following letters, JS, CM, JG, JC, JS, JG, JG, JS, and which [spring was] intended by Morgan as his using Spring.

Question by James Higgins: Are you any way interested in the establishment of this claim?
Answer: I am not.

Question by the same: What are you to have for the establishing this claim?
Answer: W[illiam] Speed came to my house and requested me to go with him to give my deposition concerning Morgans Improvement. I told him I had not gathered my corn, and that I could not go unless he would give me as much as would lure hands and pay me for the inconveniency of leaving home. William Speed agreed to give me ten Dollars for going, which was twelve Shillings per day, that being the Same I demanded of him, Spposing it would take me three in going and coming.

Question by the Same: What distance is it from here to your house?
Answer: About thirty two miles.

Question by the Same: Do you know of any more Improvements of John
    Morgans?
Answer: I do not.

Question by the Same: Were you summoned to appear here on this day?
Answer: I was.

The deponent further sayeth that the letters mentioned in deposition were made by the Commissioners who were appointed by Charles Morgan to establish the claim of John Morgan, Deceased, in the month of August 1802. Further this deponant sayeth not.
[signed] Thomas Moore

We the commissioners do certify that William Farrow, James Higgins, William Higgins, John Tatmore, James Wren, William Nelson, Henry Darnell, William Jeans [Janes] attended at the taking this Deposition. Given under our hands this 20th day of November 1802.
Matthew Thomson
Robert Scobee, disinterested Housekeepers
Thomas Pickett
Original Young, Commissioners

77.

William Bush, Benjamin D. Wheeler and John Old for Aaron Bledsoe

---

Aaron Bledsoe

Brothers Aaron and Joseph Bledsoe were born in Spotsylvania County, Virginia. Aaron (c1730-1809) married Mary Brockman. In 1771, Aaron Bledsoe of Culpeper County and wife Mary sold 106 acres of land to William Cave of Orange County. (Culpeper and Orange were formed from Spotsylvania.) Both brothers became Baptist ministers, moved to Kentucky, and became associated with the Traveling Church of Rev. Lewis Craig. Joseph was the more prominent minister, with churches in Spotsylvania County and then Garrard County, Kentucky. He died in Cumberland County in 1801. Aaron made several land entries in Kentucky between 1780 and 1784, but must have soon returned to Virginia. He reportedly died in Greene County, Georgia.[370]

Aaron Bledsoe entered 300 acres on a treasury warrant in 1780; James McMillan surveyed the tract on Lower Howards Creek in 1783; and a patent issued to Bledsoe in 1784. This land straddles Twomile Road beginning about ¾ mile south of the present corporate limits of Winchester. In 1788, Aaron Bledsoe and wife Mary of Orange County sold the 300 acres on Howards Creek to John Quisenberry for £150. Bledsoe was still living in Orange County in 1800.[371]

Benjamin Dod Wheeler

Benjamin Dod Wheeler served as a captain in the Virginia Line during the Revolutionary War. Wheeler was in Clark County by 1788, as stated in his deposition below. He lived on Lower Howard's Creek, in the area near present-day Forest Grove, on land he purchased from Rev. Andrew Tribble and Samuel Ledgerwood. Wheeler sold 50½ acres of land to Micajah Wheeler of Albemarle County, Virginia, indicating a possible connection to that county. Benjamin served as a coroner in Clark County.[372]

John Old

John Old was closely associated with Benjamin Wheeler on Lower Howard's Creek. Old was received "by experience" as a member of Providence Baptist Church on June 20, 1789. His wife, Mildred "Milly" Old, joined on June 8, the same day as neighbor Benjamin Wheeler. That year John Old signed the petition to the Virginia Assembly requesting the formation of a new county out of Bourbon and Fayette, which became Clark in 1793. Old lived on a tract of 120 acres that he purchased from James Ragland. His place was east of Boonesborough Road and north of Flanagan Station Road, adjoining the land of Thomas Burrus, Congrave Jackson and William Embree.[373] In 1818, John Old took the unusual step of "selling" his land, "all his family of Negroes" and other personal property to three trustees—John Wilkerson, Beverly Daniel and Nathaniel Ragland—to be used for the benefit of his wife and children. It further stipulated that he was

> to be furnished with a horse, bridle and saddle and from fifty to one hundred Dollars and such other things as the trustees shall think right.[374]

This document was essentially a deed in lieu of a will. Old's death date is uncertain; his wife Milly died in about 1841.[375]

Buffalo Spring

The Buffalo Spring was located on Aaron Bledsoe's claim just south of the present city limits of Winchester on a branch of Lower Howard's Creek. William Bush's deposition describes the naming of the spring in 1780, when his company found a dead buffalo bull in or near the spring. The other locational clue in the procession is the commissioners' statement that the spring was about 104 yards from "Mr. Charles Stewarts Dweling house, nearly fronting his most easterly door." The spring is not a known location today.

Deposition of William Bush [291]

> The Deposition of William Bush, being of lawful age, after being first Sworn, deposeth and saith that about the first of April 1780, he passed by this place in company with Several others, and Just below this Spring, the place we are now at, lay a Dead Buffelow bull in or near the Spring, and the Company named the Spring the *Buffelow Spring*, which Spring is one of the calls of Aaron Bledsoes Entery of three hundred acres on the Right Hand fork of Howards Creek, that he the said Deponant located [this entry] for the said Aaron Bledsoe the thirteenth of May 1780, and further the Deponant saith not.
> [signed] William Bush

Deposition of Benjamin D. Wheeler [291]

> Also the Deposition of Benjamin D. Wheeler, being of full age, and first sworn, Deposeth and Saith that some time in the year 1788, that he was Riding in Company with Mr. William Bush and passed by this Spring, the place we are now at, and there was a number of Buffelow bones about this Spring, and that Said Bush informed the said Deponant that this was called the Buffelow Spring, and

the said Spring was generally none by the name of the Buffalow Spring ever Since, [and further] the Deponant Saith not.
[signed] Benjamin D. Wheeler

Deposition of John Old [292]

Also the deposition of John Old, being of lawfull age, and first sworn, deposeth and Saith that some time in the fall of the year 1793, that he was riding in Company with Captain William Bush and others, and that Just before they got to this Spring Captain Bush asked the said deponant if he had ever heard of the Buffelow spring, and the Said deponant answered, yes, but had never seen it, and the said Bush informed the said deponant that he would shew him Said Spring, and Bush and the said deponant rode to Said Spring, and the Said deponant dismounted from his horse and drank out of the Spring, and that the Spring had generally gone by the name of the Buffelow Spring ever since, and further this deponant Saith not.
[signed] John Old

Question by Dillard Collins, who is interested in the entry of Aron Bledsoe: Mr. Olds, did you or did you not understand that the said buffelow Spring was in Aaron Bledsos Survey?
Answer By John Olds: I did not.

Clark County Sct.

Agreeable to an order of the County Court of Clark to us directed, we have cause to come before us at the Bufferlow Spring, about one hundred and four yards from Mr. Charles Stewarts Dweling house, nearly fronting his most esterly door, on the 22nd day of October 1802 & have taken the foregoing depossitions of William Bush, Benjamin D. Wheeler and John Old for the purpose of establishing the Specials calls of Aron Bledsoes entry of 300 acres lying on the right hand fork of Howards Creek, about two miles above Robert McMillians, to include the Buffalow Spring. The Word "Old" interlined before Signed. Given under our hands the day and year above Written.
Edmund Hockaday
Benjamin Combs
Thomas Berry

Clark County Sct.

Agreeable to an order of the County Court of Clark to us directed, we do cerify that we meet at the Begining corner of Aron Bledsoes Survey of 300 acres on the waters Howards Creek, and after qualifying James McMillan, who made the aforesaid Survey, and James Stevens & Garrard Townsend, Chain Carrie[r]s to said Survey, that an elm tree & Sugar tree was marked for the corner of Said Aaron Bledsoes Survey, and the Elm being dead and fallen Down, we have caused a Stone marked AB to [be] Set or erected near the road of the aforesaid elm, and from thence we proceeded to his most westerly corner, to a Mulberry and Hickory, which is a corner to Robert McMillans Settlement & preemption,

and the Said Mulberry being Dead and the Hickory being on the Decay, we have marked three Small Sugar trees and a Small hickory Standing near the aforesaid Mulberry and hickory. Given under our hands as processioners this 22nd day of October 1802.
Thomas Berry
Benjamin Combs
Edmund Hockaday

78.

Thomas Moore and Jesse Copher for Charles Morgan

Charles Morgan

The tract on Stoner Creek processioned below is the same one previously processioned in 1796 (#46). This was the claim made for John Morgan at Morgan's cabin near the mouth of Cabin Creek and, after his death, patented to his brother Charles. Charles placed the legal notice for the procession in the *Kentucky Gazette*. This is one of the few times he is known to have been in Kentucky.[376]

Deposition of Thomas Moore [295]

In persueance of a warrant from the County Court of Clarke directed to William Sudduth, James Sudduth, James Guy & Jesse Cofer, as Commissioners appointed to take Depositions to perpetuate Testimony in behalf of Charles Morgan. We the Subscribers having met at the House of James Patton in the said county of Clarke on Stoners fork, proceeded from thence to a place shewn to us as the Improvement of John Morgan, Deceased, where we took the Deposition of Thomas Moore, as follows.

The said Thomas Moore, being duly Sworn by Henry Chiles, Esquire, a Justice of the Peace for the Said County, this 20th day of August 1802, deposeth and Saith That Some time in the spring of the year 1776, this Deponant in company with Benjamin Harrison, John Morgan, Brother of Charles, Betts Collier & one Keene came down the River Ohio to the mouth of Licking, from thence proceeded up licking to Hinkston Station in a Canoe & from thence the company proceeded up this Stream now called Stoners fork to the distance, as we thought, of about twenty five miles, which the said Morgan thought would be above Gists Military Survey, he having been in this Country the year before.

The company Stoped on the Creek near a small fork coming in on the right hand Side, near the mouth of which we built a Cabbin & Covered it, Cleared about a half an acre of Land about the Cabbin & planted it in corn, intending it to be the Station or place of residence of John Morgan & Said Collier, while the rest of the company were to return up the river & move out our Families.

This Deponent has not the least doubt but that this place at which we now are is the Spot improved by us in the year 1776 for John Morgan. This Deponant is confirmed in this belief as well by his recollection of the ground around, as by his recollection of a branch or fork of the Creek coming in on the same side of the one before aluded to, and about three Hundred Yards above, and also from the appearance & Situation of the Spring from which we then got water, and which at that time was flush and Seemed as if it would afford plenty of water. The same spring rising in the bottom below James Pattons plantation about two hundred and fifty Yards from his House, at which there is an Elm & Hackberry growing close together & the letters CM, JG, JS & JC cut in the bark of the Elm with a knife. And about Sixty Yards from the old Improvement [on] a westwardly course is the one which we then called Morgans Spring & got water out of.

The Deponant saith that a Small black Locust & Small Cherry Tree, in each of which is the Letters JC, JS & JG cut in the bark with a knife, Stands near the Spot where the Cabbin was built for John Morgan.

Question by Hugh Forbis: Do you recollect whether it was up the Stream now called Hinkstons fork or the one called Stoner that the company came on which they made Morgans Improvement?
Answer: On the fork now called Stoner, but the different forks of Licking had not distinct names at that time to the knowledge of this Deponent.

Question by Same: Did you See any other Improvements on this Creek?
Answer: I did not.

Question By same: Have you not the least doubt that this is the place you then Improved for John Morgan?
Answer: I have not the least.

Question by Jessee Cofer: Where did you begin to im[p]rove?
Answer: At this place where we did more work than at any other place we did improve.

Question by Charles Morgan: When you made this Improvement, was it understood by you and the rest of the company that it was for John Morgan?
Answer: It was So understood, and intended for him and no other person, and further the deponent Saith not.

[signed] Thomas Moore

Deposition of Jesse Copher [298]

We also on the Same day and place took the Deposition of Jesse Cofer, who being first Sworn, deposeth & Saith That in the Year 1779 he in company with Benjamin Dunnaway & one Proctor came to this place, where they then found a Cabbin covered & well fixed, which was then understood by that Company to be John Morgans Improvement, and the Said Deponant hath ever Since heard it called by that name & by no other.

Question by Charles Morgan: Did you know of any other Cabbin in this part of the country in the year 1779 that was covered?
Answer: I did not.

201

Question by Same: Do you not believe that this Improvement was a place of considerable notoriety by those who frequented the woods from Boonsborough & Strodes Station in 1779 & 1780, more so then any other Improvement in this Quarter?

Answer: I do.

[signed] Jesse Copher

Clarke County Sct.

The foregoing depositions were taken before us the Subscribing commissioners appointed by the County Court of Clarke at their July Term 1802 at the place described in said Deposition on the 20th day of August 1802. It appearing to us the day for taking the Same was duly advertised in Bradfords Kentucky Gassett on the following days, to Wit, July 31st, August 6th & 13th 1802.

Also, we the said commissioners caused to be marked a black Locust & Small Cherry tree with the letters JC, JS & JG at the place Sworn to by the said Moore of the Improvement of Said Morgan & at the Spring claimed by the Deponant Moore as said Morgans Spring, they caused an Elm and hackberry growing together to be marked with the letters CM, JG, JS & JC, which was performed in the presents of Stephen Scoby, Robert Scoby & George Dean, disinterested Housekeeper, who are Subscribing witnesses here to. Given under our hands as Commissioners aforesaid, the date above written.

Robert Scobee
Stephen Scoby
George Dean
William Sudduth
James Sudduth
James Gay
Jesse Copher

79.

Ambrose Coffee, Joshua Stamper, William Clinkenbeard and John Strode for Nathaniel Bullock

Nathaniel Bullock

Nathaniel Bullock was one of Daniel Boone's saltmakers who were captured by the Shawnee on February 7, 1778. He along with Boone and ten others were conducted to Detroit by Black Fish. Bullock and Jesse Copher in company with Simon Kenton escaped Detroit in June 1779 and returned safely to Boonesborough.[377] A biographical sketch appears in Draper's *Life of Daniel Boone*:

Nathaniel Bullock was born in Virginia in 1757 and early ventured to Kentucky. After returning from his captivity, he engaged in the defense of the country and rose to the rank of captain. He married the widow Baughman, settled near Boonesborough, and died in June 1820, at the age of sixty-three—his wife surviving him a year. In height he was six feet, had high cheek bones, blue eyes, and fair skin.[378]

Bullock was eligible for a Virginia land claim by virtue of "settling in this Country in the year 1777." In December 1779 at a session of the land commission in Boonesborough, he was awarded 1400 acres for a settlement and preemption "on the South fork of licking about 5 Miles below the Salt Spring Trace that leads from this place." His settlement, processioned below, was on Strodes Creek near the claims of John Starnes, Ralph Morgan, Mathias Sphar and John Woodruff. The tract was surveyed by John Constant in 1783, with Nathaniel Bullock, marker, Samuel McMillan and Aaron Horn, chain men. This land is located 4½ miles north of Winchester in Clark County.[379]

Nathaniel and his wife Elizabeth were living in Fayette in 1815, when they deeded two tracts in Clark County to John Constant, one of 255 acres and the other 388 acres. The former adjoined Bullock's settlement on the east.[380]

Ambrose Coffee

Ambrose Coffee was an early settler who lived in Madison and Clark Counties. He provided biographical information in a deposition he gave in 1809:

> Thirty three years ago I came to Kentucky in the year of 1776 and landed at a town called Lees town on the Kentucky . . . some time in February 1777 we arrived at Boonesborough and there I continued till 1785 or 1786 I moved then out of Boonesborough into Bushes settlement stayed there a year or two from that there was two of the Martins built a mill on lower Howards creek and there I attended that mill going upon two years and then Colo. Holder bought her and after he bought her I attended her near two years and from that I moved up to the head of spencer creek near old Nicholas Anderson and from that to Slate creek where I now live near Myers mill.[381]

Coffee was present at Boonesborough during the "big siege" of 1778:

> Coffee would get up on top of the block house. [Captain David] Gass counselled him not to, suspecting that the Indians were going to fire. Fourteen bullit holes were shot thro' his clothes and yet his skin was not broke.[382]

Joshua Stamper

Joshua Stamper had one of the first cabins at Strode's Station in the winter of 1779. Based on his age stated below, he was born about 1754 and came to Kentucky when he was 25 years old. Stamper subsequently had a house near Constant's Station, which was about a mile north of Strode's, and later lived about 4 miles north of Winchester. The Stamper Meeting House was a log church that stood near their home on the land of Asa Bean. Joshua's son Jonathan was a noted Methodist minister. Joshua died in 1825, leaving a will in Clark County.[383]

William Clinkenbeard

William Clinkenbeard was the irrascible old pioneer who gave Rev. Shane an exquisitely detailed interview regarding early Kentucky events. Clinkenbeard was born about 1760, came to Kentucky from Berkeley County, Virginia, in 1779, and eventually settled a little north of Winchester on the road to Paris. Clinkenbeard was at Strode's Station from the beginning and participated in numerous military campaigns. He apparently did not have a high opinion of North Carolinians, whom he described as "all grand Tories."[384]

Deposition of Ambrose Coffee [300]

Fee to be charged to Robert Peebles.

The Deposition of Ambrose Coffee, aged about 51 years, who after being sworn, deposeth and saith that Some time in the fall of 1779 he this deponant and Nathaniel Bullock came up this creek now known by the name of Strodes Creek and encamped at this Spring, now made use of by Robert Peebles, all night, and next morning said Bullock cut the initial letters of his name on a Sugartree & lett[er]ed some trees, and Said he would lay his Settlement and preemption at this place. From that time it was known by many as Bullocks Spring & this deponant knew of no other improvement claimed by said Bullock in Kentucky.

Question by William Sudduth, one of the commissions: Do you recolect how far you then thought this improvement below the Salt trace leading from Boonsborough?
Answer: From the way we Traveled, I thought it four or five miles & further Saith not.

[signed] Ambrose Coffee
attested Robert Cunningham, Robert Hensley

Deposition of Joshua Stamper [301]

Also the deposition of Joshua Stamper, age 49 years, who after being sworn, deposeth and saith that he has known this spring eluded to in the above deposition by the name of Bullock Spring ever Since December 1779. That the first time this deponant came into these woods, it was with a William Patterson, who informed this Deponant that this was Bullocks Spring. And [he] believes about the month of December 1779 [or] beginning of the year 1780, it was known to those who generally frequented this place by the name of Bullocks Spring, as a place of notariety & further Saith not.
[signed] Joshua Stamper
attested Robert Cunningham, Robert Hensley

Deposition of William Clinkenbeard [301]

Also the Deposition of William Clinkenbeard, aged about 41 or 42 years, who after being Sworn, deposeth and Saith that Some time in the fall 1779, he this deponant in company with John Taylor and others came to this Spring & said Taylor informed this deponant & others that this Spring now used by Robert Peebles was Bullocks Spring, which is the Same Spring eluded to in Ambrose Coffees Deposition, and when they (that is, those who then frequented these parts) were in conversation, said Spring was mentioned as a place of notariety to describe their rout that they had travelled & further saith not.
[signed] William Clinkebeard his mark
attested Robert Cunningham, Robert Hensley

Deposition of John Strode Sr. [302]

Also the deposition of John Strode Sr., age about 74 years, who after being sworn, deposeth and saith that in an early period he knew this to be called Bullocks Spring, tho cannot precisely sayth what year & further Saith not.
[signed] John Strode
attested Robert Cunningham, Robert Hensley

Clarke County, To Wit,

In obedience to an order of the County Court of Clarke Court, we, William Sudduth, Daniel Harrison and John Donnaldson, Commissioners appointed for that purpose, have this day proceeded to take the depositions of Ambrose Coffee, Joshua Stamper, William Clinkenbeard & John Strode herein inclosed, in order to perpetuate Testimony respecting the Specal calls of an entry of 400 acres on Settlement right entered in the name of Nathaniel Bullock on the 17th day of January 1780, in the following words, "Nathaniel Bullock enters 400 acres in Kentucky by Virtue of a Certificate & lying on the South fork of Licking Creek about 5 miles below the Salt trace that leads from Boonsborough," previous legal notice of our meeting having been given of our meeting to Joshua Stamper, William Clinkenbeard, John Bean, Thomas Goff, John Peebles, Jacob Wilson and George Beeth, who claimed lands adjoining It, also appearing to us that the same had been duly advertized In Daniel Bradfords Kentucky Gazette on the following days, March 15th, 22nd & 29th, according to Law. Given under our hands and Seals this 3rd day of May 1803.
William Sudduth
John Donnaldson
Daniel Harrison

80.

Edward Wilson, William Sudduth, Thomas Dawson, Samuel Dawson and Samuel Hornback for Thomas Kennedy

Thomas Kennedy

Thomas Kennedy (1744-1827) was born in Frederick County, Maryland. He came to Kentucky on the Wilderness Road in 1776 and settled at Boonesborough, while in search of land for himself and brothers John and Joseph. In 1779, he brought his family out and settled at Strode's Station, remaining there until 1785. He then moved to his claim on the present Paris-Winchester Road and built a stone house on what later became the farm of Cassius M. Clay.[385] His son Jesse described his father as

> a small lean man, who . . . never weighed over 140 pounds. He had an excellent physical constitution, was energetic and hardy as a pine knot. His mental abilities were naturally good, though without polish, his education being very limited. He was a man of great hospitality and of strict moral integrity . . . The violent irrability of his temper was his greatest infirmity."[386]

The Virginia land commission awarded Kennedy a 1400-acre settlement and preemption on Strodes Creek "for Settling & raising a crop of Corn" in 1776. In 1782, Edward Wilson surveyed 400 acres on a settlement certificate and 672 acres on a preemption warrant; James Duncan was the marker, Benjamin and Frederick Couchman, chain carriers. The preemption adjoined the northwest corner of Gist's northernmost 3000-acre military survey. This land is on the Clark-Bourbon line, about 7 miles north of Winchester, about 9 miles south and a little east of Paris.[387]

Thomas Dawson

Thomas Dawson was born in Albemarle County, Virginia in 1759, served in the Revolutionary War, and later married Mary Ann Clay, a daughter of Dr. Henry Clay of Bourbon

County. Thomas was awarded a military warrant for 100 acres of land for his service in the Revolution. He owned 457 acres lying partly in Clark and partly in Bourbon, on the waters of Strodes Creek near Hornback's Mill. Thomas was listed as a resident of Christian County in 1819, when he sold this tract to John Hume. He died in Trigg County in 1829.[388]

Samuel Dawson

This could be either Samuel Dawson Sr. or his son, Samuel Jones Dawson Jr. Samuel Sr. married Martha Jones and died in Bourbon County in 1807. His will named wife Martha, daughters Priscilla and Mary, and sons Thomas (see above), Samuel Jr. and John. Samuel Jr. lived in Bourbon County.[389]

Samuel Hornback

Samuel Hornback and his brother-in-law John Reed operated a gristmill and sawmill in Bourbon County. Hornback came to Kentucky from Moorefield, Virginia (in now Hardy County, West Virginia) in about 1788. Hornback purchased some land out of Thomas Kennedy's settlement and preemption.[390]

Hornback's Mill

Samuel Hornback and John Reed petitioned Bourbon county court for a water gristmill on Strodes Creek in May 1788. In November 1788, the court ordered a survey of the "best and most convenient way" from the courthouse to Hornback's Mill.[391] The mill was described in a county history:

> [John Reed] was the first owner of a mill, which afterward passed into the hands of Mr. [Samuel] Hornback, then to Mr. Thatcher. It was a saw and gristmill, and is now [1882] owned by Matt D. Hume.[392]

The mill was located just across the Clark line in Bourbon County.

Deposition of Edward Wilson [303]

Clarke County Sct.

The Deposition of Edward Wilson, aged Sixty five years, taken at the North West corner of Gists Military survey of 3000 acres, near the roads leading from Winchester to *Hornbacks Mill*, and on the West Side of Said road, about eight feet distant from said road, for the purpose of processining & proving the corners or bounderies of a Survey of Six hundred and seventy two [672] acres, [entered] on part of a preemption Warrant and pattented the first day of July 1784 in the name of Thomas Kennedy, who after being sworn, deposeth and said That when he Surveyed Thomas Kennedys Survey of Six hundred and Seventy two acres, he had an attested copy of Gists Military Survey from [William] Prestons Office.

He this deponant found a marked line and traced it to the corner, and found that it coresponded with the copy in his possession, and that on one of the corner trees the letters TG was marked, and that the Elm Tree now standing and defaced is one of the corner trees that he found marked. We then proceeded to a white oak marked as a corner, which the said Deponant made oath was the Beginning corner to said Kennedys Settlement. The Surveyor of said County was then directed to run a line North 65 degrees East 236½ poles to a Stake in a line running South 20 degrees East from Gists North West corner, which the Deponant saith was at or near the place where said corner stood, altho no corner at this time appears & further saith not.
[signed] Edward Wilson

Deposition of William Sudduth [304]

Also the Deposition of William Sudduth, aged thirty seven years, who after being sworn, deposeth and saith that as well as he recollects, in the month of October 1787 the Deponant was shewn this corner by John Constant as the corner of Gists Survey, which this deponant has frequently seen since. That in the year 1795 or 1796 this deponant was directed by Colonel Nathaniel Gist to begin at this corner & to run the west boundrey line, in order to close the same for the purpose of Surveying 400 acres of land for Major David Bell, which this deponant run agreeable to Said Gists instruction & that in November 1802 this deponant was called on by the Heirs of Nathlaniel Gist, Deceased, to make a division of the Survey, to which this is a corner, and I run from Said corner a line North 70 degrees East the distance called for in Said Gists patent & found the corner Corrasponding with the patent as to the corner trees, and as near so as to course and distance as is usual with old lines. And that there was a marked line from this corner to the above described corner.

Question by John Donnalson: Are you acquainted with the corners & marks of
    the Survey of Gist in the neighbourhood?
Answer: I am. They are generally marked TG & the trees generally chopped in
    the same manner. This corner was before defaced, and about the same
    height of it & further saith not.

[signed] William Sudduth

Deposition of Thomas Dawson [305]

Also the deposition of Thomas Dawson, aged forty one, who after being sworn, deposeth and saith that about the year 1789 this deponant came to a corner near here, and was told by Thomas Kennedy that the corner of Gists Military Survey was at this place. And about two years afterwards, he this deponant came to this place in company with John Price, Thomas Lewis, James Bristow & John Dawson. When John Price examined his papers & found that this corner corresponded with the corner called for, and that in following the lines round was found the Distance and corner trees corresponded with the papers in John Price's possession, as far as he that deponant went, which was three corners from this place.

Question by John Donnaldson: On what occasion was John Price and James
    Bristow at this place Surveying?
Answer: I was informed that James Bristow was agent for Colonel Gist, and was
    making a division between Gist and Lewis.

Question by same: Do you recollect of this corner that is now defaced being
    marked with the letters TG?
Answer: I recollect that there was letters on some of the corners, but do not
    recollect which.

[signed] Thomas Dawson his mark

Deposition of Samuel Dawson [306]

Also the deposition of Samuel Dawson, of full age, who after being sworn, deposeth and saith that about the year 1791 he this deponant was shewn this corner by Thomas Dawson as the corner of Gists military survey. [And] that this corner which is now defaced was at the time of his first acquaintance with it was an Elm and two Sugartrees. One Sugartree was dead and the top broke off. [signed] Samuel Dawson

Deposition of Samuel Hornback [306]

Also the deposition of Samuel Hornback, of full age, who after being sworn, deposeth and said that he has been acquainted with this corner about ten years and has always known it as the corner of Gists Military Survey. That at the time of his first acquaintance with the corner [an] Elm, which is now defaced, and two Sugartrees was Standing. One of the Sugartrees was dead and the top broke off. [It was] Marked as a corner, and further Saith not. [signed] Samuel Hornback his mark

Clark County Sct.

In obedience to an order to us directed from the Worshipfull Court of Clarke County as processioners, Pursuant to an act of assembly in that case made and provided at their May Term 1803, for the purpose of taking depositions to establish the corners and Bounderies of a settlement and Preemption in the name of Thomas Kennedy & the same having been duly advertised in Bradfords Kentucky Gasette on the 7th, 14th, & 21st days of June 1803.

It was also satisfactorly proven to us that legal notice had been given to Judith C. Gist, James Bristoe, John Bristoe, William Campbell, Samuel Hornback, Benjamin Radcliff, Jeremiah Wilson, and Edward Wilson on the 13th day of June 1803. Also, Joseph Boswell acknowledged a notice to have been served on him on the 14th of June 1803. Also, Jesse Bledsoe acknowledged a notice to have been served on him the 14th day of June 1803.

We the subscribers convened at a corner shewn to us as the North West corner of Gists Military Survey, as described in the deposition of Edward Wilson, where we caused to come before us Edward Wilson, William Sudduth, Thomas Dawson, Samuel Dawson and Samuel Hornback, who after being duly sworn, deposed as inserted in their respective depositions, hereunto annexed & the corner shown to us as the North West Corner to Gists Survey was nearly destroyed. We therefore marked as Elm, which was one of the former corner trees & a Sugartree, and a red oak as Corner trees afresh in presence of David Hampton & Robert Cunningham, disinterested persons. Given under our hands and Seals this 29th day of June 1803.
Benjamin J. Taul
Original Young
Henry Chiles

81

James McMillan, Frederick Couchman, William Bradshaw and Robert McMillan for William Dryden

William Dryden

David Dryden's will, probated in Augusta County, Virginia in 1772, mentions sons William, James, Nathaniel and David and daughters Eliner, Elizabeth and Jane. A family history states that the four sons all fought in the battle of King's Mountain (1780) and that Nathaniel was killed. William came to Kentucky with his wife Mary and claimed several tracts of land on Lower Howard's Creek. He lived in Lincoln County on an improvement made by John Wilson; his claim became part of present-day Lancaster. He operated a tavern that was used as a local meeting place. Dryden died in Madison County, where his estate settlement was returned to the court in December 1805. His children were Hugh, Ruhana and Deliah.[393]

The 250-acre tract processioned below was entered in 1785 but was not surveyed by James McMillan until 1798. Dryden's survey interfered with claims of John Patrick, James Kell and William Bush. The land is 3½ miles southwest of Winchester, in the area where McClure Road crosses Lower Howard's Creek.[394]

William Bradshaw

William Bradshaw was in Kentucky by 1784, when served as a chain carrier for Bartlett Searcy on Robert Burton's survey; Hugh Bradshaw was the marker (relation unknown). William married Sallie Gray in 1796. It was not his first marriage, as his daughter Peggy married John Ramey in 1798. William owned land on the West Fork of Lower Howard's Creek. He sold 80 acres to Francis McKinney (1798) and 105 acres to William Hays (1799). The tax list for 1801 shows Bradshaw living on Fourmile Creek, on 100 acres that had been patented by William Bush.[395]

Deposition of James McMillan [308]

Fee to be charged to [John] McClure.

Agreeably to an order of the Court of Clarke County bearing date June court 1803, We, the under signed Commissioners therein named, having met at the place said to be the Beginning Corner of an entry of 250 acres entered in the name of William Dryden, proceeded to take the following deposition in order to establish the said beginning, as also the Special calls of Said entry.

The deposition of James McMillin, of lawful age, after being Solemnly Sworn, deposeth and Saith that he came to this place in June 1795, as well as he rembers, and marked said dogwood and white oak with the letter M, entering the said trees for the beginning of an entry and Survey of land, which entry was made for 250 acres in the name of William Dryden.

And this deponent further Saith that the letters aforesaid was made on a green Dogwood and on a Dead White oak. And also Saith that a white oak falen down and a Dogwood, which has Some time past had the bark taken off, shewn to us by the deponant, is the Same Trees the letters aforesaid were made on, as he this deponent surely believes.

Question by Lewis Hawks: Do you know who made this entry?
Answer: I wrote the location and Sent it by William McMillan to the [land]
office, who brought me an attested copy.

Question by same: Do you know who surveyed the land?
Answer: I surveyed it myself.

Question by same: Had you any interest in the entry when it was made?
Answer: I had.

Question by same: Have you any now?
Answer: I have no intrest at present in the land.

Question by same: Was you imployed by Dryden to make this entry?
Answer: I purchased the warrant from Dryden and entered the land, designing to hold it myself.

We then removed to near the corner of William Trimbles preemption, as called for in the third Special [call] of the above entry. And then continued the deposition of the foregoing deposition, as follows, to wit, that some time prior to entering the above entry, I marked a red oak and Sugartree, as called for in Said entry, at or very near this place.

Question by Alexander Ritchie Sr.: When you made them markes, did you not See a line runing a Northernly course that intersected the line of William Trimble that you was informed by Bartlett Searcy, prior to making the above entry, was the line of Robert Burton?
Answer: I seen a line intersecting Trimbles line at or very near this place that Searcy informed me he had made for one of the lines of Robert Burtons preemption, as assignee of Richard Searcy.

Question by John McClure: When you made the entry, did you believe that a line North 8 degrees East from this place would intersect the line of Sweringins Survey?
Answer: I did, from the information of John Fleming, believe that it would.

Deposition of Frederick Couchman [310]

Fee to be charged to John McClure.
Also the Deposition of Frederick Couchman, of Lawful age, after being Solemnly Sworn, deposeth and Saith.

Question by John McClure: Did you not know So early as the fore part of the Spring 1785 that the lines of John Fleming and William Trimble intersect at or very near the Trees Shown by James McMillion as Marker for the entry aforesaid?
Answer: I did.

Question by same: Do you recollect of Seeing the marks as proven by James McMillan early in the spring 1788?
Answer: I recollect the lines, but the marks were Some time after wards and

further this deponant sayth not.

[signed] Frederick Couchman

Deposition of James McMillan, continued [311]

Question by Lewis Hawks: When you run the line, did you run here and make a
corner at the trees marked?
Answer: When I surveyed the land, I run to the trees called for in the entry, but
the trees were marked by me before making the entry.

Question by John McClure: When you Sent the location to the office, did not the
location call for a white ash in the line of Fleming inSted of an oak, as it is
now in the entry?
Answer: It did, and the attested copy Sent to me to Survey by, agreed with the
Locaton.

Question by same: When you made the entry, did you know that the lines of
William Trimble and John Fleming intersected where you marked the
Trees for the Begining?
Answer: I Did.

We then went to the corner of William Trimbles preemption, being the
Second Special call of the foregoing entry, And continued the above deposition in
the following words.

This Deponant further Saith that he Surveyed Trimbles preemption prior
to making this entry, and then made this corner for the Said preemption, and at the
time of making the entry he entered this corner as the second Special call of Said
entry, and Farther this deponant saith not.
[signed] James McMillan

We the under signed commissioners do certify that in order to purpetuate
Testimony respecting the Beginning and Special calls of Said entry and Survey,
caused to be made by George Ritchie and Henry Hite, two disinterested
housekeepers of the County aforesaid, marks at the several Specials calls of Said
entry, to wit, at the Begining two Young walnut saplins, one marked, thus, U, and
the Second, thus, FK, and at the second Special call, a Buckeye, thus, MH, and at
the third, two Buckeyes, thus, M, and a white thorn, thus, H. We do certify that
the aforegoing depositions was taken before us as Commissioners aforesaid on the
3rd day of September 1803. Given under our hands and seals the day and Date
aforesaid.
William McMillan
Aaron Lacklin
James Hazelrigg

Deposition of William Bradshaw [313]

Charge fees to John McClure.

Agreeably to an order of the court of Clarke County bearing date June Court 1803, We the under Signed Commissioners haveing met at the third Special call of an entry of 250 acres made in the name of William Dryden, and having caused William Bradshaw and Robert McMillan to come before us, proceeded to take their Depositions in order to astablish the most east ward lines of Robert Burten, assignee of Richard Searcy, as called for in the said entry.

The Deposition of William Bradshaw, of lawful age, after being Solemnly Sworn, deposeth and Saith that he the said Bradshaw was with Bartlett Searcy when he Surveyed Robert Burtens preemtion, assignee of Richard Searcy, and as well as this deponant recollected, carried the chain for the Said Survey.

And this deponant further Saith that he perfectly recollects that the most East ward line of the Said Survey passed near to a certain Sink hole Spring on the old road from McGees Station to Strouds, which Spring is now included in the improved lands of Lewis Hawks, on which he now resides, and that the Said line passed at or very near this place, being the place proved by Colonel James McMillan as the intersection of said Burtens line and William Trimble.

Question by John McClure: Did you ever carry the chain or was you with Searcy when he Surveyed the Said land but his one time?
Answer: I never was, and further this deponant Saith not.

[signed] William Bradshaw

Deposition of Robert McMillan [314]

Also the deposition of Robert McMillan, of Lawfull age, after being Solemnly Sworn, deposeth and Saith that Bartlett Searcy informed him where to find the Begining corner of Richard Searcys land, and also the course and corners of the Eastward end of Said Survey & also the line of his preemption, which this deponant believes is patented in the name of Robert Burten, assignee of Richard Searcy.

And this deponent further saith that on examining for the Said lines and corners, he this deponant found them as discribed by Said Searcy, one of which corners stood near to this place, being the place as proven by the foregoing deposition of William Bradshaw as the most eastward line of Robert Burtens premption, as assignee of Richard Searcy.

And this deponent further Saith that from the corner he found a line running east of North, which Searcy informed him was his most Eastward line, that is the line as this deponent understands of Robert Burten, assignee of Richard Searcy.

Question by Lewis Hawks: Was you at the Surveying of William Trimbles premption?
Answer: I was, and carried the chain.

212

Question by Same: Did you trace Searcy lines before you carried the chain for Trimble?

Answer: I did.

Question By Same: Did you corner on Searcys line when you carried the chain for Surveying Trimbles lands?

Answer: We cornered on or very near Searcys line.

Question by Same: When Colonel McMillan Surveyed the land, did you not hear him say that he would enter the land Between Searcy and Trimbles lines?

Answer: I did.

Question By Same: Do you know of your own knowledge that Colonel McMillan did enter the land?

Answer: No. But I have heard him say he would, and also that he had entered the land Between Trimble line and Burtens as discribed to me by Searcy.

We then removed to the Begining corner of Said entry of 250 acres in the name of William Dryden, and then continued the forgoing deposition. This deponent Saith that he was with Colonel James McMillan when he Surveyed Trimbles premtion, and that he then Seen Colonel McMillan make letters on a dead tree this deponant believes to be an oake, and also Shaved the barke of[f] a Saplin, which he believes was a Dogwood which was living, and then make letters on Same. The letters this Deponent doth not perfu[c]tly recollect, but believes were, thus, M. And this deponent Saith that the trees as Marked by Colonel McMillan were at the intersection of Fleming and Trimbles lines, which this deponent Saith he perfectly recollects was within at most twenty yards of this place, being the place formerly proven by Colonel McMillan as the Begining corner of the entry aforesaid, and further this deponent Saith not.
[signed] Robert McMillion

Clarke County Sct.

The a foregoing depositions taken before us, commitioners appointed by the Court of the County aforesaid on the 1st day of October 1803, at the places as mentioned in the foregoing depositions. Given under our hands and seals the day and date aforesaid.
William McMillan
Aaron Lacklin

82.

Samuel Martin and John McKinney for Samuel and James Long

Samuel and James Long

Samuel and James Long claimed a 1286-acre tract on Red River and Hardwick Creek by virtue of a treasury warrant entered on January 6, 1783, surveyed by John McKinney on October 30, 1792, and granted to the Longs on May 18, 1800. Being on Red River and Hardwick Creek places the land in now Powell County, in an area south of Clay City between the two streams. David Long—relationship unknown—had 2100 acres surveyed and patented to him on Red River.[396]

Only one deed of the Longs could be found in Clark County: James Long of Robertson County, Tennessee, sold 124 acres on Millseat Creek to James McMahan of Clark County in 1804. The deed stated the land was part of the tract granted to Samuel and James Long, but did not mention what happened to Samuel's interest.[397]

Alexander Barnett

The depositions of Martin and McKinney were taken "in behalf of Alexander Barnett." There was no indication of Barnett's interest in the Longs' tract. Barnett processioned a tract of his own nearby—at the mouth of Drowning Creek on Kentucky River (#86).

Samuel Martin

His deposition indicates that Samuel Martin was born in about 1760 and was in Kentucky by 1781. In the year 1800, there were men by that name living in the counties of Bourbon, Nelson, Scott, Washington and Woodford. A Samuel Martin applied for a Revolutionary War pension from Madison County in 1834. The soldier stated that he was born in Prince Edward County, Virginia in 1745 and that he moved to Clark County in 1794, then to Madison County in 1832 where he died a month after applying for a pension.[398]

John "Wildcat" McKinney

John McKinney is best known for his fight with a wildcat while teaching school in early Lexington, but his full story is much richer than indicated by that famous event. McKinney was wounded in the Battle of Point Pleasant in 1774, for which he later received a military pension. He was in Kentucky in 1779, when he made a land claim on Stoner Creek near Paris. He married Polly Trimble in Augusta County and brought his family to Lexington in 1785, later moving to Bourbon County where he settled near Clintonville. McKinney was an elder in the Green River Baptist Church, a delegate for his county at the first statehood convention in Danville, and Bourbon's first representative to the Kentucky legislature. His main occupation appears to have been surveying. McKinney was appointed a deputy surveyor for Fayette, 1782-1786, and for Bourbon, 1792. He was once wounded by Indians while surveying on Licking River. McKinney, who was sickly in his later years, died in Bourbon in 1825.[399]

Deposition of Samuel Martin [317]

In obedience to an order of the worshipful the County Court of Clarke at their March term last, appointing Nicholas Burger, Cornelius Newkirk, Stephen Collins, James Sweeney & George Sharp, or any two of them, to take Depositions to perpetuate Testimony to establish the Special calls of an entry of 1286 acres made in the Name of Samuel & James Long on the waters of Red River, Beginning 40 poles east of the lower end of A flag Marsh on the east Sid of the said river &c. We, George Sharp & Stephen Collins, two of the above Named Commissioners, being met for the purpose afforesaid, agreeable to a notice publisshed acording to Law, as appears from the Kentucky Heralds Date March 22 & 29 & April 5th 1803, to us produced.

When we caused Samuel Martin, aged about 43 years, to come before us, who being Duly Sworn, Deposeth & Saith that in the year 1781 in the month of August, he the said Martin was on this ground in company with Alexander McClain and others, and took notice of the flag Marsh where we now are. Afterward, either in the latter end of the Year 1782, or 1783 the Beginning of, Alexander McClain Called on him the Said Martin to assist him in making out a Location of Samuel & James Longs, Beginning a certain Distance, not now remembered, eastwardly from this flag marsh.

Question By the Commissioner: Have you any Doubt of at all of this being the very Marsh called for in Longs entry, or do you know of any other flag Marsh Similar to this?

Answer: I have no doubt of its being the Same Marsh, and I know of no other like it & further this Deponent Saith not.

[signed] Samuel Martin

Deposition of John McKinney [319]

Also John McKinney, who being of Lawful age and Duly Sworn, Deposeth & saith that in the fall of the year 1792 Alexander McKlain called on him the said McKinney to Survey Samuel & James Longs land on Red River, and shewed him this flag Marsh as the Marsh called for in Longs entry.

Question by the Commissioners: Did McKlain espress any Doubt of this being the Same flag marsh called for in Longs entry?

Answer: No, not the least. He had Described it so clearly to me before we found it that I believe I should have known it by his Discription had he not been present & further this Deponant Saith not.

[signed] John McKinney

We do certify that the above Depositions were sworn to and Subscribed in our presence & that Samuel McMahan and Augustice Davis, Disinterested housekeepers of Clarke County, were present. Given under our hands & Seals this 14th day of April 1803.
Stephen Collins
George Sharp

83.

John Crittenden for Timothy Peyton's heirs

This is the same tract that was processioned for Timothy Peyton in October 1802 (#75).

Deposition of John Crittenden [320]

Fees to be charged to William Haney.
In pursuance of an order of Clarke Court to us directed, bearing Date September 1802, for the purpose of perpetuating Testimony, present Henry Chiles & George Cleveland, Commissioners, on the Lands claimed by the Heirs of Timothy Peyton, Deceased, on a preemption of one thousand acres, and at his Spring, John Crittenten, of Full age, appeared and being first Sworn, Deposeth and Saith that he is now Standing at the heads of the Spring, to the Best of his knowledge, that this Deponant Improved for Said Peyton In the years 1775 & 1776.

Question by James Matson: Is this the only Improvement you made for Timothy
       Payton In this country?
Answer: It is, and I know of no other he claimed In the Country.

Question By Same: Did not you lay in a claim for Timothy Peyton with the
       Commissioners and obtained a certificate for the above Described place?
Answer: I did to the best of my knowledge, and further this Deponant Saith not.

[signed] John Crittenden
attested Henry Chiles, George Cleveland

       We the Commissioners have marked an oak Standing about forty eight
feet above the head of the Spring, thus, C, also an Elm Near the Spring house a
Small Distance below the head of the Spring, thus, H, this 17th October 1803.
Henry Chiles
George Cleaveland

84.

David Williams for Moses Kuykendall

Moses Kuykendall

Moses Kuykendall hailed from Hampshire County, Virginia (now West Virginia). During the French and Indian War, his family built Kuykendall's Fort on the South Branch of the Potomac, about 7 miles south of Romney. Moses Kuykendall came to Kentucky and established Kuykendall's Station near Louisville in about 1782. "Kirkindol's Mill," shown on John Filson's 1784 map, was on the south fork of Beargrass Creek, and may have been located at the station. Moses is found until at least 1807 in the records of Jefferson County, where he served as sheriff and captain of the militia.[400]
Kuykendall entered 1000 acres in Fayette County on a treasury warrant in 1780. William Triplett surveyed the tract in 1783, and it was granted to Kuykendall in 1785. The tract was located on Stoner Creek, adjoining "Gists first survey of 3000 acres." In 1795, Moses and Elizabeth Kuykendall sold 100 acres of this tract to William Sudduth.[401]

David Williams

David Williams was a surveyor in Madison County who testified in numerous land cases. In 1796, he was living, about 4 miles from the mouth of Tates Creek, when he placed a notice regarding a runaway slave. In an 1808 deposition, Williams stated he came to Kentucky in 1774 with James Harrod and helped build cabins at Harrodsburg. In 1775, he accompanied James Douglass surveying on Stoner Creek. Williams had one of the earliest claims on Stoner, where he built an improvers cabin in 1775.[402]

Deposition of David Williams [321]

       Pursuant to an order to us directed from the County Court of Clarke
County as Commissioners to take Depositions to Establish the calls and boundries
of an Entry and Survey of 1000 acres in the name of Moses Kaykendall, being
conveined at the North East corner of said survey & it appearing to us that the
same had been duly advertised in Bradfords Kentucky Gazette on the following

days, June the 22nd, July the 5th & 12th.

Also it was duly proven that notice of our meeting for the purpose afforesaid was delivered to Hugh Forbes, Cornelus Skinner & Jesse Copher on the 18th day of July 1803. Also Robert Boggs acknowledged a notice to have been given him in due time.

We then caused, David Williams, aged fifty two years, to come before us, who after being sworn, deposeth and saith that in the summer of the year 1775, he was in company with James Douglas and others when Douglas made a Survey of Nathaniel Gists, Beginning on a Ridge which leads down to Bramletts lick, about three quarters of a mile from the said lick, from whence we proceeded South 70 degrees West 400 poles and cornered, thence continuing the same course 400 poles and made onother corner, thence continuing the same course 400 poles, we made another Corner, thence North 20 degrees West 400 poles and cornered, thence North 70 degrees East 1200 poles, cornering as before at every four hundred poles.

Question by William Sudduth: By what name was the Creek now called Stoner then known?
Answer: We called it Gists Creek.

Question By Same: Is this the first survey you made for Gist as discribed in your Deposition of this creek that is Stoner?
Answer: It was the first Military Survey we made for Nathaniel Gist.

Question By the same: At the time you were in Company with Douglass that he made the above Survey for Gist, did he survey any Lands adjoining said Gists Survey for John Soverns?
Answer: He did make a private survey for John Soverns for 1000 acres.

Question by same: On what part of the lines of said Gists survey did the survey of John Soverns adjoin?
Answer: It Began South 70 degrees West 400 poles from Gists Beginning corner and adjoined Gist 400 poles South 70 degrees West from Soverns beginning corner and then at right angles South 20 degrees East 400 poles for quantity.

Question: Do you believe the place we now are at is at or near the Beginning corner of Soverns Private Survey?
Answer: I do.

Question by same: Was the lines of Soverns out from Gists Survey actuly run & corners made?
Answer: The South East corner was actuly made, but as to the other I am not certain.

Question by Robert Boggs: Did you not make a survey for Gist on this Creek before you made this one described in your Deposition?

Answer: We did make a survey before we made this, which I am not certain was for Gist, which if it was, as I rather incline to think it was, he Rejected it & made no use of it.

Question By William Sudduth: Did you make any private survey for John Soverns adjoining Gist but this [one]?

Answer: Not that I remember.

Question by William Sudduth: Did you make any other private Survey adjoining Gist on this line, that is to say, the line running South 70 degrees West from the Beginning?

Answer: We did make one for Ebeneazer Soverns Beginning at Gists Beginning and running South 70 degrees West 400 poles to John Soverns corner & out at right angles for quantity South 20 degrees East.

Question by Robert Boggs: Was not the 6000 acres of Land Surveyed on this creek surveyed for Gist?

Answer: It was made for Gist.

Question by William Sudduth: Was not that 6000 acres Surveyed in two diferent and distinct Surveys?

Answer: They were.

Question by the commissioners: Are you any ways interested in the establishing any of the above mentioned claims?

Answer: Not that I know of, further this Deponent saith not.

[signed] David Williams
attested Thomas Pickett, John Donnoldson, Commissioners.

We the subscribers, disinterested persons, do certify that we were present at taking the within depositions & se[e] William Sudduth mark a redbud and ash as a corner. Given under our hands this 5th Day of August 1803.
James Sudduth
John McCreery

Clarke County, To wit,
We the subscribing commissioner do certify that the within depositions was taken, sworn to & subscribed to before us at the place shown to us as the North East corner of Moses Kuykendalls 1000 acres survey on this 5th day of August 1803.
Thomas Pickett
John Donnoldson

85.

Patrick Jordan and Elias Tolin for William Farrow

William Farrow

This procession is for William Farrow's 1000-acre preemption and the adjoining 1000-acre preemption surveyed and granted to the heirs of Thornton Farrow, both of which were previously processioned, in September 1796 (#34 and #35).

Deposition of Patrick Jordan [325]

The Deposition of Patrick Jourden taken for the purpose of perpetuating Testimony to establish the calls of an entry of 1000 acres on preemption Warrant in the name of William Farrow on Buck lick Creek, now called Grassey lick, who after being sworn, deposeth and saith that he came here in the year 1775 & fell in Company with George Rogers Clarke, John Cridenton, Thornton Farrow & other at the lick now called Grassey lick, where the afforesaid Company made an improvement by Deadning timber, marking trees & making a cabin where they encamped that night & the next day came to this place & made an improvement by marking trees & building a cabin, which improvement at this place, Thornton Farrow informed this deponant, was made for his Brother William Farrow.

And this deponent further Saith that there was a man in Company with Clarke, Farrow & others in the year 1775 at this place by the name of Guy that this deponant thought was a servant belonging to some of the Company, but was informed by said Guy that he was a hireling, came to this country for the purpose of improving lands for William Farrow of Virginia & the said Guy made application to this deponent to get leave of Thornton Farrow to let said Guy make an improvement for himself, which said Thornton refused & said he was a hirling for his Brother & that what he could do was for his Brother & the said Guy further informed this Deponant that this improvement was for his master, who had hired him.

Question by William Janes for Theodius Duling: How many improvements were made within the bounds of this claim by that Company that is William Farrows premption?
Answer: I know of none but the two mentioned in my Deposition.

Question by same: When did you fall in with that Company & how long was you with them?
Answer: I came to them at the grassey lick & in the summer 1775 [and] staid with them that day & night & the next day came with them to this place, see them make this improvement & left them and did not go any further up the creek with them.

Question by same: Was this improvement Generally known to be William Farrows at the time the claim was laid in with the commissioners?
Answer: I do not know.

Question By William Fleming: Are you looser or gainer by the determnation of
        this Claim of William Farrows with the claims it interfers with?
Answer: I am neither loosser or gainer that I know.

Question by same: Was you at that time well Acquainted with Crindenton &
        Clarke & frequently conversed with them at the time this improvement
        was made?
Answer: Yes I did & further this Deponant saith not.

[signed] Patrick Jourden his mark
attested Elias Tolin, George Yocum

Then adjourned till tomorrow 11 oclock.

Deposition of Elias Tolin [328]

We the commissioners having met agreeable to adjournment, proceeded to
take the Deposition of Elias Tolin, who after being sworn, deposeth & saith that
on the 23rd of July in the year 1775, this deponant Joined the Company with
William Lyn, Thomas Clarke, Andrew Lyn, Thomas Brazer & John Crittenden at
Wheelon [Wheeling] Fort to come to Kentucky to improve or take up land & on
the Ohio near the mouth of little Kanoway, [we] was overtaken by Thornton
Farrow, Luke Cannon & William Bennett & others who informed us they were
coming to Kentucky to take up land for themselves and some gentlemen in
Virginia & they informed Us that the hands they had under their directions were
sent by those Gentlemen in Virginia as Assistance in taking up land for those
Gentlemen in Virginia & we proceeded on in company to the mouth of Kentucky
[River] where Cannon & Bennet and their hands parted with us & proceeded
down the River Ohio.

Thornton Farrow & a man of the name of Guy, who appeared to be a
servant under said Thornton Farrow, Joined us & we proceeded up the Kentucky
River to Leestown [near Frankfort], at which place George Rogers Clarke Joined
our Company & [we] proceeded to Boonsburough, from thence out to summersett
[Creek] & encamped at or near a place now known Soverns lick. And while in
that Camp, at the absence of Thornton Farrow, some of the Company was Joking
the man by the name of Guy about his master, eluding to Thornton Farrow, to
which he Replyed, Thornton Farrow was not his master & that if the man who had
employed him (mentioning Thornton Farrows Brother) had of come out, he would
not of been treeted with that indeference he now was.

And in the time while we lay at that Camp, Thornton Farrow, John
Cridenton & George Rogers Clarke was absent From the Camp some few days &
when they returned, they informed [us] they had been making improvements
while they were absent.

The next morning this deponant went down Summersett Buffalo hunting
& got lost from the Company & wandered down on the Creek now called Grassy
lick & joined a Camp near the bank of the Creek & no person at Camp & this
deponant followed a trail from Said Camp up the Creek & came to the lick Called

Buck lick, now Grassey lick & there discovered a small cabin Built & some trees lett[er]ed & the initial letters of Thornton Farrows name cut on a tree & proceeded from thence up the Creek until the trail quit the Creek & Turned over to Summersett to the Camp.

And a few days after we concluded to divide the company, then John Cridenton, George Rogers Clarke, Thornton Farrow, the man by name of Guy & a man by the name of Paul formed one Company & William Lyn, Andrew Lyn, Thomas Clark, Thomas Brazer & this Deponant formed the other Company. And about the time of parting, the two Companys Concluded to meet again at an appointed time about 3 weeks After, at or near the forks of Summersett & Buck lick, in order to travel to Boonsburrough together & at the time appointed, the Company with the deponent came to the appointed place & found a written Paper fastened to a Buckeye informing us that the Company of Farrow & Cridenton was under necessaty of going to Boonsburrough before the appointed time, by reason of one of their company being badly scalded.

We then proceeded to go to Boonsbourrough on their trail & came up Buck Creek, now called Grassey lick Creek & founds improvements above the lick above mentioned, one at the mouth of a branch known by the Company by the name of doe lick, which is at the fork of the Creek. A small distance below here, we continued to this place & found an improvement at this place & in continuing up said Creek we see another improvement, which this Deponant thinks was about a quarter of a mile above this place, all which improvements from the marks, thus, F, we supposed to be made by Cridenton, Farrow & their Company & before we left Boonsburrough, it was agreed on by John Floyd (who was then engaged in making military Surveys) & our Company that we should be particular in making our marks, that we might not interfere with each other.

And this deponant further saith that after discovering the improvements supposed to be about a quarter of a mile above this place, the trail of the other Company bore over South to the old trail, which we had come from Boonsborrough to Summerset, we passed thro the Sassafras Grove near the head of the West Fork of summersett, but never fell in with the Company of Cridenton & others any more. [And] when we went to Boonsburrough, they had went to Harrodsburgh.

Question By William Farrow [Jr.], attorney for William Farrow: Do you know of any improvements made by any person on this creek higher up than those you have mentioned [and] marked with the marks of those you have described?
Answer: I have since I have come to live in this county seen one above, but never discovered any other marks but an aintient deadning, but do not know who it was made for by, nor when it was made. I have lived in this country about eleven years.

Question By William Janes: Do you know if Guy was with this company when these improvements was made?
Answer: No.

Question by same: Do you know of your certain knowledge by whom these improvements was made & for whose Bennefit they were made?

Answer: No.

Question By same: When you left the improvement about a quarter of a mile above this place, did the trail you pursued lead near the improvement you last mentioned & that you did not know who it was made for or by, that is the one you have discribed since you came to this Country to live?

Answer: I think the trail we pursued left that improvement about three quarters of a mile to the right.

Question by same: Do you know these improvements you mentioned on this creek were made by that Company on their rout to boonsborrough or where they made previous to that time?

Answer: I do not know, as there was three weeks space between our parting & my seeing these uper improvements.

Question By William Farrow, attorney for William Farrow: Have you not reason to believe from the information you received that those improvements were made by Thornton Farrow & company except the uper one you say you did not at that time see & that Guy was in Company with Farrow & Company at the time said improvements were made?

Answer: The improvements, I believe from the marks, were made by Thornton Farrow & Company, likewise that Guy was in Company (as he left our Company) with Farrow & Company & was no woods man & I never understood that the Company parted before the[y] went to Boonsburough.

Question By William Fleming: Does the uper improvement you mention as lat[e]ly found by you appear as old as those lower ones & did you not know of a number of improvements made by lett[er]ing trees & Deadning timber?

Answer: The deadening looks as old & [I] believe there was a number of improvements made by deadening trees.

Question by same: At the time you suppose those Improvements were made, do you know that there was a man by the name of Patrick Jourden with them, or did you hear Farrow & Company mention any thing about such a man being with them at any time?

Answer: No.

Question by William Janes: Do you think that John Soverns improvement at Soverns lick was made the same day that these you suppose were made by Thornton Farrow & Company?

Answer: No, I believe they were not made on the same day, as when the whole of us came from Boonsborrough to Soverns lick, we found Soverns improvement already made & none of our Company had parted or turned out to make improvements [at] that time.

Question By William Farrow, attorney for William Farrow: Was it a Rule with yours & Farrows Companys to make letters at each improvement you made?
Answer: It was & if we happened to omit it, we sent back & had it done (that is our Company). I never see Farrows Company make but one improvement & John Cridenton made letters at that [*left blank*].

Question By William Fleming: Would not you, from the letters made on those trees at the different improvements on this creek, believe the improvements to be made for the use of Thornton Farrow?
Answer: I never heard him say that he marked any other mans names but his own & I understood from our first meeting that it was a partnership Business.

Question by same: Was it a custom with the Companys that improved for one Man to set or mark the initial letters of his name as claiming that improvement?
Answer: As we worked in partnership, it was not material which man marked. But what was the general rule with Thornton Farrow after the company divided, I do not know.

Question by same: What was the general rule to distinguish which improvement was made for each Man of a company?
Answer: The rule of the company I was immediately concerned with was to make As many improvements as we intended to make, and then lott for them. I did not know what Thornton Farrow and companys rule was in dividing improvements.

Question By William Farrow: Did you ever hear Guy Talk of making any improvements for himself?
Answer: I never did hear him talk of making any improvements for himself, or of claiming the privilege of so doing.

Question By William Fleming: Did you ever hear Guy say that he came to make improvements for William Farrow?
Answer: I never heard Guy mention William Farrows name. I heard him say he was employed by Thornton Farrows brother & further this deponant saith not.

[signed] Elias Tolin
attested George Yocum, James Wren

We the Subscibers, commissioners appointed by the County Court of Clarke at their July term 1796 for the purpose of taking depositions to perpetuate

Testimony to establish the calls and Boundries of a preemption in the name of Thornton Farrow & a preemption of 1000 acres granted in the name of William Farrow & James French settlements and preemtion.

We having met on the 20th of December 1803 at an improvement claimed by William Farrow as the one called for in said Farrows Preemption, which is about 200 yards above William Farrows horse mill & at a spring coming out at the foot of a hill, near where said Farrow formerly lived, where we marked a red oak & sicamore with the letters WH each. Near said tree stands a white Oak marked in two places, thus, F, and a sugar tree marked the same near said white Oak & it appearing to said Commissioners that the time of taking said depositions was duly advertised in Bradford Kentucky Gazzettee on the following days, to wit, November the 29th 1803, December the 6th 1803 & December the 13th 1803.

And we the said Commissioners, being first duly sworn, proceeded on the said 20th Day of December 1803 to take the deposition of Patrick Jourden as hereunto anexed & then adjourned until the 21st day of December in the year afforesaid & having met agreeable to adjournment, we proceeded to take the Deposition of Elias Tolin, which is also hereunto anexed, which said Deposition were taken at the improvement afforesaid & in the presence of the Witnesses to said Depositions Subscribed. Given under our hands & seals this 21st day of December 1803.
William Sudduth
Henry Chiles, Commissioners

86.

Samuel Estill and Joseph Barnett for Alexander Barnett

Alexander Barnett

Alexander Barnett was born in 1754 in Culpeper County, Virginia. He was trained as a physician and served as a surgeon with the Virginia Regiment during the Revolutionary War. After the war, he moved his family to Bourbon County, Kentucky.[403] The following was taken from an 1817 deposition:

> Alexander Barnett, aged 61 years, states about the year 1789 he settled where he resides.[404]

He was one of the trustees of the Bourbon Academy, incorporated in 1798. Barnett died in 1826:

> Alexander Barnett, of Bourbon county. A native of Virginia and a soldier of the Revolution. Died October, 1826, aged 72 years.[405]

His will named wife Dorcas; son John; daughter Elizabeth Brown; Agnes Gilkey, wife of deseased son William; Martha Ward, wife of deceased son Robert; and several grandchildren.[406]

Barnett entered 500 acres on a treasury warrant 1783 and had the tract surveyed by William Orear in 1798; Barnett was the pilot and marker. He received a patent in 1799. The land was described as being on the north side of the Kentucky River several miles below the mouth of Drowning Creek, which places the tract about 10 miles northwest of Irvine in present-day Estill County. The year after receiving the patent, Alexander Barnett of Bourbon County sold the entire tract to John Alexander of Clark.[407]

Samuel Estill

Samuel Estill (1755-1837) was born in Augusta County, Virginia. His older brother, Capt. James Estill, was killed at Estill's Defeat near Mt. Sterling in 1782. Samuel came to Boonesborough, and in 1780 he and his brother James established Estill's Station 3 miles southeast of present-day Richmond. He had a long military career and served in numerous campaigns. In 1795, he was appointed lieutenant colonel commanding the 19th regiment of Madison County. He was a county judge and member of the Kentucky legislature. In 1816, the county ordered his portrait painted, which was hung in the courthouse. He was reported to stand 6 feet 2 inches and weighed over 400 pounds. Estill received a Revolutionary War pension and died in Roane County, Tennessee, in 1837.[408]

Joseph Barnett

Joseph Barnett was a deputy surveyor of Madison County, 1798-1822. He claims in his deposition below that he surveyed the tract for Alexander Barnett. Since William Orear's survey was the one filed with the land office, the purpose of this survey is unknown.[409]

Deposition of Samuel Estill [340]

In Obedience to an order of the County Court of Clarke at their March term 1803, Agreeable to an act of Assembly for the purpose of perpetuating testimony & we the undernamed Subscribers, being appointed Commissioners by said Court to attend to take depositions to establish the special calls of an Entry of 500 acres made in the name of Alexander Barnett on the North side of Kentucky river, about two miles & a half below the mouth of drownding Creek, Beginning twenty poles above the mouth of a branch whereon Stands a Honey Locust Marked AB, and to run down the river for quantity, having met agreeable to a Notice given to Achilles Eubank, agent for Richard Graham, an interfering Claimant, at the house of John Alexander on the said Land & from thence having proceeded to the Honey Locust called for in said Entry.

There having caused Samuel Estill, of Lawful age, to come before us, who being duly sworn, deposeth and saith that in the latter part of the year 1782 or the Beginning of the year 1783, I was in company with Joseph Long at this place where we encamped all night, and he marked this Honey Locust with AB, as now appears, and said he intended entering this Land for Alexander Barnett. And accordingly he went on to the [land] office, and took some papers of mine to enter for me, and informed me after he returned that he had entered this same Land for Alexander Barnett.

Question by the Commissioner: Do you consider yourself interested in any manner in this claim?
Answer: No, nor never was.

Question: Is there any other objects which you discover here beside This Honey locust that convinces you that this is the place?
Answer: Yes, the branch I seem to know, also an old Buffaloa path that crossed at this place which I can now discover, and also a Rocky or stony place in the branch which we drank at while we was encamped at this place, [and] this deponent further saith not.

[signed] Samuel Estill

Deposition of Joseph Barnett [341]

And also the Deposition of Joseph Barnett, who being of lawful age, taken at the same time and place, deposeth and saith that Joseph Long brought me to this place and shewed me this Honey Locust tree, and said it was the tree he had marked which was called for in an entry of five hundred acres in the name of Alexander Barnett, and I afterwards proceed[ed] and made the survey.

Question by Commissioner: Did he express any doubts of this being the tree he had marked?
Answer: No, he appeared to be confident of it, and appeared to have no difficulty in finding of it, and this deponent further saith [not].

[signed] Joseph Barnett

The above deposition taken and sworn to before us in the presence of James Moore and James Ashcraft, two disinterested persons. Given under our hands and seals this 28th day of August 1804.
George Sharp
Stephen Collins

87.

Josiah Collins, Aquilla White and Benjamin Dunaway for Stephen Collins

---

Stephen Collins

Willard Rouse Jillson credits Stephen Collins with erecting the first iron forge in Kentucky at his claim on Red River in the year 1787. While Jillson's claims for such an early forge cannot be substantiated, Collins' 500-acre tract, processioned below, was later the site where the Red River Ironworks was built by Robert Clark Jr. and William Smith.[410]

Collins' claim was entered at the Kentucky land office on December 3, 1782. The tract was surveyed by John McKinney on February 17, 1785; Stephen Collins was marker, Josiah "Sigh" Collins and Alexander McClain, chain carriers. A patent issued to Stephen Collins on August 20, 1786. Collin's "upper tract" of 500 acres lay in the "great bend" of Red River and included much of present-day Clay City in Powell County.[411]

Aquilla White

The pioneer hunter and woodsman Aquilla White was at Boonesborough in 1779 and later resided in what would become Estill County. He was a Revolutionary War soldier, who served in the Pennsylvania Line. He applied for a pension in 1818 at age 73, while living in Montgomery County, Kentucky, and died in 1823.[412]

Fife Lick

An early salt lick in Joseph Collins' claim, located on Fife Lick Creek which flows into Red River from the north in the vicinity of Meadow's Golf Course in Clay City.

Beaver Ponds

Beaver Ponds was the first name for Stanton. The name was changed after Powell County was formed in 1852 to something "more fitting" for a county seat.

Deposition of Josiah Collins [342]

Agreeably to an order of the Court of Clarke County to us directed, we in obedience to the order of said Clarke have on this fifth day of October 1804 Met at the place as per Entrey, mentioned agreeable to order, and have proceeded to take the deposition of Josiah Collins, being of lawfull age, deposeth and Saith that on the 25th day of December 1782 this Deponant started from McGees Station in company with a certain Aquilla White to exspore the Lands on Red River between the *Fifee Lick* & the Big *Beaver Ponds*. Said White did Inform me prior to our starting, that from The Informmation of Colonel Daniel Boon, that the above mention Land was vacant, als[o] he the said White inform this Deponent that he the Said White had made an entry for Joel Collins for 400 acres to begin at the fifee lick near Said River, and he also informed this deponent that he had made an entry of 500 acres on said river for Steven Collins and wished to shew the Beginning of said entrys to some person, as he was much exposeed to the Indians by reason of being offen in the woods.

And on our rout we came into a p[l]ain Bufferlow Road near the Indians old fields, which Road he followed to a Creek, which Creek said White Informd me was called Copprass bank Creek, and a small distance below where we struck said Creek at a Copprass bank, we gearthed a small quantity of Copprass.

We continued on Said Road down said Creek to the bottom lands of red river and thru the bottom and crossed the river at this plain. And said White Informed this Deponant that this was the ford and place which he did intend for the Beginning of an entry, made by said White for Steven Collins entry of 500 acres on said red river, dated December the third 1782.

And further said White did inform this deponant that should any accident happen so that he could not be at the directing of said survey, he this deponant must direct said Survey from this place, for it is the Beginning of said Collins entry as within mentioned.

And also this deponant further saith that, agreeable to what said White told this deponant, he this deponant did direct the survey agreeable as it is made from said place.

Question: Are you directly or indirectly Interested in this within mentioned
    Clame?
Answer: I am not, nor never was.

Question by same: Is the Creek which you at that time called Copprass bank
    Creek is that the said Creek which is at this day Called Brush Creek?
Answer: Yes, the same Creek.

Question by same: Did it appear from any part of said Whites conduct or any
    exspression that may have drapt from Said White, relative to said ford and
    place, wheather that was or was not the place during the hole of your rout?
Answer: I did at [that] day and from that to this day do believe there was not a
    doubt in said White[s] mind relative to that being the place particular.

Question by same: Was there any Buffalow road between the mouth of Copprass
        bank Creek and said ford, above mentioned, at that day?
Answer: I am confident there was not.

Question by same: Was the said Creek that was at that day called Copprass bank
        Creek known generally at that day by that name?
Answer: I knew it by no other till lately, and frequently heard it called so by
        numbers.

Question by same: On what day did said White shew you the ford & place of
        Beginning of said Steven Collins entry of 500 on said red river?
Answer: On the 26th day of December 1782.

Question by same: Has that ford as mentioned in said entry become a place of
        notiriety from that time?
Answer: With me and others I know it has.

[signed] Josiah Collins

Clark County Sct.
      This is to certify that this day Josiah Collins made oath to the above
deposition as being Just and true. Given under our hands this 5th October 1804.
Robert Clark Jr.
George Sharp
attested John Alexander, Josiah Collins Jr., William Formans, James Collins,
Alexander Collins

Deposition of Aquillia White [346]

      Agreeable to an Order of the Court of Clarke County to us Directed, we
have Proceeded to take the Deposition of Aquillia White, of Being of Lawfull
age, Deposeth and saith in the month of August 1781, this Deponant Started in
Company with Benjamin Donaway, Richard Piles, John Clemmons and Isaac
Clinkenbeard up the Kentucky River in order to make Salt Petree and Hunt on our
rout. We fell in at the Lulbergrud Old fields, now caled the Indian Old Fields, at
the said Place we came into a Buffalow Road, which Road led us to a Creek of
Red [River], and a little below where said Road Struck said creek we came to a
Copprass bank on said Creek, for which caused me to call said Creek from that
day Copprass bank Creek.
      Then following said Road down said Creek to the Botto[m] land of Red
River, the said Road leading near the foot of a nob. Following said road and
Crossing the river at this place, which Road we followed thru the Botto[m], and
this place, where we now Stand at this Identical ford on said River, is the Place I
made an Entry for Steven Collins for 500 on the 3rd day of December 1782.
      This Deponant saith that he took a Certain Josiah Collins and shewed him
this Place and Ford on the 26 day of December 1782, and told said Collins that

should any thing happen to him so that he should not be able [to] shew the Beginning of said Entry, that this Ford & Place was the Beginning of the above entry of said Collins & he must Direct it accordingley.

Question: Are you Interested either direcly or indirecly in the shewing of said Ford, Place or Entry?
Answer: I am not, nor never was.

Question by same: Was this Copprass bank as mentioned bin called and know[n] by the name of the Copprass bank Creek at that Day Genreally?
Answer: It was.

Question by same: Is this Ford, as caled for in the within Entry, a Place at that and since being a place of noteriety?
Answer: It was & is.

Question by same: Do you Know of any ford between this place & the mouth Copprass bank Creek at this day?
Answer: I do not, and am confident there is non to this day.

[signed] Aquila White

Deposition of Benjamin Dunaway [348]

Agreeable the an Order of the Court of Clarke County to us Directed, we have Proceeded to take the Deposition of Benjamin Donaway, being of lawfull age, Deposth and saith that in the month of August 1781 this Deponant in Company with Aquillia White, Richard Piles, John Clemons & Isaac Clikenbeard, this Deponant came in Company on a Plain Buffelow Road till it struck a Creek a branch of Red River a Small Distance above a Copprass bank on said Creek, and said Creek was caled Copprass bank Creek at that time & have long since be caled so, and is caled so to this day by a number of Persons.

And this Deponant further saith that he dus really beleave that this is the same Identically the same Ford and Place Mentioned by Aquillia White, as I am Confident we crossed the river at this Ford & Place on our Rout up the Kentucky.
[signed] Benjamin Dunaway

Clark County Sct.
This is to certify that the within Deposition was sworn to before us the Subscribing Justice this 5 day of October 1804.
Robert Clark Jr.
George Sharp
attested William Forman, Josiah Collins Jr., James Collins, Alexander Collins, John Alexander

88.

Samuel Boone Sr., James Patton, Peter Scholl and Abraham Scholl for Robert Boggs

Robert Boggs

Robert Boggs (1746-1825) was born in New Castle County, Delaware. He came to Kentucky as a chainman with John Floyd's surveying crew in 1774, helped build Fort Boonesborough in 1775, and later settled a few miles from Boone Creek in Fayette County. He married Sarah McCreary Huston in Greenbrier County, Virginia in 1782. Boggs' historic stone house—Cave Spring—in Fayette County, begun in the year 1792, still stands near the Athens-Walnut Hill Road. Boggs Fork, a tributary of Boone Creek, was named for him.[413]

Boggs claimed a 1000-acre tract on Stoner Creek on a preemption warrant entered in January 1783. Daniel Boone surveyed the tract in August 1783; Peter Scholl and Samuel Shortridge were chainmen, Robert Boggs was the marker. Boggs received a patent from the governor of Virginia in 1785. This land is about 5½ miles northeast of Winchester in Clark County. Boggs and his wife Sarah sold off portions of the tract at various times to Elias Myers, James Patton, Martin Judy and Jesse Copher.[414]

Samuel Boone Sr.

Samuel was Daniel Boone's brother. Samuel's Quaker wife, Sarah Day, is said to have taught Daniel "to read, spell, and write a little." Samuel was born in 1728 in Berks County, Pennsylvania, and moved to the Yadkin River in North Carolina with his parents in 1750. In 1779, he came to Kentucky with a number of other Boone and Bryan relatives. He settled at Boone's Station near Athens. Samuel died near there in about 1816; his wife Sarah died about three years later.[415]

James Patton

James Patton was awarded a 400-acre settlement on Slate Creek for making "an actual settlement in the year 1778. Patton served as a company commander in Gen. George Rogers Clark's campaigns of 1780 and 1782. He was at Boonesborough for a time and was listed as a taxpayer in Clark County beginning in 1793, the year the county was formed. He lived on Stoner Creek, in what is now the Wades Mill area. Patton died in Clark County in 1823. His will listed wife Elizabeth, son Mathew, deceased, son John, and daughter Polly Halley.[416]

Deposition of Samuel Boone Sr. [349]

The Deposition of Samuel Boone Sr., of Lawfull age, taken to establish the calls and corners of a Survey of 1000 acres in the name of Robert Boggs on Stoners fork of Licking at a high yellow bank, previous Legal notice being given in Bradfords Kentucky Gazette of September 13th & who after being sworn, deposeph and saith.

Question by Robert Boggs: How old are you?
Answer: 78.

Question by same: Is this the place Daniel Boone shewed for the High Yellow Bank noted in Boggs Entry, and the place he Began a survey of 1000 Acres made in the name of Robert Boggs?
Answer: I think it to be the place. I was at this place when Daniel Boone made the survey & [it] began within 20 yards of this place or Less. I stayed at

this place & Kept camp on that day and marked a large White Oak, near the bank of the creek & near this place, with the words "Surveyed for Robert Boggs" and the date of the year. And further saith that he Blased the said Tree and wrote on it with Gun powder the words aforesaid.

Question by William Sudduth: Did you see any of the corners of Boggs Survey marked?
Answer: No, I did not go to either of the Corners & further saith not.

[signed] Samuel Boone

Deposition of James Patton [350]

Also the Deposition of James Patton, of Lawful age, who after being sworn, deposeph and saith that he recollects that a large white oak stood in the bank of the Creek near this place and that it had been blased, and has since fell down and [been] taken off by the Creek & further saith not.
[signed] James Patton

The foregoing Depositions was taken on the bank of Stoner at the Ford near Robert Scobys Hay House on the 10th day of October 1805 & adjourned untill the 11th day of October, Met Pursuant to adjournment.

Deposition of Peter Scholl [351]

The Deposition of Peter Scholl, aged 50 years, taken at a high yellow bank on Stoner near Robert Scobys Hay House, who after being sworn, saith that he was in company with Colonel Daniel Boone when he made Robert Boggs Survey of 1000 acres and carried the chain and began at this place, which Colonel Boone said was the place alluded to in Boggs Entry.

Question by Robert Boggs: Who was in company with you when you was at this place & carried the chain after Colonel Boone?
Answer: William Hays, Samuel Boone, Samuel Shortridge, Achilles Morriss, Israel Grant, Abraham Scholl, William Scholl, Robert Boggs and myself. We left Samuel Boone at this place to keep camp, and when we returned he had taken the bark Off of a Tree and had wrote black Letters with powder on it.

We next proceeded from this place North one Hundred and Sixty poles to a large water Oak Stump, Sworn to by this deponant, which he believes to have been the North East Corner of Robert Boggs Survey of 1000 Acres, which was marked by Daniel Boone when he made the Survey. We then proceeded to a red oak and honey Locust, sworn to by this deponant, to be marked by Daniel Boone for the North West Corner of Robert Boggs survey of 1000 acres & further Saith not.
[signed] Peter Scholl

Deposition of Abraham Scholl [352]

      Also the Deposition of Abraham Scholl, age 41, who after being sworn, deposeth and saith that he was at this high yellow bank near Robert Scobys Hay house in Company with Colonel Daniel Boone, William Hays, Samuel Boone, Samuel Shortridge, Achilles Morriss, Israel Grant, Peter Scholl, William Scholl and myself, and carried the chain after William Hays when he assisted Colonel Daniel Boone to make Robert Boggs Survey of 1000 acres, and perfectly well recollects that the survey was began at this place, and that Colonel Boone said this was the place Alluded to in Boggs Entry of 1000 acres. And further saith that Samuel Boone Sr. was left at this place to keep camp, and when we returned, he had taken the bark off of a Tree and had wrote black letters with powder on it.

      We then proceeded to Two Cherry Trees Sworn to by this deponant, who saith that he was present when this was marked for the south East Corner of Robert Boggs Survey of 1000 acres marked by William Hays & further saith not. [signed] Abraham Scholl

      The Foregoing Depositions was taken in the presence of us the Subscribing Commissioners on the 10th & Eleventh days of October 1805 at that high yellow bank aforesaid and at the Different Corners aforesaid, being attended by William Sudduth, Benjamin Ely, Elias Myers, and Martin Judy Jr., Interfering Claimants. The South East Corner being in a state of decay, we marked a Buckeye & white oak, the North East Corner being cutt down, we marked a hickory & boxelder.
Benjamin J. Taul
Thomas Wornall

89.

Oswald Townsend, Joshua Stamper and William Clinkenbeard for Samuel Henderson

Samuel Henderson

      Samuel was the brother of Col. Richard Henderson, founder of the Transylvania Company. Samuel was born in Granville County, North Carolina, in 1746. He was with his brother at the Treaty of Watauga and the settling of Boonesborough in 1775. He was one of the party that rescued the Boone and Calloway girls after they were captured by the Shawnee in July 1776. Samuel, who was engaged to Betsy Calloway, was half shaved when the alarm sounded. He dropped his razor and hastened to join the rescuers. Samuel Henderson and Betsy Calloway were married on August 7, 1776, reported to be the first marriage in Kentucky. He returned to North Carolina, served in the battle of Guilford Courthouse, and attained the rank of major in the Revolutionary Army. In 1807, he moved to Tennessee, where he died in Warren County in 1816.[417]

      Samuel Henderson claimed a 400-acre settlement and 1000-acre preemption that he had marked in 1776. The land was described as "lying on the trace from Boonesborough to the lower Salt spring on licking Creek called the Sycamore Forest." The 400-acre settlement was surveyed by Joshua Bennett in December 1784, and the patent issued in 1787. The 1000-acre preemption was surveyed in January 1785, in four 250-acre tracts, and the patent issued in 1787. In 1807, Samuel Henderson was living in Franklin County, Tennessee, when he appointed James Clark of

Winchester as his attorney to handle the residue of his settlement and preemption. This land is situated on the Hancock and Johnson forks of Strodes Creek, about 5 miles northwest of Winchester.[418]

Henderson's land was later involved in a lawsuit in Fayette circuit court: *Mathew Patton and James Crocket vs Richardson Allen and Pamelia, his wife*. A map made for this suit shows the location of Henderson's settlement and preemption and Charles Tate's preemption.[419]

Matthew Patton

Matthew Patton (1728-1803) married Esther Dyer in Virginia and came to Kentucky in 1790 from the South Fork of the Potomac. He acquired part of Henderson's land claim for his home place. Patton took great interest in the scientific breeding of cattle. Patton purchased a bull (Mars) and a cow (Venus) that became legend in livestock history and sparked Kentucky's interest in shorthorn cattle. Patton died in 1803, leaving son James and son-in-law James Gay to carry on the breeding efforts he began.[420]

Matthew Patton Jr. inherited the home place from his father. Matthew Jr. had the land processioned in 1806 and placed a legal notice in the *Kentucky Gazette*. The side note by the depositions state the procession was "for Henderson by Patton."[421]

Oswald Townsend

Oswald Townsend was a Revolutionary War soldier, born in Granville County, North Carolina, in 1758. In the fall of 1775, he moved from Mecklenberg County, Virginia, to Madison County and settled at Boonesborough. Nathaniel Hart recalled him at Boonesborough:

> Oswell Towns [Opened an account at the fort] September 17, 1776. Lived in the fort. A rough, backwoods hunter. Son also a hunter, now living in Clay county, up the Kentucky. Son living in Estill County.[422]

Townsend applied for a pension in 1832 while living in Madison County and died there in 1835. He was reported to be the brother of James Townsend and uncle of Garrett Townsend, mentioned elsewhere in these Depositions.[423]

Sycamore Forest

The Sycamore Forest was a notable place name in pioneer times, being on the road from Boonesborough to Lower Blue Licks. From the depositions below we learn that the forest was situated on the ridge between Johnson Creek and Hancock Creek, near present-day Renick on Van Meter Road (KY 2888) in Clark County. The grove of sycamores was said to be about 200 yards wide and about ½ mile long.

Salt Spring Trace

One of the earliest trails in Kentucky, the Salt Spring Trace went from Boonesborough to the Lower Blue Licks, passing many landmarks along the way that are little known today. The trail went up Lower Howard Creek. Flanders Calloway's deposition stated that

> after passing the Indian Camp, the said Trace crossed the North fork of Howards Creek within one hundred Yards of the now dwelling house of Mr. William McMillan."[424]

The trail then ran north until reaching the ridge between Johnson Creek and Hancock Creek. There it turned east and passed through the Sycamore Forest, before crossing Strodes Creek, just across the Bourbon County line. The trail recrossed Strodes Creek ten more times (known as Many Crossings)—the last crossing of Strodes was called the Rocky Ford. The trail crossed Stoner Creek near the mouth of Strodes, turned east and passed by Harrod's Lick and Flat Lick, crossed Hinkston Creek above the mouth of Flat Lick Creek, then veered northeast to Lower Blue Licks. David Williams and others stated that they traveled this trail in 1776.[425]

Deposition of Oswald Townsend [355]

Pursuant to an Order to us directed from the County Court of Clarke

233

County as Commissioners to take depositions to Establish the Calls and bounderies of a Settlement & Premtion in the name of Samuel Henderson, February 3rd 1780. Samuel Henderson enters 400 acres by virtue of a Certificate & lying on the trace from Boonsborough to the Lower salt springs on Licking Cald the *Sycamore Forrest* and running Down the Creek for Quantity. 1780 June 23rd, Samuel Henderson enters 1000 acres on preemtion Lying on the trace from Boonsborough to the lower Salt Springs on Licking joining his Settlement at the Sycamore Forrest all around and to run Down the Crek for Quanty.

Being convened a[t] a honey locust, a marked tree in the sycamore forrest, and it appearing to us that the Same has been duly advertised in the Kentucky Gazett on the following day, April the 9th 1806 and April 16th 1806. Also it was proved that notice of our meeting for the purpose aforesaid was delivered to Joshua Baker on the ninth day of this present month. Thomas Kennedy also acknowledges notice, and it also appearing that Richardson Allen had notice on the 8th Instant, and Zedekiah South on the 9th Instant.

We then caused Oswald Townson, aged forty Eight, to come before us, who after being sworn, deposeth and saith That some time in the Summer 1776 or 1777 that the deponant was in Company with Richard Calloway, Samuel Henderson, Nathaniel Hart and Thomas Hardgrove.

On our Return from the Lower Salt Springs on Licking, we made a stop at the place then Cald the Sycamore Forris. At that time and place, this deponant Saw Samuel Henderson mark a tree on said trace to Boonsborough, and I have always known it Cald said Hendersons claim since.

Question by Matthew Patton: Do you believe the tree marked by Henderson was in or near the center of the Sycamore Forrest?
Answer: I think it was.

Question By same: Did the tree marked by Henderson Stand near the *Salt Spring trace*?
Answer: It did, within a few steps, I think within five.

Question By same: Did you ever know of any other place on Said trace that went by the name of the Sycamore forrest?
Answer: I did not.

Question by Thomas Kennedy: Is not the Sycamore forrest a large body of woods, and does not it extend from Hancocks fork to Johnson fork with the Salt spring trace running though it?
Answer: What I considered to be the sycamore forrest was the dividing ridge betwixt the two creeks.

Question by same: How wide do you suppose this dividing ridge to be Cald the sycamore forrest?
Answer: I suppose it to be about two hundred yards.

Question By Same: Which creek do you suppose was the creek intended to run down with Hendersons Entry?
Answer: I do not know.

Question By Mathew Patton: Do you believe that Hendersons entry fits the above described place?
Answer: I beleave it to be the place intended by Henderson. And further this deponant saith not.

[signed] Oswald Townson

Deposition of Joshua Stamper [358]

Also the Deposition of Joshua Stamper, aged fifty two, who being firs sworn, deposeth and saith that he has been acquainted with the Salt spring trace and the place Cald the Sycamore Forrest ever Since the winter 1780.

Question by Mathew Patton: Do you know that the trace from Boonsborough to the Lower Salt Springs runs throug the center, or nearly so, of the sycamore forrest?
Answer: I do suppose it was nearly through the Center.

Question By same: Do you know of any other place on said trace that bore the name of the Sycamore Forrest?
Answer: I do not.

Question by same: Was there not Sycamores on each side of the ridge, both on the waters of Hancok & Johnson?
Answer: There was.

Question by Thomas Kennedy: Was not the Sycamore forrest a large body of wood extending from Hancock fork to Johnsons fork with the Salt spring trace runing through it?
Answer: I conceived the dividing rid[g]e to be the sycamore forrest betwixt the two creeks.

Question By same: How wide do you conceive the distance to be when you first entered the sycamore forrest on one side before you left it on the other?
Answer: I think about half Mile the way the trace run.

Question By same: Which of the two Creeks, Hancock or Johnson, was intended for Hendersons Entry to run Down?
Answer: I do not know.

Question By Mathew Patton: Do you beliave that Hendersons entry fits the above Described place?
Answer: I think it does.

Question By same: How near did the Salt spring trace go to the marked Honey Locust, said to be marked by Henderson in the Sycamore forrest?
Answer: It went very near to it. And this deponant further saith not.

[signed] Joshua Stamper

Deposition of William Clinkenbeard [360]

Also the Deposition of William Clinkenbeard, aged about forty five, who being first sworn, deposeth and saith That he has been acquainted with the Salt Spring trace and the place Cald the Sycamore Forrest Ever since the winter of 1780.

Question By Mathew Patton: Do you know that the trace from Boonsborough to the lower Salt Springs run through the center (or nearly so) of the Sycamore forrest?
Answer: I beleave it did.

Question By Same: Do you know of any other place on said trace that bore the name of the Sycamore Forrest?
Answer: I do not.

Question by Same: Was there not sycamores on each side of the ridge, both on the waters of Hancock and Johnson?
Answer: There was.

Question By Thomas Kennedy: Was not the sycamore forrest a Large body of wood extending from Hancocks fork to Johnsons fork with the salt spring trace runing through it?
Answer: It was a large body of wood, but I do not think they extended to either.

Question By Thomas Kennedy: Which of the two Creeks, Hancock or Johnson, would you suppose was intended for Hendersons Entry to run Down?
Answer: I do not know.

Question By Mathew Patton: How near did the salt spring trace go to the marked Honey locust, said to be marked by Henderson in the Sycamore forrest?
Answer: It went close to the trace. And this deponant further Saith not.

[signed] William Clinkenbeard his mark

We the subscribers Commissioners Do certify that the foregoing Depositions was taken and subscribed this 25th day of April 1806.
John Donnoldson
John Bean
James Young, Commissioners

We also proceeded to plant a Stone marked SH at the aforesaid marked Honey locust, it being did in the presents of Joshua Stamper & William Clinkenbeard, disinterested persons. Given under our hands and seals the date above.

John Donnoldson
James Young
John Bean

90.

John J. Judy, Edward Wilson, William Clinkenbeard and Joshua Stamper for Mathias Sphar

This is the same tract of 500 acres previously processioned for Mathias Sphar in June 1796 (#29).

Taylor's Creek

Taylor's Creek or Taylor's Branch was an early name for a fork of Strodes Creek that was later called Woodruff Creek. May have been named first for John Taylor who had a 426-acre preemption at the mouth of the branch. The later name was probably for John Woodruff (also spelled Woodroff, Woodrough, etc.) who had a 400-acre preemption on the creek, joining Taylor's. Sphar's 500-acre claim, which joined Woodruff's, was also on the creek.[426]

Deposition of John Jacob Judy [362]

The Deposition of John J. Judy taken to perpetuate Testimony to establish the calls of an entry & survey m[a]de in the name of Mathias Sphar, which entry is in the following words, to wit, "June 16th 1780, Mathias Sphar, assignee of James Duncan, enters 500 acres upon a Treasury Warrant to include a white oak Marked MS Standing near *Taylor branch* of Licking about 2½ miles above Said Taylors Spring. [Judy] being aged 40 years and first duly sworn, Deposeth and saith that in the year 1782 this deponant was one who carried the chain when Mathias Sphars land was Surveyed, and that the begining of the Said Survey is at a large white Oak & Sugar tree, which begining I was this day at and shewed to the commissioners, and the said corner is still fresh in my memory.

I then went with the commissioners to the Second corner, which calls for 4 ash trees coming out of the same root, which trees are all down and some antient marks on them, which I believe to be the corner that we made when we made the Survey.

We then proceeded to the 3rd corner which the patent calls for, a forked white oak, and at the place that we supposed the corner ought to be, we found a forked white oak which is dead and down, and this deponant verily believes the said tree to be the corner or very near where the corner stood.

And this deponant then proceeded to the 4th corner, which is in cleared Land, and the laying of the Land is familiar to this deponant, and he believes that the place where the Commissioners fixed a stone is the place or very near where the corner stood.

We then proceed to the 5th corner, which is an elm, and this deponant believes the said tree to be the corner that was made when we made the Survey, for the Looks of the place and lying of the Land is still fresh in his memory.

We they proceeded to the 6th corner, which the patent calls for 2 elms, and this deponant cannot recollect the Said corner.

Question by Daniel Sphar: In the year 1780 was not the branch I now live on, And which runs through this Survey That we have been around this day, Called and Known by the name of *Taylors Creek*?
Answer: From my first acquaintance and until Several years after it was called Taylors Creek, but do not recollect which [name] I knew it as [in] early 1780, but I did in the year 1782.

Question by same: Did you know Taylors spring? And if you did, where is it?
Answer: Near the mouth of this creek is the spring called Taylors Spring, which creek was formerly called Taylors Creek, but [is] now known by the name of Woodruff.

Question by Richard Hawley [Halley]: Do you know the large white oak and Sugar tree that Stands near this branch to be the Begining of Mathias Sphars Survey of 500 acres, which trees we are at this day?
Answer: To the best of my knowledge they are the begining. And this deponant further saith not.

[signed] John J. Judy

Deposition of Edward Wilson [365]

Also the Deposition of Edward Wilson, aged Sixty eight years, and first sworn, deposeth and saith that in the year 1782 I was called on and made a Survey for Mathias Sphar, which begining is near a creek now called Woodruff, but at the time I made the Survey it was called Taylors Creek, which begining is on a large white Oak and sugar tree, which I shewed the commissioners this day.

And I went with them to the second corner, which was four ash trees coming from the same root, but said trees are now down and has ancient marks on them, which trees I believe I marked for the corner where I made the said survey.

We then proceeded to the th[i]rd, fourth and fifth corners, but this deponant recollects nothing about them. We then proceeded to the sixth corner, which is two elms marked and one of them dead and down, which trees I believe is the corner that I made when I made the survey, as the ground they stand on is fresh in my memory.

Question by Daniel Sphar: Was the Creek now Known by the name of Woodruff generally Known by the name of Taylors in the year 1782?
Answer: I believe it was.

Question by the same: Do you know Taylors spring? And if you do, where is it?
Answer: It is near the mouth of this branch which is now called Woodruff, but

formerly known by Taylors Creek. And further this deponant saith not.

[signed] Edward Wilson

Deposition of William Clinkenbeard [366]

Also the Deposition of William Clinkinbeard, aged forty five years, being first duly Sworn, deposeth and being interrogated.

Question By Daniel Sphar: Do you know Taylors Spring, and if you do, where is it?
Answer: It is near the mouth of this Creek, which is the Spring Colonel Donoldson now makes use of.

Question By the same: How early was you acquainted with the said spring?
Answer: In the fall 1779. And this deponant further saith not.

[signed] William Clinkenbeard his mark

Deposition of Joshua Stamper [367]

Also the Deposition of Joshua Stamper, age 53 years and first duly sworn, deposeth and Saith that from my first acquaintances in this country which was in the Winter 1780, I knew the creek that is now called Woodruff to be called and known by the name of Taylors Creek.

Question by Daniel Sphar: Do you know Taylors Springs, and if you do, where is it?
Answer: It is near the mouth of the creek now called Woodruff, and I have known the spring ever since the winter of 1780.

Question by same: Do you know if the corner that you was at this day with the commissioners, which is a large white oak & sugar tree and said to be the begining of Mathias Sphar Survey of 500 acres, is a corner of John Woodruffs Survey?
Answer: It is a corner made for John Woodruffs survey. And this deponent further saith not.

[signed] Joshua Stamper

Clarke County, to wit,
We the under named Subscribers, Commissioners appointed by the Honorable County Court of Clarke at their June Court 1807 to assertain the boundary and procession the Land &c of Daniel Sphar, which Land was entred & Survey in the name of Mathias Sphar, do certify that we this day met at the House of Daniel Sphar, and then went to the begining corner of said survey, which is a large white oak & sugar tree.
We then proceeded to the Second corner which his patent calls for, 4 ash

trees coming from the same root, and we found them all fell down and Some ancient marks on some of them, and we marked for a corner a Large black ash, Small Elm & white oak.

We then proceeded to the 3rd Corner, which the patent calls for a forked white oak, and we found a forked white oak which was dead laying down and much rotten, that we ancient marks on it, and at that place we fixed a stone for a corner.

We then proceeded to the fourth corner which the pattent calls for a forked Elm, and we had the course & Distance measured, which took us into a cleared field claimed by Mr. Richard Hawley [Halley], and we had the fourth line reversed and at this intersection of the 2 lines, we placed a Stone for a corner.

We then proceeded to the fifth corner, which the pattent calls for an elm, which we thought to be in a state of decay at which place we marked 2 sugar trees as corner trees.

We then proceeded to the sixth corner tree, which the patent calls for 2 Small Elms, and we found one of the Elms dead & down, but it had antient marks on it, at which place we marked a small Sugar tree & white hickery as corner trees.

And also certify that the foregoing Depositions of John J. Judy, Edward Wilson, William Clinkinbeard & Joshua Stamper was this day taken before us, and that the notices given by [Daniel] Sphar is filed with those Depositions, and that John Smith & Henery Smith are disinterested House Keepers who went around the said survey and Saw the corner trees marked. Given under our hands this 27th day of March 1807.
Thomas Pickett
John Dannoldson
Thomas Wornall

91.

Thomas Moore, Lawrence Harrison, Ambrose Coffee, Original Young, Robert McMillan, Thomas Burrus Sr. for Benjamin Harrison

Benjamin Harrison

Benjamin Harrison was born in southwest Pennsylvania at a time when that area was still considered to be part of Virginia. In 1776, Benjamin was commissioned a captain in the "West Augusta Volunteers," the 13th regiment of the Virginia Line. During that year, he found time to visit Kentucky for the purpose of locating land. He fought in the battles at Brandywine and Germantown in 1777. After the war, in about 1785, he settled in Bourbon County. His residence was located about 6 miles south of present-day Cynthiana. He served as one of the county's first justices, was the first sheriff and represented his county at the Kentucky convention in Danville in 1787 and again in 1788. In 1792, he was commissioned a brigadier-general in the Kentucky militia, and that same year he served as a representative to the Kentucky constitutional convention. In 1793, he was elected to the Kentucky legislature. The following year, Harrison County was formed from Bourbon and named after Benjamin Harrison. In 1801, Harrison removed to the Spanish Province of Louisiana. He died in Washington County, Missouri, in 1808.[427]

Harrison claimed a preemption for his 1000-acre improvement on a branch of Stoner made in the year 1776. As stated in the deposition below, Thomas Moore actually made the improvement. The tract was described by the land commissioners as

> lying at the head of the West fork of Licking Creek about 3 Miles from John Morgans Cabbin, on a branch [Little Stoner] which empties into the Creek about 1 quarter of a mile above the said Cabbins.[428]

The tract was surveyed by George Lewis in 1787; Lawrence Harrison and John Judy, chain carriers, Benjamin Harrison, pilot and marker. A patent issued to Harrison in 1789. This land is situated at the head Little Stoner Creek, between Ecton Road (KY 1960) and Ironworks Road (KY 15), about 4 miles east of Winchester. In 1800, Benjamin and his wife Mary sold 150 acres of his preemption to the heirs of Archibald Tanner. In 1839, Col. Thomas Hart had a 134-acre tract processioned that was patented by Harrison.[429]

Lawrence Harrison

Lawrence Harrison was Benjamin's brother. He lived near Benjamin and was a resident of Harrison County until 1800.

Original Young

Original Young was living in Fauquier County, Virginia, in 1793, when he purchased 750 acres on Stoner Creek that had been patented by William Eustace. Shortly thereafter Young moved to Clark County, where he appeared on the tax list for the first time in 1794. He was one of the justices of the court of quarter sessions. In 1810, Young's household consisted of him and his wife—both over 45 years old—and ten slaves[430]

Thomas Burrus

The parents of Thomas Burrus were Thomas Burrus Sr. (1720-1789) and Frances Tandy (c1731-1816). Thomas Jr. lived on Twomile Creek in Clark County, where he had several large patents. He was born in Orange County, Virginia, in 1757, married Elizabeth Stevens there in 1778, and died in 1836 leaving a will in Clark County. Six of his sisters married Kentucky pioneers: Fanny married John Embree, Mildred married Joseph Embree, Elizabeth married John Brockman, Sarah Ann married Rev. Andrew Tribble, Jane married Rev. James Quisenberry, and Frances married William Bush. These families were closely associated with Capt. Billy Bush's settlement and the Providence Baptist Church. Thomas gives additional biographical information in his deposition below.[431]

Garrett Townsend

Much information about Garrett Townsend comes from the depositions below. Thomas Burrus stated that Townsend was the first person he met when he arrived in Boonesborough in 1779 and that he frequently went out hunting with Townsend to provide meat for the fort. William Sudduth recalled that he lived with Townsend at Boonesborough in 1780 and that Townsend appeared to be 16 or 17 years old at the time.

Garrett Townsend is found in close association with James Townsend, who has been proposed as being his father. Both signed petitions to the Virginia General Assembly in 1787 to create a new county out of Fayette, Bourbon and Madison and another in 1789 to form a new county out of Fayette and Bourbon. Both appear on the tax list for Fayette County in 1787, 1788 and 1790, and for Clark County in 1793. Garrett reportedly married Elizabeth Hall.[432]

Pittman's Station

Pittman's Station was settled in the fall of 1779 or the spring of 1780. William Pittman's 500-acre entry on a treasury warrant in 1780 mentions the station, the land being situated "on pitmans creek, a branch of green river, including pitmans station about the center of the land." It was located close to the Green River, near the mouth of Pittman's Creek, about 5 miles below Greensburg in now Green County.[433]

Deposition of Thomas Moore [370]

Clarke County Sct. October 15th 1806

  We, Original Young & Joseph Miller, commissioners appinted by the county court aforesaid pursut to an act of assembly entitled an act for assertaining the boundries of an entry of Land of 1000 acres on a premtion warrent entred by Benjamin Harrison, now at two springs, the one on the one side of the said Branch & the other on the other sid and near a Large Hickrey near one of the said Spring[s], which we have caused to be marked with the Letter, thus, M, the said Springs & Hickroy now in a corn field called Wilmores.

  And have caused to come before us, Thomas Moor, a witness, which being first Sworn, Dep[o]seth & saith In the year 1776 Early in the spring, proverably in March, I proceeded Down the river Ohio in Company with Mr. John Morgan, Benjamin Harrison, Bets Coler [Collier], Keen & myself to the mouth of the Licking Creek, from thence proceeded up Licking Creek to the Fork, thence up the South fork to Hinksons station. There we rested a day or two, thence up this creek to Morgans cabin. There we stoped and emproved and made morgans cabin, as said.

  And after we had done that improvement, Benjamin Harrison and my self proceeded on up the same stream to a fork, and then took the rite hand fork. In order to improve, [we] went up to where the streem come up to this place & I myself made the emprovements for Benjamin Harrison by choping trees that was round about the spring and planting a number of Hills of corn.

  After making our improvements, [we] proceeded to return back to John Morgans cabin, then Benjamin Harrison, Keen & myself returned to Hinksons Station. And [we] left John Morgan and Collar at John Morgans Cabin, while we returned by Hinksons Station Home.

Question by Samuel Morton: By what athority did Benjamin Harrison obtain the certificate?
Answer: In consquence of his Emprovement mad by me in the year 1776, as I understood by General Harrison.

Question by James Stevens, agent for John Stevens: Whether did you & General Harrison make any other improvements beside this?
Answer: Yes.

Question by Same: Do you know that this improvement was aluded to in Harrisons Entery?
Answer: Yes.

Question by same: Do you no where Benjamin Harrisons Entry is?
Answer: Yes, this place where we are at now, these two Springs.

Question by same: Do you no where Benjamin Harrisons begining of his Entry that is called for in his Location?
Answer: I [know no] other than these Springs.

Question by Captain Benjamin Ashby: How many improvements did you make on these warters?

Answer: I assisted to make three, one for John Morgan, one for myself & one for Benjamin Harrison.

Question by same: Had Harrison any other Emprovements?

Answer: None as I know off.

Question by Same: If you had been requested to shown Benjamin Harrisons Emprovements Shortly after your return to Kentucky, wood you have shown the one we now are at in preferance to any other Emprovements made by Benjamin Harrison & yourself & company in the year 1776?

Answer: I should.

Question by same: What compensation are you to have to show this claim?

Answer: I do not no, but Expect the gentlemen who is consernd will pay me for my trouble & expense for tending at the place.

Question by Mr. James Stevens: Did you not refuse shewing this place untill there was some Satisfaction made you?

Answer: I refused doing bussiness for the Gentleman who employed [me] to come on the bussiness, untill they agreed to satisfy me for my trouble.

Question by Captain Benjamin Ashby: What were the marks or letters made at these improvements by which they could of been distinguished from other improvements?

Answer: I do not particularly charge my memory now with the particular letters or marks & further the deponent saith not.

[signed] Thomas Moore

Clarke County Sct.

The foregoing Deposition being taken before us, Original Young & Joseph Miller, commissioners appinted by the County Courts of Clarke, and on the Land of 1000 acres claimed by Benjamin Harrison at a Emprovement made by Thomas Moore for Said Harrison at two Springs, the one on the north side & the other on the south side [of] the Branch, and the one Spring on the south Side near a large Hickory, which we have caused to be marked with the letter M. As witness our hands this 15th day of October 1806.

Original Young

Joseph Miller

Deposition of Lawrence Harrison [374]

Clarke County Sct. September 15th 1806

We, Original Young, Henry Chiles & Joseph Miller, Commissioners appinted by the county court aforesaid pursuant to an act of assembly entitled an act for assertaining the Boundries of an entry of Land of 1000 acres on a premtion warrant entred by Benjamin Harrison & for other purposes, being convened on the said Mentioned Land claimed by the said Harrison at a black walnut, Elm, Honey Locus & white Hickry marked.

Laurence Harrison, a witness, and being Sworn, Depo[s]eth & saith I was present when the said walnut, Elm, Honey Locass & white Hickery trees was marked by George Lewis, who Surveyed the Same for Benjamin Harrisons begining corner, and also I myself [was] one that carried the chain.

Question by James Stevens, Agent for John Stevens: What date was it at the time the said corner was marked?
Answer: I cant answer to the day of the month, but it was nineteen years past, I think, this Last winter.

Question by same: Do you no and did you see the above mentioned 4 trees marked for the Entry of Benjamin Harrison for the 1000 acres as above mentioned?
Answer: I do not know wheather he had a Entry or no.

Question by Captain Dillard Collins: Were you ever at Benjamin Harrisons Emprovement of his 1000 acres made for the said Harrison?
Answer: I have been at the Emprovement that was said to be Benjamin Harrisons Emprovement, but was not there When it was made.

Question by same: Was you present when Morgans cabin was made, which this Entry of Benjamin Harrison has alusion too?
Answer: I was not.

Question by same: Do you no that the warters that ran from this place at the marked trees, to wit, walnut, Elm, Honey Locass & White Hickrey, is the warters of this Branch aluded to in Benjamin Harrisons Entry as before mentioned?
Answer: I do not no wheather it does or not.

Question by Samuel Morton: Do you no wheather the emprovements, such is said to be Benjamin Harrisons down the said Branch from there aluded to in the entry, runs into Stoner above the place that is called Morgans cabbin as presented in the entry?
Answer: It does.

[signed] Laurence Harrison

Clarke County Sct.
The foregoing Dep[osi]tion being taken before us, Original Young, Henry Chiles, Joseph Miller, Commissioners appinted by the county court of Clarke &

on the Lands of 1000 acres of Benjamin Harrison at a walnut & Elm, Honey Locass & white Hickory, shewed by Laurance Harrison, as above Mentioned, at the said 4 trees as above, in the presents of Thomas chisim, John Williams, Nicholas Aldridge, Disinterested Witness, on the 15 day of September 1806. As witness our hands & seals the day above Writen.

Thomas Chisholm
John Williams
Nicholas Aldridge
Original Young
Henry Chiles
Joseph Miller

Deposition of Ambrose Coffee [377]

Clarke County, State of Kentucky September 10th 1807

We, Original [Young], Henry Chiles & Joseph Miller, commissioners appinted by the County Court of Clarke pursuant to an Act of assembly entitled [an] act for assertaining the Boundries of Land of said entry made by Benjamin Harrison of 1000 acres on a premption warrant & for other purposes, being conveined on the said Land Mentioned or Claimed by the said Harrison, and at two springs, the one on one side of a Branch & the other on the other side of said Branch & near a large Hickrey, Which we have caused to be marked, thus, M. The said springs & Hickory now in a corn field called Wilmors.

[We] have caused to come before us Ambros Coffee, a Witness, who being first sworn, Deposeth & saith that in the year Eighty [1780] he was at this place in Company with Colonel Richard Callaway & I asked him if he knew this place. He answered, yes, he understood it belonged to one Benjamin Harrison. I apply to him, who was this Benjamin Harrison? He replyd to me that he did not Know, only by information. Then said I to him, we shall no when we come into these woods when we come to this place? Yes, says he, we shalle know it. Then I and Callaway returned from this place to Boons Bourough.

[A]fter some time in the said year Eighty [1780], myself and Pembleton [Pemberton] Rollins came Hunting in these woods and happened to come by the Spring and camped all night. Rollins asked me if I noad who claimed this place. My answer to him was that it was I was informed by Colonel Richard Callaway that it belonged to Benjamin Harrison. The place was very much taken with cain but Low. In the morning, we went to get our horses & came to the other Spring, the one on the one Side of the Baranch & the other on the different Side [of] said Branch & so went from this place to Boonsbourough.

And some time in eighty two [1782] I came here with Robert McMillion & we camped here that night. I did not expect that Robert McMillion was acquainted with the claim calld Harrisons. [I] says, I herd [this] is a fine piece of Land, do you Know who claimes it? His answer to me was, by information, it belonged to one Benjamin Harrison. Then said I will make a mark that you should Know it & then took my tomahawk and marked a stooping Lyn tree, which we are now at, I think. I remember well that and [a] Blue Ash tree stood at that time near a large Hickory that is now standing & near the spring, which I think was marked MH & if I mistake not, the Hickrey then standing was marked with M, but the tree Belted was at the spring on the other side of the Branch & that this place has been known by me ever since [as] a place of noteriety.

Question by Samuel Morton: Did you here other Hunters at Boonsbourough Say that they Knowd this place?
Answer: I did here them say they were acquainted with it as Benjamin Harrisons Claim so calld.

Question by same: Did you consider Garrott Townson as a woodsman at that time in eighty [1780]?
Answer: I did.

Question by same: Where wood you gon or come to have found the west fork of Licking in the year Seventy nine [1779]?
Answer: I wood have come to Stoner.

Question by Dillard Collins: Was not What We now call Stoner Known by the Hunters &c to be Calld Stoner in the year 1779 & 1780 and also by your self and also by the Locators that you were acquainted with at that time?
Answer: I answer I cant tell what others may call it or did call it, and to myself I formerly Knowd it by the west fork of Licking & this deponent further saith not.

[signed] Ambros Coffee

Deposition of Original Young [380]

Deposition of Original Young, of full age, being sworn, Deposeth & saith.

Question by Dillard Collins: Was you not told that Samuel Morton was to give Thomas Moor 60 Dollars to prove this place as Benjamin Harrisons improvement?
Answer: I, as one of the Commissioners, was at this place waiting to enter on the business and wated untill late in the Evening, as I thought. And Mr. Samuel Morton came to me or I calld on him to Know what was the reason we could not go the business. Mr. Samuel Morton, who had just left conversing with Thomas Moor, told me that Moor asked them [for] 60 dollars before he wood prove the claim, which I told Morton I thought it wood Destroy his testimony.

Question by Radford McCargo: Did you here Thomas Moor say he was to get 60 dollars?
Answer: No.

Question by same: Did you here Samuel Morton say he promised or paid him 60 Dollars or any other unlawfull sum?

Answer: No, and further this Deponent saith not.

[signed] Original Young

Clark County Sct.

The foregoing two depositions Being taken before us, Original Young and Henry Chiles and Joseph Miller, Commissioners appinted by the County Court aforesaid, and on the Land of 1000 acres claimed by Benjamin Harrison at an improvement made and certified by Ambrose Coffee at 2 springs, the one on the north side & the other on the south side the Branch, which is mentioned in Harrisons Certificate, with the commisioners to be [convened at] a Branch of the warters of Licking. The Spring on the south side neer a large Hickory, which we have caused to be marked with the letter M, and near a Crooked Lyn, which the said Ambrose Cofee Declears he marked, now standing & near to the Said Large Hickrey. As Witness our hands this 10th day of September 1807 [1806].
Original Young
Joseph Miller
Henry Chiles

Deposition of Robert McMillan [382]

Clarke County Sct. December 16th 1806

We, Original Young, Henry Chiles & Joseph Miller, Commissioners appinted by the county court of Clarke pursuant to an Act of assembly entitled an act for assertaining the boundries of an entry of Land of 1000 acres on a premtion warrant, entred by Benjamin Harrison, and for other purposes, being conviened on the said Land mentioned or claimed by the said Harrison now at the place mentioned in said entry.

We have caused to come before us, the said Commissioners, Robert McMillon, a witness, who being first sworn, Deposeth & Saith that to the best of my recolection, som time in the fore part of 1780 I was at this place in company with Garrard Townson & John Vivians [Vivion]. I think then that Garrard Townson calld it Harrisons Emprovement& I think I heard it called Harrisons Improvement in 1783 & 1784.

Question by William Sudduth: Where did you reside in 1779 or 1780?
Answer: I came to BoonsBourough, as well as I recolect, on the 21st of March 1780, and resided there untill about August following.

Question by same: At what time of the year 1780 do you think Garrett Townsend informed you this was Harrisons improvement?
Answer: I think in April or May.

Question by same: Did Townsend inform you this was Benjamin Harrisons improvements?
Answer: I am not certain that he said Benjamin Harrisons improvement, but I have since heard it called Benjamin Harrisons improvement.

Question by same: Do you think this improvement was noteriously Known by the name of Benjamin Harrisons improvement in the month of April and May 1780 at Boonsborrough, McGees & Strodes Station among your acquaintances?

Answer: I do not Know that it was & further this deponent saith not.

[signed] Robert McMillion

Deposition of Thomas Burrus [383]

Also the Deposition of Thomas Burriss Sr., of full age, being first sworn on the Judgment that he is not as he Knows of interested in the Lands of John stevens & Benjamin Harrisons preemtion so far as they interfere & then being sworn as a witness, deposeth & saith, the year I became acquainted with Garrard Townsen was in the year 1779, a few days before Christmas, the first of our acquaintance, we got at Boonsbourough.

And in Som short time after, we moved to William Bushes emprovement where Lewis Griggby now lives. Garrard Townson & my self Hunted together & killed meet untill about the 20 of March following. Then I myself went & lived With Captain Gest [David Gass] in Boonsbourogh in the fort there. Then I left Boonsbourough 29th day of March 1780. I started to go to Virginia. On holdston [Holston River] I met William Bush, John Stevens & several others & I returned back with them to Boonsbourough again.

And in a few days after we returned to William Bushes place again, where Lewis Griggsby now lives, from thence I in company With Garrard Townson, John Vivans & others came over on the warters of stoner, [this] being the first time that ever John Vivans and Garrard Townson ever was on these warters as I know off.

Question by James Stevens, agent for John Stevens: Did not John Vivans return from Bushes Cabbin, where Lewis Griggsby now lives, with yourself & others?

Answer: . . . [*text apparently omitted*] . . . to Boonsborough and from that to *Pitteys Station* on the Warters of Green river [and] from thence John Vivans, as I was informed, set off to Virginia, which said Vivans I left at Pitteys station in June 4th 1780.

Question by William Sudduth: At the time you were first acquainted with Garrard Townsend, did you believe him to be a woods man?

Answer: No.

Question: What time did you leave this county in the year 1780?

Answer: First I left it in march 1780 & went to Holdston & then returned to Boonsborough in the last of April 1780 & continued at Boonsbourough & lived with Garrett Townsend fu[r]ther, untill about the 20th May. I then went to Pettetts [Pittman's] Station on the waters of Green river.

Question by same: In May 1780 did you consider Garrett Townsend as a
        woodsman or Conversan[t] with Locators or as a man of information?
Answer: No.

Question by same: How old do you suppose Garrard Townsend was in May 1780
        from his appearance?
Answer: About 16 or seventeen.

Question by same: At what time did he come to this county?
Answer: In the fall of 1779, and this Deponent further saith not.

[signed] Thomas Burriss

Clarke County Sct.
        The Deposition of Thomas Burris, of full age, taken before us, Original
Young & Joseph Miller, Commissioners appinted by the County Court of Clarke,
and on the Land Claimed by Benjamin Harrison. As witness our hands this 16th
December 1806.

Clarke County Sct.
        The Deposition of Robert McMillion, of full age, taken before us Original
Young & Joseph Miller, Commissioners appinted by the Clarke County Court &
on the Land Claimed by the Said Benjamin Harrison. As witness our hands this
16th day of December 1806.
Original Young
Joseph Miller

        Agreed by Samuel Morton for Benjamin Harrison, James Stevens, agent
for John Stevens & William Sudduth, who claims under the Heirs [of]
Berthaloman Dupe [Dupuy], to pospone and ajuorn mutualy consent from the
16th December 1806 untill the 3rd monday in February next, and then appear at
the house of Absalom Hanks at usual day agreed before we the said
Commissioners.
Original Young
Joseph Miller

92.

Ralph Morgan, Benjamin Dunaway, William Clinkenbeard, Joshua Stamper and Thomas Kennedy for Charles Tate

Charles Tate

More is known about Samuel Tate than the other early Kentucky Tates—Charles, Robert and John. It is uncertain if they were all related. Samuel opened an account with the Henderson Company store at Boonesborough in April 1775. Nathaniel Hart's notes give a brief biography:

From Carolina. Gave name to Tate's Creek, Madison Co. Tates Cr., Madison Co., fired upon by the Indians. Two men killed. . . . He escaped by running into the water and following the stream.[434]

Samuel Tate marked and improved a claim on Stoner Creek in 1775, then assigned his right to a settlement and preemption to John Hall. Robert Tate was awared a settlement and preemption on Silver Creek in what is now Madison County for his raising a crop of corn there in 1775. John Tate received a settlement and preemption on Paint Lick Creek in Madison, based on his raising corn there in 1776. Finally, Charles Tate received a preemption of 400 acres, the tract processioned below, for "Making an Actual Settlement in April 1779." Charles lived in Bedford County, Virginia, where he witnessed William Bramblett's will in February 1779 before coming out.[435]

Charles Tate's claim in Clark County was surveyed by Ralph Morgan in 1785, with Benoni Swearingen listed as marker and Charles Snell and John Row, chain carriers. The tract was described to the Virginia land commissioners as "lying on Strodes fork of licking Creek about One Mile below Strodes Station." "Below" is used to mean "downstream of" and not "south of," as is sometimes thought. A patent issued to Tate in 1786. The land is located on Van Meter Road, about 1 mile north of U.S. 60.

Tate had died by 1807, when Joel Preston of Bedford County, acting as the representative of Tate's heirs, sold 225 acres of this tract to Thomas Constant. Preston was given power of attorney by Caleb and Edmund Tate of Franklin County and Obediah, Nancy and Pamelia Tate of Bedford County, who were all heirs of Charles Tate.[436]

Thomas Constant

Thomas Constant served as the Tates' attorney for this procession. He lived on Constant's Fork of Strode Creek in Clark County. He was a son of Capt. John Constant, who came to Kentucky seeking land in 1779 with a party from Berkeley County, Virginia. John Constant resided at Strode's Station until establishing his own station about a mile to the north. He died there in 1788. Thomas joined other Constants and Morgans migrating to Ohio and then to Illinois.[437]

Deposition of Ralph Morgan [387]

Pursuant to an order to us directed from the County Court of Clarke County at their July Court 1808 appointing us commissioners to take depositions to perpetuate the calls and boundaries of a premption of 400 acres in the name of Charles Tate, entered with the Commissioner for adjusting the title to unpattented lands in the district of Kentucky on the 29th day of December 1779, and entered with the Surveyor of Fayette County on the 15th day of October 1783, Surveyed on the 6th day of May 1785, and pattented on the 18th day of June 1786.

We the Commissioners having met at the house of Thomas Constant on the first day of August 1810, and it appearing unto us that the time and place of taking Depositions to establish the calls and boundry of the above enteries and Surveys had been duly advertised in Smiths Kentucky Gazzette, who is successor to Daniel Bradford, on the following days, to wit, on the 3rd day of July 1810, on the 10th day of July 1810, and on the 17th day of July 1810, and also that Notice thereof had been duly Delivered in writing to those having claims interferring or adjoining.

We from thence proceeded agreeable to said notice to the White Oak and white Ash, Beginning corner to said Tates Preemption in John Strodes line and corner to John Constants corn right, where we caused to come before us Ralph Morgan, age 52 years, who after being sworn, deposeth and saith that he made the original Survey of the Charles Tates preemption, which trees are plainly and aintiently marked.

From thence we proceeded to the West Corner of said 400 acres preemption, a hickory, sugar tree and white hickory, corresponding with the patent and shewn by Ralph Morgan as a Corner marked by him at the time he made said Tates Survey, and as a corner for the same, and the hickory being a state of Decay, we caused to be marked afresh a sugar tree and black ash with the letters YS.

We then proceeded to the north corner of said 400 acres preemption, a sugar tree, Mulberry & honey locust, shown by said Ralph Morgan as a corner made by him for said Tates preemption and corresponding with the pattent, and the mulberry being in a state of Decay, we caused to be marked afresh a sugartree with the letters YS.

We then proceeded to the East Corner of said Tates 400 acres preemption in Constants line, a shell bark hickory and box elder, the hickory being in a state of Decay, we caused to be marked two young elms as corners on the side fronting said Corner.

We then proceeded to a place shewn by said Ralph Morgan as Charles Tates spring and improvement.

Question by Thomas Constant, agent for Charles Tate heirs: How early did you
    Know this place as Charles Tates spring and improvement?
Answer: In the year 1780.

Question by same: Was there any appearance of corn having been raised at said
    Improvement when you were first acquainted with it?
Answer: Yes.

Question [by] same: How far above the improvement you have this day shown as
    Charles Tates do you suppose Strodes Station stood?
Answer: I think about three quarters of a mile & further this deponent saith not.

[signed] Ralph Morgan

Deposition of Benjamin Dunaway [388]

Also the Deposition of Benjamin Dunaway, of lawfull age, who being first duly sworn, deposeth and saith that in the month of May 1779 the deponant saith that in company with William Bramblett, Charles Tate, Thomas Shald & John Henderson, they made the improvement for Charles Tate. The spring where I have this day seen the young Groth cut of off & marks on an Elm which much resemble the marks made by the afforesaid Company of Bramblett and others & the place I have this day shewn the Commissioners is where the improvement was made.

And this deponant further saith that to the best of his Knowledge at the time they made the afforesaid improvement, they planted corn at the same & there was a noted hunters trace from Strodes Station passed by said Spring & improvement in 1780. And further this deponant saith not.

[signed] Benjamin Dunaway his mark

Deposition of William Clinkenbeard [388]

Also the deposition of William Clinkenbeard, aged 47 years, who after being duly sworn, deposeth and saith that he has always heard this place shewn by Ralph Morgan & Benjamin Dunaway called Tates Improvement from the year 1779 & that in the fall of 1779 there was the stalks of corn in said Improvement that had grew there that year, namely 1779 & this Improvement has been Known to the deponant by that name to the present day, and further the deponent saith not.
[signed] William Clinkenbeard Jr. his mark

Deposition of Joshua Stamper [390]

Also the deposition of Joshua Stamper, aged 56 years, who after being duly sworn, deposeth and saith that he has always heard this place shewn by Ralph Morgan and Benjamin Dunaway called Tates improvement from the fall 1779 & that in the fall 1779 there was the stalks of corn in said improvement that had grew there that year, namely 1779. And this improvement has been Known to this deponant by that name to the present day & further this Deponent saith not.
[signed] Joshua Stamper

Adjourned to the 9th of August 1810 to meet at the house of Thomas Constant at 10 oclock &c.

Deposition of Thomas Kennedy [390]

We the Commissioners having met at the house of Thomas Constant, agreeable to adjurnment, on the 9th day of August 1810, we from thence proceeded to a white oak and white ash in the line of John Strodes preemption, corner to John Constants preemption of 400 acres, being the first corner named in the foregoing Deposition of Ralph Morgan, where we caused to come before us Thomas Kenaday, aged 66 years, who being first sworn, deposeth and saith that to the best of his Knowledge the survey of the said 400 acres of John Constants preemption was made in the winter of 1783, and that he this deponant was chain carrier and Benjamin Ashby surveyor, and that the white oak and white ash before mentioned is the second corner of said survey.

Question by Thomas Constant: Did you or did you not live at Strodes Station when you carried the chain round said survey?
Answer: Yes.

Question by same: How long did you live at Strodes Station after the said survey was made?
Answer: I think I lived there till the winter 1785.

Question by same: Could or could not any person by inquiring at Strodes Station

252

have found the corner while you lived at said Station?

Answer: I supose they could.

Question by same: How far do you suppose it is from Strodes Station to this corner?

Answer: I suppose scearcely half a mile.

Question by same: Did you not consider the said Constant survey to be a noted survey?

Answer: I Did.

Question by same: How long has it been since the first improvements was made on the said Constants survey?

Answer: I think it was made in the spring of the year 1780, and further this deponant saith not.

[signed] Thomas Kenneday

Given under our hands this 9th day of August 1810.

Thomas Scott

Original Young, Commissioners

93.

Joshua Stamper and William Sudduth for Nathaniel Gist

Nathaniel Gist

Nathaniel Gist, the son of explorer Christopher Gist, served as a scout in Gen. Edward Braddock's ill-fated expedition (1755) and as a colonel in George Washington's Continental Army (1777). While trading among the Cherokee, he reportedly became the father of Sequoyah, inventor of the Cherokee alphabet. Nathaniel married Judith Cary Bell in Virginia and, in 1793, moved to Clark County where he built a fine mansion—Canewood—on his military survey. Canewood was famous for its beautiful grounds, extensive gardens and the lavish hospitality of the Gists. He died in 1796. His widow married Charles Scott in 1807, and Scott was elected governor the following year.[438]

In the summer of 1775, the Fincastle surveyors were in Kentucky locating prime tracts of land for veterans of the French and Indian War. James Douglass made two surveys of 3000 acres each for Nathaniel. The first survey was on military warrants issued to Christopher Gist and assigned to Nathaniel "as oldest son and heir-at-law"; the second was for military warrants issued to Nathaniel. His brother Thomas was present when the land was located and surveyed. These adjoining tracts were located on "Gist's Creek"—now Stoner Creek—in what is now Clark and Bourbon counties, straddling the county line.[439]

Judy's Mill

In 1804, Martin Judy petitioned the Clark county court for permission to erect a water gristmill on Stoner Creek "about one mile above Brambletts Lick." The court gave Judy permission to build a dam 10 feet high. The following year, the court ordered a road viewed from "Winchester towards Brambletts Lick by Judas Mill." Martin Judy died in 1831. The mill was later known as Wade's Mill.[440]

Deposition of Joshua Stamper [392]

       The undersigned being appointed by an order of the Clarke County Court [as] Commissioners to perpetuate Testimony Respecting two military surveys of 3000 acres each on Stoners fork, formerly called Gists creek, made by Virtue of the King of Great Britains proclamation of 1763, lying in Clarke County, the one made for Nathaniel Gist as heir at law to Christopher Gist, the other for said Nathaniel in his own name & Right notices having been given to the adjoining claimants & also duly advertised in the Reporter.

       We on the 4th day of April 1810 convened at *Martin Judys mill* & proceeded from thence to the beginning Corner of the upper survey, being the south east [corner] & Josiah Hart & Jacob Vert, two disinterested house Keepers being present we caused to come before us, Joshua Stamper, aged 56 years, who deposeth & saith that he was shewn this corner, a Red oak & two hickories, in the year 1783 or 1784 by Captain Benjamin Ashby as Gists Corner & he has frequently since heard it called a corner to Gists military survey & further this deponent saith not.

[signed] Joshua Stamper his mark

       When we adjourned untill tomorrow nine oclock to meet on the Road leading from Paris to Winchester near Colonel Donnaldson, on the lower line of said upper survey near to the said West Corner.

April 5th 1810

       The commissioners met pursuant to adjournment and having proceeded to make some experiments in running the lines of one of said surveys, and no testimony being their offered, adjourned untill tomorrow morning nine oclock, to meet at the beginning or south East Corner of the upper survey.

Deposition of William Sudduth [393]

April the 6th 1810

       The commissioners met pursuant to adjournment, and James McClannahan and William Goben, two disinterested house Keepers being present, caused William Sudduth, aged about 44 years, to come before them who being duly sworn, deposeth and saith that then and now standing at this place, a Red Oak and two hickories, anciently marked as a corner, and Coresponds with the call of Nathaniel Gists Patent, as heir at Law to Christopher Gist. The Red Oak is dead but standing with the bark on, and has marked on it the letters TG, apparently as ancient as the Corner and line marks of said survey. And we caused two hickories to be marked on this day, in addition to said Corner, so as to include said dead oaks about the center of the new and old marked Trees.

       That the deponent has been acquainted with said Corner by the name of Gists Corner from about the year 1790 or 1791, and that about the year 1803 or 1804 he was shewn the said Corner by David Williams as Gists beginning Corner, who stated he was present when it was made for him by Douglas in Company with Thomas Gist and others in the year 1775.

       And the Deponent further states that when he first became acquainted with said Corner in 1790 or 1791, the marks then appeared ancient, and from their appearance would indicate them to have been made about the year 1775. That he has executed several surveys either by order or Request, which Surveys call for the beginning Corner of the survey, and he has allways started from the place as Gist beginning corner.

The deponant says that he does not Recollect to have been acquainted with the south west Corner of said survey, or red oak, white oak and Hickory, untill the year 1798, at which time the hickory was dead but marks plainly appeared as a Corner on each of those trees, and Corresponded to the Corner Called for. The hickory is now down and nearly Rotten. The red oak is down with the marks plain on it, and the letters TG, apparently equally ancient with the other marks, are also marked on it. The white oak only is standing.

This Deponent does not recollect to have seen the North West Corner of the said survey, claimed three hickories, untill the year 1795 or 1796. From that time he has heard it Called Gists Corner. The marks from their age and direction would answer for a corner of said survey. They, however, as to the Kind of tree do not correspond. There was two which are generally called the white hickory, the other a scaly bark hickory.

This deponent saith that he has been acquainted with the North West Corner of the lower Survey, a sugar tree and Elm, ever since the year 1787, at which time it was shewn to him as a corner of Gists lower survey by John Constant, and he has heard it so calld ever since.

This deponent says he does not recollect to have seen the North East corner of the lower survey, a sugar tree and two white oaks, untill about 5 to 6 years ago. The marks on these trees together with the old lines in each direction leading to them corresponded to shew it to be the corner Called for. One of the white oaks are now down, on which the old marks plainly appear. This deponent saw this Corner when all the trees were standing, though the white oak now down, shewn to the surveyor by me on the 5th of the present month, was then dead.

This deponent does not recollect to have ever seen the division Corner of the two three thousand acres surveys on the Eastern ends untill the 5th of the present month. There is at that place, in addition to the spanish oak and hickory called for, [a] large Burr oak standing between those two Trees, anciently marked like the others as a Corner.

Question by Colonel John Donnaldson: What was the situation of the north west Corner of the lower survey when you saw it in 1803?

Answer: In Riding from my house to Paris, being long acquainted with that Corner as shown to me by John Constant, I discovered the sugar tree was cut down & about as much of it removed or taken away as would have contained the marks as a Corner, agreeably to the usual hight of marking in Gists military Surveys. The Elm so defaced by chops on the old marks that I considered the Corner destroyed. I am not certain whether I met Colonel Donnaldson at Paris or met him shortly afterwards, but the first time I saw him I informed him of the state of the Corner & advised him to procession his land, as I thought some malitious person had destroyed the

Corner & that at some future day he might be injured by it.

Question by same: On what side of Strodes Creek is the above Corner & what distance is it from the Creek?

Answer: On the East side about one quarter of a mile from the Creek, as well as my recollection serves me. I never measured it, and further the deponant saith not.

[signed] William Sudduth

April the 7th 1810

The Commissioners met according to Adjournment & this day being Rainy & unfit for business, they adjourn till Monday next at nine oclock, to meet at the south west Corner of the upper survey.

Clarke County, to wit,

We the Commissioners having no further Testimony offered to us, offer the above as our Report, so far as we have progressed. Given under our hands and seals.

Thomas Scott
William Sudduth
John Bean

94.

John Conkwright and Isaac Oliver for John Newland

Thomas Maxwell

Thomas and Bazeleel Maxwell were residents of Montgomery County, Virginia, in 1782. Thomas purchased John Gilliam's military warrants for 600 acres and used the warrants to acquire three surveys located by John Floyd in November 1775. All three tracts, 200 acres each, were on Upper Howard's Creek in Clark County "about eight miles above Boonsborough." In 1795, Maxwell sold his patent at the mouth of Upper Howard's Creek to John Howard, the same John Howard who was awarded a preemption at the mouth of Lower Howard's Creek and after whom both streams are named. Maxwell lived in Madison County, where he left a will probated in 1796. The following year his executors, wife Agnes and brother Bazeleel, sold one of his Upper Howard Creek tracts to Peter Tabler of Clark County.[441]

The processioned tract was about two miles above the mouth of Upper Howard's Creek. In 1794 Maxwell sold this land for 100£ to John Newland Jr. of Wythe County, Virginia. This land is about 8 miles southeast of Winchester.[442]

John Newland

John Newland Sr. (1743-1833) raised his fourteen children in Wythe County, Virginia. "John Newland Jr. of Wythe County" purchased Thomas Maxwell's 200 acres on Upper Howard Creek in 1794. John Jr. appeared on the Clark County tax rolls for the first time in 1797 and was listed in the census for Clark County in 1810 and 1820. In 1798, he married Sarah Bush, daughter of James and Lydia Bush. In 1817 he was an inspector of tobacco at Howard's Warehouse at the mouth of Upper Howard's Creek. John and Sarah were still living in Clark County in 1827 when he sold land to Pleasant Bush.[443]

In July 1813, John Newland made a motion in Clark county court to procession 200 acres surveyed and patented to Thomas Maxwell; at October court the depositions from the procession were ordered recorded.[444]

John Conkwright

John Conkwright (1776-1847) was a son of Hercules Conkwright. Hercules, who was born in Holland, settled on Upper Howard's Creek in Clark County. John was born in Mecklenburg County, North Carolina, and came to Kentucky with his parents in about the year 1789. In 1799, he married Keturah "Kitty" Lewis. He became a Methodist preacher. John's land adjoined Isaac Oliver's on Upper Howard's Creek. John was buried next to his father in the graveyard on his place.[445]

Isaac Oliver

Isaac Oliver, the son of James Oliver, was born in about the year 1765 and lived in Rowan County, North Carolina. Isaac married John Conkwright's sister Rachel, and his son Isaac Jr. married John's daughter Elizabeth. Isaac owned land on Upper Howard's Creek purchased from John Holder's heirs. He may have been a blacksmith, as a deed to his son Joseph mentions "the blacksmith shop of Isaac Oliver." Isaac died in 1835, leaving a will in Clark County.[446]

Isaac was the brother of Richard Oliver (1752-1847), who was born in Virginia, moved to North Carolina, and came to Kentucky in about 1790. Richard's homeplace was on Bull Run Creek, and some of his children settled on Fourmile Creek. Isaac gave a deposition in Richard's Revolutionary War pension application in 1833. Richard married John Conkwright's sister Hannah.[447]

Deposition of John Conkwright [396]

Clarke County, to wit,

In pursuant of a warrant Issued from the Clerk of the said County by Virtue of an order made by the court of the county aforesaid at their July court 1813 and in conformity of an act of the General Assembly of the Commonwealth of Kentucky entitled as act to reduce into one the Several acts to ascertain the boundaries of and for processioning Lands, approved December 19th 1796. We, the commissioners appointed in Said order, and whose names are hereunto Subscribed on this 30th day of September 1813, attended with John Newland, whose name is mentioned in Said Warrant and on whose motion the said order of Court was made, at the first Begining corner of two hundred acres of land, pattented to Thomas Maxwell by patent from the Commonwealth of Virginia dated the 20th day of July 1780, and founded on a Survey bearing date the 18th day of November 1775.

And then & there [we] pesceeded to take such proof as the said Newland did offer in relation to the said boundary of said land, as follows, to wit,

The Deposition of John Conkwright, of lawful age, being first duly Sworn, deposeth and Saith that between five and ten years ago this deponant hapened at this Spot in Company with others, and at which place there stands large Stump, at least some large old roots nearly rotten, which this deponant Says is the remaining part of a large Syckamore, near to which formerly stood a hoopwood tree, and that when he was here betwen 5 & 10 years ago both those trees were Standing, or else the Sycamore was Standing & green & that the hoopwood was Dead, but whether the hoopwood was Standing or down he does not recolect. He further States that at that time he saw Chops on Said Sycamore resembling those generally made on corner trees, but does not recolect Seeing Chops on the hoopwood, as the bark was then off and the tree in a roting State. This deponant further states that at that time he was told and has often been told that those two trees was the Begining corner of Maxwells Survey of 200 acres.

And further this deponant states that about 14 years ago a certain Fielding Combs offered to sell to this deponant a tract of land, which he Combs said lay above and adjoining to the said Maxwells 200 acres tract, and that said Combs then described the said Corner trees as being one of the corners of said 200 acres tract, and that the said corner trees was in his Combs line, and to which corner Combs offered to sell land, but no further.

We the commissioners thence proceeded to the 2nd corner called for in said patent, to wit, 3 White oaks Standing on the side of a hill. Here this deponant States that the said white oak has often been Shewed to him as the Second corner called for in said patent. And further Saith [not].
[signed] John Conkwright

Deposition of Isaac Oliver [397]

Also the Deposition of Isaac Oliver, of Lawful age, who being first duly sworn, and being at (as it is said) the 5th corner called for in Said patent, being a white oak and ash standing on a hill side near the Creek, Deposeth and Saith that the white oak, which we are now at and which is fallen down & some decayed, was Shewn to the deponant as one of the said corner trees called for in said patent as aforesaid by the said Newland about 12 years ago, and the said white oak was then Standing and was dead, but that then the top was broke off. And further saith not.
[signed] Isaac Oliver

Given under our hands.
Thomas Scott
John B. Lawrence, Commissioners

95.

Lawrence Thompson, Jacob Dooley and Martin Johnson for Achilles Eubank

Nathaniel Hart

Nathaniel Hart (1734-1782) and his brothers Thomas and David were members of the Transylvania Company, the abortive effort led by Richard Henderson to claim the area south of the Kentucky River. Nathaniel settled in North Carolina, residing at his estate he called Red House. He came to Boonesborough with Henderson in 1775 and brought his family out in the fall of 1779. They settled at his place on Otter Creek known as White Oak Station. He was killed by Indians not far from his home in July 1782. He had made out a will the month before. Nathaniel left a widow, the former Sarah Simpson, and nine children.[448]

The 400-acre tract processioned below and an adjoining 500-acre tract on the Kentucky River were entered for Hart's heirs in 1782, but were not surveyed by Asa Massie until 1798. The 400-acre tract began about 1 mile above the mouth of Fourmile Creek. The land is about 8½ miles south and a little west of Winchester.[449]

Achilles Eubank

Achilles Eubank was a Clark County pioneer, who resided on Twomile Creek. He was born in Goochland County, Virginia, and saw extensive service during the Revolutionary War. He came to Kentucky with Col. John Bowman's regiment in 1777 and later fought at Guilford Courthouse and Yorktown. He moved to Kentucky after the war and became a prominent figure in Clark County, where he served as sheriff and justice of the county court. He represented Clark County in the Kentucky House of Representatives in 1799-1800. Eubank acquired significant land holdings in the Twomile-Fourmile area and had a gristmill and warehouse on Fourmile Creek. He moved to Missouri and was living in Cooper County when he received a Revolutionary War pension. His death notice states:

> Achilles Eubank of near Booneville, Missouri, formerly Clark county, Kentucky. Died August 16, 1844, aged 91 years.[450]

His role in this procession is explained in a Clark County deed. James McMillan and William Hoy located the two tracts claimed by Hart and were entitled to one-half the land for their services. McMillan sold his interest to Achilles Eubank. In 1802, the Clark County court ordered William Sudduth, commissioner, to divide Hart's land among Eubank, Hoy and Hart's heirs.[451]

Jacob Dooley

Jacob Dooley served in Capt. Thomas Buford's company of Bedford County, Virginia, volunteers in Dunmore's War, 1774. In 1795, Dooley served as a "lieutenant with a sergeant and 15 privates on the frontiers of Clarke," for which he later received compensation by the Kentucky legislature. In 1818 at age 63, Dooley applied for a Revolutionary War pension while living in Madison County. He died in Madison in 1842, and his wife Nancy applied to receive his pension.[452]

Martin Johnson

Martin Johnson (sometimes spelled Johnston in the records) was born in 1758, the son of William and Sarah Johnson. Martin enlisted in the Virginia Line in Culpeper County, Virginia, in 1779. He settled in Clark County and had a plantation near the junction of Fourmile Creek and the Kentucky River. He applied for a Revolutionary War pension from Clark County in 1818 and died there in 1820. Johnson was involved in the Red River Millstone Quarry near Pilot Knob with Spencer Adams and others.[453]

Deposition of Lawrence Thompson [397]

Pursuant to an Order of the County Court of said Clarke County made at their May Court 1814 Appointing us commissioners to establish and perpetuate Testimony of the calls of an entry, which entry is in the following words and figures, to wit, "December 10th 1782, Nathaniel Hart, assignee, enters 400 acres on treasury warrant Number 5824 On the Kentucky [River] about 4 miles above Boonsborrough, to begin about 30 poles above on an old improvement on the river, to run out and down the river for quantity."

We David Hampton, James Sympson, Lewis Grigsby and Benjamin Heronomous, commissioners named and appointed in said order on warrant, have met at the House of Ambrose Eubank this 21st day of July 1814, Agreeable to a publication printed in Lexington in the Reporter, giving notice of the time and place of meeting, and we having caused to come before us by an proper warrant Laurance Thompson, Jacob Dooley and Martin Johnson at the house of said Ambrose Eubank.

We thence proceeded Accompanyed by Lewis Hood and John Woollery, two disinterested witnesses, to the Beginning calls of said entry, it being about

259

One mile above the mouth of the four mile Creek, within 20 poles of the Kentucky river, close to the foot of the river hill, and within or about five poles from the head of a spring down the river from the same. At which place there was to us the evident marks of an old improvement, and we proceeded about 30 poles from said improvement up the river, and found on the bank at high water mark a large white poplar and two sugar trees marked as beginning corners to the Survey. One of which Sugars was dead and must fall in a short time.

We thence returned to the improvement before mentioned near the spring, and the before named Lawrance Thompson, who being of full age, and first sworn, deposeth and saith that in May 1781 he was at this place in company with a James McMillion, at which time he the said Thompson made a location for Nathaniel Hart of 400 acres, in pursuance of which location the before recited entry was made.

And he the said Thompson further saith that there was an improvement at this place at the time he made the above Location, consisting of about One half acre, now cleared, and some deaded timber and the body of a cabbin raised 4 or 5 logs high, all which appeared to be done about 2 years past.

Question by Achillis Eubank: Was you at the time you made the above location acquainted between the mouth of 2 mile Creek and Howards upper creek? And if you was, say if you know of any other improvements on the river but the one we are at.

Answer: I was in the habit of Spying from Boonsborough and was frequently up and down the river at the time I made the above Location. And never did [I] see any improvement on the river between the mouth of 2 mile creek and Howards upper creek but the one we are at. And further this deponant saith not.

[signed] Lawrence Thompson

Deposition of Jacob Dooley [399]

Also the deposition of Jacob Dooley taken at the same time and place to establish the before calls & who being of lawful age and first sworn, deposeth and saith that he was at this place about 26 or 27 years past, and at that time their was the body of a cabin about waist high and about half an acre of ground that had been cleared adjoining the same.

Question by Achillis Eubank: Was you in the time you first saw this improvement acquainted on the river between the mouth of 2 mile creek and Howards upper creek? And if you was, say if You know of any improvement but this one.

Answer: I was acquainted on the river between 2 mile creek and howards upper creek [at] the time I first see this improvement and did not know of any but this one in the bounds. And further this deponant saith not.

[signed] Jacob Dooley

Deposition of Martin Johnson [400]

The deposition of a Martin Johnson taken at the same time and place for the same purpose, who being of full age and first sworn, deposeth and saith that about 25 years past he was at this place, at which time there was a cabbin wall four or five logs high and about half an acre of old cleared ground adjoining said Cabbin.

Question by Achillis Eubank: Was you, about 25 years past, acquainted on the Kentucky river between the mouth of 2 mile Creek & Howards upper creek? And if You was, did you ever see any Other improvement but this?
Answer: I was acquainted, at the time above, on the river between the mouth of 2 mile creek and Howards upper creek and never knew of any improvement but the one we are at. And further this deponant saith not.

[signed] Martin Johnson

We whose names are hereto set, Commissioners as herein before named, do certify that the before named Lawrence Thompson, Jacob Dooley and Martin Johnson did subscribe to the foregoing depositions before us this 21st day of July 1814.
James Sympson
David Hampton
Lewis Grigsby
Benjamin Heronimus, Commissioners

96.

Joseph Berry and John Henry for Aaron Lewis

Aaron Lewis

The tract on Red River, processioned below, was surveyed for Aaron Lewis by his father-in-law, John South, in 1785. John Taylor was the marker, Joseph Berry and Sigismund Stribling, chain carriers. This tract was the subject of a lawsuit in Fayette circuit court in 1796, *Aaron Lewis vs Thomas Halsey, in ejectment*, which meant Lewis was attempting to remove Halsey from the property. No decision was recorded. In 1814, Lewis was living in Christian County when he sold part of this tract to William Daugherty. This land was located near the mouth of Red River, about 11 miles southeast of Winchester. According to local historian Bessie Taul Conkwright, Lewis' tract was known as "Marshy Bottom," which is shown on contemporary topographic maps as "Marsha Bottom."[454]

Joseph Berry

Joseph Berry gave an informative deposition in another land case in 1807. He was living in Mason County at the time and stated that "in the year 1782 he came to this country [Kentucky] and resided at Holder's station on the Kentucky River and traveled the road from Bryant's station to the Lower Blue lick in company with about 500 men on a tour to bury the dead killed at Blue lick in the year 1782 in the month of August." He was appointed a deputy surveyor for Fayette County and stated, "In the year 1784 I was accustomed to entering and surveying lands."[455]

John Henry

Insufficient information is available to positively identify this John Henry. He states in his deposition below that he assisted Philip Detheridge, a deputy surveyor of Clark County, conduct a survey of Aaron Lewis' Red River tract in the year 1797. There was a John Henry residing in Clark County at that time—listed on the tax rolls between 1794 and 1800—however, no marriage, deed or will could be found for him in the county.

Deposition of Joseph Berry [401]

Pursuant to an Order of the County Court for Clarke County passed at their February term 1814 Appointing us Commissioners to Establish and Purpetuate Testimony of the Beginning corner and special Calls of a 1000 acres, Land office Treasury warrant Survey (Number 9798) issued the 11th day of December 1781, and pattented the 21st day of May 1787, and pattented in the name of Aaron Lewis, and named in the grant as lying and being in the County of Fayette, now Clarke County, On the waters of Red River.

We, David Hampton, William Poor and James Wood, three of the commissioners named and Appointed in said Order and warrant, have met at the house of William Lane in the said county On the said Waters of red river the 12th day of April 1814, agreeably to a publication printed at Lexington in the Reporter of the time and place of meeting, and have caused to come before us by our proper Warrant Joseph Berry at the said Lands, together with Luke Philbert and John Lane, two disinterested witness out of the County of Clarke. We thence proceeded to the Beginning corner of said 1000 acres Survey, it being a white oak marked HC, a buckeye and Hickory trees named and called for in the grant of said Survey.

The said Joseph Berry, being of lawful age and first duly sworn, deposeth and saith that he is the same Joseph Berry who was returned by John South Jr. as a chain carrier to said 1000 acres survey in the month of March 1785. And at that time John South Jr. was Deputy Surveyor to Colonel Thomas Marshall for the County of Fayette, and in said month of March (this deponant does not recollect what day) he attended the said South, Surveyor aforesaid, together with John South Sr., John Taylor and William Stribling at the place which we now are. And that the said White Oak marked HC, Which was shewn and made Known to him in the said month of March 1785 as the Beginning corner of said 1000 acres Survey, and that there were other trees marked at the same time and designated as the Beginning corner, but this deponant does not recollect the number nor what Kind of trees they were.

Question by Lewis's Attorney: Do You or do You not Know this to be the place where the said white oak tree was marked as the Beginning Corner of the said 1000 acres Survey in the month of March 1785?
Answer: The principal things that convince me that this is the place, and that this is the same white oak tree that is now standing that was shown and made known to me at that time, is that I marked the two first letters of my name on a white oak close by the corner, And I now see the same tree with the same letters on it. I also know the situation of the ground and this lick, and I also know that we encamped about one hundred yards up this little

branch that puts in this Other main branch.

Question by same: Was or was not this place Known at that time by the name of Clay lick?

Answer: This place was notoriously Known at that time by the name of a Lick, but I dont recollect whether it was called Clay Lick or Mud Lick, but was at that time called by one of those names.

Question by same: Do You or do You not recollect at this time whether there were any old traces leading up to or from this lick?

Answer: I recollect seeing at that time a Number of old traces leading to and from this Lick. I suppose they were principally made by Buffaloe and Other wild game resorting the lick.

Question by same: Do You or do You not believe this buckeye and hickory that have been cut down and now lie here are the same buckeye and hickory trees that was Called for in the grant as the Beginning corner?

Answer: I have seen a buckeye and hickory that have [been] cut down at this corner, and from the ancient chops on them in the shape of a corner, I think they were the same trees called for in the grant and marked at that time as the Beginning corner trees of said Survey.

We then adjourned until the next day at 9 oClock A.M.

Wednesday, 13th April 1814

Met pursuant to an adjournment, together with the said Lane and Philbert, Witnesses aforesaid, and Berry, the deponant, and proceeded along a line of said Survey South 40 degrees West 160 poles, the course and distance called for in the grant, to another corner of said Survey on the bank of aforesaid river, of which the said deponant further saith that the said ash, hickory and elm trees at which we now are is the second Corner of said Survey and was marked and designated as Such at the time When he helped Survey the same March 1785.

We thence proceeded with the said witnesses and deponant along another line of said Survey North 50 degrees West 500 poles, the course and distance called for in the grant, and after a diligent Search we found no corner at the end of the said distance.

We then went with the said Witnesses and deponant to the 5th corner of said Survey, it calling for two ashes and hickory, of which the said trees were lying on the earth and nearly rotten, to which deponant further saith that from the Situation of the ground and from the Knowledge he had of the groath of timber and other circumstances, he believes the place at which we are is the identical place where the Corner did stand at the time when he helped survey the same March 1785.

Deposition of John Henry [404]

Also the Deposition of John Henry, of lawful age and first duly sworn,

deposeth and saith that he helped run out the said 1000 acres Survey about the Year of 1797, and [he] was at that time Shewn the place at which we now are by Philip Detheridge, the Surveyor who wase at that time resurveying the same, and the two ashes that are called for in the grant were at that time lying upon the ground and had ancient chops on them in the shape of corner trees, and was informed by said Detheridge, the Surveyor, that the said ashes and hickory that was lying down were the same Corner trees called for in Aaron Lewis's grant of 1000 acres Survey. And further this deponant saith not.
[signed] John Henry his mark

We then adjourned until the next day at 9 Oclock A.M.

Deposition of Joseph Berry [405]

Thursday, the 14th day of April 1814

    Met pursuant to an adjournment and proceeded with the said Witnesses and deponant Berry along another line of said Survey covering the course called for in the grant, North 50 degrees West 500 poles, the course and distance called for in the grant, to another corner of said Survey, it being on two locusts and Walnut. The said corner trees were standing, of which the said deponant further saith that from the situation of the ground and from all other appearances, he believes the said corner tree at which we now are is the 4th corner of the said Survey, and was marked and designated as such at the time when he helped survey the same.

    We thence proceeded with the said Witnesses and deponant along another line of said Survey, South 40 degrees West 320 poles, reversing the course called for in the grant the same course and distance untill we intersected the Second line (South 40 degrees West) And finding no corner, the deponant further saith that he believes that the place where the lines intersect each other is the place where the corner did stand. We then marked and designated a sugar tree to stand in the place of the right corner, supposed to be rotted down.
[signed] Joseph Berry

[attested]
Luke Philbert, John Lane, Witnesses
David Hampton
William Poor
James Wood [Commissioners]

Sampler of Maps Showing the Location of Processioned Tracts

Eleven maps taken from land cases showing some of the tracts processioned in Clark County. Maps often show other features, such as streams, licks, mills, houses, etc. Note the North arrow in each figure.

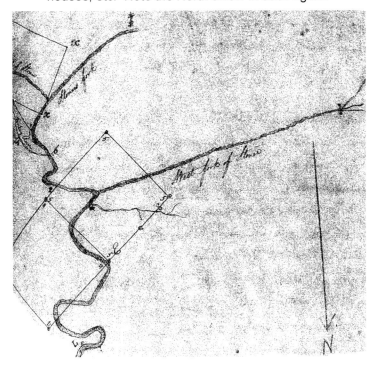

5555—John Morgan's 1,000-acre preemption on Stoner Creek patented to Charles Morgan (processions #46 and #78). Inside the tract, ★, Morgan's cabin at the mouth of Cabin Creek. Bottom of figure, at L, Bramblett's Lick. (Kentucky Land Trials A:342)

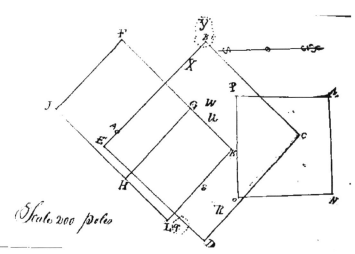

OPMN— John Morgan's 1,000-acre preemption on Stoner Creek patented to Charles Morgan (processions #46 and #78). Y—Original Young's house (deposition in procession #91). (Clark County Land Trials, 1812-1815, p. 41)

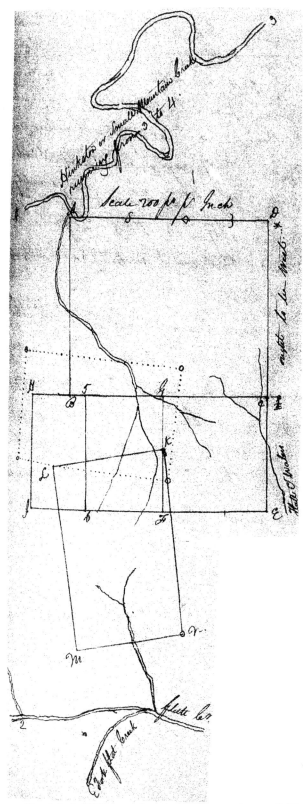

KLMN—James Davis' 1,000-acre tract on the waters of Flat Creek and Hinkston Creek (procession #18). Davis interfered with *CEFG*—James McMillan's 600 acres and FGHJ—William Trimble's 750 acres. (Kentucky Land Trials A:465)

266

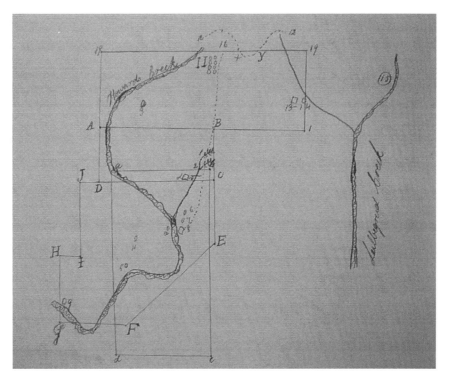

ABCD—Cuthbert Combs' 400-acre settlement and *CDJIHGFE*—Combs' 1,000-acre preemption on Upper Howard's Creek (procession #59). *abcd*—Thomas Porter's 1,076⅔ acres. *8*—Beasley's cabin on Upper Howard's Creek and *13*—Beasley's cabin on Lulbegrud. *I I*—the gate posts in the "Old Indian Town," or Indian Old Fields. (Clark County Land Trials, 1812-1815, p. 488)

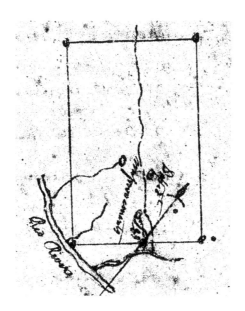

Aaron Lewis' 1000-acre survey on Red River, beginning at the Clay Lick on Log Lick Creek (procession #96). (Kentucky Land Trials, 1791-1810, p. 2)

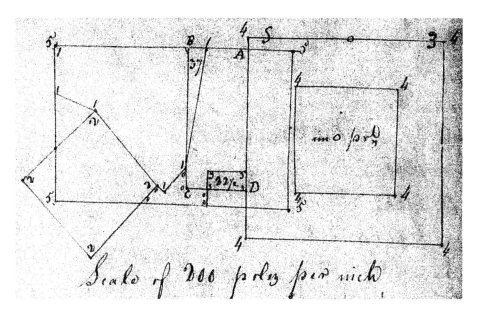

4444—Samuel Henderson's 400-acre settlement, *inner square*, and 1,000-acre preemption, *outer area* (procession #89). *2222*—Charles Tate's 400-acre preemption (preemption #92). *5555*—William McCrackin's 1,400-acre settlement and preemption, interfering with both. (Kentucky Land Trials A:4)

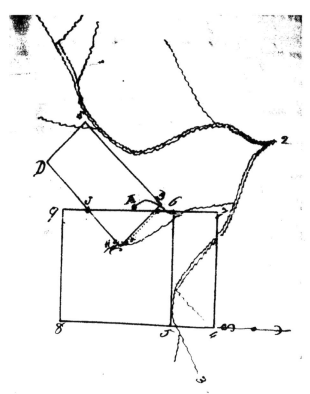

4576—Daniel Boone's 400-acre settlement and *5698*—his 1,000-preemption on Georges Branch of Stoner Creek, patented to William Scholl (procession #50). *ABCD*—John Price's 500 acres (procession #51). (Kentucky Land Trials C:44)

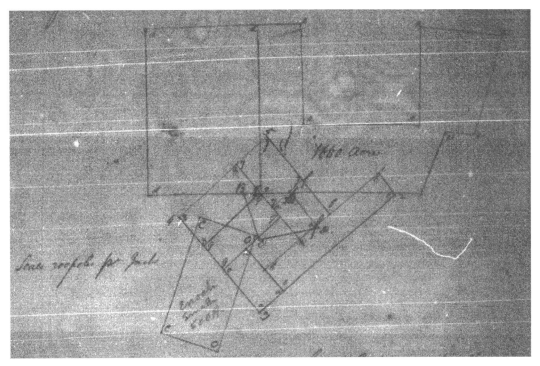

Tract labeled "1640 acres" is John Marshall's patent (procession #69), and *123456* is George Winn's 1,000 acres (procession #21), both located just north of Winchester. (Kentucky Land Trials B:452)

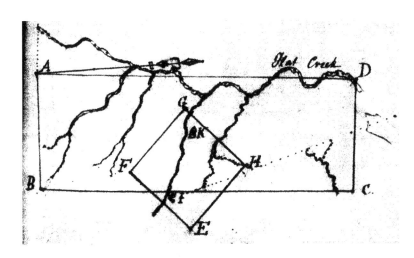

EFGH—Forrest Webb's 500-acre tract on branches of Flat Creek (procession 62). Webb interfered with *ABCD*—John Wilkerson's 3,050-acre tract (procession #32). (Kentucky Land Trials, 1791-1810, p. 55)

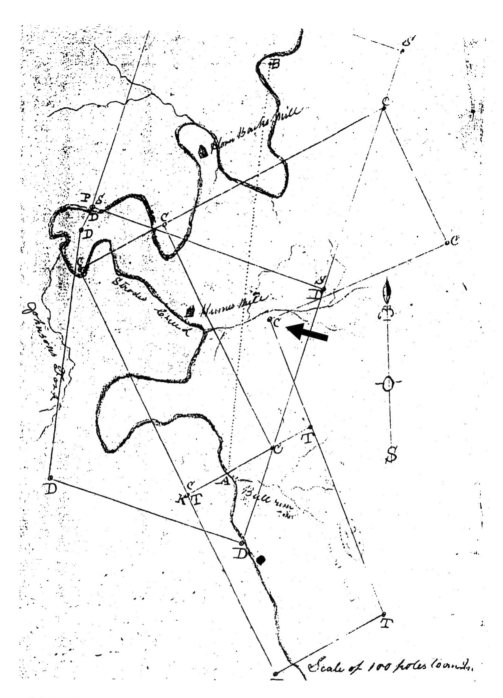

CCCCC—Thomas Kennedy's 400-acre settlement and 672-acre preemption on Strodes Creek (procession #80). Shows the location of Hornback's Mill and Hume's Mill. Arrow points to *C*, the northwest corner of Nathaniel Gist's upper 3,000-acre survey (procession #93). (*James Duncan vs Thomas Kennedy and Thomas Dawson*, Bourbon Circuit Court, 1804)

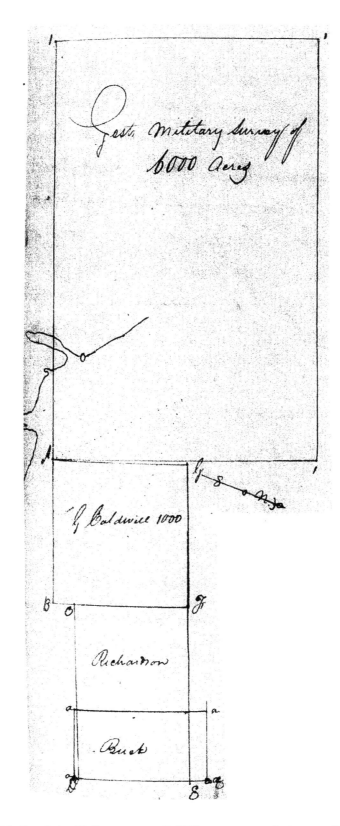

A111—Nathaniel Gist's upper 3,000 acres and lower 3,000 acres (procession #93), and *ABFG*—George Caldwell's 1,000 acres (procession #64). (Kentucky Land Trials A:527)

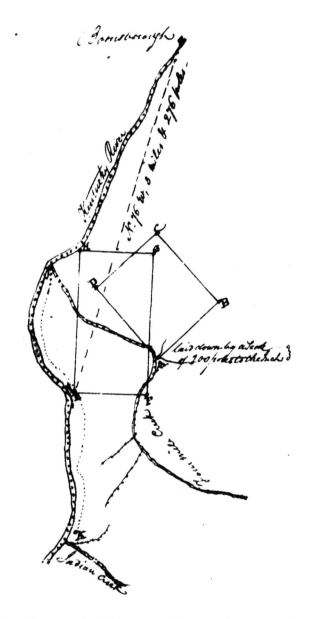

EFGH—Tilley Emerson's 750-acre claim on the Kentucky River at the mouth of Fourmile Creek (procession #24), showing interference with *ABCD*—Joseph Wright's 562 acres. (Kentucky Land Trials, 1791-1810, p. 43)

Bibliography
Short Titles and Abbreviations

The following list explains the short titles and abbreviations used for frequently cited references throughout the Notes.

500 Old Families—Kathryn Owen, "Five Hundred Old Families of Clark County," unpublished manuscript (1963-1964) in possession of the author.

Certificate Book—Kentucky Historical Society, *Certificate Book of the Virginia Land Commission, 1779-1780* (Frankfort, 1981).

Clark County Chronicles—a series of articles prepared by the Clark County Historical Society and published in the *Winchester Sun.*

Cornstalk Militia—G. Glenn Clift, *The "Cornstalk" Militia of Kentucky, 1792-1811* (Frankfort, 1957).

DB—deed book.

Death notices—G. Glenn Clift, *Kentucky Obituaries, 1787-1854* (Baltimore, 1979).

Draper MSS—Lyman C. Draper manuscripts on microfilm at M. I. King Library, University of Kentucky, Lexington.

Early Kentucky Surveyors—B. R. Salyer, "Early Kentucky Surveyors and Deputy Surveyors" (2004) at www.kysos.com/ADMIN/LANDOFF.journal.asp.

EB—entry book.

FCHQ—*Filson Club History Quarterly.*

History of Fayette County—William Perrin, editor, *History of Fayette County, Kentucky* (Chicago; 1882).

History of Kentucky—Richard H. Collins, *History of Kentucky, Volume* 2 (Covington, 1874).

Kentucky Encyclopedia—John E. Kleber, editor, *The Kentucky Encyclopedia* (Lexington, 1992).

Kentucky Land Trials—the record of law suits filed in the District Court at Lexington, all dealing with land cases, on microfilm at the Kentucky Libraries and Archives, Frankfort. Abstracts of these cases were published by Charles R. Staples, "History in Circuit Court Records," *RKHS* (1930-1935) Volumes 28-33.

Life of Daniel Boone—Lyman C. Draper, *Life of Daniel Boone,* edited by Ted Franklin Belue (Mechanicsburg, PA, 1998).

Littell's Laws—William Littell, *Statute Law of Kentucky, 5 Volumes* (Frankfort, 1809).

Marriage Bonds of Clark County—George F. Doyle, *Marriage Bonds of Clark County, Kentucky, from the Formation of the County in 1793 to 1850* (Winchester, 1933).

Morgan's Station—Harry G. Enoch, *In Search of Morgan's Station and "The Last Indian Raid in Kentucky"* (Bowie, MD, 1997).

OB—order book.

Old Kentucky Entries and Deeds—Willard R. Jillson, *Old Kentucky Entries and Deeds* (Louisville, 1926).

Petitions—James Rood Robertson, *Petitions of the Early Inhabitants of Kentucky to the*

General Assembly of Virginia, 1769 to 1792 (Louisville, 1914).

RKHS—*Register of the Kentucky Historical Society.*

Stockading Up—Nancy O'Malley, *"Stockading Up": A Study of Pioneer Stations in the Inner Bluegrass Region of Kentucky* (Frankfort, 1987).

Virginia Baptist Ministers—William S. Simpson Jr., *Virginia Baptist Ministers, 1760-1790, Volumes 1-5* (Richmond, VA, 1990).

WB—will book.

Notes

[1] George Thompson, Revolutionary War pension application, S.31416, Virginia; George M. Chinn, *History of Harrodsburg and "The Great Settlement Area" of Kentucky, 1774-1900* (n.p., 1985), p. 75; Mercer County OB 3:484; Enoch, *Morgan's Station*, pp. 118-119.

[2] *Lexington Observer & Reporter*, May 1, 1834.

[3] Old Virginia Surveys 4:182; Old Virginia Grants 2:274; Clark County DB 1:340.

[4] Kentucky Land Trials A:537; plat recorded in *Quintain Moore vs John Fowler et al.,* Montgomery Circuit Court, 1813.

[5] Kentucky Land Trials, A:242, 283, 525, 778.

[6] Robert M. Rennick, *Kentucky Place Names* (Lexington; 1984), p. 229; Carrie Myers, "How Peeled Oak Got Its Name," *Bath County News-Outlook,* August 24, 1961.

[7] J. Winston Coleman Jr., *Stage-Coach Days in the Bluegrass* (Berea, KY, 1935, 1976 reprint), p. 32.

[8] See Enoch Smith's deposition for Edward Payne, procession #12.

[9] *Frankfort Weekly Journal*, September 23, 1846.

[10] Lloyd D. Bockstruck, *Virginia's Colonial Soldiers* (Baltimore, 1988), pp. 15, 30. Fauquier County was formed in 1759 from an area that had been part of Prince William County.

[11] Certificate Book, p. 160.

[12] Old Virginia Surveys 11:29; Old Virginia Grants 3:203; Clark County DB 6:543.

[13] Salyer, "Early Kentucky Surveyors"; Old Virginia Surveys 3:527, 7:28; Clark County DB 1:369, 591; Kentucky Land Trials B:274.

[14] Daniel Bryan interview, Draper MSS 22C10, 14(17).

[15] Stratton O. Hammon, "John Hammon, Revolutionary Soldier and Kentucky Pioneer," *FCHQ* (1949) 23:202; *Petitions*, No. 6; Samuel M. Wilson, et al., *Kentucky in Retrospect* (Frankfort, 1942), p. 188.

[16] Certificate Book, p. 184.

[17] Clark County OB 1:207; *James Berry et al. vs Robert Gunnell*, Lexington District Court, 1799, papers in the Special Collections, University of Kentucky Library, Lexington; Old Kentucky Surveys 5:78, 79; Old Kentucky Grants 11:42-49.

[18] Montgomery County DB 2:10, 15, 21.

[19] Old Virginia Surveys 2:356; Old Virginia Grants 7:117-118.

[20] Harry Mills, "Early Families," *Mt. Sterling Advocate*, August 20, 1975; Elias Tolin, Revolutionary War pension application, S.37492, Virginia.

[21] R. S. Cotterill, "Battle of Upper Blue Licks," *FCHQ* (1927) 2:29.

[22] Augusta Fothergill and John Naugle, *Virginia Tax Payers, 1782-87* (Richmond, VA, 1940); Old Virginia Surveys 4:240; Old Kentucky Grants 1:446; Joan Brookes-Smith, *Index for Old Kentucky Surveys & Grants* (Frankfort, 1974); Sarah G. Clark, "The Chiles

and Allied Families," *RKHS* (1938) 36:26-53, 128-156, 376-378; "A Family Record of Chiles, Carr and Davis," *RKHS* (1918) 16:55-57.

[23] Lloyd D. Bockstruck, *Virginia's Colonial Soldiers* (Baltimore, 1988), p. 185.

[24] Jillson, *Old Kentucky Entries and Deeds,* p. 187; Old Kentucky Surveys 3:216; Old Kentucky Grants 6:46; Lyman Chalkey, *Chronicles of the Scotch-Irish Settlement in Virginia, Vol. 3* (Baltimore, 1912, 1974 edition), pp. 160-169; procession #72.

[25] Clark County OB 1:209; Clark County DB 5:255.

[26] John Mack Faragher, *Daniel Boone, Life and Legend of an American Pioneer* (New York, 1992), p. 286.

[27] William Watson, Revolutionary War pension application, S.17752, Virginia; Clark County DB 3:19, 10:288.

[28] Jillson, *Old Kentucky Entries and Deeds,* p. 305; Old Kentucky Surveys 7:524; Old Kentucky Grants 13:467.

[29] Jillson, *Old Kentucky Entries and Deeds*; Salyer, "Early Kentucky Surveyors"; Willard R. Jillson, "Land Surveys of Daniel Boone," *RKHS* (1946) 44:86; John Mack Faragher, *Daniel Boone, Life and Legend of an American Pioneer* (New York, 1992), p. 239.

[30] See for example, Michael A. Lofaro, *Life and Adventures of Daniel Boone* (Lexington, 1978), pp. 57-63.

[31] Draper MSS 7C72, 88, 99, 103.

[32] Margery H. Harding, *George Rogers Clark and His Men, Military Records 1778-1784* (Frankfort, 1981), p. 117; Clark County DB 16:337, 17:295, 18:25; Owen, "500 Old Families"; Hazel Boyd, "Montgomery County Notes, *Mt. Sterling Advocate*, February 19, 1981; Clark County Chronicles, *Winchester Sun*, June 14, 1923.

[33] Old Virginia Surveys 2:472.

[34] Old Virginia Grants 4:423.

[35] Kentucky Land Trials C:451.

[36] Hazel Boyd, "Montgomery County Notes," *Mt. Sterling Advocate,* February 19, 1981; Halley family papers and "Journal of John Halley, His Trips to New Orleans Performed in the Years 1789 & 1791," Special Collections, M. I. King Library, University of Kentucky; William Clinkenbeard interview, Draper MSS 11CC54; Nancy O'Malley, *Searching for Boonesborough* (Lexington; 1989, revised 1990).

[37] Christopher Barton family of Ireland at members.aol.com/swinfield9/barton.htm.

[38] Certificate Book, p. 88.

[39] Henry Clay Connor Jr., *Life and Times of Leonard Hall* (Indianapolis; 1981); Bedford County (VA) DB 9:271; Barren County WB 1:106.

[40] Certificate Book, p. 88; Old Virginia Grants 7:108; Old Virginia Grants 6:417, 9:353.

[41] John Gass interview, Draper MSS 11CC11.

[42] Nathaniel Hart interview, Draper MSS 17CC200.

[43] Ibid.

[44] H. Thomas Tudor, *Early Settlers of Fort Boonesborough* (Richmond, KY, 1975); *Petitions*, No. 9; Montgomery County OB A, court held May 5, 1789; Barton family history at www.hardylaw.net/Bogard.html.

[45] Certificate Book, p. 88; Old Virginia Surveys 4:314; Old Virginia Grants 3:355.

[46] Draper, *Life of Daniel Boone,* p. 487; Old Virginia Surveys 3:409; Old Virginia Grants 2:369.

[47] William S. Bryan and Robert Rose, *A History of Pioneer Families of Missouri* (St. Louis, 1876), p. 225.

[48] Homer Musselman, editor, Chopawamsic Baptist Church Record (Fauquier County, VA); Enoch, *Morgan's Station*, pp. 14, 62, 168, 182-183; Montgomery County DB 2:51, 400.

[49] Old Virginia Surveys 1:271; Old Virginia Grants 1:409.

[50] Holly W. Sphar, *The Sphar Family* (n.p., 1984), pp. 61-64.

[51] Beal Kelly, Revolutionary War pension application, S.15490, Virginia; Clark County Court of Quarter Sessions OB 1:413.

[52] James Wade interview, Draper MSS 12CC11; Enoch, *Morgan's Station*, pp. 14, 17, 36, 62, 168, 176, 183; Montgomery County WB E:51.

[53] Certificate Book, p. 70; Old Virginia Surveys 1:174; Old Virginia Grants 3:52.

[54] John Rankin interview, Draper MSS 11CC31; "Corn Compact," 29CC59; Enoch, *Morgan's Station*, pp. x, 14, 62, 168, 182-183; Montgomery County WB A:398.

[55] Old Virginia Surveys 1:149; Old Virginia Grants 6:77.

[56] Montgomery County DB 8:256.

[57] Will of James Hardage Lane in Loudoun County (VA) WB C:280.

[58] Certificate Book, p. 42.

[59] James Wade interview, Draper MSS 12CC11.

[60] Perrin, *History of Fayette County*, pp. 671-674; Draper MSS 15CC233; *Kentucky Gazette*, August 23, 1788; Fayette County DB R:252.

[61] *Kentucky Gazette*, January 16 and May 20, 1806.

[62] Old Virginia Surveys 4:557; Old Virginia Grants 10:132.

[63] Brooke Payne, *The Paynes of Virginia* (Harrisonburg, Virginia, 1977), pp. 258-259; Clark County DB 1:488.

[64] Payne, *The Paynes of Virginia* , pp. 254-256; Perrin, *History of Fayette County*, pp. 672-673.

[65] Payne, *The Paynes of Virginia* , pp. 253-254; Perrin, *History of Fayette County*, pp. 672-673; Fayette County OB 1:268.

[66] H. Thomas Tudor, *Early Settlers of Fort Boonesborough* (Richmond, KY, 1975); Certificate Book, p. 72, Kentucky Land Trials A:194-201.

[67] Old Virginia Surveys 6:114; Old Virginia Grants 6:482.

[68] William E. Ellis et al., *Madison County, 200 Years in Retrospect* (Richmond, KY, 1985), pp. 7, 10-11, 24, 98.

[69] Certificate Book, p. 72; William Clinkenbeard interview, Draper MSS 11CC54; Enoch, *Morgan's Station*, pp. 35-37, 46-48.

[70] James Corn, "The Corn Family of Mercer County, Kentucky," *RKHS* (1946) 44:70; Robert McAfee to Lyman Draper, Draper MSS 4CC87(4); Clark County Chronicles, April 26, 1923; Clark County WB 7:36.

[71] Patrick Scott interview, Draper MSS 11CC5.

[72] Certificate Book, p. 280; Old Virginia Surveys 2:446; Old Virginia Grants 6:220; Clark County DB 1:124, 2:11.

[73] O'Malley, *Stockading Up*, pp. 178-189; George M. Chinn, *Kentucky Settlement and Statehood, 1750-1800* (Frankfort, 1975), pp. 273-276.

[74] Kleber, *Kentucky Encyclopedia*, p. 475.

[75] Culpeper County (VA) DB V:324; Bourbon County OB H:192; Bourbon County WB G:268; Otto Basye, *The Basye Family in the United States* (Kansas City, MO, 1950), p. 253.

[76] Benjamin Allen interview, Draper MSS 11CC67; Littell, *Littell's Laws, Vol. 1*, p. 187; Clark County DB 2:19, 5:10; Trustee Minutes of the Town of Winchester, February 6, 1794.

[77] Certificate Book, p. 277; Old Virginia Surveys 2:447; Old Virginia Grants 6:211.

[78] William Calk deposition, *John Chiles vs William Halley's heirs*, Clark Circuit Court, 1808.

[79] Jackie Couture, *Madison County, Kentucky, Order Book A, 1787-1791* (Bowie, MD, 1996), pp. 5, 7, 15, 89.

[80] Certificate Book, p. 276; Old Virginia Surveys 2:441; Old Virginia Grants 7:104; Kentucky Court of Appeals DB F:381.

[81] Certificate Book, p. 280.

[82] George Robinson, *History of Greene County, Ohio* (Chicago; 1902), pp. 228-229.

[83] *Petitions*, No. 9.

[84] Old Virginia Surveys 8:126; Old Virginia Grants 14:123.

[85] Kentucky Land Trials A:644; Clark County DB 6:200, 607.

[86] Certificate Book, p. 53.

[87] Kentucky Land Trials A:538.

[88] George M. Chinn, *History of Harrodsburg and "The Great Settlement Area" of Kentucky, 1774-1900* (n.p., 1985), p.246; *Kentucky Gazette,* November 14, 1789, September 26, 1795; Mercer County OB 3:484.

[89] Old Virginia Surveys 2:64; Old Virginia Grants 5:315; Clark County DB 1:305.

[90] Kentucky Land Trials D:212; Margery H. Harding, *George Rogers Clark and His Men, Military Records 1778-1784* (Frankfort, 1981), p. 187; Clift, *Cornstalk Militia*, p. 2; Salyer, "Early Kentucky Surveyors."

[91] Clark County DB 11:361; John P. Landers, *Poingdestre-Poindexter, A Norman Family Through the Ages, 1250-1977* (n.p.; c1977); Samuel Morris interview, Draper MSS 12CC199; Simpson, *Virginia Baptist Ministers, Vol. 1*, p. 54.

[92] Daniel Boone's survey book, Draper MSS 25C58; Old Kentucky Surveys 1:357; Old Kentucky Grants 3:604.

[93] Jesse Daniel interview, Draper MSS 11CC93.

[94] Draper, *Life of Daniel Boone*, p. 455.

[95] Jesse Copher deposition, Kentucky Land Trials D:215; Draper, *Life of Daniel Boone*, pp. 470, 483, 488; David Todd to Lyman C. Draper, Draper MSS 44J57; Boone County (MO) WB A:120.

[96] Draper, *Life of Daniel Boone*, p. 488.

[97] Certificate Book, p. 74; Old Virginia Surveys 6:254; Old Virginia Grants 6:501, 10:294.

[98] Marty Hiatt and Craig R. Scott, *Loudoun County Virginia Tithables, 1758-1786, Vol. 2* (Athens, GA, 1995); Fayette County tax lists, 1785-87; Clark County WB 1:74; Fayette County WB A:44, B:35.

[99] Jillson, *Old Kentucky Entries and Deeds*, p. 309; Old Virginia Surveys 2:245, 264, 268; Old Virginia Grants 2:175-177.

[100] Old Virginia Surveys 2:245, 264, 268.

[101] Margaret Hopkins, *Index to the Tithables of Loudoun County, Virginia* (Baltimore; 1991), p. 43; Marty Hiatt, *Early Church Records of Loudoun County, Virginia* (Westminster, MD; 1995), p. 275.

[102] Jillson, *Old Kentucky Entries and Deeds;* Old Virginia Surveys 3:36; Old Virginia Grants 3:192-193.

[103] Clark County DB 7:65, 67, 76, 8:41, 42.

[104] Much of this information comes from the website of the Gen. Philemon Thomas Chapter of the Louisiana Society of the Sons of the American Revolution; also Clift, *Cornstalk Militia*, pp. 55; Collins, *History of Kentucky*, p. 547; Mason County DB C:13.

[105] Clark County OB 2:44.

[106] W. T. Black, "Ancestry of John Bell Hood," *RKHS* (1953) 51:305; "Kentucky Tombstone Inscriptions," *RKHS* (1929) 27:527.

[107] Lucien Beckner, "A Sketch of the Early Adventures of William Sudduth in Kentucky" *FCHQ* (1928) 2:43-70; Draper MSS 14U114-139; Mary Sudduth Stoddard, *The Stoddard-Sudduth Papers* (n. p., 1959); Clift, *Cornstalk Militia*, p. 74; death notice in *Lexington Observer & Reporter*, September 3, 1845.

[108] Benjamin Allen interview; Draper MSS 11CC67.

[109] Montgomery County WB E:5; Harper family notes by Mrs. William Everett Bach in the Mt. Sterling Public Library; Hazel Boyd, "Harper Families of Montgomery," undated clipping from the *Mt. Sterling Advocate*.

[110] Fayette County EB 1:25.

[111] Clark County OB 2:50.

[112] Kentucky Land Trials 1791-1810, p. 45.

[113] Old Kentucky Surveys 4:62; Kentucky Land Trials 1791-1810, p. 42; Clark County DB 5:458, 6:233.

[114] Clark County WB 4:43.

[115] Doyle, *Marriage Bonds of Clark County*; George F. Doyle, "Clark County Tombstone Records," unpublished manuscript (1935) at M. I. King Library, University of Kentucky, Lexington, p. 39.

[116] Cecil O'Dell, *Pioneers of Old Frederick County, Virginia* (Marceline, MO, 1995), pp. 83-86; William Clinkenbeard interview, Draper MSS 11CC54; O'Malley, *Stockading Up*, p. 161.

[117] *Kentucky Gazette*, August 20, 1805.

[118] Certificate Book, p. 90; Old Virginia Surveys 1:188; Old Virginia Grants 7:44.

[119] Malania E. Reynolds, "Clan Duncan Then And Now!" unpublished manuscript (2000) at the Kentucky History Center, Frankfort.

[120] Julia Ardery, *Kentucky Court and Other Records, Vol. 2,* (Lexington, 1932), p. 113.

[121] Kentucky Land Trials D:237.

[122] Draper MSS 11CC54.

[123] Old Virginia Grants 6:97; Certificate Book, p. 90; Clark County DB 6:410.

[124] Salyer, "Early Kentucky Surveyors"; Old Virginia Surveys 1:272; Old Virginia Grants 6:108; Clark County DB 1:139, Certificate Book, p. 90; William Clinkenbeard interview, Draper MSS 11CC54; Kentucky Land Trials B:445; D:217.

[125] Kentucky Land Trials D:217.

[126] Clark County DB 6:266.

[127] Draper MSS 11CC54; O'Malley, *Stockading Up*, p. 161.

[128] Boyd Crumrine, *History of Washington County, Pennsylvania* (Philadelphia; 1882), p. 645; Kentucky Court of Appeals DB J:30; Old Virginia Grants 7:385, 398.

[129] Certificate Book, p. 281.

[130] Old Virginia Surveys 7:89, 385, 398; Old Virginia Grants 6:482.

[131] *Kentucky Gazette*, May 14, 1796; Kentucky Land Trials 1791-1810, p. 5.

[132] Lucien Beckner, "Eskippakithiki: The Last Indian Town in Kentucky," *FCHQ* (1932) 6:355; A. Gwynn Henderson et al., *Indian Occupation and Use in Northern and Eastern Kentucky during the Contact Period (1540-1795): An Initial Investigation* (Frankfort, 1968), pp. 63-102; Old Virginia Surveys 4:261.

[133] Samuel M. Wilson, et al., *Kentucky in Retrospect* (Frankfort, 1942), pp. 139, 147; Clark County Chronicles, July 19, 1922; Fayette County WB B:57; Clay Lancaster, *Antebellum Architecture of Kentucky* (Lexington, 1991), p. 143.

[134] Old Virginia Surveys 3:49; Old Virginia Grants 5:211.

[135] Danske Dandridge, *Historic Shepherdstown* (Charlottesville; 1910), pp. 22, 33; Danske Dandridge, *George Michael Bedinger, A Kentucky Pioneer* (Charlottesville; 1909), pp. 43, 76.

[136] Old Virginia Surveys 4:132; Old Virginia Grants 5:426.

[137] *Kentucky Gazette*, April 30, 1796.

[138] R. S. Cotterill, "John Fleming, Pioneer of Fleming County," *RKHS* (1951) 49:193.

[139] John Craig interview, Draper MSS 12CC146; Clift, *Cornstalk Militia*, pp. 15, 72; Clark County WB 7:186.

[140] John A. Richards, *History of Bath County, Kentucky* (Yuma, AZ, 1961), pp. 7, 362; Old Virginia Surveys 7:385; George Stone, Mt. Sterling, personal communication.

[141] Ellen Eslinger, "Migration and Kinship on the Trans-Appalachian Frontier; Strode's Station, Kentucky," *FCHQ* (1988) 62:52; Daniel Sphar interview, Draper MSS 11CC107.

[142] William Clinkenbeard interview, Draper MSS 11CC54.

[143] Jefferson County EB 1:389.

[144] Old Virginia Surveys 1:199; Old Virginia Grants 6:100.

[145] Daniel Sphar interview, Draper MSS 11CC107.

[146] John Crawford interview, Draper MSS 12CC156.

[147] Clark County DB 29:440.

[148] Draper MSS 11CC54.

[149] Collins, *History of Kentucky*, p. 232.

[150] Halifax County (VA) WB 1:312, 332; Anthony Buckner family group record at www.familysearch.org; *Kentucky Gazette*, July 2, 1796; Clark County OB 2:44.

[151] Certificate Book, p. 107; Old Virginia Surveys 11:483, 485; Old Virginia Grants 11:384, 392.

[152] William Foster, Revolutionary War pension application, W.2986, Virginia; Clark County DB 7:640, 18:228; Clark County OB 8:88.

[153] Old Virginia Surveys 11:483, 485.

[154] Simpson, *Virginia Baptist Ministers, Vol. 1*, p. 32; Jillson, *Old Kentucky Entries and Deeds,* pp. 130-131, 258; Clark County DB 1:220, 262, 566; Kentucky Court of Appeals DB H:546.

[155] Old Virginia Surveys 3:174; Old Virginia Grants 5:213.

[156] *Petitions*, No. 47; Madison County DB A:61, F:178; Anne Crabb, editor, *Land Entries for Madison County, Kentucky, 1780-1793* (Richmond, KY, 1996), p. 73; *Kentucky Gazette,* December 11, 1806; Jonathan T. Dorris, "A 1792 Offer for the Location of the Capital of Kentucky at Boonesboro," *RKHS* (1933) 31:174; Clift, *Cornstalk Militia*, p. 122; Collins, *History of Kentucky*, p. 776.

[157] Old Virginia Surveys 2:247.

[158] Simpson, *Virginia Baptist Ministers, Vol. 3*, p. 111; "Reminiscences from the Life of Col. Cave Johnson," *RKHS* (1922) 20:207; Daniel Bryan interview, Draper MSS

22C14(17); Daniel Boone Jr. interview, Draper MSS 22C10; Bedford County (VA) Will Book 1:351.

[159] Certificate Book, p. 77.

[160] Old Kentucky Surveys 4:368; Old Kentucky Grants 8:262.

[161] Certificate Book, p. 97; *Kentucky Gazette,* December 5, 1795; Robert M. Rennick, *Kentucky's Bluegrass, A Survey of the Post Offices* (Lake Grove, 1993), p. 80.

[162] Certificate Book, p. 284; George W. Ranck, *History of Lexington, Kentucky* (Cincinnati, 1872), p. 73.

[163] Fayette County EB 2:263.

[164] Old Virginia Surveys 8:253; Old Virginia Grants 14:507;

[165] Collins, *History of Kentucky*, pp. 11, 147, 765; Dianne Wells, et al., *Roadside History, A Guide to Kentucky Highway Markers* (Frankfort, 2002), p. 192; Kleber, *Kentucky Encyclopedia*, p. 240; J. Winston Coleman Jr., *Historic Kentucky* (Lexington, 1968), p. 132.

[166] Martin D. Hardin, *Reports of Cases Argued and Adjudged in the Court of Appeals, 1805-1808* (Cincinnati, 1869), p. 52.

[167] Certificate Book, p. 223; Old Virginia Surveys 11:233; Fayette County District Court DB A:40; Montgomery County DB 2:357.

[168] *Kentucky Reporter*, November 17, 1819.

[169] Certificate Book, p. 307; Old Virginia Surveys 7:384; Old Virginia Grants 6:512.

[170] Clift, *Cornstalk Militia*, pp. 46, 130, 172; *Kentucky Gazette* November 6, 1801; Collins, *History of Kentucky*, p. 632; U.S. Census, 1820, Fleming County, Kentucky.

[171] Kentucky Land Trials B:461.

[172] W. H. Perrin, J. H. Battle and G. C. Kniffin, *Kentucky, A History of the State* (Louisville and Chicago; 1887-88); Hardin family papers at the Kentucky History Center, Frankfort.

[173] Certificate Book, p. 286.

[174] Old Kentucky Surveys 1:202; Old Kentucky Grants 3:320; Clark County Chronicles, June 7, 1923.

[175] Neal O. Hammon and Richard Taylor, *Virginia's Western War 1775-1786* (Mechanicsburg, PA, 2002), p. 15; Certificate Book, pp. 189, 216.

[176] "Lipscomb Family" by Hazel Smith Bonner at worldconnect.rootsweb.com.

[177] Old Kentucky Surveys 1:447, 450.

[178] Clark County OB 2:87; *Kentucky Gazette*, October 8, 1796.

[179] Jackie Couture, *Madison County, Kentucky, Order Book A, 1787-1791* (Bowie, MD, 1996), pp. 5, 55, 104; Madison County WB D:83.

[180] Kentucky Land Trials B:354.

[181] Old Kentucky Surveys 1:448; Old Kentucky Grants 4:111.

[182] Old Virginia Grants 12:273 (Myers).

[183] Lawrence Thompson, Revolutionary War pension application, R.10546, North Carolina; Jane G. Buchanan, *Thomas Thompson and Ann Finney of Colonial Pennsylvania and North Carolina* (Oak Ridge, TN, 1987), pp. 145-166; Draper MSS 17CC213.

[184] Draper MSS 17CC197.

[185] Draper MSS 28C32, 34; Clift, *Cornstalk Militia,* pp. 5, 55, 81; Certificate Book, p. 93; Salyer, "Early Kentucky Surveyors."

[186] Old Virginia Surveys 5:322; Old Virginia Grants 10:308.

[187] *Petitions,* Nos. 47, 65; Juanita Townsend's notes in Ellen and Diane Rogers, *The Rogers Book,* (Stanton KY, n.d.), p. 660; Clark County WB 1:27, 33.

[188] Walter Chiles Carr at freepages.genealogy.rootsweb.com/~markfreeman/chiles.html; Perrin, *History of Fayette County,* pp. 64, 69, 540, 775.

[189] *Lexington Observer & Reporter,* December 8, 1838.

[190] Old Virginia Surveys 4:254; Old Virginia Grants 4:458; Clark County DB 1:671.

[191] W. W. Abbot, editor, *Papers of George Washington, Colonial Series Vol. 5* (Charlottesville; 1988), p. 268; Neal O. Hammon, *Early Kentucky Land Records,* 1773-1780 (Louisville; 1992), pp. 44, 46, 259, 271; *Samuel Meredith vs John McChord et al.,* Kentucky Land Trials F:263-292.

[192] *Virginia Gazette,* May 24, 1783.

[193] Kentucky Land Trials A:235; Hazel Dicken Garcia, *To Western Woods; The Breckinridge Family Moves to Kentucky in 1793* (Rutherford, NJ; 1991), pp. 114-153; Clift, *Cornstalk Militia,* pp. 4, 32; *Kentucky Gazette,* June 2, 1798, November 13, 1815; Clay Lancaster, *Ante Bellum Houses of the Bluegrass* (Lexington, 1961), p. 58; Draper MSS 17CC12-13.

[194] Old Virginia Surveys 11:273; Old Kentucky Grants 2:198.

[195] *Kentucky Gazette,* September 24, 1796.

[196] Wilson Maddox, Revolutionary War pension application, S.8413, Kentucky; Bettye Lee Mastin, *Lexington 1779, Pioneer Kentucky as Described by Early Settlers* (Lexington, 1979), pp. 76, 89.

[197] J. M. Armstrong & Co., *Biographical Encyclopedia of Kentucky* (Cincinnati, 1878), p. 11.

[198] Jean Calvert and John Klee, *Towns of Mason County, Their Past in Pictures* (n.p., 1986), p. 17; Willard R. Jillson, *Pioneer Kentucky* (Frankfort; 1934), p. 83.

[199] Kleber, *Kentucky Encyclopedia,* p. 488.

[200] Neal O. Hammon, "Kentucky Pioneer Forts and Stations," *FCHQ* (2002) 76:563.

[201] Old Virginia Surveys 5:296; Old Virginia Grants 10:465.

[202] Jefferson County EB 1:441.

[203] Old Virginia Surveys 5:296.

[204] William Risk interview, Draper MSS 11CC87; Clark County OB 2:63.

[205] Nathaniel Hart interview, Draper MSS 17CC201; Draper, *Life of Daniel Boone*, p. 276.

[206] Benjamin Combs' deposition and maps in Clark County Land Trials 1812-1815, pp. 474-523; Draper MSS 11CC81; O'Malley, *Stockading Up*, p. 153.

[207] Peter Houston, *Sketch of the Life and Character of Daniel Boone*, edited by Ted Franklin Belue (Mechanicsville, PA; 1997), pp. 30-31, 66-67.

[208] Nicholas Brent Porter, Revolutionary War pension application, S.23454, Virginia.

[209] Certificate Book, p. 309.

[210] Old Virginia Surveys 11:384; Joan E. Brookes-Smith, *Master Index Virginia Surveys and Grants* 1774-1791 (Frankfort, 1976); p. 20.

[211] Certificate Book, p. 85; Old Virginia Surveys 2:62; Old Virginia Grants 5:190.

[212] Kentucky Land Trials A:570; Bourbon County OB A:516; Harry Mills, "Early Families of Montgomery County and Pioneer Kentucky," *Mt. Sterling Advocate*, April 4, 1946; Enoch, *Morgan's Station*, pp. 8-9, 14-15, 18, 20, 52-54.

[213] Certificate Book, p. 42; Old Virginia Surveys 1:189; Enoch, *Morgan's Station*, pp. 53, 180.

[214] "Descendants of William Morgan," unpublished manuscript provided to the author by Betty Knorr of California (BettyKn@aol.com).

[215] W. W. Abbot, editor, *Papers of George Washington, Confederation Series, Vol. 3*, (Charlottesville, 1992-1997), p. 309, *Vol. 4*, p. 314; *Retirement Series, Vol. 2* (Charlottesville, 1999), pp. 296, 552, *Vol. 4*, p. 395; Donald Jackson, editor, *Diaries of George Washington, Vol. 2* (Charlottesville, 1976), p. 294; Lucien Beckner, "Letter from George Washington to Charles Morgan of Kentucky, 1795," *FCHQ* (1928) 3:23; Kentucky Court of Appeals DB 5:244; Allegheny County (PA) WB 1:241.

[216] Certificate Book, p. 151.

[217] Old Virginia Surveys 3:177; Old Virginia Grants 5:294.

[218] Old Virginia Surveys 3:177; Kentucky Land Trials A:339-340.

[219] Certificate Book, p. 108; May R. King and David L. Ringo, *Ringo Family History, Vol. 2* (Alhambra, CA, 1980), pp. 219-229.

[220] Certificate Book, pp. 51, 257; Old Virginia Surveys 10:235; Old Virginia Grants 11:494-495; Montgomery County DB 2:118.

[221] John Crawford interview, Draper MSS 12CC156.

[222] Richard Reid, *Historical Sketches of Montgomery County* (Lexington, 1926), pp. 15-16.

[223] Certificate Book, p. 309; Old Virginia Surveys 11:326.

[224] Doyle, *Marriage Bonds of Clark County*.

[225] Perrin, *History of Fayette County*, p. 492; S. J. Conkwright, *History of the Boone's Creek Baptist Association of Kentucky* (Winchester, 1923), p. 44; *Kentucky Gazette*, December 24,1791, May 11,1793; Collins, *History of Kentucky*, p. 170; Fayette County WB D:305.

[226] Old Virginia Surveys 2:289; Clark County DB 23:419.

[227] Clark County OB 2:488.

[228] Certificate Book, p. 82.

[229] Old Virginia Surveys 6:20; Old Virginia Grants 2:174, 210.

[230] John W. Scholl, *Scholl-Sholl-Shull Genealogy, The Colonial Branches* (New York, n.d.), pp. 6-9; S. J. Conkwright, *History of the Boone's Creek Baptist Association of Kentucky* (Winchester, 1923), p. 42.

[231] Clark County Chronicles, May 31, June 14 and June 21, 1923; O'Malley, *Stockading Up*, pp. 159-169; Clark County DB 7:419, 614, 9:231; Owen, "500 Old Families."

[232] Neal O. Hammon, editor, *My Father Daniel Boone; Draper Interviews with Nathan Boone* (Lexington; 1999); William D. Brown, "Capture of Daniel Boone's Saltmakers: Fresh Perspectives from Primary Sources," *RKHS* (1985) 83:1.

[233] Samuel Boone, Revolutionary War pension application, S.1168, North Carolina; Clark County WB 10:279; Sarah R. S. Rockenfield, *Our Boone Families—Daniel Boone's Kinfolks* (Evansville, IN, 1987), p. 382.

[234] Clark County DB 25:285.

[235] Kentucky Land Trials B:469.

[236] Littell, *Littell's Laws, Vol. 1*, p. 58; Clark County DB 10:200.

[237] *Kentucky Reporter*, September 16, 1822.

[238] Old Virginia Surveys 3:187; Old Virginia Grants 10:93; Clark County DB 7:250.

[239] Chester R. Young, *Westward into Kentucky, The Narrative of Daniel Trabue* (Lexington, 1981), pp. 75, 175; William E. Railey, *History of Woodford County, Kentucky* (Versailles, 1968), p. 39; Simpson, *Virginia Baptist Ministers, Vol. 1*, p. 14; *Kentucky Gazette* July 29, 1797.

[240] Jillson, *Old Kentucky Entries and Deeds*, p. 201; Old Virginia Surveys 2:60, 63; Old Virginia Grants 1:458, 3:208; Clark County DB 7:458.

[241] Collins, *History of Kentucky*, p. 367; Clark County DB 3:539, 4:192; Kentucky Court of Appeals DB N:318.

[242] Clark County DB 6:74, 10:130, 265, 267, 276, 298, 299, 410, 11:25, 44; *Kentucky Reporter*, April 13, 1831.

[243] Old Virginia Surveys 2:512, 513; Montgomery County WB B:173.

[244] Jefferson County EB 1:424.

[245] Clark County OB 2:73; Old Kentucky Surveys 4:344.

[246] Old Virginia Surveys 11:116; Old Kentucky Grants 1:112; *Robert Wickliff vs George Ensor et al*, Nicholas Circuit Court.

[247] Kentucky Land Trials A:542.

[248] Bath County DB G:1.

[249] Will of Thomas Swearingen, recorded in Kentucky Court of Appeals DB V:257; Clark County DB 19:363, 28:289.

[250] Old Virginia Surveys 1:407; Old Virginia Grants 1:403; Clark County DB 1:607.

[251] Trustee Minutes of the Town of Winchester, February 13, 1794; Salyer, "Early Kentucky Surveyors"; Enoch, *Morgan's Station*, p. 30; S. D. Mitchell, "Sketch of Josiah Hart, Father of Joel T. Hart," *RKHS* (1944), p. 19; Kathryn Owen, *Old Graveyards of Clark County, Kentucky* (New Orleans, 1975), p. 128.

[252] *Petitions*, No. 78; Clark County DB 1:345, 6:275.

[253] "William Calk his Jurnal," transcription at the Kentucky History Center, Special Collections and Archives, Frankfort.

[254] J. H. Spencer, *History of Kentucky Baptists, Vol. 1.* (Cincinnati, 1885), p. 264 and *Vol. 2*, pp. 96-97, 100; Frances Faulconer interview, Draper MSS 11CC135-139; Mason County WB H:118.

[255] Old Virginia Surveys 3:59; Old Virginia Grants 2:284; Clark County DB 1:712-713.

[256] State of Maryland, *Calendar of Maryland State Papers, Number 4, Part 1, The Red Books* (Annapolis, 1950), p. 50; Henry Peden, *Revolutionary Patriots of Baltimore Town and Baltimore County, Maryland* (Silver Spring, MD, 1988); Certificate Book, p. 255; Collins, *History of Kentucky,* p. 102; Joan E. Brookes-Smith, *Master Index Virginia Surveys and Grants 1774-1791* (Frankfort, 1976); Enoch, *Morgan's Station,* pp. 26-37.

[257] Old Virginia Surveys 2:317; Old Virginia Grants 4:449.

[258] Danske Dandridge, *Historic Shepherdstown* (Charlottesville, 1910); Danske Dandridge, *George Michael Bedinger, A Kentucky Pioneer* (Charlottesville, 1909); Bedinger Papers, Draper MSS 1A1; Enoch, *Morgan's Station,* pp. 21-26, 30-35.

[259] Bath County OB A:349; Clark County Court of Quarter Sessions, October 22, 1793; Clift, *Cornstalk Militia,* p. 47; Enoch, *Morgan's Station,* pp. 109, 133.

[260] Harry Mills, "Montgomery Family," *Mt. Sterling Advocate,* January 31, 1973; Montgomery County DB 2:445; James Wade interview, Draper MSS 12CC11.

[261] Enoch, *Morgan's Station,* pp. 87-89, 106-108.

[262] Certificate Book, p. 80.

[263] Old Virginia Surveys 6:39, 8:333, 11:246.

[264] Draper MSS 11CC279, 12CC256; Salyer, "Early Kentucky Surveyors"; Madison County WB A:81; Certificate Book, p. 89.

[265] Clark County OB 2:51 *Kentucky Gazette,* July 9, 1796.

[266] Kleber, *Kentucky Encyclopedia,* p. 363; J. Winston Coleman, *Historic Kentucky* (Lexington; 1968), p. 185.

[267] Clark County Chronicles, March 20, 1924; Clark County WB 1:166.

[268] Clark County Chronicles, March 27, 1924; Kentucky Land Trials A:577, B:54; Clift, *Cornstalk Militia,* p. 4; William Clinkenbeard interview, Draper MSS 11CC54.

[269] Old Virginia Surveys 3:477, 502, 4:328.

[270] Josiah H. Combs, *Combs, A Study in Comparative Philology and Genealogy* (Pensacola, FL, 1976), p. 127.

[271] Draper, *Life of Daniel Boone,* p. 348.

[272] Thomas Eastin interview, Draper MSS 11CC95-97.

[273] George W. Ranck, *Boonesborough* (Louisville, 1901), p. 178.

[274] Certificate Book, p. 14; Clark County WB 3:427.

[275] Draper MSS 11CC80.

[276] Draper MSS 11CC86; Clark County DB 5:67.

[277] Lewis H. Kilpatrick, "William Calk, Kentucky Pioneer," *Kentucky Magazine* (1918) 2:33; Lewis H. Kilpatrick, "Journal of William Calk, Kentucky Pioneer," *Mississippi Valley Historical Review* (1921) 7:363.

[278] Enoch Smith deposition, procession #22.

[279] Benjamin Combs' deposition and maps in Clark County Land Trials 1812-1815, pp. 474-523.

[280] *Kentucky Gazette*, May 24, 1788.

[281] *Kentucky Gazette*, August 15, 1795; Joan E. Brookes-Smith, *Master Index Virginia Surveys and Grants* 1774-1791 (Frankfort, 1976); Harry G. Enoch, "Charles Morgan's Mill," *The Millstone* (Fall 2003) 2:31; Muhlenberg County WB 2:193.

[282] Old Virginia Surveys 9:180; Old Virginia Grants 10:286; *Kentucky Gazette,* February 7, 1809.

[283] Draper MSS 11CC54.

[284] Kentucky Land Trials A:807, 809; Clark County DB 2:40, 4:223, 10:29.

[285] Joseph Proctor, Revolutionary War pension application, S.11270, Virginia; Draper MSS 12CC208.

[286] Harry G. Enoch, "The Travels of John Hanks, Recollections of a Kentucky Pioneer," *RKHS* (1994) 92:131.

[287] Old Virginia Surveys 11:97; Old Kentucky Grants 1:120.

[288] Clark County DB 1:391, 393, 2:190.

[289] Kleber, *Kentucky Encyclopedia*, p. 195.

[290] Brenda Reed, "Updated Kith & Kin of VA, NC, etc.," at worldconnect.rootsweb.com; Montgomery County DB 4:413.

[291] Old Virginia Surveys 7:314; Old Virginia Grants 12:156; *Kentucky Gazette,* August 13, 1796.

[292] Kentucky Land Trials A:537.

[293] Kentucky Land Trials A:542.

[294] Emma B. Nunnelly, "The Collins' and Prewitts', Pioneer Patriots Jointly Sketched," *RKHS* (1932) 30:93; Billie Adams, "Collins Documentation," unpublished manuscript (c1990) at the Kentucky History Center, Frankfort; Willard R. Jillson, *Red River Iron Works* (Frankfort, 1964); Kentucky Land Trials E:96; Fayette County District Court DB A:131, 344, B:454, C:485; Fayette County Circuit Court DB A:2.

[295] Old Virginia Surveys 6:246-247 (Stephen), 6:99-100 (Joel), 10:437 (Elisha).

[296] Patrick Scott interview, Draper MSS 11CC5; Bourbon County OB B:260, 468; *Stewart's Kentucky Herald*, March 21, 1797; Fayette County Circuit Court DB B:520;

Littell, *Littell's Laws, Vol. 2*, p. 279; Clark County OB 2:386, 405; *Thomas Constant vs James Swinney*, Clark Circuit Court, 1803.

[297] Abstract provided by Norwood Thorpe of Estill County, source unknown.

[298] Montgomery County DB 3:498; Clark County OB 3:395.

[299] Draper MSS 12CC64; Bettye Lee Mastin, *Lexington, 1779. Pioneer Kentucky as Described by Early Settlers* (Lexington, 1979), pp. 46-48.

[300] Kentucky Land Trials D:322.

[301] *Petitions*, No. 17; Kentucky Supreme Court DB B:76.

[302] Old Virginia Surveys 5:46, 11:22; Old Virginia Grants 6:541.

[303] Clark County DB 4:27.

[304] Kentucky Land Trials A:523.

[305] Jefferson County EB 1:381.

[306] Old Virginia Surveys 5:301, 305; Old Virginia Grants 8:315, 403; Clark County DB 1:676, 668, 6:547; Mercer County OB 3:296, Madison County WB A:490.

[307] Samuel Shelton, Revolutionary War pension application, W.8716, Virginia.

[308] Bessie Taul Conkwright, "Captain Billy Bush," *Winchester Democrat*, October 15, 1915; Draper, *Life of Daniel Boone*, pp. 335, 428; George F. Doyle, "A Transcript of the First Record Book of Providence Church, Clark County, Kentucky" unpublished manuscript (1924) at the M. I. King Library, University of Kentucky, Lexington, p. 2.

[309] Clark County Chronicles, April 10, 1924; Kentucky Land Trials B:344; Old Virginia Surveys 3:460; Old Virginia Grants 10:80, 85; Clark County WB 3:55.

[310] O'Malley, *Stockading Up,* p. 27; Certificate Book, pp. 91, 96, 116; George M. Chinn, *History of Harrodsburg and "The Great Settlement Area" of Kentucky, 1774-1900* (n.p., 1985), p. 230; Clark County DB 4:425, 430; Neal O. Hammon and Richard Taylor, *Virginia's Western War 1775-1786* (Mechanicsburg, PA, 2002), pp. 69-70, 106.

[311] Old Virginia Surveys 7:233.

[312] Edgar Woods, *Albemarle County in Virginia* (Harrisonburg, VA, 1978 edition), p. 387; Archibald Woods, Revolutionary War pension application, S.37492, Virginia; Harry G. Enoch, *The History of Weddle's Mill and Other Old Mills Located near Doylesville on Muddy Creek in Madison County, Kentucky* (Clay City, KY, 2004), p.3.

[313] Madison County OB C:4, D:531.

[314] Old Kentucky Surveys 5:118; Old Kentucky Grants 11:118.

[315] Old Virginia Grants 11:490; Littell, *Littell's Laws, Vol. 2*, pp. 179, 376; *Vol. 3*, p. 390; James Speed, *The Political Club* (Louisville, 1894), p. 95.

[316] Josiah H. Combs, *Combs, A Study in Comparative Philology and Genealogy* (Pensacola, FL, 1976), p. 127; Deposition of Benjamin Combs, 1813, in *Cuthbert Combs Sr. vs Thomas Porter's heirs,* Clark County Land Trials, 1812-1815, pp. 474-523; Clark County DB 3:296, 299.

[317] Certificate Book, p. 14.

[318] Clark County DB 1:320.

[319] Old Virginia Surveys 1:11 (Maxwell), 6:324 (Combs); Fayette County Survey Book B:131 (Howard); Clark County DB 1:461, 584.

[320] Old Virginia Surveys 1:15 (Maxwell), 3:443 (Moore).

[321] *Lexington Observer & Reporter*, December 12, 1838.

[322] Thomas Eastin interview, Draper MSS 11CC95-97; Littell, *Littell's Laws, Vol. 1*, p. 187; Kathryn Owen, *Old Graveyards of Clark County, Kentucky* (New Orleans, 1975), p. 23; Kleber, *Kentucky Encyclopedia*, p. 219.

[323] Lewis Collins, *Historical Sketches of Kentucky* (Maysville, 1847), pp. 234-235; Harry G. Enoch, *John Howard of Howard's Creek; Biography of a Clark County Pioneer* (to be published, 2005).

[324] Cuthbert Combs' claim on Upper Howard's Creek and William Bush's claim on Lower Howard's Creek in October 1779 and December 1779, respectively, in Certificate Book, pp. 14, 80.

[325] Collins, *History of Kentucky*, p. 168.

[326] Certificate Book, p. 72; Old Virginia Surveys 10:104; Old Virginia Grants 13:469.

[327] J. M. Armstrong & Co., *Biographical Encyclopedia of Kentucky* (Cincinnati, 1878), p. 353.

[328] *Kentucky Gazette*, June 15, 1801; Clark County DB 11:276.

[329] J. Winston Coleman, *Historic Kentucky* (Lexington; 1968), p. 166; William E. Railey, *History of Woodford County, Kentucky* (Versailles, 1968), pp. 178, 306; Collins, *History of Kentucky*, pp. 393, 542.

[330] W. M. Paxton, *The Marshall Family* (Cincinnati, 1885).

[331] Jefferson County EB 1:425.

[332] W. M. Paxton, *The Marshall Family* (Cincinnati; 1885).

[333] Old Virginia Surveys 1:396, 2:206; Old Virginia Grants 2:85, 5:97; Clark County DB 4:220.

[334] Chloe McNeill, "Africa, Illinois" at www.illinoishistory.com/africa.html; Augusta County OB 17:231, 265; Isaiah Slavens, Revolutionary War pension application, S.16529, Virginia; Clark County DB 4:220.

[335] Clark County DB 4:220.

[336] Neal O. Hammon, editor, *My Father Daniel Boone; Draper Interviews with Nathan Boone* (Lexington; 1999), p. 109.

[337] Jefferson County EB 1:342; Old Kentucky Surveys 7:66-67; Old Kentucky Grants 15:169, 171.

[338] Clark County DB 3:506, 9:37, 14:210, 27:285.

[339] *Kentucky Gazette*, April 13, 1801; Old Kentucky Surveys 7:66.

[340] William E. Railey, *History of Woodford County, Kentucky* (Versailles, 1968), p. 130.

[341] Railey, *History of Woodford County*, pp. 130-131; Fayette County WB E:216.

[342] Jefferson County EB 1:424; Old Virginia Surveys 5:335; Old Virginia Grants 6:511.

[343] Bessie Taul Conkwright, "Conkwright," unpublished manuscript (1935) at the Kentucky History Center, Frankfort.

[344] Old Kentucky Surveys 5:483; Old Kentucky Grants 13:41; Clark County DB 10:438.

[345] George M. Chinn, *History of Harrodsburg and "The Great Settlement Area" of Kentucky, 1774-1900* (n.p., 1985), pp. 67, 224, 227, 230, 232, 237, 255; Mercer County OB 2:195; Collins, *History of Kentucky*, p. 326; William and Mary Kennedy family files, Campbell County Historical Society at www.rootsweb.com.

[346] *Kentucky Gazette,* May 30, 1799.

[347] Clark County OB 3:30.

[348] Old Kentucky Surveys 5:358; Clark County DB 5:304, 306, 308.

[349] Clark County DB 6:102; *Kentucky Gazette*, January 15, 1802.

[350] R. S. Cotterill, "Battle of Upper Blue Licks," *FCHQ* (1927) 2:29; Kentucky Land Trials A:12, B:338; Old Virginia Surveys 11:255.

[351] Old Virginia Grants 2:194; Reuben T. Durrett, *Bryant's Station* (Louisville, 1897), p. 49; Clark County WB 1:14.

[352] Clark County Chronicles, March 27, 1924, April 3 and 10, 1824; Benjamin Allen interview, Draper MSS 11CC67; Anderson C. Quisenberry, *Kentucky in the War of 1812* Frankfort, 1915), p. 162; *Lexington Observer & Reporter,* March 10, 1836; George F. Doyle, "Clark County Tombstone Records," unpublished manuscript (1935) at M. I. King Library, University of Kentucky, Lexington, p. 19.

[353] O'Malley, *Stockading Up,* p. 158; Kentucky Land Trials D:225.

[354] Salyer, "Early Kentucky Surveyors"; Edna Barney, "Virginia Descendants of Henry Peyton" at members.aol.com; Jeptha Kemper interview, Draper MSS 12CC128; Dr. Louis Marshall interview, Draper MSS 16CC242.

[355] John Rankin interview, Draper MSS 11CC82.

[356] Jeptha Kemper interview, Draper MSS 12CC128; Bourbon County WB A:17.

[357] Certificate Book, p. 284; Old Virginia Surveys 8:323; Old Virginia Grants 15:326; Clark County DB 1:204, 7:4.

[358] Owen, "500 Old Families"; H. Thomas Tudor, *Early Settlers of Fort Boonesborough* (Richmond, KY, 1975); Certificate Book, p. 74; Old Virginia Surveys 5:100.

[359] Draper MSS 11CC112.

[360] Clark County DB 3:223; George F. Doyle, "A Transcript of the First Record Book of Providence Church, Clark County, Kentucky" unpublished manuscript (1924) at the M. I. King Library, University of Kentucky, Lexington, p. 7; Clark County WB 4:382.

[361] Fred Simpson, *Back of the Cane, Early Virginia Surveys in Today's Garrard County, Kentucky* (Utica, KY, 1993 edition), p. 292; Draper MSS 15CC233; James Speed, *The Political Club* (Louisville, 1894), p. 66; Forest Calico, *History of Garrard County and Its Churches* (New York, 1947), p. 26.

[362] *Kentucky Gazette*, October 1, 1811.

[363] Old Virginia Surveys 8:529, 11:3.

[364] Clark County DB 3:65, 10:31.

[365] Kentucky Land Trials A:332.

[366] H. Thomas Tudor, *Early Settlers of Fort Boonesborough* (Richmond, KY, 1975); James A. James, editor, *George Rogers Clark Papers, 1781-1784, Collections of the Illinois State Historical Library, Volume XIX, Virginia Series, Volume IV* (Springfield, IL, 1912), pp. 338, 408; Margery H. Harding, *George Rogers Clark and His Men, Military Records 1778-1784* (Frankfort, 1981), p. 84; Kentucky Land Trials A:189, 337, 805, D:260; Clark County Court of Quarter Sessions, July 22, 1794; Montgomery County WB B:203.

[367] Holly W. Sphar, *The Sphar Family* (n.p., 1984), p. 75; *Petitions*, No. 26.

[368] Kentucky Land Trials A:340.

[369] O'Malley, *Stockading Up*, p. 241.

[370] Orange County (VA) DB 15:310; Simpson, *Virginia Baptist Ministers, Vol. 2*, p. 64; *Kentucky Gazette,* July 20, 1798.

[371] Old Virginia Surveys 1:253; Old Virginia Grants 1:286; Kentucky Supreme Court DB A:495; Kentucky Court of Appeals DB F:165.

[372] Hamilton J. Eckenrode, *Virginia Soldiers of the American Revolution, Vol. 1* (Richmond, VA, 1989 edition), p. 466; Clark County DB 1:537, 3:362, 6:582.

[373] George F. Doyle, "A Transcript of the First Record Book of Providence Church, Clark County, Kentucky" unpublished manuscript (1924) at the M. I. King Library, University of Kentucky, Lexington, p. 11; *Petitions*, No. 65; Clark County DB 7:546.

[374] Clark County DB 14:471.

[375] Clark County WB 9:603.

[376] Old Virginia Grants 5:294; *Kentucky Gazette*, July 30, 1802.

[377] Draper, *Life of Daniel Boone,* pp. 460-484.

[378] Ibid., p. 488.

[379] Certificate Book, p. 89; Old Virginia Surveys 4:298; Old Virginia Grants 3:420.

[380] Clark County DB 11:318.

[381] Madison County DB 1:95.

[382] John Gass interview, Draper MSS 11CC14.

[383] William Clinkenbeard interview, Draper MSS 11CC54; Kathryn Owen, *Old Homes and Landmarks of Clark County, Kentucky* (Lexington, 1967), p. 32; Clark County WB 6:55.

[384] Lucien Beckner, "Reverend John D. Shane's Interview with Pioneer William Clinkenbeard," *FCHQ* (1928) 2:95-128.

[385] "Memoirs of Jesse Kennedy," unpublished manuscript at the John Fox Jr. Library, Paris; "Scott's Papers," *RKHS* (1953) 51:154.

[386] "Memoirs of Jesse Kennedy."

[387] Certificate Book, p. 91; Old Virginia Surveys 3:74.

[388] *Cadiz Record*, April 3, 1902; Bourbon County DB O:285; Dawson family file, Clark County Public Library, Winchester.

[389] Bourbon County WB C:316; Dawson family file, Clark County Public Library, Winchester.

[390] Mrs. Pierce interview, Draper MSS 13CC7; George Trumbo interview, Draper MSS 12CC114.

[391] Bourbon County OB A:128, 206.

[392] William Perrin, editor, *History of Bourbon, Scott, Harrison and Nicholas Counties, Kentucky* (Chicago, 1882), p. 138.

[393] Augusta County (VA) WB 4:521; Fred Simpson, *Back of the Cane, Early Virginia Surveys in Today's Garrard County, Kentucky* (Utica, KY, 1993 edition), pp. 106-107; Frances Ferguson and Miriam Luke, "David Dryden, The Tailor, 1729-1777, and His Family," unpublished manuscript (1979) at the Kentucky History Center, Frankfort; Madison County WB A:330; Kentucky Land Trials C:155.

[394] Old Kentucky Surveys 7:530; Old Kentucky Grants 15:613.

[395] Old Virginia Surveys 11:246; Doyle, *Marriage Bonds of Clark County*; Clark County DB 3:146, 3:390.

[396] Old Kentucky Surveys 6:456-457; Old Kentucky Grants 13:567, 575.

[397] Clark County DB 5:189.

[398] Samuel Martin, Revolutionary War pension application, S.38238, Virginia.

[399] John McKinney, Revolutionary War pension application, R.6768, Virginia; Mrs. Ware interview, Draper MSS 11CC75; Collins, *History of Kentucky*, pp. 225-226; Certificate Book, p. 155; Otto Rothert, "John D. Shane's Interview with Mrs. John McKinney and Her Son Harvey, Bourbon County," *FCHQ* (1939) 13:157; Salyer, "Early Kentucky Surveyors."

[400] William H. Ansel Jr., *Frontier Forts Along the Potomac and Its Tributaries* (Parsons, WV, 1984), p. 118; Draper MSS 8CC4; Willard R. Jillson, *Pioneer Kentucky* (Frankfort; 1934), p. 89; Jefferson County DB 6:172; Jefferson County Minute Book 1:55.

[401] Old Virginia Surveys 2:386; Old Virginia Grants 9:125; Clark County DB 2:117.

[402] Salyer, "Early Kentucky Surveyors"; *Kentucky Gazette*, October 22, 1796; Kentucky Land Trials D:210, E:153.

[403] "Death of One of the Early Pioneers, Alexander L. Barnett Joins the Silent Majority" (DeWitt County, IL), April 30, 1886, at www.rootsweb.com.

[404] Julia Ardery, *Kentucky Court and Other Records, Vol. 2,* (Lexington, 1932), p. 110.

[405] *Kentucky Reporter*, November 6, 1826.

[406] Littell, *Littell's Laws, Vol. 2*, p. 227; Bourbon County WB G:433.

[407] Old Kentucky Surveys 5:470; Old Kentucky Grants 13:29; Clark County DB 4:124.

[408] Alma Wilson, "Estill Family," *RKHS* (1945) 43:121; Neal O. Hammon, "Kentucky Pioneer Forts and Stations," *FCHQ* (2002) 76:546; Clift, *Cornstalk Militia*, p. 22; Samuel Estill, Revolutionary War pension application, S.12876, Virginia.

[409] Salyer, "Early Kentucky Surveyors."

[410] Willard R. Jillson, *The Red River Iron Works* (Frankfort, 1964).

[411] Old Virginia Surveys 6:246; Old Virginia Grants 8:479; Harry G. Enoch, "Clay City Area, 1782, as Described by Aquilla White and Josiah Collins," *Red River Historical Society & Museum Newsletter* (2002) 10(2):28.

[412] Aquilla White, Revolutionary War pension application, S.37533, Pennsylvania.

[413] Samuel Cassidy, *Story of a Log House* (Lexington; 1976); Clay Lancaster, *Antebellum Architecture of Kentucky* (Lexington, 1991), p. 47.

[414] Old Virginia Surveys 2:417; Old Virginia Grants 2:156; Clark County DB 6:632, 7:219, 13:53-54.

[415] John Mack Faragher, *Daniel Boone, Life and Legend of an American Pioneer* (New York, 1992), pp. 16-17, 219, 221; Sarah R. S. Rockenfield, *Our Boone Families—Daniel Boone's Kinfolks* (Evansville, IN, 1987), p. 382.

[416] Certificate Book, p. 38; Margery H. Harding, *George Rogers Clark and His Men, Military Records 1778-1784* (Frankfort, 1981), pp. 53, 119; John McIntire deposition in procession #76; Clark County WB 5:324.

[417] Draper, *Life of Daniel Boone,* pp. 416, 423, 567.

[418] Certificate Book, p. 77; Old Virginia Surveys 7:232, 10:452-454; Old Virginia Grants 8:605, 9:561, 565, 10:520, 11:75; Clark County DB 10:198.

[419] Kentucky Land Trials A:1.

[420] Holly W. Sphar, *The Sphar Family* (n.p., 1984), p. 104; Perrin, *History of Fayette County*, p. 179; Thomas D. Clark, *Clark County, Kentucky, A History* (Winchester, 1995), p. 125; Clark County WB 1:315.

[421] *Kentucky Gazette,* April 9, 1806.

[422] Draper MSS 17CC204.

[423] Oswald Townsend, Revolutionary War pension application, W.605, Virginia; Madison County WB F:222; Juanita Townsend's notes in Ellen and Diane Rogers, *The Rogers Book*, (Stanton KY, n.d.), pp. 660, 687.

[424] Procession #57.

[425] Kentucky Land Trials D:210 (David Williams), D:211 (Patrick Jordan), D:215 (Jesse Copher); D:220 (Oswald Townsend), D:223 (Stephen Hancock); D:285 (William Bush).

[426] Old Virginia Surveys 1:274, 2:183.

[427] Collins, *History of Kentucky*, p. 331; Kleber, *Kentucky Encyclopedia,* p. 411.

[428] Certificate Book, p. 304.

[429] Old Virginia Surveys 10:283; Old Virginia Grants 14:154; Clark County DB 5:138; Clark County Processions, p. 427.

[430] Micah Taul, "Memoirs of Micah Taul," *RKHS* (1929) 27:356; Clark County DB 1:395; U.S. Census, 1810, Clark County, Kentucky.

[431] Bess Hawthorne, "Thomas Burris, Ancestor of Kentucky Pioneers," *RKHS* (1926) 24:182; S. J. Conkwright, *History of the Boone's Creek Baptist Association of Kentucky* (Winchester, 1923), p. 21; Old Virginia Grants 1:285, 2:64; Clark County WB 8:481.

[432] *Petitions*, Nos. 47, 65; Juanita Townsend's notes in Ellen and Diane Rogers, *The Rogers Book*, (Stanton KY, n.d.), p. 660.

[433] Willard R. Jillson, *Pioneer Kentucky* (Frankfort; 1934), p. 98; Jefferson County EB 1:408.

[434] The Henderson Company Ledger, Draper MSS 17CC191.

[435] Certificate Book, pp. 64, 73, 78, 94; Bedford County (VA) WB A:351.

[436] Certificate Book, p. 94; Old Virginia Surveys 4:486; Old Virginia Grants 4:616; Clark County DB 6:151, 161.

[437] Mabel Carlock, "John Constant, A Kentucky Pioneer," *RKHS* (1934) 32:23; Gerald Collins and Ann Tuohy, *The John Morgan Family* (Silver Spring, MD, 1995); Bourbon County WB A:11.

[438] Clark County Chronicles, January 4, 1923; Albert Goodpasture, "The Paternity of Sequoya, the Inventor of the Cherokee Alphabet," *Chronicles of Oklahoma* (1922) 1:121.

[439] Philip F. Taylor, *A Calendar of the Warrants for Land in Kentucky, Granted for Service in the French and Indian War* (Baltimore, 2001 reprint), pp. 75, 101; David Williams' deposition, Kentucky Land Trials D:210; Neal O. Hammon, "Fincastle Surveyors in the Bluegrass," *RKHS* (1973) 71:293.

[440] Clark County OB 3:282, 296, 330; 4:63; Clark County WB 7:653.

[441] Philip F. Taylor, *A Calendar of the Warrants for Land in Kentucky, Granted for Service in the French and Indian War* (Baltimore, 2001 reprint), p. 71; Old Virginia Surveys 1:11, 12, 15; Madison County WB A:111; Clark County DB 3:37.

[442] Clark County DB 1:138.

[443] Sharon Louisa Cantrall, "John Newland, Revolutionary War Patriot" at worldconnect.rootsweb.com; Clark County DB 1:138, 22:324; Doyle, *Marriage Bonds of Clark County;* Clark County OB 6:51.

[444] Clark County OB 5:106, 128.

[445] Bessie Taul Conkwright, "Conkwright," unpublished manuscript (1935) at the Kentucky History Center, Frankfort; Clark County WB 11:221, 347.

[446] Owen, "500 Old Families"; Bessie Taul Conkwright, "Conkwright," unpublished manuscript (1935) at the Kentucky History Center, Frankfort; Clark County DB 27:1; Clark County WB 12:272.

[447] "Richard Oliver of Clark County, Kentucky," unpublished manuscript at the Kentucky History Center, Frankfort; "Genealogy of the James Oliver Family," unpublished manuscript (c1981) at the Clark County Public Library, Winchester; Richard Oliver, Revolutionary War pension application, S.31282, North Carolina.

[448] Draper, *Life of Daniel Boone*, p. 572.

[449] Old Kentucky Surveys 7:44, 48.

[450] Achilles Eubank, Revolutionary War pension application, W.27743, Virginia; Clark County OB 3:211, 230, 6:39, 49; Clark County DB 1:8, 7:376; *Lexington Observer & Reporter*, September 4, 1844.

[451] Clark County DB 7:736.

[452] Draper MSS 2ZZ36; Littell, *Littell's Laws, Vol. 3*, p. 516; Jacob Dooley, Revolutionary War pension application, W.1837, Virginia.

[453] Martin Johnson, Revolutionary War pension application, W.436, Virginia; Old Kentucky Surveys 4:62; A. Goff Bedford, *The Proud Land; A History of Clark County, Kentucky* (Mt. Sterling, KY, 1983), p. 603.

[454] Old Virginia Surveys 8:560; Old Virginia Grants 10:491; Kentucky Land Trials A:1; Clark County DB 11:137; Bessie Taul Conkwright, "Conkwright," unpublished manuscript (1935) at the Kentucky History Center, Frankfort.

[455] Kentucky Land Trials D:295.

Index

For a listing of processions, depositions, biographical sketches and place names, see the Table of Contents. Note: Multiple spellings of names in the depositions are not separately indexed here. Some names had more than a dozen different spellings and indexing each would have made a much longer and more difficult to use list. Some common variations (but by no means all) are included below in parentheses.

Mary, 130
Nancy Ann, 130
Dyer, Esther, 233

Easton, Parthena, 123
Edwards, William Sr., 173
Elliott, John, 8-13
Martin, 192
Ellis, William, 98-100, 102-104, 112, 157
Ely, Benjamin, 232
Isaac, 57
Embree, Fanny, 241
John, 241
Joseph, 241
Mildred, 241
William, 198
Embry, John, 181-182
Richard, 181-182
Emerson, Diana, 67
Francis, 67
James, 67
Tilley, 66-68, 272
William, 67
England, David, 87
Estill, James, 49, 174, 176-177, 225
Samuel, 176-177, 225
Eubank, Achilles, 163, 225, 258-261
Ambrose, 259
William, 55-56
Eustace, William, 7-9, 241
Evans, Mayberry, 185
Ewing, Samuel, 169

Farrow, John, 6
Sarah, 91
Thornton, 89-92, 158, 219-224
William, 89, 91-92, 197, 219-224
William Jr., 91-92, 221-223
Faulconer, Frances, 140
Fields, Barnett, 133
Filson, John, 89, 152
Finley, John, 73
Fishback, Jacob, 146
Fleming, John, 37, 41, 45, 72, 79-80, 89, 91,
194, 210-211, 213
Lucy, 79
William, 220, 222-223
Floyd, John, 1, 105, 171, 230, 256
Forbes (Forbis), Hugh, 9-10, 81, 113-114,
116, 119-122, 194, 201, 217
Joseph, 181-182
Forman, William, 228-229
Fort, Peter, 62-63, 66
Foster, Sarah, 84
William, 84
Fowler, James, 148

Fox, Arthur, 105-107, 192
Frakes, Joseph, 90-91
Frame, William, 14-15, 50
Frazier (Frazer), David, 55, 149-151
David Jr., 149
James, 56, 149, 152
William, 56, 149, 152
French, James, 3-4, 6-7, 23-25, 27-29, 58-
59, 84-85, 155, 171, 191, 224
Keziah, 23
Richard, 38
Thomas, 134, 136
Fryer, David, 123
Elizabeth, 123
James, 123
Jane, 123
Leah, 123
Nancy, 123
Parthena, 123
Peggy, 123
Polly, 123
Robert, 123-124
Robert Jr., 123
Fugate, Jonas, 134
Josiah, 136-138
Josiah Jr., 12-13

Gadey, Elijah, 147
Galloway, James, 45-48, 72, 75-76
Rebecca, 45
Garrard, Elizabeth, 146
James, 146-149
Gass, David, 203, 248
John, 115
Gay, James, 202, 233
George, Margaret, 191
Nicholas, 113, 191-192
Nicholas Sr., 191
Whitson, 191
Gibson, John, 8
Gilkey, Agnes, 224
Charles, 153
Gill, Thomas, 53-54
Gilliam, John, 256
Gist, Christopher, 253-254
Judith C., 208, 253
Nathaniel, 1, 8, 78, 164, 207, 217, 253-
256, 270-271
Thomas, 253-254
Glover, Alice, 130
Job, 130
John, 130
Goben, William, 254
Goff, Thomas, 205
Goodwin, Patrick, 62-63, 66, 188
Graham, Richard, 225

White, Aquilla, 87, 162, 189, 226-229
    Benjamin, 36-37
    Charles, 37
    John, 44, 99-100, 174-175
    Margaret, 147
Whitledge, Robert, 2, 33, 150
Whitson, Margaret, 191
Wilkerson, Aletha, 28
    John, 18, 58, 85-87, 128-129, 198, 269
    William, 86
Williams, Daniel, 29
    David, 52, 93, 216-218, 233, 254
    Edward, 22-29, 36-37, 50-51, 60, 101-
        102, 119, 147-148, 153, 156-157,
        160-161
    Jemima, 23
    John, 162-164, 245
Wills, Frances, 60
    Frederick, 60
    James, 120, 170
Wilmore, __, 242
Wilson, Edward, 69-71, 81-83, 139, 205-
        206, 208, 238-240
    Jacob, 205
    Jacob Jr., 129
    James, 188
    Jeremiah, 208
    John, 169-170, 188-191, 209
    John Sr., 169
    Patrick, 169
    Samuel, 169, 188

Winn, Daniel, 180
    George, 57-58, 178, 269
    Owen, 57-58, 178
    Thomas Sr., 57
    Thomas, 17, 57-58, 178
    William, 18
Wood, James, 17, 262, 264
    John, 17
Woodruff (Woodrough), John, 81-82, 203,
    237
Woods, Archibald, 99, 169-170
Woollery, John, 259
Wornall, Thomas, 232, 240
Wren, James, 184, 197, 223
Wright, Joseph, 67, 272
Wyatt, Francis, 155-157

Yates, Joshua, 90
    Joshua Jr., 92
Yocum, George, 220, 223
Young, James, 8-10, 19-20, 132, 236-237
    John, 14-15, 18, 21-22, 57, 70-72, 82-
        86, 118, 121-122, 133, 139-140
    Lawrence, 97
    Original, 14-15, 18, 21-22, 39-47, 49,
        57-58, 70-72, 74-78, 82-83, 88, 90-
        92, 94-95, 97, 113-114, 116, 121-
        122, 134, 136, 170, 180, 184-186,
        188, 193-197, 208, 241-247, 249,
        253, 265

Made in the USA
Columbia, SC
03 January 2021